Growing Up the Chinese Way

FREDERICK LEONG, PH.D.
THE OHIO STATE UNIVERSITY
DEPARTMENT OF PSYCHOLOGY
142 TOWNSHEND HALL
1885 NEIL AVENUE MALL
COLUMBUS OHIO 43210-1222

D0614785

Growing Up the Chinese Way:
Chinese Child and Adolescent Development

Edited by
Sing Lau

The Chinese University Press

ISBN 962–201–659–6

First edition 1996
Second printing 1997

THE CHINESE UNIVERSITY PRESS
The Chinese University of Hong Kong
SHA TIN, N.T., HONG KONG
Fax: +852 2603 6692
+852 2603 7355
E-mail: cup@cuhk.edu.hk
Web-site: http://www.cuhk.edu.hk/cupress/w1.htm

Printed in Hong Kong

For Siu Ying and Hin Hin
with love.

we

were

once

a

child

Contents

Part I: Context of Development: Chinese Culture and Tradition

Part II: Cognitive Development: Academic Achievement

Preface

There seems to be a place for children in everyone's heart.

Magically, they can bring us laughter and tears of joy. They can, of course, also bring us troubles and worries as they grow older. But despite all the headaches, we tend to welcome their coming into our lives. They are able to bring back memories of ourselves, and we can see shadows of ourselves in them. Each of us was, indeed, once a child.

And China has millions of children. It is just fascinating, capturing the process of their development.

To all nations, children are the most important natural resource; but the outcome depends on how we treat them. They can be assets if they are allowed to develop to their fullest potential. They can, however, be liabilities if their normal development is stifled. Chinese children, like all children, are born with different talents: They can develop into useful citizens and professionals in all walks of life. A wrong turn in childhood, however, could tell a different story, of wasted lives: delinquency, drug addiction, school drop-out, suicide, and other forms of negative development.

This volume is a collection of research on Chinese child development. Since Chinese social science has been through decades of stagnation because of political suppression, the research reported in this volume represents a rare source of information.

Despite the absence of a reasonably systematic period of empirical study, there is no shortage of old Chinese and Asian wisdom and insight on Chinese child development for us to draw upon. The following is an excerpt from an Asian philosopher-poet:

> "Your children are not your children.
> They are the sons and daughters of Life's longing for itself.
> They come through you but not from you.
> And though they are with you, yet they belong not to you.

You may give them your love but not your thoughts, for they have their own
thoughts.
You may house their bodies but not their souls, for their souls dwell in the
house of tomorrow which you cannot visit, not even in your dreams.
You may strive to be like them, but seek not to make them like you.
For life goes not backward nor tarries with yesterday."

Kahlil Gibran
'The Prophet', 1923

I wish to thank all the authors for their concerted effort and "parent-ing". The present volume may be seen as a beginning, and it is hoped that it will serve as a prelude to further research in the future.

A philosophical outlook on child development characterizes this volume, and much patience has been needed to bring it to life. The helpful comments and advice given by Professor Robert McCall of the University of Pittsburg are greatly appreciated. Last but not least, the capable assistance provided by Wing-ling Li and Patricia Yeung is also greatly valued.

Introduction

China is emerging as a modern nation of great significance and influence. Its people and its culture are what the world wants to know more about. But the world itself is undergoing tremendous change: Lines are being redrawn between East and West both geographically and ideologically. Previous knowledge about China, about East and West, has thus become insufficient to enable us to fathom modern China.

What the world makes of China, however, could begin with China's offspring, the development of its new generation of children. For one thing, children are the product of their culture and environment. For another, children are the most potent force in shaping the present and future of a nation. This volume is about Chinese children. It is believed that by understanding how Chinese children develop, we can understand China and its people better.

Chinese children have in their own right, caught the attention and fascination of the Western world. Their sheer numbers alone makes them hard to ignore: One in every four children in the world is Chinese. Their outstanding academic achievements have made them the envy of Western educators: By most estimates and by most national and international standards, they top the list in academic excellence, particularly in science and mathematics. They are living in a vastly different world — a world of over-night change — and China is changing rapidly too. To understand Chinese children of this era, we need to acquire a broader and more modern perspective. Old knowledge, built on stereotyped simple cultural beliefs, is just not adequate.

This volume presents controversies: It re-examines long-held beliefs and preconceptions about Chinese culture; it takes issue with simple demarcations of East and West; it draws forth incompatible pictures and contradictory facts about Chinese children; it points to neglected areas of research; it draws attention to new problems of the modern Chinese family.

Unsettled feelings are aroused by the incongruous images which emerge. This is inevitable since that is the world we are facing today.

Our ways of understanding Chinese people and their younger generations have to change along with global change. The West is facing a new breed of Chinese offspring. They are no longer passive and submissive. They behave in ways which contradict what would be predicted from traditional depictions in cross-cultural literature. Their longing for freedom and democracy, for one thing, defies the adage of how traditional Chinese culture prescribes, shapes, and molds obedient offspring. The student movements, striving for basic human rights, do not seem to be accidental or isolated. In fact they sprang up on campuses across Asia almost instantaneously. Korea, Japan, Taiwan, Mainland China, Hong Kong, Thailand, and Burma all found their young people spelling out their wishes loud and clear. This would not have been predicted by the theory so favoured in the literature, that Asian cultures are strictly authority-abiding. Suddenly it seems as if the old obedient sons and daughters are gone and have been replaced by a new generation so similar to its Western counterparts.

We may ask: Is this simply transitory or unprecedented behaviour? Or is our previous knowledge so misled simply wrong or one-sided? Have we been so misled by our preference for neat and tidy cultural truths that we have failed to acknowledge the diversities? Protests against authority by young people, for one thing, are not a new invention but have a long history: They are simply not included in the theorizing about Chinese children. Other over-sights are every bit as evident when examined in actual contexts. Our understanding of Chinese people, or children, from cross-cultural research needs to be more didactic. The "fortune-cooky" and "Confucius-says" mode, however, remains strong.

Focus and Structure

The focus of this volume is three-fold. First, it aims to re-examine and question some of the commonly held beliefs about Chinese culture and Chinese child development. Second, it aims to stimulate new thinking on developmental theories in general and on the development process of the Chinese child in particular. Incompatible phenomena and controversies on the achievement and failure of Chinese children are brought forward, and hypotheses are proposed to reconcile the opposing facts. Third, the present volume aims to bring forth some new issues and problems that Chinese families and children are facing in modern times.

The volume is significant in reviewing and extending our current knowledge about child development. Western scholars are becoming increasingly aware of the need for cross-cultural developmental research. The current volume brings together researchers to write on their own and others' work on different aspects of Chinese child development. Readers will be informed of the work currently being done and the conceptual issues and controversies involved.

The structure of the volume consists of four parts. In the first three chapters, the importance of culture on child development is highlighted. Attention is drawn to the understanding and misunderstanding surrounding Chinese culture and children. Broader perspectives are referred to in the cultural context of understanding Chinese children.

The next four chapters review the literature on the cognitive development of Chinese children. In particular, the authors focus on the reasons for the outstanding academic performance of Chinese students. One chapter confines itself to the context of learning, the next to the cognitive attribution of success and failure. The third focuses on the learning style of Chinese children. And the fourth examines the truth in the role of parenting in Chinese students' academic success. All four chapters attempt to bring forth controversial facts and to resolve them by proposing probable hypotheses.

The third part's focus is on the social-emotional development of Chinese children. Two chapters are concerned with the mental health and psychopathology of Chinese children. A third chapter is on delinquency. These chapters thus include reviews of both positive and negative development of Chinese children.

The fourth part of the book comprises three chapters relating to some modern issues and problems of the Chinese family. Two chapters focus on Chinese who live in Western countries: The adjustment of adolescents and intergenerational conflict in Chinese families. The other chapter relates to the paramount one-child policy in Mainland China and its effects and implications.

The present volume is the first of its kind in the scope of Chinese societies it covers. In particular, readers are introduced to the research on Chinese children residing in Mainland China, Taiwan, Hong Kong, Singapore, Australia, and the United States. Authors of this volume are in the forefront of research on Chinese child development. Their insight is evident in the way they present research facts, bring up controversies, and pinpoint neglected and misunderstood areas. It is believed that this volume will serve the needs of psychologists, educators, social service professionals, sociologists, and cross-cultural scholars with respect to their concern for the well-being of Chinese children.

It is necessary to point out some controversies and points of departure in this book. In reading through this volume, readers might be become aware of some shortcomings or dilemmas. First of all, it is impossible to cover all aspects of Chinese children's development.

Second, China is a vast country consisting of many ethnic groups, and it is scarcely possible even to glimpse Chinese children in all regions. Nonetheless, the contributors to this volume have tried their best to include all published works that have a strong empirical base. The development of social science research, psychology in particular, has lagged behind Western research. This has made the task of locating valid and reliable research difficult.

Third, readers may either agree or disagree with the contributors' interpretations of various aspects of Chinese children's development. This is precisely the point: controversies are inevitable. The editor of this volume intentionally refrains from drawing a coherent line of thinking among the chapters. Take the case of academic performance as an example: although Chinese children tend to give a general impression of being top students, the rate of illiteracy is nonetheless staggering, especially in Mainland China. Even disregarding other factors (such as poor opportunity to go to school, and inadequate teaching resources), the sheer number of Chinese children makes the figure of illiterate Chinese children (especially in remote areas of China) hard to imagine in absolute terms. And even in modernized areas such as Hong Kong (with better availability of schooling and resources), the drop-out rate and poor performance of students do not go unnoticed (*Education Commission Report No. 4*, 1990). Moreover, the education systems of Chinese societies, and of other Asia countries (such as Japan) as well, tend to stifle creativity and to produce an environment described as "exam hell".

Finally, in this volume, Chinese children's development is compared with that of Western children. Readers may find "Western" too broad a term. We need therefore to delimit it to refer to just a generic term. In most chapters, "Western" refers to American children. This is mainly due to the fact that most published comparative works in the West involve this group of children. The contributors to this volume have tried their utmost to also include research involving children in Australia and Europe.

All in all, this volume should serve as a road map, albeit it a rough one, for research on Chinese children's development. The map is exceedingly complex, with innumerable interconnecting roads and sideroads; but with greater concerted efforts, we will be able, in the future, to trace a main route amidst all the fascinating trends of development in this modern age.

Reference

Education Commission (1992). *Education Commission Report No. 4.* Hong Kong: Education Commission.

Parental Control:
Psychocultural Interpretations of Chinese
Patterns of Socialization

David Y. H. Wu

This chapter examines the one-child-per-family policy in China and its impact on three areas of childhood socialization: (1) current child-rearing practices; (2) the meaning of "spoiling" and; (3) the socialization process in preschool and at home. Findings from several research projects will be presented to demonstrate aspects of continuity of cultural tradition in promoting a socialization process that emphasizes parental control and consistent monitoring. This chapter also addresses the national concern about childhood from historical and political points of view and discusses the symbolic relationship in Chinese society between parental control and state control.

Methodological Issues in the Study of Contemporary Chinese Socialization

The study of Chinese patterns of socialization has been a rather neglected and fragmented area in the field of Chinese psychology. Psychologist David Y. F. Ho has made substantial contributions in this area in research and in synthesizing relevant literature available in both Chinese and English publications since the 1950s (Ho, 1981, 1986, 1989; Ho and Kang, 1984). Ho and his colleagues' recent review work, *Chinese Patterns of Behavior: A Sourcebook of Psychological and Psychiatric Studies* (Ho, Spinks, and Yeung 1989) contains more than a thousand annotated bibliographical entries. However, less than a few dozen of these deal with Chinese socialization or child rearing and personality. Early works on Chinese socialization include anthropological reports based on observation and description (e.g., Hsu, 1981; Wolf, 1970; Wu, 1966, 1981, 1983); psychological research

based on testing or measurement (see Ho, 1989; Wu, 1985b); and political
science surveys, testing, and interviews (e.g., Saari, 1990; Solomon, 1971;
Wilson, 1970, 1974). Much of the early research was conducted outside of
Mainland China, although these analyses often shed light on all Chinese
societies. Adding to the methodological diversity are different levels of
theorization about the characteristics of Chinese child development, Chinese
patterns of socialization, personality, and child training, and implications for
political institutions (see Ho, 1986, 1989).

At the height of Cultural Revolution in the early 1970s, groups of
American psychologists were allowed to visit China. A glimpse of Chinese
children in kindergartens and nurseries offered foreign delegates oppor-
tunities to make grand theoretical speculations about dramatic changes in
Chinese patterns of child development and how they were transforming
Chinese society (see Baum and Baum, 1979; Ho, 1974; Honig, 1978;
Kessen, 1975; Sidel, 1972, 1982).

Dramatic speculation concerning changing childhood socialization
also had an indigenous source when, from the early 1980s, China's media
began to expose the psychological ill consequences of the one-child-
per-family policy on a new generation of single children. National concern
generated new research on children in the rehabilitated disciplines of
psychology and psychiatry in China, and foreign scholars also arrived to
carry out field research. As shall be highlighted below, research by Chinese
scholars has espoused the official and popular view of the problems of the
"spoiled brats."

Given the paucity of pre-1980 research on Chinese socialization
processes, the varieties and different levels of interpretation of Chinese
behavior and psychology, and the dynamics of economic-social-political
change in China, the complexity of research design is quite obvious. In
this chapter, to address single-child issues and current child-socialization
patterns, I therefore take into consideration all these background factors
in formulating psychocultural presentations. My work has relied not only
on interdisciplinary method but also experimental explorations. I also take
account of relevant, broad Chinese historical and political implications in
offering my explanations of contemporary socialization and its environment, agent, and consequences.

This chapter consists of five parts: (1) discussion of the national concern about the ill effects of rearing single children and past and recent
research findings; (2) reports on my collaborative work (Wu, 1985b, 1991 in
particular) with Chinese health practitioners on contemporary child-rearing

practices in both rural and urban settings; (3) my investigation and findings on child socialization in Chinese kindergartens (see Tobin, Wu, and
Davidson, 1989; Wu, 1992); (4) reports on an ongoing project that involves
a team of international scholars comparing early childhood socialization
within Chinese homes in China and among several Chinese communities
overseas;[1] (5) discussion of "parental control" as a key concept to characterize current socialization of single children. Finally, the concluding part
of this chapter brings in additional macro, socio-political considerations,
interpreting how aspects of Chinese cultural tradition continue to be
manifest in both family socialization and in political discourse in China
today.

The central argument of this chapter is that this complicated Chinese
phenomenon cannot be adequately understood by relying on quantitative
methods based on hypothesis testing and psychological measurement. It is
necessary to examine this phenomenon in the context of Chinese national
discourse in the modernizing process; The central concept of Chinese as an
ideal people; and the ideal socialization methods through which to train
ideal Chinese children. Furthermore, it is necessary to understand how the
academic research on Chinese child-rearing is seen as an integral part of
China's political struggle against the hegemonic domination of Western
social science (see Paranjpe et al., 1988).

The Spoiled Single Children?

During the 1980s Chinese newspapers and popular magazines carried many
articles portraying single children as problems. The media soon termed this
problem the "4-2-1 syndrome": four grandparents and two parents pouring
their attention onto one spoiled child. Chinese say that a child indulged by
as many as six doting adults is likely to come to think of himself or herself
as "a little sun" or, little "emperor" of the home. This line of reporting
continues to this day and is repeated by foreign media reports. For example,
a recent article in the *New York Times* has the headline: "For China, It's the
Year of the Spoiled Children" (Dunn, 1991). It is reported that only children

---

[1] The author is grateful to research support provided by the East-West Center,
Honolulu, which enabled the author to organize collaborative research with major
institutions in China, including Beijing Medical University and Shanghai Institute of Mental Health.

have become more pampered because parents have spent more money on children's toys.

The national discourse of the 1980s reflects a common fear that children in one-child families are spoiled by their parents and grandparents, leading to unavoidable and undesirable social and economic outcomes (Wu, 1983, 1985b, 1992). Is too much attention (or love) harming the child? Yes, definitely, answer many experts. How can children growing up without siblings learn to cooperate, share, and treat their fellow citizens as brothers and sisters? How can a generation of single children be taught to be socially responsible, to survive in a society based on the principles of socialist collectivity, selflessness, and comradeship?

To confirm Chinese authorities' claims of the ill effects of single-child socialization, the academic community produced "scientific" evidence.[2] In the early 1980s leading mental health researchers from China presented research findings at East–West Center conferences about traits of the spoiled single child:[3]

> Only children are usually viewed as selfish, spoiled, unsociable, maladjusted, narrow-minded, self-centered, conceited, fragile, and cowardly. (Wang 1984)

> Marked food preferences, short attention span, obstinacy, demands for immediate gratification of their wishes, disrespect for elders, bossiness, lack of initiative, and outbursts of temper …. (Tao and Chiu, 1985)

> Overdependence on parents and adults; sluggishness in daily life; nail sucking and biting …. (Yu, 1985)

> Only children are more egocentric …. (Jiao, Ji, and Jing, 1986)

It is incredible that these harsh words are used to characterize young children no more than six years old. One cannot help but ask: aren't these shortcomings universal traits of children at young ages? (The cultural conceptions of childhood behavior deserves cross-cultural investigation.)

These research reports of the early 1980s left much to be desired. Most studies were based on crude subjective observations or simple tests in

---

[2] Brown (1981) documented how the Chinese psychologists, since the Anti-Rightist Movement, claimed to be carrying out "scientific" or "biological" research — hence politically correct.

[3] The following quotes are from professors and directors of leading institutions of psychology, psychiatry, and children's mental health.

Table 1.1:   Samples of the Target Children

		K-School	Non-K
Urban (N = 228)	Single	66	67
	Non-S	53	42
Rural (N = 240)	Single	62	61
	Non-S	57	60

kindergartens. They were not based on long-term comparative study of both single children and children with siblings. Nor were any studies carried out in homes to look into parental child-care practices. Some experts were aware of these shortcomings and began to conduct research on child-rearing methods in homes. As I will now discuss, I participated in a large-scale study where results contradict popular beliefs.

Child-rearing Practices Studied

A joint project by Chinese mental health experts and American anthropologists was carried out in 1984 to study child-rearing practices in Shanghai and in two villages in a neighboring county.[4] Based on a questionnaire I developed from previous studies on child socialization in several cultures,[5] we interviewed parents of 468 families (randomly selected out of 7,542 sampled families with children 3–6 years old).

Containing 60 questions, the questionnaire enabled us to address five areas of concern in interviews with parents of four-year-old children. They are:

1. Methods and practices of child care: Who is the main caretaker? How many caretakers are involved? Does the child go through a

---

[4] Participating researchers (excluding assistants) are Zhenyi Xia, Rene Xi, Shoukang Chen, Yiqin Tang, Jiequ Liu, Wei-lan Wang, and David Y. H. Wu. Sampled target children were drawn from two Shanghai municipal districts (*jiedao* units) and two villages of a county neighbouring the larger Shanghai city.

[5] The questionnaire was constructed in part on the basis of earlier ones by Landy (1959); Sears, Marcoby, and LeVin (1957); and Wu (1968, 1981, 1985a, and 1985b). Each answer is rated on a 1 to 9 scale in terms of degree of applicability, intensity, or quantity.

period of swaddling? How frequently does the mother change the baby's diaper? How long does breast feeding and the drinking of milk? Feeding schedule? What are the sleeping arrangements for the child now and at infancy?

2. Methods of training of the young child: toilet training, training in independence, sociability training, and training of separation from parents.

3. The child's behavior, with special emphasis on bonding behavior with parents: What about how do parents deal with the child's clinging? Crying, temper, apprehension of being alone, and *sajiao* (撒嬌).[6] We also asked whether or not the child is particular about certain foods.

4. Disciplinary measures: parents' definition of a good and bad child, parent's punitive actions, demands for the child's obedience, measures to deal with the child's aggressive behavior, favored punitive measures, age discipline begins, different methods of punishing boys and girls, and parental definition of "spoiling".

5. Parental attitudes and value of children: reasons for wanting children, energy and money invested, and expectations of the child's future position. There were also questions regarding the sources of parents' child-rearing knowledge as well as generational differences between the parents and the grandparents in practice and in values.

Interview questions were also designed to cover child-socialization practices that are regarded in the psychological and anthropological literature as "traditional" ways of child care in Chinese society. Having summarized the characteristics of traditional Chinese child-rearing practices in my earlier studies, I shall not repeat them here (Wu, 1981, 1985a, and 1985b).

The design of our study allowed us to do comparative analysis concerning four fundamental questions (considered as main independent variables): (1) whether or not single-child and non-single-child (predominantly of two-child) families practice child care differently; (2) whether or not there is a difference in child rearing between urban and rural areas; (3) whether boys and girls are raised in a different manner; and (4) whether those who were cared for at home (who never attended a nursery or kindergarten) are different from those who were under the care of a nursery or kindergarten?

Our findings were presented in two international conferences (see Wu,

1985b and 1991; see also summary in Ho, 1989). Our key question was whether single children are brought up in a drastically different manner from non-single children. We found little evidence that such is the case. We did find, however, that only children's parents are better educated and made special efforts in bringing up their only child. Worry about the "spoiled" single child is not warranted, according to this study, except in that such children were more particular about foods and were less likely to receive a beating from their parents.

It is also interesting to discover that boys and girls were cared for in a similar manner by parents and other adults, be it in the city or in the rural region. Only four variables are statistically significant in showing a difference between the raising of boys and of girls: (1) number of caretakers in raising the child; (2) self-reliance training in dressing or washing; (3) obedience training; and (4) punishment of aggressive behavior against parents (see Table 1.2 and Table 1.3).

Our most significant findings are seen in the marked difference between children who have never attended a nursery or kindergarten and those who have, as well as between urban children and rural children. The latter contrast is based on such an overwhelming number of behavioral and attitudinal variables (22 out of 26) that it is almost impossible to dismiss the results as accidental (see Table 1.2 and Table 1.3). Our analysis demonstrates how the parents of these two groups of children are different in education and occupation, in the way they looked after their infants, and in the methods they used to control their children's behavior.

Since more than 70 percent of China's population resides in rural areas, our findings in rural China provide certain important clues to the maintenance of Chinese cultural tradition through child-rearing practices. For instance, our rural samples show more intensive physical and affective bonding behavior between parents and children, such as prolonged breast feeding period (over one year); lengthier period of children sleeping with parents on the same bed, and even under the same blanket; more frequent change of diapers when the child was an infant; and higher tolerance of young children's crying or temper tantrums. Almost all rural infants have undergone swapping (in blankets or towels). Toilet training started earlier in the cities, but both groups of children learned the habit of control at the age of one and a half years. Both groups of children predominantly slept with their mother when young; in the countryside some children were found to be spending the nights sleeping with their grandmother.

In terms of discipline, which may reflect parental concern or lack of

Table 1.2:   Questionnaire Variables

Variable code name	Meaning
Child background	
1. RESD	Residence: urban vs. rural.
2. CHDSEX	Child's sex: male vs. female.
3. CHDNO	Single vs. non-single child.
4. GROW	Whether the child grows up at home or in a nursery/kindergarten.
Child rearing methods	
5. CARETKR3	Who takes care of the child when under 3 years old?
6. HELPER4YR	Who gives help when child is 4 years old?
7. BLNKT	Swaddling (was infant wrapped in a blanket).
8. DIAPERNT	At 6 months, frequency of changing diapers at night.
9. MILPRD	Period of feeding milk.
10. SOLIDFD	Age started solid food.
11. FXFEED	Was child fed by fixed schedule?
12. SLPARGA	Sleeping arrangement: with whom does the child usually sleep?
13. SLPARMA	Sleeping arrangement: since when did the child sleep in a separate room?
14. SELFTOT	At what age was child toilet trained?
15. CHRSASGN	Training of the child with household chore assignment.
16. SELFCARE	Can the child dress/wash himself?
17. PLAYGOA	Where does the child play?
18. NIGHTOUT	When parents go out at night, do they take the child along?
19. BABYSIT	Who looks after the child when parents go out?
Child's behavior	
20. CLINGING	How much does the child cling to the mother?
21. CRYING	Did the child cry very much?
22. TEMPER	Does the child often throw a temper tantrum?
23. FEAR	Is the child often fearful of something?
Discipline	
24. BEDTIME	Is there a fixed bedtime for the child at home?
25. OBEY	How obedient is the child?
26. RESPTKBK	If the child talks back, what do parents do?
27. PUNFTKID	How would the parents punish the child for fighting with others?
28. DSCPLINE	Which methods do you agree for punishing the child?
Value of children	
29. WHYCHD	Why do you want children?
30. QUES52	Expectations of the child in the future.

concern about the "spoiled single-child" issue, urban parents appeared to be stricter. In the countryside, as mentioned above, young children were reported to cry more, cling to their mothers more often, and be more demanding or have temper tantrums. In traditional Chinese society, there

Table 1.3: Significant Level of Correlation Analysis (x^2) between Chinese Child-rearing Practices and Four Sets of Independent Variables

Variables	Single/non-single	Male/female	Home/nursery	Rural/urban
Child background				
1. RESD	0.1482	—	—	—
2. CHDSEX	0.7914	—	0.7219	0.1878
3. CHDNO	—	—	—	—
4. GROW	0.7539	—	—	0.6370
Child rearing methods				
5. CARETKR3	0.6360	0.7956	0.0005**	0.0000**
6. HELPER4YR	0.6153	0.0396*	0.0000**	0.0258*
7. BLNKT	0.9210	0.0571	0.6707	0.0006**
8. DIAPERNT	0.9892	0.1819	0.8917	0.0000**
9. MILPRD	0.9150	0.8968	0.0556	0.0001**
10. SOLIDFD	0.6252	0.2511	0.0199*	0.1318
11. FXFEED	0.2812	0.5598	0.5270	0.0971
12. SLPARGA	0.5272	0.7051	0.0013**	0.0000**
13. SLPARMA	0.0021**	0.8911	0.6227	0.0000**
Child training methods				
14. SELFTOT	0.3651	0.7449	0.0637	0.1320
15. CHRSASGN	0.3722	0.3771	0.0000**	0.0000**
16. SELFCARE	0.2482	0.0480*	0.0000**	0.0000**
17. PLAYGOA	0.1168	0.1025	0.0000**	0.0001**
18. NIGHTOUT	0.0087**	0.5668	0.0561	0.0000**
19. BABYSIT	0.0004**	0.7420	0.4635	0.4137
Child's behavior				
20. CLINGING	0.9207	0.1038	0.5430	0.0001**
21. CRYING	0.6047	0.7774	0.0098**	0.0003**
22. TEMPER	0.1940	0.1565	0.1498	0.0011**
23. FEAR	0.1686	0.8739	0.1168	0.0000**
Discipline				
24. BEDTIME	0.2759	0.6267	0.0000**	0.0000**
25. OBEY	0.0273*	0.0097**	0.0002**	0.0000**
26. RESPTKBK	0.3070	0.0011**	0.0056**	0.0000**
27. FUNFTKID	0.4556	0.4496	0.0027**	0.0010**
28. DSCPLINE	0.5010	0.7125	0.0332*	0.0000**
Value of children				
29. WHYCHD	0.3434	0.6478	0.1644	0.0000**
30. QUES52	0.0003**	0.0181	0.6034	0.0000**

Note: * $p < 0.05$
    ** $p < 0.01$

was no strict bed-time training for young children (see Wu, 1985a for a discussion of the implications of attachment or affective closeness). The rural Chinese parents in our study still kept this habit, whereas some parents in the city have begun to require their child to go to bed at an assigned time. In contrast to the city parents, fewer rural parents reported food-picking behavior exhibited by their child (it is proposed that indulgence in picking food implies affective display on the part of parents). Another area often mentioned in the "indulgence" of children is the perceived lack of self-reliance or independence training on the part of children in washing and dressing themselves. In this area, we found that the city parents emphasized earlier training: they also required of their children some household chore (such as tidying up their rooms or sweeping the floor). A multivariant (Smallest Space) analysis of our data reveals that training in this area correlates with the mother's level of education; the higher the mother's level of education, as in the cities, the earlier and stricter the training. We must further explain these contrasting attitudes in the context of the nation-wide "single-child discourse." I suspect that urban parents, in appearing to be more demanding in children's independence training in these areas, are reflecting their awareness of the popular, negative discourse on single-child "spoiling" (i.e. they consider the lack of independence training as the parents' fault). It could also be due to the fact that more children in the city attended kindergartens: they received training from strict teachers (as observed at child care centers and kindergartens, children are able to dress and undress themselves by the age of four). Rural parents may be more spontaneous, as exemplified in their answers to another question about children's inclination to exhibit *sajiao* behavior, or showing dependence, cuteness, or vulnerability.[6] More rural parents reported that their young children frequently display *sajiao*. The rural environment was also con-ducive to more traditional child socialization in providing opportunities for children to play with other children in the neighborhood. Naturally, children in the city were more inclined to play at home by themselves or herself. Another item that indicates the more traditional attitudes of rural parents is obedience training. Rural parents are either very strict or do not care about young children's aggressive behavior against parents. Urban parents appear to be loose in their demands for obedience. The significance

---

[6] Ho (1989, p. 156) cites my research and relates this concept to his definition as "sweet, perhaps somewhat naughty, behaviour calculated to élicit an affectionate response from initimate persons by whom one can presume to be loved." A similar concept of *amaeru* is said by Doi (1987, 1986) to be the key to under-standing Japanese culture).

of the parents' answers lies in their revelation of how conservative the parents can be in conducting child training at home, rather than in what they say they actually do. Rural parents' answers in our survey reveal a higher degree of retention of cultural traditions than do those of their urban counterparts. When asked about how early children should receive parental control and active training (*guanjiao* 管教), the city parents believed in the earliest interference possible, and the majority maintained that discipline should begin when the child reaches one and half years of age (see Ho and Kang, 1984 and Wu, 1981 for the meaning of "the age of understanding"). Rural parents considered children unmanageable until they reach at least two to three years of age. To discipline children at a young age, urban fathers were most often responsible, while rural mothers were more likely to be in charge. Again, it is common knowledge that traditionally a Chinese father would not fulfill his role as a strict disciplinarian until the child was older than six or seven years (see Wolf, 1970; and Solomon, 1971 on the "golden age" when young children are not subject to physical punishment).

As to sources of child-rearing knowledge, rural mothers are more inclined than urban mothers to say that they still seek advice from their mothers-in-law. A further question about young mothers' perceptions of change and continuity in child-rearing practices as compared to those of their own parents' generation (i.e. grandparents) also yielded answers showing generational continuity among rural mothers. In contrast, the urban mothers tended to perceive changes in the way parents discipline their children: young mothers accuse the old folks using "beatings and scolding" to deal with children.

On the question of the value of children, rural parents again reflect the influence of traditional culture. In spite of state propaganda to the contrary, many rural parents still believe that carrying on the clan and ancestral lines (*chuanzong jiedai* 傳宗接代) is the most important reason for having children. Some of them also dare to say that they desire more boys than girls (against years of government teachings). Only boys can carry on the ancestral lines according to traditional kinship structure as well as Confucian thinking (see Hsu, 1967 and 1981). The city parents appear to be better educated (i.e. in greater confomity to government teachings) in their answers; they say: "both boys and girls are fine, because the reason to have children is the pleasure of enjoying family life."

When we closely examine the variations of behavior in children cared for at home and those under the care of a nursery or kindergarten, we can clearly see the active role of institutionalized child care in changing children's habits. According to parents in our study, in the kindergartens children have been trained to such an extent that they become more group-oriented, less self-centred, more orderly and obedient, and more altruistic. Yet, these children are more inclined to be emotionally dependent or manipulative in soliciting adults' attention. In two open-ended questions we asked parents to list the most desirable and undesirable behaviors of their children. In their answers, it was apparent that the idea of obedience (*fucong* 服從 or *tinghua* 聽話) or disobedience (*bu fucong* 不服從 or *bu tinghua* 不聽話) still preoccupied parents. This idea coincided with the same emphasis in the kindergartens, as shall be discussed below.

In individual interviews I conducted at various places in China, young parents often admitted their ignorance about how properly to rear and educate their child: they admitted that parents were responsible for today's children becoming overindulged (*jiaozong* 嬌縱). In many interviews, parents appeared to agree with the government authorities, teachers, and doctors that institutionalized child rearing is the only hope to correct undesirable or even wrong psychology, habits, and behavior. "The kindergarten gives my child the needed experience of collective life (*jiti shenghuo* 集體生活)", was a typical response. Since popular Chinese opinion holds that, institutionalized child care is the key to behavioral change for single children, I turn in the next section to the role of preschools in the single-child problem and its solutions.

Preschool and Socialization

In the past decade I have visited more than twenty cities and rural areas in China to observe preschool education in order to understand contemporary Chinese childhood socialization. Between 1984 and 1988, in collaboration with colleagues, I conducted a project to compare preschools in China, Japan, and the United States.[7] This study applied qualitative methods of visual and reflexive ethnography. We searched for a deeper understanding of the interplay of cultural values, the role of parents and teachers, and the prevalent socialization process. We published the research findings in the form of a book (Tobin, Wu, and Davidson, 1989) and a video tape. The

---

[7] In China numerous people gave generous help to my research. However, due to the sensitivity of the subject matter and the uncertainty of political consequences, I decided in our *Preschool* book to use pseudonyms to report people involved.

following briefly summarizes our findings with special reference to the corrective solution to spoiling as perceived by parents, teachers, and authorities.

Chinese authorities and experts have promoted preschools as a solution to spoiling presented by the single-child family. Both authorities and ordinary parents believe that preschools provide single children with the chance to interact with other children and that teachers are best qualified to correct the negligence or errors of single-child parents. Educators are quite explicit about this. A sociological study reports: "Since the inception of the new population policy, the number [of Chinese schools] has been greatly increased with the aim of raising the quality of the population while controlling the quantity" (Wang, 1984, pp. 3–4).

During field observations, children in Chinese kindergartens exhibited orderly and obedient behavior in the classroom and during collective learning activities. Group life and collective rules fulfill the policy of collective child care and education, which was especially prominent for the whole care program in which children go home only once every three days (Wednesday evenings) or one day a week (on Sundays). Teachers and nurses maximized their corrective role in the collective life of kindergartens.

It is a Chinese tradition that parents are preoccupied with training children to control impulses (Ho, 1986). This preoccupation prevails in today's kindergartens. The concept of governing, monitoring, interfering, and controlling (*guan* 管) summarizes teachers consistent actions to maintain order and discipline in the classroom. A responsible teacher must create an orderly environment to enable children to concentrate on learning. Chinese may argue that *guan* has a very positive connotation. It can mean also "to care for" or even "to love." To a Western visitor to the Chinese preschools, "regimentation" is perhaps the best word to describe the classroom (see the detailed discussion in the book by Tobin, Wu, and Davidson, 1989). A common method of teaching in Chinese preschool is learning by rote or recitation in unison with the entire class. School is a place for learning, not for fun. Parents appreciate serious teaching of words, story telling, drawing, arithmetic exercises, singing, and dancing and believe that it gives their child an edge when entering primary school. Teachers also consistently apply methods of comparison and appraisal to arouse children's enthusiasm for learning and for conforming to the rules. Achievement through competition is most regularly used in group play and outdoor games (see Wu, 1992). With only one child to carry on the father's and mother's wishes — wishing the son to become a dragon (*wangzi chenglong* 望子成龍) — preschool training gives their child a competitive edge for later schooling.

I propose to stress the concept of guan as the characteristic feature of Chinese socialization. One may argue with this oversimplified generalization, saying that China is full of regional, linguistic, and ethnic diversities. How can one concept apply to all China? Indeed, one study in Guangzhou reports that there is no single way of Chinese socialization when, in a single city like Guangzhou, there are different styles of kindergartens with varying standards of facilities, teacher qualifications, and children's backgrounds. However, this is a misleading picture, as we can see strong common cultural characteristics in all the preschools in China. Ekblad's research on kindergartens in China (1985, p. 19) supports my view: "Although the (child care) centres vary considerably in terms of physical aspects, such as space, furnishings, and comfort, there is an extremely high degree of uniformity throughout the country in the philosophy and techniques of child-training in day-care centres." Furthermore, I base my generalization on cross-cultural comparisons. If we take any Chinese preschool and compare it with the preschools in Japan and the United States, as did I in our research, the Chinese regimentation and collectivity will clearly stand out. By way of reflexive questionnaires, we learned from Chinese teachers and parents who revealed their own cultural bias (or preference) by criticizing American teachers as irresponsible and American classrooms as chaotic when they saw on video of American preschool teachers allowing free choice, independence, and individuality. Chinese teachers were upset to see on video a Japanese teacher's non-interference when a boy repeatedly hit another boy and caused a disturbance among his classmates. The Japanese teacher (as was explained to us later) was deliberately teaching the children to experience groupism by solving interpersonal problems among peers. This, in the eyes of Chinese teachers, was interpreted as the teacher's irresponsibility and as an inexcusable failure to care and to constantly monitor children's behavior and relationships. "How could a teacher allow one child to bully another?" Chinese teachers asked. One may explain the Japanese technique of group socialization as focusing on the training of self-regulated social life. One may then characterize the Chinese socialization as other (teacher)-regulated (see Wilson, 1970; Yang, 1989).

Both the manner of teaching in Chinese preschools and parents' expectations are "traditional." Even some Chinese educators themselves were critical of the conservative preschool education. It was pointed out that even in China's most modernized city of Shanghai the conventional methods of preschool teaching can be summarized in four words: *guan, guan, bao, and tong* (Jiang, 1986). School regulations and teachers' restrictions keep children at bay at all times (*guan*); unimaginative teaching emphasizes stuffing (*guan* 灌) children with incomprehensible materials and leaves no room for children's creativity or self-expression; teachers patronize of students and monopolize the initiation of activities (*bao* 包); and conformity and requirements of unity (*tong* 同). A leading propaganda magazines published in English — *China Today* — recently admitted (Li, 1991) that rigid teaching methods demanding order and obedience have made Chinese kindergarten children "lifeless." Strangely enough, there is a new theory in the West that regards this kind of learning as an alternative way of "creativity."[8]

The essence of the modern Chinese preschool, despite its socialist dogma and modern textbooks, reminds one of the Chinese traditional studio prior to the twentieth century, where young children recited classical texts of the sages. This was the first step of training in moral character as well as literacy, aimed toward the potential glory of passing the national civil service examination to join the officialdom. The teacher at the old studio was always a male who would play the role of an awesome father in moral indoctrination. Although today's kindergartens promote the image of the teachers, who are always females, as substitutes for kind and affectionate mothers, they are more likely to be feared by children in the same way the father was feared by his children as a disciplinarian in traditional Chinese families (see Ho, 1981, 1986; Wu, 1981). A long tradition of Chinese parents' preoccupation with training children to control impulses (Ho, 1986) prevails in today's kindergartens. However the traditional moral teaching in the neo-Confucian tradition (since the fifteenth century), the so-called learning for children (*xiaoxue* 小學) was not required for

---

[8] It is interesting to note that American educational scholar Howard Gardner (1989) has taken this traditional, rigid teaching method as an alternative way for children to learn "creatively," especially in regard to art, music, and mathematics. Gardner was quoted to say: "creativity depends as much on culture and society as on your inborn talents" (Cromie, 1990, p. 15).

I have discussed elsewhere (Wu, 1992, p. 20) Chinese educators' argument about what creativity is: "the properties of creativity are for children to be consistent, and show perserverance, self-control, self retinance, and a sense of responsibility."

children before they reached the age of six or seven. Today, the strict training of young children in kindergartens has pushed the age of *xiaoxue* to as early as three.

The Essence of Child Socialization in China

Has indulgence run wild in Chinese homes, as the authorities have claimed? What behavior and psychology characterize young parents in raising their single child? Is the indulgence indeed a departure from the traditional Chinese ways of rearing children? These are some of the questions that led us into a new research project at the East–West Center. In 1990 I initiated a project to launch an international collaboration in the study of Chinese childhood socialization and family education. Since 1991 field research has been conducted by research teams in southern Taiwan, Shanghai, Singapore, Bangkok, Los Angeles, and Honolulu. The teams used the methods of visual and reflexive ethnography and conducted a community surveys of parental attitudes and behavior. Data collection is still proceeding, but I can discuss some preliminary observations on the basis of my visits to families and video taping in China. The essence of the style of socialization marked by constant *guan* certainly prevails among several single-child families observed during two field trips in 1990 and 1991.

Adult attention and care toward the child highlights family life, whether it is in a nuclear family consisting of two generations or a three-generation family including grandparents, parents, and a young child. It is true that these days a single child enjoys better food and clothing, and the number of toys in a single child's possession is also beyond imagination (we counted more than 100 toys for one six-year-old boy). However, the popular notion of the 4-2-1 syndrome provides only a one-side view of overindulgence in affection and care. What we saw in the single-child family is another unreported aspect of intensified *guan*. Contrary to today's popular belief in overindulging young parents, we saw parents constantly attempting to control, monitor, and correct their (only) child's behavior. Tradition dies hard among authoritarian Chinese parents, although affective bonds between parents and children are reinforced as compared to the old days. In the old days, when a mother had five children, she might not have the energy to pay attention to each one of the five at all times. Now that the number of children is reduced to only one, the child coming home from kindergarten can indeed receive full attention from parents and grandparents. At meal-time, for instance, parents try all kinds of tricks to induce the child to eat more. In leisure time, parents or grandparents often demand that the child demonstrate skills learned in school as well as do "homework," such as reading, writing, singing, playing the piano (in the late 1980s China's piano stores could not meet the market demand), drawing, or reciting the English alphabet or even learning English words. They hope parental efforts and homework will insure the child's outperforming other children in school and being competitive enough in the future to guarantee a higher level of education.

In one family we observed, when a six-year-old boy got up in the morning, his parents played at a loud volume a tape recording of English lessons. The boy had memorized the English alphabet and dozens of English words that his parents had taught him, using a popular text published in Shanghai. In another nuclear family, a six-year-old boy was a slow eater at dinner time. We saw his father, after failing to talk him into eating faster, display an angry face. The display of his displeasure was followed by verbal threats, including a threat to report to the police and the boy's school teacher. A five-year-old girl in yet another family was questioned about her "homework" by her father on the morning of the Chinese New Year's day, when the entire nation was supposed to be relaxing. The father nagged his young daughter continuously until she gave up watching television and did some "winter vacation homework" (i.e., school and parental assignment for holidays). Later on the same day, when the girl was taken to her grandparents' home to pay them New Year's respect, the grandfather, again, asked her whether she was doing well in her kindergarten.

In short, these single children not only enjoyed no freedom at the kindergartens when they returned home they received further demands and instructions from parents as well as grandparents. What follow is a short transcription of conversations among family members during our visit to a single child's family.

(The family consists of grandfather, grandmother, father, mother, and a four-year-old girl. While the guests were chatting with the adults, the hosts offered apple slices to guests.)

> Father (toward the girl): "Come here; wipe your mouth (with a towel)." (The girl did not respond.)
>
> ......
>
> Mother (toward the girl): "Wipe your mouth, OK?" (No response.)
>
> Father: "Come, wipe your mouth."

Mother: "That is enough" (The girl was grabbing the apple slices.)

Father: "Don't touch that." (The father grabbed the girl and wiped her face.)

(The girl offered apples to a guest)

Guest 1: Thank you.

Grandfather (toward the girl): "What are you supposed to say?" (The girl kept silent.)

Mother: "What should you say?"

Grandfather: "What do you say when the guest said thank you?"

Girl: "You are welcome."

Grandfather: "Such an unworldly girl."

Grandmother: "Today (you, the girl) is not familiar with the guest and does not know what to say." (Turns to the girl) "You are quite capable of speaking (polite words) ordinarily, aren't you?"

(Adults engaged in conversations.)

(The girl offered another piece of apple to another guest.)

Guest 2: Thank you.

Grandmother: "What do you say? 'You are welcome.' Why can't you talk?"

Grandfather, father, mother (at the same time): "Don't grab another one."

Grandfather: "Take it to the guest."

Father: "Why are you so disobedient (*bu tinghua*)?"

Girl: "I want another, again," (Grabs; father lets her.)

Grandmother (orders the girl): "Don't touch the rabbit (toy), you will break it."

……

Grandmother: "How about singing a song?"

Grandfather: "Can you really sing?"

Grandmother: "How about dancing a modern disco," (Turns to the girl) "*Guai, guai* (good girl), stand still."

Grandfather: "Stand up; stand up."

Grandmother: "Stand up and give us a performance."

Mother: "Come, stand here, do a good performance…. How about reciting a poem?"

Girl (recites a classic poem): "Hoe the rice seeds at noon, sweat mixed with the seeds and buried in the dirt. Who knows that every single rice in the plate comes out of hardship."

Mother: "How about another one. Stand at the centre of the room."

Girl: "Goose,, goose, goose, singing on the water. White feathers on green water; red palms push light whirls."

Grandmother: "The voice is too low. You usually have a loud voice."

Father: "Louder, as much as possible. How come your voice is so low?"

Girl (reciting louder): "Goose, goose, goose, singing on the water. White feathers on green water; red palms push light whirls. This is it"

Father: "What else? louder?"

Grandmother: "How about singing a song? How about that 'My family has four members.' How do you sing that one?"

......

(The girl performs)

Grandfather: "How about dancing a dance?"

Girl: "Ai ...,(sigh)"

Grandfather: "Then, how about telling us a story?"

Mother: "Let's tell a story, OK? Tell the story of the feathers."

Grandmother: "Last time you told the story to X about the Y story. Isn't that one interesting? That feather something?"

Grandfather: "Tell a story about the little rabbit! You can do it very well."

Grandmother: "Whatever story (you tell us) ... How about the one about the Snow White ...?"

Mother: "Otherwise (if you don't tell a story), then why should we buy so many books for you?"

Discussion: Socialization and Political Culture — Persistence of Chinese Tradition

Only children in China are not more spoiled, more indulged, or reared significantly differently from children with siblings. This is the conclusion we can draw from the three research projects presented above. Major differences in socialization exist between rural and urban children and between the preschool environment and the home environment. It is encouraging to know that other scholars' research has reached similar results (see Falbo and Poston, this volume; Poston and Yu, 1985). As Falbo and Poston explain (1989, p. 493): "A factor motivating this study was the widespread concern that Chinese only children have less desirable personalities than those with sibs. The results of these two surveys suggest that only children are developing normal personalities and that they possess no less virtue according to Chinese standards, than those with sibs." They predict that despite the fact that research has shown no significant difference between only children and children with siblings, the myth about single children will continue both in the West and in China. Lately in China, however, the press has begun to report Chinese research findings that contradict popular beliefs. An article (Cai, 1991) in *China Daily* quoting a survey conducted by sociologists at Beijing University bears the headline: "Flaws in Little Emperor Theory." It reports that only children are not more pampered in the amount of pocket money and television-watching time they are given, but that their parents do have higher aspirations for their child's future.

On the basis of my own research and others' studies, I began to realize that the problem lies not with single children but with their parents, and grandparents, and with the political élites. There may be adverse effects on child development and psychological orientation of parental control in the form of extreme attention, overprotection, constant monitoring of a child's behavior and desires, and high expectations of school performance and future aspirations. It may also be that the authoritarian political system may be correlated with the increased parental control of children, young and old.

Socialist revolution may have changed profoundly Chinese social organizations and bureaucracy, but current Chinese political culture and social ethics still reflect the legacy of a powerful Chinese cultural tradition. Aside from class struggle, Mao's Marxism emphasizes the teaching of moral character, which closely resembles Confucian teachings of collectivism, selflessness, and altruism. The national concern for the problems of spoiled single children illustrates the legacy of many aspects of the Chinese cultural tradition: the traditional Chinese conception of children; the legacy of the Confucian theory of childhood socialization; and the continuation of cultural and political discourse on the Chinese concept of self as well as ideal personhood — to be human (*chengren* 成人). Childhood socialization today by no means departs from Chinese characteristics: the strength of cultural tradition carries on in spite of communist revolution (Tobin et al., 1989; Wu, 1991). In this presentation of the single-child phenomenon, I stress the meaning of political discourse, rather than taking the problem of spoiling for granted. How the Chinese tradition persists shall be further discussed in the historical context of "spoiling."

In European cultures, the concept of "child" did not come into being until after the thirteenth century: before that time, children were perceived as "little adults" (Aries, 1962). Chinese, on the contrary, have since the beginning of written history, have maintained a conception of child and childhood. It has been frequently reported in anthropological and sociological literature that due to both natural catastrophe and man-made suffering Chinese held a dim view of the life of young children. This view is reiterated in a recent historical study by Saari of child socialization in the late Qing and early Republican periods: "Throughout the years of childhood, the basic pattern of Chinese childrearing was governed by the image of children as weak, vulnerable, and dependent beings that had to be closely protected and strictly instructed if they were to survive and become worthy adults. A period of early indulgence and protective restraint, from conception to age six, when various taboos were observed and children kept close, satisfied, and out of any conceivable danger, was followed by a period of strict instruction in the ways of life that ended around age fourteen. During this entire period, adults attempted to control the milieu of children, to shield them from dangers and temptations in the outer world that could destroy and corrupt their emerging lives ..." (Saari, 1990, p. 8).

We are reminded that concern about spoiling in China did not suddenly emerge with the single-child family. Long before the 1949 revolution, Chinese child-rearing texts warned of the dangers of "drowning [a child] in love" (*niai* 溺愛) (Solomon, 1971, p. 65; Wu, 1981, p. 154). Under Confucian influence, Chinese adults are apprehensive of the ill effect of pouring too much love on their children. In the literature of anthropology and psychology, Chinese fathers are well known for deliberately keeping an affective distance from their sons as soon as they reach the age of about six — an age at which children are supposed to begin "understanding things" (*dongshi* 懂事) (Ho, 1989; Wu, 1981). The innate human filial devotion toward parents (later toward superiors and rulers) can be nurtured in a child only by way of teaching and training during childhood.

> The *Classic of Filial Piety* implies that two early emotions point toward *hsiao* [孝]: affection (*ch'in* [情]) and awe or reverence (*yen* [嚴]). Affection is believed to be a natural admiration of children for parents, while awe or reverence seems to be derivative of this, and learned in practice. The former is related to the mother, the latter to the father, though not exclusively in either case. (Saari, 1990, p. 28)

Attachment training as the source of affection and awe toward parents was recently discussed in Yang's review article on the psychological process of Chinese filial piety (Yang, 1989, pp. 55–58) and my own earlier

work on Chinese early childhood socialization process (Wu, 1981, 1985a).
Yang categorically states that filial devotion (*xiao* 孝), is one of the
most conspicuous characteristics of Chinese culture, being the foundation
of the Chinese style of collective life. Both as a social attitude and as
cultural behavior, filial devotion is learned through socialization (Yang,
1989, pp. 39–50). We may add to this the further assertion that parents' and
teachers' demands of discipline and obedience in modern Chinese kindergartens indicate the continuation of traditional filial piety in action. Political
discourse also demonstrates this tradition of socialization for filial piety
which still prevails in China today. The state, symbolizing not just the
political authority but also the ideal father figure, must take over when
single children's real fathers have failed their ideal role in training children to become filial, loyal, friendly, selfless, independent, and obedient
members of a prosperous, modern China. The state leaders in their speeches
to educate the people still espouse this traditional goal of ideal Chinese
socialization. The essence of ideal Chinese children lingered on, for instance, in the mind of the national leader of child and youth welfare, Song
Qingling 宋慶齡 (Madame Sun Yat-sen). She wrote in the mid-1980s in "A
Letter to Children" on the occasion of the thirtieth anniversary of *Ertong
Shidai* 兒童時代 (Children's Times): "I wish you from your early age to be
obedient to father and mother; respect teachers; to have good thoughts
and good moral character. All in all, I wish you to be like uncle Lei Feng
(雷鋒), to grow up healthy. To grow up to be successors of revolution; well
rounded in morality (*de* 德), intelligence (*zhi* 智), physically (*ti* 體), and
beauty (*mei* 美)" (Zhongyang, 1984).

Since the 1950s the focus on children's moral education by the Chinese
authorities has reflected the persistence of the Confucian tradition. During
the Ming and Qing dynasties, Neo-Confucian philosophers promoted
education for children between the ages of seven and fourteen (*xiaoxue*).
They believed that at this stage children can be indoctrinated and nourished
by the thoughts of the sages and learning to become an acceptable man
(*zuoren* 做人) (Saari, 1990, p. 30). However, today's kindergartens have
pushed moral education and the indoctrination of patriotism for children as
young as three years old. The Neo-Confucians believed in the theory of
stuffing young children with moral learning before they could understand
things (*dongshi*). Once they were stuffed with the correct thoughts, there
would be no room left for immoral or inappropriate thoughts. By the
1920s, after the May Fourth Movement, an enlightened new generation of
scholars dismissed child socialization by stuffing (Saari, 1990, pp. 38–39).

Yet, traditional Chinese thinking on early education seemed to have gained favor among later-day communist élites. Even the contents of communist moral education for young children reflect the anti-imperialist and nationalistic ideology of late nineteenth and early twentieth century intellectual discourse (Wu, 1992).

Today's parents support the idea of early indoctrination in the preschool, believing in the benefit of teaching and discipline to improve their child's intelligence. When asked to list skills by which children in China are identified as being "intelligent," teachers in several cities of China said: "immediate memory for words, pitcures and poems, language development, motor skills and knowledge of science and mathematics" (Brown, 1981, p. 224). At home, parents may not be strict disciplinarians, but they nevertheless exert great pressure on their single child to achieve. (Ho and Kang's study in Hong Kong [1984] points out that "the age of understanding", hence the potential time to begin learning, is considerably younger in the minds of today's fathers.) Among the families we have observed, single children received so many pressures and demands and so much interference that their socialization hardly matches the image of indulgence. This pressure for achievement is a continuation of the emphasis in traditional Chinese culture (see Ho and Kang, 1984; Wu and Tseng, 1985).

Finally, there is an additional point on the relationship between the Chinese style of socialization that I summarized in one word, *guan*, and the Chinese political system. Political scientists who study Chinese socialization often refer to collectivity and the development of authoritarian psychology. Western scholars like Solomon (1971), Metzger (1981), and Saari (1990) continue to refer to the Chinese struggle from childhood for a balance between autonomy and dependency. The emphasis on filial piety (*xiao*) and demands of obedience (*fucong*) to adults or superiors (*tinghua*) continues to play an important role in the patterns of child training in China, Taiwan, Hong Kong, and overseas Chinese communities (Ho, 1981, 1986, 1989; Ho and Kang, 1984; Tseng and Wu, 1985; Yang, 1989). The emergence of single children has so far made no serious changes in patterns of Chinese socialization. In my opinion, it has further rein-forced personal characteristics of authoritarianism, collectivism, control of temperament, competitiveness, and achievement. The psychological effects on single children of reinforced control in the school, along with increased restrictions and pressure at home, in time will either prompt the expansion of dependence on authority or rebellion for autonomy. This should be one area of interest for future research.

Perhaps the whole issue of the Chinese apprehension of spoiled single children, and preschool as a counter measure, reflects the Chinese conception of selfhood. The emphases in Chinese preschools on "experience in a group" (which is assumed to be lacking in the home environment today) and "learning to be a good citizen" are closely related. They are conceptually part of a more encompassing concern in Chinese society, both traditional and modern, that young children must be taught to identify with something larger (hence more significant) than themselves and their families. Chinese have always faced concern about balancing the personal and the communal. In the Chinese understanding, children belong not only to parents, but also to society (thus filial piety refers to both parents and the emperor). Chinese preschools and the ongoing debate about self and collectivity summarize the continual search for this balance. However, as Chinese students in modern schools have been taught for decades (both in China and in Taiwan), one must sacrifice one's "smaller self" (*xiaowo* 小我) for the sake of a "larger self" (*dawo* 大我) — the collective, the society, and the nation. Confucian ideas of collective self prevailed in Chinese conceptions of education (Wu, 1992). Chinese authorities and educators today still express the Confucian ideal of a person as an insignificant self submitting to a significant larger self of (Chinese) collectivity. Chinese preschools are in this sense ideal agents of cultural conservation rather than change. Preschool in China functions to conserve rather than transform the value of collectivity, which is fundamental to a Chinese and communist society.

Psychiatrists Baum and Baum (1979) conjectured over a decade ago that adult political behavior projects the cultural models of child socialization; Chinese political behavior can be explained in terms of the psychological theory of latent defense mechanisms that are observed in the early experience of communist children. We may not agree with their psychoanalytical interpretations of a functional model of Chinese child socialization, but they are correct to emphasize the continuity in Chinese parental bonding with young children as a characteristic Chinese style of socialization (see also Wu, 1985a).

The revived promotion of the ideal communist hero — Lei Feng — since 1989 serves to exemplify the official discourse of political metaphors and cultural symbols of the parent–child bond. The meaning of the following poem attributed to the national hero Lei Feng is self-evident:

> *To the Party, I sing a folk song.*
> *To the Party, I compare to my mom.*

My natural mother gave me a body.
The Communist Party gave me a glorious life.

Chinese socialization reflects the conservative Chinese cultural tradition, as many scholars have argued (see Ho, 1981, 1989; Parish and Whyte,
1978; and Wolf, 1970). The growing up of Chinese boys and girls who are
the only child in the family, the worries of young Chinese parents about the
future of their only child, and the political discourse of the spoiled generation all are part of the ideological manifestation of China's struggle to
become modern. Parents take good care of their only child, hoping to take
total control of the child and its future; the state desires China to become
modern and prosper with citizens who obey, listening to their leaders. No
matter how the social and political discourse claims other- wise, today's
Chinese childhood socialization still holds important clues to understanding
common Chinese patterns of psychology in the milieu of a die-hard
authoritarian, collective, nationalistic political culture.

References

Aries, P. (1962). *Centuries of childhood.* (R. Baldick, Trans.). London: Jonathan
Cape.
Baum, C. L., and Baum, R. (1979). Creating the new communist child. In
R. Wilson (Ed.) *Value change in Chinese society* (pp. 98–121). New York:
Praeger.
Brown, L. B. (1981). *Psychology in contemporary China.* Oxford: Pergamon.
Cai, Y. (1991, July 19). Flaws in little emperor theory. *China Daily*, p. 4.
Cromie, W. J. (1990, February). A question of creativity. *Harvard Alumni Gazette*,
pp. 15–16.
Doi, T. (1971). *The anatomy of dependence.* Tokyo: Kodansha.
———. (1986). *The anatomy of self.* Tokyo: Kodansha.
Dunn, S. W. (1991, February 17). For China, it's the year of the spoiled children.
New York Times, p. 5.
Ekblad, S. (1985). *Social determinants, restrictive environment and aggressive
behaviour.* Stockholm: Huddinge Hospital.
Falbo, T., Poston, D. L., Jr., Ji, G., Jiao, S., Jing, Q., Wang, S., Gu, Q., Yin, H., and
Liu, Y. (1989). Physical, achievement and personality characteristics of
Chinese children. *Journal of Biosocial Science*, 21: 483–495.
Gardner, H. (1989). The key in the slot: creativity in a Chinese key. *Journal of
Aesthetic Education*, 23 (1): 141–158.
Han, J. (1985, September 3). Kindergartens in China. *World Journal* (Los Angeles),
p. 16.

Hare-Mustin R. T. (1986). Family change and the concept of motherhood in China. *Journal of Family Issues*, 7 (1): 67–82.

Ho, D.Y.F. (1974). Early socialization in contemporary China. In *Proceeding of the twentieth international congress of psychology* (1st ed., 1972, p. 442). Tokyo: University of Tokyo Press.

———. (1981). Traditional patterns of socialization in Chinese society. *Acta Psychologica Taiwanica*, 23 (2): 81–95.

———. (1986). Chinese patterns of socialization: A critical review. In M. H. Bond (Ed.), *The psychology of the Chinese people* (pp. 1–37). Hong Kong: Oxford University Press.

———. (1989). Continuity and variation in Chinese patterns of socialization. *Journal of Marriage and the Family*, 51 (1): 149–63.

Ho, D.Y.F. and Kang, T. K. (1984). Intergenerational comparisons of child-rearing attitudes and practices in Hong Kong. *Developmental Psychology*, 20 (6): 1004–1016.

Ho, D.Y.F., Spinks, J. A., and Yeung, C.S.H. (Eds.). (1989). *Chinese patterns of behavior: A sourcebook of psychological and psychiatric studies*. New York: Praeger.

Honig, A. S. (1978). Comparison of child-rearing practices in Japan and in the Republic of China: A personal view. *International Journal of Group Tensions*, 8 (1–2): 6–32.

Honig, E., and Hershattar, G. (1988). *Personal voices: Chinese women in the 1980's*. Stanford: Stanford University Press.

Hsu, F.L.K. (1967). *Under the ancestor's shadow*. New York: Doubleday.

———. (1981). *Americans and Chinese*. Honolulu: University of Hawaii Press.

Jiang, Y. (1986). Youeryuan Jiaoyu Gangyau [Guidelines of kindergarten education]. *Youer Jiaoyu* 1: 4–5.

Jiao, S., Ji, G. P., and Jing, Q. H. (1986). Comparative study of behavioral qualities of only children and sibling children. *Child Development*, 57 (2): 357–361.

Kessen, W. (1975). *Childhood in China*. New Haven: Yale University Press.

Kwong, J. (1985). Changing political culture and changing curriculum: An analysis of language textbooks in the People's Republic of China. *Comparative Education*, 21 (2): 197–208.

Landy, D. (1959). *Tropical childhood: Cultural transmission and learning in a rural puerto rican village*. Chapel Hill: The University of North Carolina Press.

Li, X. (1991). Kindergartens that nurture with care. *China Today*, 40 (6): 8–11.

Martin, R. (1975). The socialization of children in China and Taiwan: An analysis of elementary school textbooks. *China Quarterly*, 62: 242–262.

Metzger, T. A. (1981). Selfhood and authority in Neo-Confucianism political culture. In A. Kleinman and T. Y. Lin (Eds.), *Normal and abnormal behavior in Chinese culture* (pp. 7–27). Dordrecht, The Netherlands: D. Reidel.

Paranjpe, A. C., Ho, D.Y.F., and Rieber, R. W. (1988). *Asian contributions to psychology*. New York: Praeger.

Parish, W. L., and Whyte, M. K. (1978). *Village and family in contemporary China*. Chicago: University of Chicago.

Poston, D., and Yu, M. Y. (1985). Quality of life, intellectual development and behavioural characteristics of single children in China: Evidence from a 1980 survey in Changsha, Hunan province. *Journal of Biosocial Science*, 17: 127–136.

Saari, J. L. (1990). *Legacies of childhood*. Cambridge, MA.: Council on East-Asian Studies, Harvard University.

Sears, R. R., Maccoby, E. E., Levin, H. (1957). *Patterns of child rearing*. Illinois: Row, Peterson and Co.

Sidel, R. (1972). *Women and child care in China*. New York: Hill and Wang.

———. (1982). Early childhood education in China: The impact of political change. *Comparative Education Review*, 26 (1): 78–87.

Smith, D. C. (1989). *Children of China*. Taipei: Pacific Cultural Foundation.

Solomon, R. H. (1971). *Mao's revolution and the Chinese political culture*. Berkeley: University of California Press.

Tao, K., and Chiu. (1985). The one-child-per-family policy: A psychological perspective. In W. S. Tseng and D.Y.H. Wu (Eds.), *Chinese culture and mental health* (pp. 153–66). Orlando: Academic Press.

Tobin, J., Wu, D.Y.H., and Davidson, D. (1989). *Preschool in three cultures: Japan, China, and the United States*. New Haven: Yale University Press. (Video tape on three schools by the same press in 1991)

Tseng, W. S., and Wu, D.Y.H. (Eds.). (1985). *Chinese culture and mental health*. Orlando and London: Academic Press.

Wang, N. Z. (1984, August). *The socialization of the only child in China*. Paper presented at the Conference on Child Socialization and Mental Health, East–West Center, Honolulu, HI.

Wang, Q., Gu, H., Yin, and Liu Y. (1989). Physical, achievement and personality characteristics of Chinese children. *Journal of Biosocial Science*, 21: 483–495.

Wilson, R. W. (1970). *Learning to be Chinese*. Cambridge: M.I.T. Press.

———. (1974). *The moralo state: A study of the political socialization of Chinese and American children*. New York: The Free Press.

Wolf, M. (1970). Child training and the Chinese family. In M. Freedman (Ed.), *Family and kinship in Chinese society* (pp. 37–62). Stanford: Stanford University Press.

Wu, D.Y.H. (1966). Cong renleixue guandian kan muqian Zhongguo ertong yangyu [An anthropologist looks at Chinese child training methods]. *Thought and Word* (Taipei), 3 (6): 741–745.

———. (1968). Child training among the Eastern Paiwan. *Bulletin of the Institute of Ethnology, Academia Sinica*, 25: 55–107.

————. (1981). Child abuse in Taiwan. In J. Corbin (Ed.), *Child abuse and neglect: A cross-cultural perspectives* (pp. 139–165). Berkeley: University of California Press.

————. (1983, November). *Child rearing in China*. Paper presented at the Annual Meeting of the American Anthropological Association. Chicago.

————. (1985a). Child training in Chinese culture. In W. S. Tseng and D.Y.H. Wu (Eds.), *Chinese culture and mental health* (pp. 113–134). Orlando and London: Academic Press.

————. (1985b). Modernization of Chinese family and child rearing. In J. Chiao (Ed.), *Proceedings of the Conference on Modernization and Chinese Cultural Studies* (pp. 31–40). Hong Kong: The Chinese University of Hong Kong, School of Social Sciences.

————. (1991). Population policy in China and rearing of single children. In J. Chiao (Ed.), *Chinese family and its change* (pp. 277–286). Hong Kong: The Chinese University of Hong Kong, New Asia College.

————. (1992). Preschool education in China. In S. Feeney (Ed.), *Early childhood education in Asia and the Pacific: A sourcebook* (pp. 1–26). New York: Garland.

Wu, D.Y.H., and Tseng, W. S. (1985). Introduction. In W. S. Tseng and D.Y.H. Wu (Eds.), *Chinese culture and mental health* (pp. 3–13). Orlando and London: Academic Press.

Yang, K. S. (1981). The formation and change of Chinese personality: A cultural-ecological perspective. *Acta Pscyhologica China*, 23 (1): 39–55.

————. (1989). The analysis of Chinese concept of Xiao. In K. S. Yang (Ed.), *Chinese psychology* (pp. 39–73). Taipei: Guiguan.

Yu, L. (1985). An epidemiological study of child mental health problems in Nanjing district. In W. S. Tseng and D.Y.H. Wu (Eds.), *Chinese culture and mental health* (pp. 305–314). Orlando and London: Academic Press.

Zhongyang jiaoyu kexue yanjiusuo. (Ed.). (1984). *Song Qingling lun shaonian ertong jiaoyu* (Song Qingling's essays on education for youth and children). Beijing: Jiaoyu chubanshe.

2

Understanding Chinese Child Development: The Role of Culture in Socialization

Sing Lau and Patricia P. W. Yeung

The relation between culture and socialization is undisputed especially in anthropological works (Brown and Reeve, 1985; Cazden, John, and Hymes, 1975; Ogbu, 1982). Developmental researchers who have worked in different cultures have also become convinced that human functioning cannot be separated from the cultural and immediate context in which children develop (Lamb, Sternberg, Hwang, and Broberg, 1992; Rogoff and Morelli, 1989). As Cole stated in 1981, the zone of proximal development is "where culture and cognition create each other." Not only is the diversity of cultural backgrounds in our world a resource for building the future, it is also a resource for scholars to study how children develop.

Recent interest in psychological research has shifted more and more toward cross-cultural comparisons. The reason behind this expanded interest seems to lie in the hope of broadening the understanding of child development. Many anthropologists and developmental psychologists have found themselves in alignment with Vygotsky's theory (Rogoff and Morelli, 1989), in which the focus is on the sociocultural context of a child's development. This theory offers a picture of human development that stresses how development is inseparable from human social and cultural activities (Vygotsky, 1978). Indeed, children develop through socialization, and their immediate families or peers thus become the main social agents for them to grow up with (Steinberg, Dornbusch, and Brown, 1992).

In recent years, a growing number of researchers have concentrated their studies particularly on the socialization processes in Chinese culture (Berndt, Cheung, Lau, Hau, and Lew, 1993; Ho, 1989; Kelley and Tseng, 1992; Lau, 1992; Lau and Cheung, 1987; Lee, 1992). One important factor that might have attracted their attention is the notable achievements of Chinese people. Recent studies on academic achievements in America have reported the remarkable performance of Asian-American students who exceed their White, African-American, and Hispanic counterparts (Sue and Okazaki, 1990). The superior school performance of Chinese and other Asian students has fascinated many psychologists and served as an impetus to search for an answer which may help to raise the academic performance of American students.

Another reason why scholars are spending more time and effort investigating the socialization of Chinese children is simply due to the fact that Chinese people constitute a great majority of the world's population. By estimation, one out of every four children in the world is Chinese (Ho, 1989). In other words, for theoretical and practical reasons, the understanding of Chinese culture and socialization has become an essential area of research for developmental psychologists.

In the following sections, we will first briefly review the theoretical basis underlying research on Chinese child development. Both the similarities and differences of Western and Chinese perspectives on child development are highlighted. Second, we will provide a critique of the theoretical assumptions (from Confucianism in particular) adopted by Western psy-chologists, and outline the ways in which the scope should be broadened. Third, we will highlight and bring to the attention of Western developmental psychologists the different aspects and issues of Chinese child development. In particular, we argue that the focus of the theoretical basis is too narrow and that the process or aspects of development as described in the Western literature are too lopsided.

Theories of Development: Western and Chinese Perspectives

From a Western perspective, development is viewed as a lifelong process. It is the circumstances of our lives and the way we deal with these circumstances that continually shapes us as unique individuals (Shaffer, 1989). Thus, developmental psychologists are interested in examining wide aspects of human psychological development. In the Western perspectives of development, there are in general well-defined boundaries: one can be approached in terms of specific domains (e.g. cognitive, social, moral) or theories (e.g. behaviorism, psychoanalysis) of development. Overall, domains and theories are often enmeshed and are empirically based. For brevity's sake, we will mention some of the more commonly known theories just to highlight the contrast with Chinese perspectives on development.

In the Western literature there are some well-established theoretical frameworks or approaches. For example, in terms of the psychoanalytic approach, psychologists like Freud, Jung, Adler, and Erikson, are particularly interested in discussing human personality structures and dynamics: this approach has remained the most comprehensive and influential theory of personality ever established (Shaffer, 1989). By contrast, in the social learning and behavioristic approach, the emphasis is on the importance of the environmental determinants of behaviour through modelling and stimulus-response associations. How a human behaves is therefore the result of a continuous interaction between personal and environmental variables. Some major theorists who are interested in this approach include Watson, Pavlov, Skinner, and Bandura (Shaffer, 1989).

In terms of domains such as cognitive development, it is suggested that a child's ability to think and to reason progresses through a series of distinct stages. Each stage has its own unique characterization, yet it could vary considerably depending on intelligence, cultural background and socioeconomic factors. Piaget (Shaffer, 1989) is a major contributor to this theoretical approach. A similar stage theory of development is also found in moral reasoning, as exemplified by the works of Kohlberg, and in personality, by Erikson and Maslow (Shaffer, 1989).

Another framework in studying child development is the ethological perspective. Ethology is the study of the biological bases of behavior, including its evolution, causation, and development. This theoretical approach arose because some zoologists argued that other theorists had overlooked or ignored the importance of biological contributions to human and animal behavior. Two of the most influential theorists in this approach are Ainsworth and Bowlby (Shaffer, 1989).

Even though the above approaches are considered to be the "grand theories" in Western developmental psychology, there are some areas which still remain controversial. These include the questions of nature (biological forces) versus nurture (environmental forces); inherently good versus inherently bad; or children actively involved in the developmental process versus passively involved, etc. (Shaffer, 1989).

When referring to Chinese perspectives of child development, Chinese scholars adopt similar approaches or frameworks to those used by Western theorists. Yet one marked difference is that they tend to be predominantly intuitive in their thinking, and they also do not diversify the viewpoints and distinctly label them into different psychological categories. Instead, Chinese perspectives seem to build solely upon some integrative framework, such as that of Confucianism. Despite the fact that studies of Chinese child development have lacked theoretical bases as well as empirical support, Confucianism is one Chinese ideology that has been widely adopted by both Chinese and Western researchers. Some major concepts include: supreme moral person (Lei, 1993; Metzger, 1992); filial piety (Hsu, 1981; Kelley and Tseng, 1992); interpersonal harmony (Domino, 1992); collective decision making (Stander and Jensen, 1993); self-fulfillment (Kelley and Tseng, 1992; Suzuki, 1980); good manners, and the importance of education (Chiu, 1987; Ekblad, 1986; Ho, 1989).

In ancient Chinese writings, attention to stages or hierarchy of development in learning and interpersonal relationships is also noted in Confucianism (*The Record of Rites*; Liu, 1991). For example, in terms of cognitive development, there is emphasis on progressive learning (shaping or learning by steps), timing (maturation or learning the right things at the right time), and a human instinct or capacity to learn (nurturing). In terms of moral development, there is emphasis on respect for authority and a well-defined hierarchy of human relationships in government, society, and at home. It is the latter aspect, morality, that Western psychologists pay the greatest attention to.

Suffice to say, unlike Western theories of development, there is a notable lack of an empirical base from which Chinese thinking on child development is structured. In brief, Chinese perspectives on child development are more like philosophies than theories of nature. Although Confucianism has been viewed as the most traditional ideology in Chinese history, it is still worth questioning to what extent it is applicable in contemporary Chinese society. China is a nation that has gone through many upheavals in recent centuries. In other words, today's Chinese culture is definitely not the same as that experienced by our great-grandfathers, and the ways of life prescribed by Confucianism may need some re-thinking.

Since Chinese history is not the area we want to spend time on in this chapter, readers who are interested in gaining further information on this topic can refer to other sources (Baker, 1979; Hsu, 1948; Tu, 1984, 1985).

Theoretical Basis of Chinese Developmental Research

As we have mentioned earlier, Confucianism seems to be the main focus as a theoretical framework for Chinese child development. Thus, researchers have paid less attention to other schools of thought such as Taoism and Buddhism, that have also been of great influence in Chinese culture (Rea,

Chao, and Good, 1981). The single-minded focus on one ideology has created a phenomenon whereby researchers tend to over-generalize the influence of Confucianism. Perhaps worse of all, it may even generate misconceptions in the process of investigating Chinese culture and child development. The following are some illustrations.

Let us take parental control and family harmony in Chinese culture as an example. Some researchers have suggested that children who live in societies founded on Confucianism do perceive a parent's right to exert control and dominance over them as acceptable, and subsequently perceive parental control and dominance as an expression of parental warmth (Rohner and Pettengill, 1985). Nevertheless, some Asian scholars have disputed the fact and claim that this might not be completely true after all. Instead, studies have shown that Chinese children, like their Western counterparts, do resent strict and authoritarian parenting (Berndt, Cheung, Lau, Hau, and Lew, 1993; Ho, 1987; Lau and Cheung, 1987; Lau, Lew, Hau, Cheung, and Berndt, 1990). Therefore, the ideology of Confucianism can easily be overgeneralized if it is not investigated carefully.

Meanwhile, other studies have cast doubt on the hypothesis that because of the old teachings of Confucianism and traditional Chinese culture, Chinese are basically collectivistic with no individualistic or personal wishes. In a recent study, Lau (1992) has found that Chinese in Mainland China, Singapore, and Hong Kong do place great emphasis on personal values (such as freedom and personal achievement), no less so (and on some values even more) than American college students. These results are consistent with previous studies on similar topics (Bo, 1985; Feather, 1986; Fei, 1948; Lau, 1988; Stipek, Weiner, and Li, 1989).

The fight for freedom and the democracy movement in Mainland China in 1989 serves as another excellent example. Most notably, the one million people who turned up in street marches, voluntarily, in support of the 1989 freedom movement in Hong Kong (a Chinese society generally regarded as the least patriotic and the least concerned about human justice and liberty because of its "colonial" background) surprised everybody and defied the general laws from Confucian dictum. In fact, the whole world was touched by the human rights action in China and Hong Kong. The movement should be seen as reflecting some kind of common human wishes among Chinese and should not be dismissed as some isolated or temporary incident. In fact, when we look at China's recent history, similar movements can be found. The feelings are there; they are just waiting for the right moment to surface.

Lam and Yang (1989) have also pointed out that Wheeler's (1988) article over-generalized some Chinese traditional behaviour and falsely interpreted the cultural differences, and had consequently "seriously misled his audience and the journal's readership." (p. 642) These incidents have proven once again that it is possible to be trapped in the traditional and stereotypic modes of thought when the focus is solely on one aspect of Chinese culture. Especially in view of the lack of empirical basis, these off-hand concepts may lead to unnecessary misunderstanding rather than providing a better understanding of Chinese child development.

We have been discussing Chinese tradition for quite a while, but what exactly is it? Is Chinese culture totally different from Western culture? Are there any similarities between Chinese culture and other cultures whatsoever? Sure enough, Chinese tradition has its own uniqueness; yet one cannot deny that there are some areas that are comparable with other cultures as well. For instance, a McDonald's hamburger seems to be enjoyed by almost every child in the world regardless of what nationality he or she is. This is definitely a very interesting phenomenon: young children from China, America, Japan, the Soviet Union, or Hong Kong are all fond of sinking their teeth into a juicy hamburger and munching it along with those golden, crunchy French fries. This could perhaps lead to a suggestion that all cultures possess their own uniqueness and yet all are inter-related.

Research in a variety of cultures has also provided evidence of impressive regularities across cultures in the field of development. For instance, there is marked similarity across cultures in the sequence and timing of sensorimotor milestones in infant development, smiling, and separation anxiety (Gewritz, 1965; Goldberg, 1972; Konner, 1972; Super, 1981; Werner, 1989) and also in the order of stages in language acquisition (Bowerman, 1981; Slobin, 1973). Meanwhile there are also consistent findings that children's behavior and development in terms of specific patterns or ways of manifestation may vary according to cultural context (Rogoff and Morelli, 1989).

Confucianism Revisited

The ideology of Confucius has been the backbone of studying Chinese culture (Kelley and Tseng, 1992). But if we move one step further and examine it in depth, we may discover some flaws within this ideology. It seems that Confucianism only covers the areas of family, society, the moral person, self-fulfillment, and happiness, etc. (Suzuki, 1980). As Ekblad

(1986) has described, the Chinese orientation toward children tends to be moralistic rather than psychological. The ideology might have neglected, for example, teaching and learning, or the psychological development of an individual.

The following excerpt may offer us a glimpse of the concept that Confucius wanted to pass on to his followers and the world. As Confucius described, "... when the perfect order prevails the world is like a home shared by all ... a sense of sharing displaces the effects of selfishness and materialism ... the door to every home need never be locked and bolted by day or night. These are the characteristics of an ideal world, the commonwealth state ..." (*The Record of Rites*). Regardless of how original Confucianism stands in relation to Chinese culture, there are limitations. Many articles or research studies have only focused on the positive side of Confucianism — how it productively effects Chinese culture. Yet they have neglected its other sides — the ideology has also brought forth some controversial issues.

For instance, Westerners always look up to Chinese child rearing practices especially with regard to their positive relation to education. Chinese students seem to attain more distinguished achievements in the academic setting than Western school children (Mordkowitz and Ginsburg, 1987; Sue and Okazaki, 1990). And Asian immigrants have also succeeded in North American schools for many decades and continue to do so (Tharp, 1989). In the study by Steinberg, Dornbusch, and Brown (1992), Asian-American students were described as those "who were the most successful in school ... devote relatively more time to their studies, are more likely to attribute their success to hard work, and are more likely to report that their parents have high standards for school performance. They spend twice as much time each week on homework as do other students, and report that their parents would be angry if they came home with less than an A-." Interestingly enough, as Steinberg and his colleagues have concluded (1992), what distinguishes Asian-American students from others is not so much their stronger belief that educational success pays off, but their stronger fear that educational failure brings forth negative consequences.

In fact, the education system in Asian countries is often described as an "Exam Hell" (Cherry, 1983). Thomas Rohlen (1983), an anthropologist, described the situation in Asian countries as one in which "students are not going to be examined on expressive or critical skills, but on diligence in the mastery of facts ... in sum, the lecture format in high schools teaches students patient listening; it underlines the authority of the teacher as the superior in learning" (p. 30). Chinese culture and tradition always enshrine the entrance examination system (Cherry, 1983). This has become a rather heavy burden to Asian students. At its worst, it has led to a rising suicide tendency in Hong Kong children and youth (Hong Kong Samaritan Befrienders, 1981–1991).

Frankly speaking, Chinese culture is not as glorious as Westerners perceive it to be. It also has its dark side, problems, and difficulties: for example, infanticide, delinquency, teenage pregnancy, single-parenthood, and families with divorced parents, etc. Similar to other Western countries, Chinese societies are not immune to all these issues. Researchers should try to take note of the diversity of Confucianism — how it has exerted positive influence, and on the other hand, how it may also elicit many controversial matters in the Chinese population as well.

To sum up, to rely on a single ideology to study Chinese culture and child development is simply not appropriate. First, the ideology may not be all-perfect. Thus if one decides to use it as a theoretical base, both positive and negative aspects should be taken note of. Second, the ideology may not be all encompassing. In Western psychological literature, one does not find or depend on a single dominant ideology. In the United States, for example, even though every coin has an "In God We Trust" inscription, researchers would not start with the assumption that all Americans are Christian or religious in their life-orientation. Similarly, even with the theoretically well-grounded concept of the Protestant Work Ethic, together with a solidly established scale, researchers would also not start with the assumption that all or most Americans uphold such a belief toward work. To be exact, if one wants to use any religious or cultural ideology as a basis for studying certain behaviours, one would first ask about it, or get some measure on it, rather than just assume that everyone falls under its influence. Similarly, researchers should not assume that all Chinese uphold Confucian beliefs to the same extent, not to mention that there are other dominant ways of thinking (such as Taoism and Buddhism). Assumption should be empirically measured and tested. Real understanding of Chinese child development would benefit from real empirical studies. It is beyond the scope of this chapter to discuss other major thinking. As Confucianism so often appears in Western literature, the present chapter thus places greater emphasis on it, to draw attention to the pitfalls that might be involved in such research or thinking. It is just too convenient to rely on one ideology to guide research on Chinese behavior. If we look at the history of Western psychology, we find no such parallel: There is no Plato here Plato there,

Christ here Christ there, or Darwin everywhere. All Western theories (e.g., cognitive dissonance, frustration-aggression, social comparison) tend to be based on insights drawn from commonplace observations rather than on any single ideology.

The Modern Chinese: New Destinies

Studies have shown that the value orientation and life goals of modern Chinese are creating another chapter in Chinese history. In a recent study (Lau, Nicholls, Thorkildsen, and Patashnick, 1995), it has been found that Chinese high school students showed a greater preference for the idea that school should teach them to be more creative in facing challenges than did their American counterparts. It was also found that they regarded interest and effort to be more important factors for success in work than did American students. They also perceived having personal assets, such as good fate (success), intelligence, and wealth, as essential. And putting in enough effort, being smart, and being lucky could help in attaining success at work as well. The study also showed that Chinese students were more self-confident than their American counterparts. Other studies of value orientation have also shown that both Chinese college and high school students treasure personal goals such as freedom and achievement (Feather, 1986; Lau, 1988, 1992; Lau and Wong, 1992).

Many researchers have shown that adolescents raised in authoritative homes do indeed perform better in school than their peers from non-authoritarian homes (Dornbusch, Ritter, Liederman, Roberts, and Fraleigh, 1987; Lamborn, Mounts, Steinberg, and Dornbusch, 1991). However Steinberg, Dornbusch, and Brown (1992) have found that virtually regardless of their parents' practices, Asian students received higher grades in school than other American students. In other words, this study has found that students' beliefs about the relation between education and life success influence their performance and engagement in school. And for Asian students, it is their fear that educational failure will lead to negative consequences that motivates them to strive for excellence (Steinberg et al., 1992).

In terms of educational aspiration and attainment, Chinese students view school as a place which prepares them to earn money, acquire luxuries, and eventually enter high status colleges and thus establish an outstanding career (Lau et al., 1995). By contrast, American high school students are more likely to view school as a place which should teach them to understand science, improve their critical thinking, and make them useful to society.

Another study has examined the value preference of Chinese high school students (Lau and Wong, 1992). The result has indicated that these adolescents placed greater emphasis on personal and competency values. They tended to favour a joyous, comfortable, free, and enjoyable lifestyle. The four most important terminal values for them were: freedom, true friendship, happiness, and a comfortable life. These findings were a complete contrast to the general collectivistic depiction of Chinese in relation to adolescent development (Lau and Wong, 1992). The modified values and goals of the new Chinese generation have confirmed to us once again that, indeed, a new destiny is gradually being sketched out. Perhaps these young Chinese are tired of following the rigid and traditional cultural formats and want to escape them.

Meanwhile, these young people are in search of something — in search of a good life, or in search of an identity (Ho, 1989). The latter is especially applicable to Chinese who have immigrated overseas or who were born in foreign countries, as shown in the root-finding mentality depicted in novels and films written or produced by overseas Chinese. As Amy Tan (1989), who was born and grew up in San Francisco, wrote in her novel *The Joy Luck Club* about her experience of visiting China for the first time:

> The minute our train leaves the Hong Kong border and enters Shenzhen, China, I feel different. I can feel the skin on my forehead tingling, my blood rushing through a new course, my bones aching with familiar old pain. And I think, my mother was right. I am becoming Chinese … I was a sophomore at Galileo High in San Francisco and all my Caucasian friends agreed: I was about as Chinese as they were. But my mother had studied at a famous nursing school in Shanghai, and she said, "… once you are born Chinese, you cannot help but feel and think Chinese." "Someday you will see," said my mother. "It is in your blood, waiting to be let go."

The paragraph above clearly reflects the feelings of the author, a typical ABC (American Born Chinese): Who am I? And where can I seek my own family roots? Am I Chinese or American? Or both? Sometimes these Chinese–Americans are caught in the middle of two cultures. Self-identification is a question for hard contemplation. These problems not only apply to Chinese immigrants, but also even to Chinese who are born and raised in Taiwan, Hong Kong, Singapore, or Malaysia. Since Western culture has had an impact on these countries, traditional Chinese rules and values have diminished bit by bit. People become less and less aware of their origins and self-identity: Where are they from? What province do their ancestors belong to?

When one looks at the recent history of China, one can not fail to realize the upheavals Chinese have gone and are going through. Nowadays, some Chinese are apprehensive or anxious about the future because of the past, and they are desperately in search of a good life (mostly in overseas countries). Other Chinese are bewildered or lost in the present also because of the past, and they are in search of a new self-identity (finding their roots at home). These are the generations of young people and children we need to study.

Conclusion: Beyond the Perfect Face

Chinese children first caught the attention of Western psychologists because of their unusually high academic achievement. If education is the backbone of a country's development in terms of human resources, it is no wonder that Western scholars turn to the East for remedies to stem the falling school standards in their own countries.

Yet, beyond the seemingly perfect face, Chinese children do manifest many problems of growing up. Suffice to say, gangs, juvenile delinquency, and other self-destructive antisocial behaviors (especially organized crimes) are becoming daily items of local and international news (Feldman, Rosenthal, Mont-Reynaud, Leung, and Lau, 1991; Lau 1990; Lau and Leung, 1992a, 1992b; Leung and Lau, 1989). The depiction of the perfect Chinese family is also unreal too. China has a long history of child and wife abuse. The inequality of the two sexes (with male being more superior) is also notorious and can be traced back to ancient times. These and similar issues are covered in other chapters in this volume.

Lying ahead of Chinese people is great uncertainty — a brave new world. Nobody knows what changes will have taken place in China ten years from now or twenty years from now. But everybody is seeking a better life — a life that leads to success and self-fulfillment. Many scholars have predicted that the next few centuries will be very crucial for China, in terms of social, political, and economic development (Meisner, 1986; Spence, 1990; Terrill, 1992). And perhaps traditional Chinese culture will thus be effected and modified over and over again. This new world may eventually be shaped by the new generations of Chinese children and hence lead us to a brand new destiny — a new chapter that the world is longing to see and to experience.

References

Baker, H. D. (1979). *Chinese family and kinship*. New York: Columbia University Press.

Berndt, T. J., Cheung, P. C., Lau, S., Hau, K. T., and Lew, W. (1993). Perceptions of parenting in mainland China, Taiwan, and Hong Kong: Sex differences and societal differences. *Developmental Psychology*, 29 (1): 156–164.

Bo, Y. (1985). *Choulou de Zhongguo ren* [The ugly Chinese]. Taipei: Lin Bai.

Bowerman, M. (1981). Language development. In H. C. Triandis and A. Heron (Eds.), *Handbook of cross-cultural psychology* (Vol. 4, pp. 93–185). Boston: Allyn and Bacon.

Brown, A. L., and Reeve, R. A. (1985). *Bandwidths of competence: The role of supportive contexts in learning and development* (Tech. Rep. No. 336). Champaign: University of Illinois at Urbana–Champaign, Center for the Study of Reading.

Cazden, C. B., John, V. P., and Hymes, D. (Eds.). (1975). *Functions of language in the classroom*. New York: Teachers College Press.

Cherry, K. (1983, October). Exam hell. *Winds*, 17–24.

Chiu, L. H. (1987). Child-rearing attitudes of Chinese, Chinese–American, and Anglo–American mothers. *International Journal of Psychology*, 22: 409–419.

Cole, M. (1981). *The zone of proximal development: Where culture and cognition create each other* (Report No. 106). San Diego: University of California, Center for Human Information Processing.

Domino, G. (1992). Cooperation and competition in Chinese and American children. *Journal of Cross-Cultural Psychology*, 23 (4): 456–467.

Dornbusch, S. M., Ritter, P. L., Liederman, P., Roberts, D., and Fraleigh, M. (1987). The relation of parenting style to adolescent school performance. *Child Development*, 58: 1244–1257.

Ekblad, S. (1986). Relationships between child-rearing practices and primary school children's functional adjustment in the People's Republic of China. *Scandinavian Journal of Psychology*, 27: 220–230.

Feather, N. T. (1986). Value systems across cultures: Australia and China. *International Journal of Psychology*, 21: 697–715.

Fei, X. T. (1948). *Xiang tu Zhongguo* [Rural China]. Shanghai: Quanchashe.

Feldman, S. S., Rosenthal, D. A., Mont-Reynaud, R., Leung, K., and Lau, S. (1991). Ain't misbehavin': Adolescent values and family environments as correlates of misconduct in Australia, Hong Kong, and the United States. *Journal of Research on Adolescence*, 1: 109–134.

Gewritz, J. L. (1965). The course of infant smiling in four child-rearing environments in Israel. In B. M. Foss (Ed.), *Determinants of Infant Behavior* (Vol. 3, pp. 205–248). London: Mathuen.

Goldberg, S. (1972). Infant care and growth in urban Zambia. *Human Development*, 15: 77–89.

Ho, D. (1989). Continuity and variation in Chinese patterns of socialization. *Journal of Marriage and the Family*, 51: 149–163.

Ho, D.Y.F. (1987). Fatherhood in Chinese culture. In M. E. Lamb (Ed.), *The father's role: Cross-cultural perspectives* (pp. 227–245). Hillsdale, NJ: Erlbaum.

Hong Kong samaritan befrienders. (1981–1991). Annual Reports. Hong Kong: Hong Kong Samaritan Befrienders.

Hsu, F.L.K. (1948). *Under the ancestors' shadow: Chinese culture and personality*. New York: Columbia University Press.

————. (1981). *American and Chinese: Passage to differences* (3rd ed.). Honolulu: University Press of Hawaii.

Kelley, M. L., and Tseng, H. M. (1992). Cultural differences in child rearing: A comparison of immigrant Chinese and Caucasian American mothers. *Journal of Cross-Cultural Psychology*, 23 (4): 444–455.

Konner, M. (1972). Aspects of the developmental ethology of a foraging people. In N. Blurton-Jones (Ed.), *Ethological studies of child behavior* (pp. 285–328). Cambridge: Cambridge University Press.

Lam, D. J., and Yang, C. F. (1989). Social behavior in real Hong Kong. *Personality and Social Psychology Bulletin*, 15 (4): 639–643.

Lamb, M. E., Sternberg, K. J., Hwang, C. P., and Broberg, A. G. (Eds.). (1992). *Child care in context: Cross-cultural perspectives*. Hillsdale, NJ: Lawrence Erlbaum.

Lamborn, S. D., Mounts, N. S., Steinberg, L., and Dornbusch, S. M. (1991). Patterns of competence and adjustment among adolescents from authoritative, authoritarian, indulgent, and neglectful families. *Child Development*, 62: 1049–1065.

Lau, S. (1988). The value orientations of Chinese University students in Hong Kong. *International Journal of Psychology*, 23: 583–596.

————. (1990). Crisis and vulnerability in adolescent development. *Journal of Youth and Adolescence*, 19: 111–131.

————. (1992). Collectivism's individualism: Value preference, personal control, and the desire for freedom among Chinese in mainland China, Hong Kong, and Singapore. *Personality and Individual Difference*, 13 (3): 361–366.

Lau, S., and Cheung, P. C. (1987). Relations between Chinese adolescent's perception of parental control and organization and their perception of parental warmth. *Developmental Psychology*, 23 (5): 726–729.

Lau, S., and Leung, K. (1992a). Relations with parents and school and Chinese adolescents' self-concept, delinquency, and academic performance. *British Journal of Educational Psychology*, 62: 21–30.

————. (1992b). Self-concept, delinquency, relations with parents and school, and Chinese adolescents' perception of personal control. *Personality and Individual Differences*, 13: 615–622.

Lau, S., Lew, W.J.F., Hau, K. T., Cheung, P. C., and Berndt, T. J. (1990). Relations among perceived parental control, warmth, indulgence, and family harmony of Chinese in mainland China. *Developmental Psychology*, 26: 674–677.

Lau, S., Nicholls, J. G., Thorkildsen, T. A., and Patashnick, M. (1995). *Chinese and American adolescents' perception of the purposes of education and beliefs about the world of work*. Manuscript submitted for publication.

Lau, S., and Wong, A. K. (1992). Value and sex-role orientation of Chinese adolescents. *International Journal of Psychology*, 27 (1): 3–17.

Lee, L. C. (1992). Day care in the People's Republic of China. In M. E. Lamb, K. J. Sternberg, C. P. Hwang, and A. G. Broberg (Eds.), *Child care in Context: Cross-cultural perspective* (pp. 355–392). Hillsdale, NJ: Lawrence Erlbaum.

Lei, T. (1993, November). *Metzger's model for the modern moral man*. Paper presented at the International Conference on Moral and Civic Education, Hong Kong.

Leung, K., and Lau, S. (1989). Effects of self-concept and perceived disapproval on delinquent behavior in school children. *Journal of Youth and Adolescence*, 18: 345–359.

Liu, I. S. (1991). The dragon is not willing to grow up. In L. Y. Tsze (Ed.), *Parenting in Chinese culture* (In Chinese) (pp. 1–24). Taipei: Living Psychology Magazine.

Meisner, M. J. (1986). *Mao's China and after: A history of the People's Republic*. New York: The Free Press.

Metzger, T. (1992). The thoughts of Tang Chun-i (1909–1978): A preliminary response. In *Proceedings of the International Conference on Tang's thoughts* (pp. 165–98). Hong Kong: Fa-tzu.

———. (1993). *The legitimization of the three marketplace as important part of modernization: A research note with regard to the question of Chinese modernization*. Unpublished manuscript. Hoover Institution at Stanford, California.

Mordkowitz, E., and Ginsberg, H. (1987). Early academic socialization of successful Asian–American college students. *Quarterly Newsletter of the Laboratory of Comparative Human Cognition*, 9: 85–91.

Ogbu, J. U. (1982). Socialization: A cultural ecological approach. In K. M. Borman (Ed.), *The social life of children in a changing society* (pp. 253–267). Hillsdale, NJ: Erlbaum.

Rea, J. C., Chao, D. W., and Good, C. (1981). Evangelizing Taiwan-Chinese college students. In C. Wagner and R. Dayton (Eds.), *Unreached People '81*. Elgin, IL: D. C. Cook.

Rogoff, B., and Morelli, G. (1989). Perspectives on children's development from cultural psychology. *American Psychologist*, 44 (2): 343–348.

Rohlen, T. P. (1983, October). The facts just the facts. *Winds*, 26–36.

Rohner, R. P., and Pettengill, S. M. (1985). Perceived parental acceptance–rejection and parental control among Korean adolescents. *Child Development*, 56: 524–528.

Shaffer, D. R. (1989). *Developmental psychology: Childhood and adolescence* (2nd ed.). Pacific Grove, CA: Brooks / Cole.

Slobin, D. I. (1973). Cognitive prerequisites for the development of grammar. In C. A. Ferguson and D. I. Slobin (Eds.), *Studies of child language development* (pp. 175–200). New York: Holt, Rinehart and Winston.

Spence, J. D. (1990). *The search for modern China*. New York: Norton.

Stander, V., and Jensen, L. (1993). The relationship of value orientation to moral cognition: Gender and cultural differences in the United States and China explored. *Journal of Cross-cultural Psychology*, 24 (1): 42–52.

Steinberg, L., Dornbusch, S. M., and Brown, B. B. (1992). Ethnic differences in adolescent achievement: An ecological perspective. *American Psychologist*, 47 (6): 723–729.

Stipek, D., Weiner, B., and Li, K. (1989). Testing some attribution — Emotion relations in the People's Republic of China. *Journal of Personality and Social Psychology*, 56: 109–116.

Sue, S., and Okazaki, S. (1990). Asian–American educational achievements: A phenomenon in search of an explanation. *American Psychologist*, 45: 913–920.

Super, C. M. (1981). Behavioral development in infancy. In R. H. Munroe, R. L. Munroe, and B. B. Whiting (Eds.), *Handbook of cross-cultural human development* (pp. 181–270). New York: Garland.

Suzuki, B. H. (1980). The Asian–American family. In M. D. Fantini and Cardenas (Eds.), *Parenting in a multicultural society* (pp. 74–102). New York: Longman.

Tan, A. (1989). *The joy luck club*. New York: Ivy Books.

Terrill, R. (1992). *China in our time: The people of China from the communist victory to Tiananmen Square and beyond*. New York: Touchstone.

Tharp, R. G. (1989). Psychocultural variables and constants: Effects on teaching and learning in schools. *American Psychologist*, 44 (2): 349–359.

The record of rites, book IX: The commonwealth state. Singapore: Confucius Publishing Singapore Pte. Ltd.

Tu, W. M. (1984). *Confucian ethics today: The Singapore challenge*. Singapore: Federal Publications.

———. (1985). *Confucian thought: Selfhood as creative transformation*. Albany, NY: State University of New York Press.

Vygotsky, L. S. (1978). *Mind in society*. Cambridge, MA: Harvard University Press.

Werner, E. E. (1989). A cross-cultural perspective on infancy. *Journal of Cross-cultural Psychology*, 19 (1): 96–113.

Wheeler, L. (1988). My year in Hong Kong: Some observations about social
     Behavior. *Personality and Social Psychology Bulletin*, 14: 410–420.

3

Gender Role Development

Fanny M. Cheung

Gender roles are prescribed in traditional Chinese societies where stereotypic gender roles are socialized primarily in the family, and reinforced by other social institutions. The only place delegated to women was in the family where they would play the instrumental and supportive roles of managing the home and supplying male heirs. The patrilineal continuation of the family and the cultural tradition of reserving inheritance to sons and not to daughters have resulted in greater values attached to sons in the Chinese family. Despite rapid social changes in contemporary Chinese societies, the cultural prescriptions for gender roles have lagged behind external social conditions. This chapter will review these traditional gender stereotypes, introduce the literature on sex-typed values, motives, and behaviors in contemporary Chinese societies, and examine the role of various socialization agents in the development of these roles and stereotypes.

Traditional Gender Concepts

The Chinese ideology of feminine inequality considers women to be inferior and subordinated to men by nature, and hence should be subjected to a double standard of marriage and related matters. The denial of women's right to divorce and remarriage was advocated. A wife could be divorced if she committed one of seven "wrongs", including failure to serve well or disobeying parents-in-law, failure to give birth to a son, and jealousy. Chiao (1989) noted that this ideology developed in the Han dynasty by Confucian scholars as an "involution" process reaching a peak in the late Ming and early Qing dynasties. Despite the revolution against feminine inequality in China in the early twentieth century, there is a lack of progress towards gender equality in modern Chinese societies due to the entrenched ideology. Even in the People's Republic of China where gender equality was enshrined in the national constitution, the revolution for women has been set aside and remains at the theoretical level without any working programme. With the majority of its population in the rural patrilocal community, daughters are considered temporary commodities who will move away to the homes of their husbands when they marry. Women are put into a dependent class by the strength of the traditional Chinese family (Lindsey, 1990). Given the "survival of the patrilineal kinship system", the "ancestral cult in China", and the "inadequacy of the socialist revolution", women in China still experience discrimination at work and within the home (Hong, 1976).

The contemporary Women's Movement in Taiwan started in the 1970s along with the increased opportunities for women in education and employment. Despite higher educational achievement and greater economic participation by women in Taiwan, women scholars noted that equal partnership for women and men in all aspects of social life remained a distant objective. Women's new social roles conflict with traditional familial values, and thus limit their standards of achievement and cause role conflicts and stress (Chiang, 1989; Ku, 1988). The traditional achievement for Chinese women is to be married to a good provider for herself, to bear male children for his family, and hope these children will be successful. This supportive role continues to be reinforced in modern Chinese society through newspapers, television, movies, and the school system which sends the message that the women's place in the world is to be a mother. Her value is judged first by the success of her husband and then by the success of her children (Yu and Carpenter, 1991).

One would expect that in the British colony of Hong Kong, the influence of Western culture would enhance the role of women. However, the colonial government has avoided bringing major changes to the local culture especially those traditions related to the family. The Hong Kong government was the last among major Chinese societies in outlawing polygamy and adopted the Marriage Reform Ordinance only in 1971 whereas marriage reforms protecting the rights of women have been enacted by the Chinese Republic in 1911 and by the People's Republic of China in 1949 (Cheung, Wan, and Wan, 1994). Up till 1994, the colonial government still endorses the traditional Chinese custom of land inheritance among indigenous villagers and allocation of small house entitlement within the village along the male line only (Hong Kong Government, 1993).

The preference for sons over daughters is epitomized in the One-Child policy in the People's Republic of China planned parenthood programme.

With strong vestiges of ancestor worship, Chinese believe that there can be no descendants without a son. Female infanticide is noted to be on the rise after the adoption of this policy (Croll, 1983). Women who bore daughters instead of sons tend to be devalued (Chinese Women Social Status Survey Group, 1993). In Hong Kong, preference for sons over daughters is also evident in the attitudes of parents although the explicit rejection of daughters is less apparent (Family Planning Association of Hong Kong, 1984, 1989).

In traditional Chinese families, the two sexes were segregated from an early age. Socialization of sons and daughters differed from birth. The social structure of the family revolved around the father-son relationship. Yu and Carpenter (1991) described the two general principles which govern this kinship structure, which in turns forms the basis of gender identification: the patrilineage generational principle, and the principle of "estrangement between the sexes and sex inequality". Boys are socialized to take over power and responsibility while girls are subject to subordination to males and to other women in the family hierarchy. In Western culture which is also a male-oriented culture, there is greater pressure for boys than girls to conform to narrowly defined sex-appropriate standards (Hetherington and Parke, 1986). However, in traditional Chinese culture which also accorded greater esteem, privileges, and status to the masculine role, there are more restrictive prescriptions for the role of women. Women submerge their individuality to the family, following the orders of their fathers when young, their husbands when married, and their sons when widowed. The virtues to be followed as a woman are defined clearly in her function as wife and mother.

Although education is an important value in Chinese culture, aspirations for educational achievement are focussed on boys rather than on girls. Women were not allowed nor encouraged to receive formal education until the beginning of the twentieth century. Even when free and compulsory education up to the ninth grade has opened up educational opportunities for women in the Chinese societies in the 1970s, school is not a priority for girls especially when the family is limited in financial resources. Older daughters often have to give up their studies and go out to work to support their younger brothers' schooling (Tang, 1981).

Gender-typed behaviors

Similar to findings in Western studies, gender typing and stereotypes are observed among young Chinese children. One of the earliest studies was initiated by Keyes (1979, 1984) who developed a Chinese Sex-Role Inventory based on the Bem Sex Role Inventory (BSRI; Bem, 1974) as well as adding items she found relevant to Chinese children in Hong Kong. The 104-item rating scale consisted of school subjects and activities the students deemed important for a boy and a girl to be good at, and qualities of character a boy and a girl should possess. She studied school children aged 10, 13, and 16 and found that these children could specify distinct stereotypes of male and female personality traits and activities. Male character terms included active, ambitious, brave, career-minded and persevering. Male activities were ballgames, soccer, sports, Ping-Pong, model-making, and photography. Female character terms included kind and approachable, conforms to and sensitive to others' needs, generous, and presentable. Female activities were minding children, singing, housework, cooking, needlework, and dressmaking. These stereotypes were more clearly articulated by the older children.

Keyes' (1979, 1983, 1984) studies were among the few which studied gender differences in cognitive abilities among Chinese children. She found biological sex differences in patterns of cognitive test performance, including spatial ability, fluency, and verbal ability. Adolescent boys performed better on spatial ability and girls performed better on fluent production. These patterns of ability were not related to sex role identification. However, Keyes noted that conflict and maladjustment would be related to discrepancy between one's abilities and normative sex role and suggested that these aspects should be further investigated.

These findings were consistent with Western findings of actual sex differences in cognitive development. Based on summaries of classic and recent studies, Hetherington and Parke (1986) differentiated among mythical, equivocal, and actual sex differences. In the area of cognitive development, actual differences were confirmed in verbal abilities including vocabulary, reading comprehension, and verbal creativity, in which girls are superior from infancy and the superiority increases rapidly in high school years. Boys, on the other hand, are found to excel in visual-spatial ability such as manipulating objects in two- or three-dimensional space, reading maps, or aiming at a target, from about age 10, and to excel in mathematics beginning at about age 12 (p. 626).

In terms of social and emotional development, the areas of actual sex differences highlighted by Hetherington and Parke (1986) include aggression, especially physical aggression in which boys are more often the aggressors as well as the victims; compliance to adult demands for girls, and nurturance towards younger children among girls (p. 626). Similar gender differences in social and emotional behaviors of young Chinese children were also found in one of the few in-depth studies of Chinese childrearing practices and children's behavior (Cheung, Lam, and Chau, 1990). In an intensive observational study of the interactions of young children with their caretakers and with their peers, Cheung and her associates found that 6-year-old boys already exhibited more assertive behavior than girls. While verbal and physical aggression were rare among the children and tend to be controlled by the caretakers, girls were much less prone than boys to express any form of aggression. These gender differences in general aggressive behavior and aggression control were also found in a study of primary school children in China using an aggression inventory (Ekblad, 1989).

Gender Stereotypes in Children and Adolescents

Apart from Keyes' early studies, Cheung (1986) studied a larger group of Hong Kong students with a wider age range. 561 primary 1 to 6 school children and 1145 secondary 1 to 7 children were selected from schools drawn from a stratified random sample. The Sex Stereotype Measure II (SSM II), a 32-item forced-choice instrument in pictoral format developed by Best and her Associates (Best, Williams, Cloud, Davis, Robertson, Edwards, Giles, and Fowles, 1977) in a cross-national study was used with the primary school subjects. For the secondary school children, the translated version of the Pancultural Adjective Checklist developed by Williams and Best (1982) for their 30-nation cross-cultural study was used. Cheung found that even for young primary school children, distinctive gender stereotypes were formed. Both boys and girls described males as typically adventurous, disorderly, cruel, boastful, coarse, confident and strong on the SSM II. Females were described as emotional, weak, gentle, meek, excitable, soft-hearted, and dependent.

Gender stereotypes were found to increase with age. Secondary school children described the typical male as active, adventurous, capable, confident, courageous, determined, enterprising, humorous, initiating, and robust. The typical female was described as affectionate, charming, emotional, gentle, kind, mild, touchy, and warm. Cheung (1986) noted that these gender-based stereotypes conformed with the "competency-strength cluster" associated with the male stereotype and the "warmth-expressiveness cluster" associated with the female stereotype found in other Western studies (Broverman, Vogel, Broverman, Clarkson, and Rosenkrantz, 1972).

The secondary school subjects in Cheung's (1986) study perceived the typical male and typical female in more gender-stereotypic terms than they viewed themselves. Although boys scored higher on masculine characteristics than girls, they were also likely to describe themselves in terms of expressive characteristics. Girls, on the other hand, described themselves much more in terms of feminine characteristics than masculine characteristics. Similar to their perception of gender stereotypes, the school children's own identification with gender stereotypes also increased with age. Older male subjects identified with more masculine adjectives while older female subjects identified with more feminine adjectives.

The Hong Kong findings were comparable to the results obtained for 100 5-year-old and 100 8-year-old children in Taiwan by Williams and Best in their cross-national study (1990). While children at age 5 were able to differentiate between male and female characteristics, 8-year-olds perceived more differences in the psychological makeup of girls and boys than their younger counterparts. However, compared to the other 24 international samples, the degree of gender differentiation found among Taiwan subjects was moderately low. In the cross-national comparison, the countries with the highest degree of gender differentiation were Pakistan, England, and New Zealand, while the countries with the lowest degree of differentiation were Thailand, Nigeria, and Venezuela (p. 202). The mean common variance for the Taiwan subjects with all the other international samples was 67.5, indicating that their responses were fairly typical of children in most other countries. The samples which shared the highest common variance with the Taiwan 8-year-old sample were the Netherlands, Norway, Peru, Canada, and England. The sample with the lowest common variance was India. It is interesting to note that the Japanese sample, coming from a culture which is often assumed to share the same Confucian roots, only shared a moderate common variance with the Taiwan sample.

In the Williams and Best's (1990) study, a small sample of 100 university students in Taiwan was asked to fill in a 52-item short-form of the Adjective Check List (Gough and Heilbrun, 1965) which was used to identify gender stereotypes. The short-form consists of 26 items which were highly associated with males and 26 items which were highly associated with females in three English speaking countries: U. S., England, and Ireland. The degree to which the responses of the Taiwan subjects corresponded with the gender association of the adjectives in these three countries was calculated in terms of M% for the male-associated adjectives and F% for the female-associated adjectives. While the total percent of stereotyped responses for the Taiwan subjects was 85%, the M% was 91%, much higher than the F% of 79%, showing higher cross-cultural agreement for the male stereotype than for the female stereotype. 19 of the 26 "Amengire" (America, England, and Ireland) male-associated adjectives were rated by over 90% of the Taiwan subjects. The adjectives most often attributed to males were active, adventurous, autocratic, boastful, coarse, courageous, enterprising, independent, reckless, and strong. In contrast, only 10 of the 26 female-associated adjectives were rated correspondingly by the Taiwan subjects. These adjectives were also more likely to be negative in nature, including dreamy, emotional, frivolous, fussy, nagging, sensitive, soft-hearted, submissive, and timid.

Ward (1990) also used the Sex Stereotype Measurement II by Williams and Best (1982) in her study of Singaporean children. Her subjects consisted of 40 5-year-old and 40 8-year-old boys and girls with ethnic Chinese composing 87.5% of the sample. She found that the male stereotype was more readily identified than the female stereotype. These stereotypes were more accurately identified by the same-sex than opposite-sex subjects in the 5-year-old sample. However, the 8-year-old girls' stereotype of boys increased with age more than their stereotype of girls. Compared with the results of the Williams and Best's (1982) cross-cultural study, the contents of the Singaporean children's stereotypes were similar to those of other countries, with boys being perceived as aggressive, adventurous, cruel, loud, strong, and jolly, and girls being viewed as emotional, appreciative, gentle, meek, excitable, and dependent. At 5 years of age, Singaporean children were found to be particularly well informed about gender stereotypes.

After completing their original 30-nation cross-cultural study, Williams and Best (1990) added a further sample of 100 Singaporean university students which consisted of 90% ethnic Chinese, using the 300-item Adjective Check List. The common variance for the genderized responses of the Singaporean subjects with those of the other 25 countries in the original study was 79%, indicating that the gender differentiation of the subjects was very typical. However, a comparison with the Taiwan sample in the original study was not possible since only the short-form of the Adjective Check List was used in the Taiwan study. Further analysis of the favorability scores of the stereotypes among the Singaporean subjects indicated that the favorability of the male stereotype was relatively high while that of the female stereotype was relatively low with a large discrepancy score between the two. Comparisons of the strength scores of the stereotypes between Singapore and the other countries showed that the male stereotype was seen to be stronger than average and the female stereotype to be below average in terms of strength.

Studies among Chinese college students confirm similar patterns of gender stereotypes. Li (1985) expanded the list of adjectives in the Bem Sex Role Inventory (Bem, 1974) to a total of 186 adjectives and asked 191 college students in Taiwan to rate the gender-appropriateness of each characteristic. Among the 60 adjectives which indicated gender differences, those attributed to masculine characteristics were instrumental in nature and were related to the development of the individual's career achievement. Adjectives attributed to feminine characteristics were affective and temperamental in nature, and related to the development of intimate interpersonal relationships. Li, however, found in an earlier study that among 502 college students who were asked to describe themselves based on 20 masculine and 20 feminine characteristics, the distinction between male and female students were less pronounced. A sizable proportion of the subjects could be classified as androgynous or undifferentiated whereas only 35% of the males and 36% of the females were classified exclusively according to their respective gender role (Li, 1985). Again, the perception of gender stereotype is more differentiated than one's own identification with these stereotyped characteristics.

Gender stereotypes in Chinese societies have remained quite constant despite rapid changes in the role of women especially in Western countries. In a cross-cultural study on sex-role stereotypes and social desirability among U.S. and Chinese college students (Lii and Wong, 1982), the Chinese students' rating of the female role maintained a more traditional view of women who possessed "warm" and "expressive" attributes. In contrast, American students described the female sex-role with more "agentic" and "competent" attributes, reflecting a more "liberated" view of women. In both the U.S. and the Chinese groups, the male subjects tend to emphasize the male stereotype as more socially desirable, while the female subjects did not make the differentiation.

Gender and Esteem

Gender role orientation is recognized as being an important aspect of one's self-esteem (Whitley, 1983). The social values attached to gender roles affect the development of self-worth of males and females. In Cheung's (1986) secondary school study, more masculine traits were selected by male and female students in their descriptions of the ideal-self. Fewer of the feminine traits were chosen as ideal while more of them were seen as unfavorable. The reverse was found with masculine traits. Although there were sex differences in the preference for characteristics associated with one's own gender, the preference for masculine characteristics was greater than for feminine characteristics for both male and female students. This is consistent with the result of Whitley's (1983) review that optimal well-being is a result of the strength of the masculinity dimension.

Current research on the relation between gender role and self-esteem has pointed to a more complex pattern of relationships involving different domains of self-esteem (Marsh, Antill, and Cunningham, 1987). Different domains of the adolescents' self-esteem are related to their gender roles. Lau (1989) included five distinct domains — academic, appearance, physical ability, social, and general self-esteem — in his study of 191 16-year-old students in Hong Kong. He found a strong positive relation between masculinity and all five self-esteem domains. The correlations between femininity and self-esteem were much lower, with no significant relations found for physical ability and appearance. The masculine and androgynous groups of subjects were superior to the feminine and undifferentiated groups in academic, appearance, and general self-esteem. These results also support the masculinity model (Whitley, 1983): that masculinity is strongly associated with self-esteem and psychological well-being.

The feminine stereotype, on the other hand, is often associated with a sense of inferiority. Crittenden (1989) studied the attributional patterns of female university students in Taiwan and found that their attributions were more self-effacing than those of male students. Compared with their American counterparts, the Taiwanese women students maintained more "traditional Asian virtues" and were more external and self-effacing in their attributions. The author concluded that these findings fit those of gender role stereotypes in which women are characterized as socially responsible but relatively incompetent. She further argued that Chinese women conform to the feminine gender role to enhance their public and private esteem. This may be reflected in the observation that empirical gender differences in attributional style were smaller and more subtle than differences between gender-role stereotypes (Crittenden, 1991).

In the People's Republic of China, a national survey on the social status of women was conducted in 1990 by the All China Federation of Women (Chinese Women's Social Status Survey Group, 1993) using a sample of 11,211 females and 10,661 males aged 18 to 64. The survey covered objective indicators and subjective perceptions of gender equality. In the section on self-esteem, questions included perception of one's ability and accomplishments. There was little gender difference in terms of the respondents' belief about their ability to achieve a higher position. At the same time, over 60% of the rural respondents of both genders felt that they lacked a special skill. However, the gender differential in the urban areas was more distinct with more of the urban female than male respondents expressing this deficit. The majority of the respondents of both genders did not believe that males were inherently stronger than females. This attitude was particularly prevalent among the young age group (18 to 19) and the well-educated respondents. Although it is apparent that the perception of male superiority in ability and strength is no longer prevalent, in the perceived level of gender equality in the domain of social attitudes, the majority (58%) of the respondents regardless of gender considered that men held more superior status than women, although they found greater equality in other social domains especially legal status. Overall speaking, women still peferred to have been born as a male (41%) than a female (20%) if they had the choice especially in the rural areas. In contrast, only 8% of the male respondents wished they were born as a female as opposed to a male (54%).

Gender Differences in Values and Aspirations

The impact of gender role conflict on achievement motivation has received much attention since Horner's (1972, 1974) original thesis on the motive to avoid success acquired by women in early life. Horner noted that success poses an approach-avoidance conflict for females: On the one hand, success is desirable for its associated rewards; on the other hand, it is perceived as a male goal and may lead to "unfemininity", and thus, social and sexual rejection. The implications on women's educational and career aspirations have received much attention.

Wang and Creedon (1989) examined attributes for success and failure, fear of success, and goal setting in 77 male and 87 female Chinese college students. They found that Chinese women were more likely to endorse statement expressing fear of success than Chinese men. The women also tend to attribute their achievement success to luck and failure to a lack of ability. Although the most important personal goal for both male and female college students was that of career success, Chinese men placed greater importance than women on achieving wealth and their expectancy of actually becoming wealthy was higher.

Other studies in Taiwan and Hong Kong have examined gender differences in achievement aspirations. Tsai and Chiu (1989) investigated the average level of educational aspiration among university students in Taiwan and found that much fewer female students aspired to enroll in graduate studies. While both male and female college students aspired towards professional jobs, the aspiration to the positions of employer and executive is much higher among males.

Similar differences in aspiration have been noted by Chow (1988) in her follow-up survey of university graduates at the Chinese University of Hong Kong. She found that female university graduates entered jobs that were steady and secure, while male graduates were more likely to choose jobs which offered advancement and entrepreneurship despite lower pay initially. The female graduates were also less confident about their ability and future career prospects. Similar gender differences were found in her comparative study of Hong Kong and Shenzhen university graduates (Chow, 1991). She found that fewer female students have made definite career plans before college graduation, reflecting lower family expectation for girls to start a career. The female students also had lower achievement aspirations in terms of long-term expected salaries, lower self-confidence, and less favourable assessment of their job-related attributes. These gender discrepancies were consistent in both Hong Kong and Shenzhen.

The development of identity and self-worth in adolescents has been found to be related to their identification with gender role. There are differences in value preferences between boys and girls with boys being more concerned with achievement and being smart, and girls being more concerned with interpersonal relationships and being liked (Maccoby and Jacklin, 1974; Stewart, 1982). The relations between value and sex role orientation among Chinese high school students in Hong Kong were studied by Lau and Wong (1992) using the Rokeach Value Survey (Rokeach, 1973). They found that sex-role orientation of adolescents is more closely related to their instrumental value system. While masculine and feminine adolescents were similar in their terminal value systems, they were very dissimilar in their instrumental value systems. Masculine adolescents preferred more agentic and personal values while feminine adolescents preferred more expressive and communal values. Androgynous adolescents were very similar to the masculine adolescents in terms of their terminal and instrumental values. While they were also more similar to the feminine adolescents in terms of their terminal values, they were less similar in the instrumental values. Results from the regression analysis showed that masculinity had more pervasive effects than femininity on value preference among the students. The authors concluded that the stronger relationships between instrumental values and sex-role orientation support Feather's (1984) expectancy-value theory which stipulated that gender role differences were based mainly in the preferred modes of conduct (instrumental values) rather than in the end-states of existence (terminal values).

Attitudes Towards Gender Roles in Chinese Societies

Women's self-esteem is, to a large extent, affected by society's attitudes towards women as members of the female gender. Attitudes towards women have changed with social times, and as such, have been included in measures of a person's Traditionality-Modernity in Chinese societies (Yang, 1986). Studies in Taiwan have found that Male Dominance/Superiority is one of the major factors identified on the Traditionality subscale and Sex Equality is a factor on the Modernity subscale (Yang, 1988).

Adolescents' attitudes towards women have been investigated in a number of community surveys in Hong Kong. An earlier survey in the 1970s (Breakthrough Research Group, 1976) found that only 35% of the female respondents and 20% of the male respondents supported the pursuit of tertiary education for women. Generally, more girls than boys supported the principles of equal pay for equal work, universal suffrage for both genders, and women's right to stand for elections. Even in the late 1980s, a survey of adolescents found that 75% of the respondents still supported the traditional patriarchal value that a wife belongs to the husband while over 10% believed that men and women should not have equal rights.

Chia, Chong, and Cheng (1986) studied the relationship between modernization and attitudes towards marital roles among male and female college students. They found that women held more modern values and more egalitarian attitudes towards the marital role. While there was a significant relationship between traditionality-modernity and marriage-role attitudes, the relationship was much stronger for women than for men.

The more positive view by females towards women's roles is confirmed in other studies comparing gender differences in attitudes towards women. In a study relating attitudes towards women to attitudes towards rape victims, Lee and Cheung (1991) found that female subjects were more supportive than males towards women in general and rape victims in particular. In addition to gender differences in these attitudes, occupational differences were also found, with clinical psychologists and social workers being more supportive than nurses and police officers, even when gender of the respondents were controlled.

However, in the work sphere, masculine characteristics are still preferred over feminine characteristics. Francesco and Hakel (1981) investigated the preference for gender characteristics in 3 gender-typed jobs among college students. In general, masculine applicants of both sexes were preferred over androgynous applicants, who in turn were preferred over feminine applicants. For a neutral job, androgynous applicants were the most preferred. Feminine applicants were rated lowest in all the jobs.

Differential Socialization of Boys and Girls by Parents

Maccoby and Jacklin's (1974) classic book summarized early theories of gender socialization which pointed to the roles of the home environment, peers and teachers in the acquisition of gender differences in behavior and attitudes. Contrary to the popular view that sex-typed behavior is primarily "shaped" by parents, they concluded that the role of direct socialization was crucial "not only in its own right but also in establishing the foundation upon which later self-socialization is based" (p. 303). As such, the impact of parental reinforcement on gender role socialization was found to be restricted to the narrowly defined areas of sex-typed behavior such as play activities and toy choices. However, due to the narrative nature of their reviews, their conclusions have been subject to strong criticism (Block, 1983).

Lytton and Romney (1991) reviewed the recent literature in a meta-analysis of 172 studies on parents' differential socialization of boys and girls. They found that most of the effect sizes were small and non-significant, supporting Maccoby and Jacklin's earlier conclusions. The only areas where significant effects were found were in parental encouragement of sex-typed activities and in greater use of physical punishment on boys. There was little evidence of differential socialization of cognitive and social characteristics.

The research literature on parental socialization of gender-typed behavior in Chinese societies is mostly limited to small-scaled and observational reports. Educationists noted that parents had differential expectations on the behavior and career development of boys and girls. Boys are taught to use tools to help their fathers mend furniture and appliances while girls help their mothers with washing and cooking in the kitchen. Boys are expected to be doctors, engineers and take up scientific jobs; girls are expected to be nurses, housewives, or work in the service sector. When resources are scarce, educational opportunity is reserved for sons because they are considered to be future bread-winners (Luk, 1981). Lam's (1982) study of the pattern of child-rearing practices in low-income families also showed that parents held differential expectations of the educational attainment of their sons and daughters. More of the parents wished their sons to attain tertiary education and to become doctors. They were also more likely to respect the interest and ability of their sons in choosing their future career. In contrast, if parents had any specific career aspirations for the daughters, it would be in the traditional feminine profession of nursing.

The thesis that given limited family resources, there would be differential opportunity of educational attainment for sons and daughters has been verified in Tang's (1981) empirical study. In these families, older daughters had to give up their studies to work in order to support the education of their brothers. When the family's financial resources improved partly as the result of the contributions of the older girls, there would be less gender differences in terms of access to education. Similarly, Mak (1991) noted the interaction between social class and gender in predicting women's access to higher education. Women who attended university came from a higher socioeconomic background. In poorer families, sibling order would compensate for the disadvantage of being a daughter so that younger daughters had similar access to education as their brothers. Although these reports did not investigate the behavioral aspects in the process of parental socialization, these patterns of outcome point to the direct impact of parental decisions in the allocation of family resources along gender lines. These gender-based decisions pronounce a differential set of values on sons and daughters, and directly channel their course of development.

Parents may affect the academic choice as well as performance of their children through their beliefs and expectations. Lummis and Stevenson (1990) studied gender differences on tests of cognitive abilities and tests of achievement in reading and mathematics in students in kindergarten, grade 1 and grade 5 in Taiwan, Japan, and the U.S. Although few gender differences were observed on curriculum-based tests of mathematics computation and reading, children as well as their mothers tended to believe that boys were better at mathematics and girls were better at reading. These beliefs were found as early as grade 1 and were consistent across the three cultures.

Gender Socialization in Schools

In studies of identification with gender stereotype among school children, its has been found that gender differentiation increases with age. Given the major proportion of a young person's life being occupied by the school system, the important role of schools in addition to the home environment in shaping and reinforcing gender differences has been recognized (Lytton and Romney, 1991). In particular, teachers and school textbooks are noted to be major sources of influence on the development of children's sex roles.

Analyses of textbooks used in primary and secondary schools in Hong Kong show that not only are gender stereotypes abound, but also that women are underrepresented in many areas. Au (1993) reviewed the contents of the most popular textbooks used in three primary school subjects: Chinese Language, Social Studies, and Health Education. She found that male characters appeared about twice as often as female characters. Of the characters who were engaged in economic activities, only 30% were females, much lower than the actual rate of labour force participation by females in Hong Kong. Moreover, the jobs in which the female characters were portrayed were few and repetitive with none in high level professional positions. In terms of sports activities, women were not represented at all. The family roles depicted in these textbooks conformed to traditional stereotypes without recognition of the changing status of women in society or the increasing participation of fathers in parenting. There were few women included as prominent role models among the world-famous figures quoted in these textbooks. Even when some of these female characters were noted, they were often recognized as the mothers or wives without citing their own names. Au's findings were confirmed in similar studies on primary school textbooks in China and Taiwan (Awakening Foundation, 1988; Zhang, 1984), and in analyses of children's readers in Hong Kong kindergartens (Ma, 1991) and in Taiwan (Chiang, 1989).

An earlier study of junior secondary textbooks for Chinese History and Social Studies in Hong Kong by Yau and Luk (1988) identified strong biases against women. Over 95% of the characters depicted in Chinese History books were males. Women only appeared in one of five main categories: the concubines of emperors who added to people's suffering and brought down the imperial dynasty; the ruthless empress dowagers; traditional forms of female labor such as child care, weaving, and tending to silk worms; the virtuous wife and mother; and matrilineal societies in ancient times. The two categories of women in the imperial court were the most common. In Social Studies, males were presented more than twice as often as females. When female roles were presented, only about one quarter was engaged in the labor force. Even then, the women were depicted in low-level positions with very few in professional jobs including those of teaching where females were over represented in reality. Only a handful of women were mentioned among famous figures in science, medicine, social reform, and philosophy.

Similar criticisms were lodged against junior secondary textbooks in Taiwan (Awakening Foundation, 1988). Women were not represented in ancient history or in contemporary discussions of human rights issues. The activities in which women were portrayed included singing, sewing, washing dishes, and watering plants; the male activities were more diversified in nature, including ballgames, fishing, hiking, reading, painting, and conducting experiments.

These gender stereotypes in textbooks limit the role models for girls and boys and distort the social reality of gender relationships in modern society. Research in the West has established a clear relationship between children's perception of sex-role appropriateness of specific educational activities and their motivation to achieve in these tasks (Huston, 1983; Stein and Bailey, 1973). Although no study has been undertaken in Chinese societies to demonstrate this set of relationships, the outcome in gender streaming in terms of subject preferences and in academic aspirations is apparent. It has been shown in a previous section that female university students had lower academic and career aspirations despite similar level of academic performance as male students. Other than parental expectations and stereotypes in school textbooks, the role of teachers in gender socialization has often been cited.

Given the domination of female teachers in the primary school, one would expect that the "feminine" culture would value qualities that are appropriate to the feminine role, and thus girls would perform better in their academic work (Hetherington and Parke, 1986). This is in fact often observed to be the case in primary schools. However, the advantage enjoyed by girls in the early grades is short-lived. Girls' achievement levels have been shown to decrease with growth. At the secondary level, girls were found to be less confident and less willing to undertake difficult tasks (Rogers, 1987). By the university level, the proportion of underachievers among female students exceeds that among male students (Hetherington and Parke, 1986). Rogers drew attention to the role of teacher expectations and in particular, prescriptive expectations in relations to gender roles in shaping students' behavior. Prescriptive expectations are what teachers believe boys and girls ought to be and are found to be more likely to become self-fulfilling prophecies. Although not necessarily deliberate, these prescriptive expectations takes on the force of a "moral imperative" in determining the patterns of behaviors for boys and girls in schools.

Chang (1976) examined the effect of sex-role identification based of the sex of teachers on the learning experience of school children in grades 4, 5, and 6 in Taiwan. Results showed no difference in the students' intellectual abilities measured by the Raven's Progressive Matrices between those taught by male and female teachers. Lower form students taught by female teachers did better on classroom Chinese and mathematics examinations while higher form students taught by men had higher scores in classroom examinations and achievement tests. Teachers believed that their own behavior influenced students of the same sex the most. While teachers identified boys as troublemakers and attributed less favorable characteristics to them, they also expected boys to achieve more than girls and would be more disappointed when boys failed.

In Hong Kong, the streaming of students into different subjects beginning in Form 4 (Grade 10) may be a reflection of the interplay of the expectations of teachers, parents, and peers, and one's identification with gender-appropriate roles regardless of one's aptitude and interest. Girls are often encouraged to develop more in Arts subjects while boys are encouraged towards Science subjects. Boys feel ashamed when assigned to the Arts stream, and will be frowned upon for choosing Domestic Science which is a girl's subject (Luk, 1981). In most secondary schools, only boys take Woodwork classes while only girls take Domestic Science. In prevocational schools, only male students are allowed to take Woodwork, Metal Work, Technical Drawing, and only female students are allowed to take Typewriting and Dressmaking courses.

The result of gender-based streaming in the choice of subjects can be seen clearly in the pattern of gender segregation in examination subjects at school leaving and in the choice of major subjects in the university. In the Hong Kong Certificate of Education Examination (HKCEE) taken by students in Form 5 (Grade 11), males dominate in numbers in the Science subjects including Physics, Chemistry, Additional Mathematics, and Engineering Science, and in technically-oriented subjects such as Electronics and Electricity, Metalwork, Woodwork, and Technical Drawing. Females dominate in Arts subjects, including Chinese History, Chinese Literature, History, and English Literature, and in service-oriented subjects such as Shorthand, Needlework, Dressmaking, Home Economics, and Typewriting. This differential pattern of gender domination becomes even stronger in the Hong Kong Higher Level Examination (HKHLE) taken in Form 6 (Grade 12), and the Hong Kong Advanced Level Examination (HKALE) taken in Form 7 (Grade 13). At the university level, males dominate in the Faculties of Engineering, Science, Dentistry, and Medicine, while females dominate in the Faculties of Arts and Law (Chan, 1989).

Summary

In the past 40 years, societal conditions for Chinese women have changed in many aspects. Women's opportunities for education and economic participation have expanded women's traditional role beyond that exclusive to the family. However, there is still a huge cultural lag in attitudes towards their gender roles. Gender stereotypes are polarized. Girls are often perceived as subordinate to boys and in terms of weaker and inferior attributes. The lower expectations of girls in turn are reflected in the lower aspirations and esteem among girls. These traditional gender concepts are maintained through the socialization practices of parents and the educational system.

The gender gap in Chinese societies are in many ways similar to those found in Western societies. Results reported by the existing studies on gender stereotypes, self-esteem, values, and aspirations of boys and girls in Chinese societies confirm the trends found in Western studies. The extent of research on gender role development in the Chinese context has, however, been limited. Many of the earlier studies are mainly descriptive in nature, reporting simple gender differences without full exploration of a theoretical framework to analyze the data in the Chinese cultural context or in a cross-cultural context. A large number of the studies were conducted by scholars in other social science disciplines or by social advocates. The wider topic of the psychology of gender roles itself is under-developed, reflecting a relative lack of interest among Chinese psychologists on gender issues in psychology. Including gender role development as a key component in the study of Chinese developmental psychology would provide the impetus for setting an overall research agenda.

References

Au, K. C. (1993). *A study of gender roles as defined in primary school textbooks in Hong Kong* (In Chinese) (Occasional Paper No. 18). Hong Kong: The Chinese University of Hong Kong, Hong Kong Institute of Asia–Pacific Studies.

Awakening Foundation. (1988). *Manual for equal education across gender* (In Chinese). Taipei: Awakening Foundation.

Bem, S. L. (1974). The measurement of psychological androgyny. *Journal of Clinical and Consulting Psychology*, 42: 155–162.

Bernard, M. (1979). Does sex-role behavior influence the way teachers evaluate student? *Journal of Educational Psychology*, 71: 553–562.

Best, D. L., Williams, J. E., Cloud, J. M., Davis, S. W., Robertson, L. S., Edwards, J. R., Giles, H., and Fowles, J. (1977). Development of sex-trait stereotypes among young children in the United States, England, and Ireland. *Child Development*, 48: 1375–1384.

Block, J. H. (1983). Differential premises arising from differential socialization of the sexes: Some conjectures. *Child Development*, 54: 1335–1354.

Breakthrough Research Group. (1976). Views of the two sexes on the female role (In Chinese). *Breakthrough*, 3 (3): 6–9.

Broverman, I. K., Vogel, S. R., Broverman, D. M., Clarkson, F. E., and Rosenkrantz, P. S. (1972). Sex-role stereotypes: A current appraisal. *Journal of Social Issues*, 28: 59–78.

Chan, J. (1989). Are boys late developers? *Convocation Newsletter, No. 2*. Hong Kong: University of Hong Kong.

Chang, C. H. (1976). Sex differences of children in school learning as related to sex differences of teachers: An analytical study of effect of availability of sex-role identification model on children's school learning. *Bulletin of Educational Psychology*, 9: 1–20.

Cheung, F. M. (1986). Development of gender stereotype. *Educational Research Journal*, 1: 68–73.

Cheung, F. M., Lam, M. C., and Chau, B.T.W. (1990). Caregiving techniques and pre-school children's development in Hong Kong families (Occasional Paper no. 29). Hong Kong: The Chinese University of Hong Kong, Centre for Hong Kong Studies.

Cheung, F. M., Wan , P. S., and Wan, O. C. (1994). The underdeveloped political potential of women in Hong Kong. In B. Nelson and N. Chowdhury (Eds.), *Women and politics worldwide* (pp. 326–346). New Haven, Conn.: Yale University Press.

Chia, R. C. , Chong, C. J., and Cheng, B. S. (1986). Relationship of modernization and marriage role attitude among Chinese college students. *Journal of Psychology*, 120: 599–605.

Chiang, L. H. (1989). The new social and economic roles of Chinese women in

Taiwan and their implications for policy and development. *Journal of Developing Societies*, 5: 96–106.

Chiao, C. (1989). Involution and revolution in gender equality: The Chinese experience. In Christian Academy (Ed.), *The world community in post-industrial society: Vol. 1. Changing families in the world perspective* (pp. 138–153). Seoul: Wooseok Publishing Co.

Chinese Women's Social Status Survey Group. (1993). *Zhongguofunu shehuidiwei gaiguan* [An overview of the social status of Chinese women]. Beijing: Chinese Women Press.

Chow, G. (1988). *Report on a study of the career aspiration of 1987 graduates with special regard to their entrepreneurial inclinations.* Hong Kong: The Chinese University of Hong Kong; Office of Student Affairs.

——— . (1991). Gender differences in career preference and achievement aspiration: A case study of Chinese University and Shenzhen University. In F. M. Cheung, P. S. Wan, H. K. Choi, and L. M. Choy (Eds.). *Selected papers of Conference on Gender Studies in Chinese Societies* (pp. 71–81). Hong Kong: The Chinese University of Hong Kong, Hong Kong Institute of Asia–Pacific Studies.

Crittenden, C. S. (1989). Attributional patterns of women university students in Taiwan: Asian self-effacement or feminine modesty. *Proceedings of the Conference on Gender Roles and Changing Society* (pp. 229–261). Taipei: National Taiwan University, Population Studies Center, Women's Research Program, and National Tsing Hua University, Institute of Sociology and Anthropology.

——— . (1991). Asian self-efficacement or feminine modesty? Attributional patterns of women university students in Taiwan. *Gender and Society*, 5: 98–117.

Croll, E. (1983). *Chinese women since Mao*. Armonk, NY: Sharpe.

Ekblad, S. (1989). Stability in aggression and aggression control in a sample of primary school children in China. *Acta Psychiatrica Scandinavica*, 80: 160–164.

Family Planning Association of Hong Kong. (1984). *Family planning knowledge, attitude and practice in Hong Kong, 1982.* Hong Kong: Family Planning Association.

——— . (1989). *Report on the survey of family planning: Knowledge, attitude and practice in Hong Kong, 1987.* Hong Kong: Family Planning Association.

Feather, N. T. (1984). Masculinity, femininity, psychological androgyny, and the structure of values. *Journal of Personality and Social Psychology*, 47: 604–620.

Francesco, A. M., and Hakel, M. (1981). Gender and sex as determinants of hireability of applicants for gender-typed jobs. *Psychology of Women Quarterly*, 5: 747–757.

Gough, H. G., and Heilbrun, A. B., Jr. (1965). *Adjective check list manual.* Palo Alto, CA: Consulting Psychologists Press.

Hetherington, E. M., and Parke, R. D. (1986). *Child psychology: A contemporary viewpoint* (3rd ed.). New York: McGraw-Hill.

Hong Kong Government. (1993). *Green paper on equal opportunities for women and men.* Hong Kong: The Government Printer.

Hong, L. K. (1976). The role of women in the People's Republic of China: Legacy and change. *Social Problems*, 23: 545–557.

Horner, M. S. (1972). Toward an understanding of achievement-related conflicts in women. *Journal of Social Issues*, 78: 157–176.

––––––. (1974). The measurement and behavioral implications of fear of success in women. In J. Atkinson and J. Raynor (Eds.), *Motivation and achievement* (pp. 41–70). New York: Wiley.

Huston, A. C. (1983). Sex-typing. In P. H. Mussen (Ed.). *Handbook of child psychology* (Vol. 4, pp. 387–467). New York: Wiley.

Keyes, S. (1979). The development of spatial ability in Hong Kong Chinese adolescents: Sex-role stereotypes and patterns of cognitive ability. *Hong Kong Psychological Society Bulletin*, 2: 21–26.

––––––. (1983). Sex differences in cognitive abilities and sex-role stereotypes in Hong Kong Chinese adolescents. *Sex Roles*, 9: 853–870.

––––––. (1984). Measuring sex-role stereotypes: Attitudes among Hong Kong Chinese adolescents and the development of the Chinese sex-role inventory. *Sex Roles*, 10: 120–140.

Ku, Y. L. (1988). The changing status of women in Taiwan: A conscious and collective struggle toward equality. *Women's Studies International Forum*, 11: 179–186.

Lam, M. C. (1982). *Changing pattern of child rearing: A study of low income families in Hong Kong.* Hong Kong: Department of Social Work, The Chinese University of Hong Kong in association with UNICEF.

Lau, S. (1989). Sex role orientation and domains of self-esteem. *Sex Roles*, 21: 411–418.

Lau, S., and Wong, A. (1992). Value and sex-role orientation of Chinese adolescents. *International Journal of Psychology*, 27: 3–17.

Lee, H. B., and Cheung, F. M. (1991). The attitudes toward rape victims scale: Reliability and validity in a Chinese context. *Sex Roles*, 24: 599–603.

Li, M. C. (1985). Changes in the role and personality of Chinese women in Taiwan. *Proceedings of the Conference on the Role of Women in the National Development Process in Taiwan: Vol. 2.* Taipei: National Taiwan University, Population Studies Center.

Lii, S. Y., and Wong, S. Y. (1982). A cross-cultural study on sex-role stereotypes and social desirability. *Sex Roles*, 8: 481–491.

Lindsey, L. L. (1990). *Gender roles: A sociological perspective.* Englewood Cliffs, NJ: Prentice-Hall.

Luk, B. (1981). Tuixing renjin qicai de nannü pingdeng jiaoyu [Advocation for equal education opportunity for full development of potentials]. *Ming Pao Monthly Magazine*, 16 (6): 41–44.

Lummis, M., and Stevenson, H. W. (1990). Gender differences in beliefs and achievement: A cross-cultural study. *Developmental Psychology*, 26: 254–263.

Lytton, H., and Romney, D. M. (1991). Parents' differential socialization of boys and girls: A meta-analysis. *Psychological Bulletin*, 109: 267–296.

Ma, T. F. (1991). *Report of the study on father's image in Hong Kong primary and kindergarten textbooks* (In Chinese). Hong Kong: Hong Kong Christian Service.

Maccoby, E. E., and Jacklin, C. N. (1974). *The psychology of sex differences.* Stanford, CA: Stanford University Press.

Mak, G.C.L. (1991). The schooling of girls in Hong Kong: Progress and contradictions in the transition. In G. A. Postiglione (Ed.), *Education and society in Hong Kong* (pp. 167–180). New York: M. E. Sharpe.

Marsh, H. W., Antill, J. K., and Cunningham, J. D. (1987). Masculinity, femininity, and androgyny: Relations to self-esteem and social desirability. *Journal of Personality*, 55: 101–123.

Rogers, C. (1987). Sex roles in education. In D. J. Hargreaves and A. M. Colley (Eds.), *The psychology of sex roles* (pp. 159–175). Cambridge, U.K.: Hemisphere Publishing Corporation.

Rokeach, M. (1973). *The nature of human values.* New York: Free Press.

Stein, A. H., and Bailey, M. M. (1973). The socialization of achievement orientation in females. *Psychological Bulletin*, 80: 345–366.

Stewart, A. J. (1982). Sex difference in human social motives: Achievement, affiliation, and power. In A. J. Stewart (Ed.), *Motivation and society.* San Francisco: Jossey-Bass.

Tang, S.L.W. (1981). *The differential educational attainment of children: an empirical study of Hong Kong.* Unpublished doctoral dissertation, University of Chicago.

Tsai, S. L., and Chiu, H. Y. (1989). Gender and achievement aspirations: The case of NTU students. *Proceedings of the Conference on Gender Roles and Changing Society* (pp. 133–169). Taipei: National Taiwan University, Population Studies Center, Women's Research Program, and National Tsing Hua University, Institute of Sociology and Anthropology.

Wang, T. H., and Creedon, C. F. (1989). Sex role orientations, attributions for achievement, and personal goals of Chinese youth. *Sex Roles*, 20: 473–486.

Ward, C. (1990). Gender stereotyping in Singaporean children. *International Journal of Behavioral Development*, 15: 309–315.

Whitley, B. E., Jr. (1983). Sex role orientation and self-esteem: A critical metaanalytic review. *Journal of Personality and Social Psychology*, 44: 756–778.

Williams, J. E., and Best, D. L. (1982). *Measuring sex stereotypes: A thirty-nation study*. Beverly Hills: Sage.

———. (1990). *Measuring sex stereotypes; A multination study* (Revised ed.). Newbury Park, CA: Sage.

Yang, K. S. (1986). Studies on Chinese individual traditionality and modernity: I. The construction of multidimensional scales (In Chinese). Unpublished manuscript. National Taiwan University, Department of Psychology, Taiwan.

———. (1988). Will societal modernization eventually eliminate cross-cultural psychological differences. In M. H. Bond (Ed.), *The cross-cultural challenge to social psychology* (pp. 67–85). London: Sage.

Yau, L.L.B., and Luk, B. (1988). *Gender roles as defined in current history and social studies subjects textbooks at the junior secondary level in Hong Kong.* (In Chinese) (Occasional Paper no. 24). Hong Kong: The Chinese University of Hong Kong, Centre for Hong Kong Studies.

Yu, L. C., and Carpenter, L. (1991). Women in China. In L. L. Adler (Ed.), *Women in cross-cultural perspective* (pp. 189–203). New York: Praeger.

Zhang, D. (1984). *Xingbie jiaose de shejiaohua diaocha.* [Survey on the socialization of gender roles]. Unpublished manuscript, Chinese Northeast Normal University, Department of Education.

Academic Achievement and Motivation of Chinese Students: A Cross-National Perspective[*]

Chuan-sheng Chen, Shin-ying Lee, and
Harold W. Stevenson

In this chapter we describe the high status attained by Chinese students in international studies of academic achievement and discuss some of the factors related to their remarkable performance. To do this, we rely primarily on a series of studies we and our American colleagues have conducted during the past decade in collaboration with associates in Mainland China and Taiwan. By examining children's lives at home as well as at school, we have attempted to discover how Chinese culture influences the beliefs, attitudes, and practices that distinguish the motivation of Chinese children from that of their peers in the United States and Japan.

Chinese Participation in Cross-national Studies

Although China enjoyed a long history of educational, scientific and technological achievement in the pre-modern era (Needham, 1954–1988), today's educational system in China was actually introduced from the West around the turn of the present century. One of the consequences was that

[*] Research reported in this chapter was supported by funds from William T. Grant Foundation, National Institute of Mental Health, and National Science Foundation. We are grateful to our collaborators throughout the years, James Stigler of the University of California at Los Angeles, Chen-chin Hsu of National Cheng Kung University, Taiwan, Seiro Kitamura and Susumu. Kimura of Tohoku Fukushi University in Sendai, Japan, and Fang Ge, Tong Lequan, and the late Liu Fan of the Institute of Psychology, Chinese Academy of Sciences.

Chinese education shifted from its traditional emphasis on Chinese classics to a broader curriculum that included mathematics and physical sciences. Schools expanded rapidly, but little was known until recently about how successfully Chinese students mastered this new curriculum. Chinese students had been left out of the early cross-national comparisons of academic achievement, thereby precluding their evaluation from an international perspective. For example, Chinese students were not included in the twelve-nation First International Mathematics Study (FIMS) (Husen, 1967). Nor did they participate in the subsequent Six Subject Study involving twenty one countries (Walker, 1976).

Only during the last decade did Chinese students begin to participate in international comparisons of academic achievement. Our research group included students in Taiwan in a three-country comparative study (Stevenson, Lee, and Stigler, 1986; Stigler, Lee, Lucker, and Stevenson, 1982). At about the same time, Chinese students in Hong Kong participated in the Second International Mathematics Study (Garden, 1987). Students from Mainland China were among the participants in the most recent study by the International Assessment of Educational Progress (Lapointe, Mead, and Askew, 1992), and students from Mainland China and Hong Kong will participate in the Third International Mathematics Study to be conducted in the 1990s.

The presence of Chinese students in cross-national research on academic achievement is a result of many social, political, economic, and educational factors, including China's opening up to the outside world and the rapid economic development in East Asia. Three factors are of special importance.

First, Chinese students did remarkably well in the first few studies in which they participated. Whether they were from Hong Kong, Taiwan, or Mainland China, or whether they were beginning elementary school or finishing high school, Chinese students have been among the top performers in cross-national comparisons, especially in mathematics.

Second, students of Chinese descent who are attending school in other countries have been found to display an extraordinarily high level of academic achievement compared to other ethnic groups. This is especially evident in the United States and Canada (see Chao and Sue's chapter in this volume; Sue and Okazaki, 1990; Yee, 1992). Asian-Americans have been labeled the "model minority" or "super minority" (Ramirez, 1986) and Asian-American children have been called "whiz kids" (Lord and Linnon, 1988).

Third, Chinese students have also gained prominence in other types of international comparisons involving academic subjects, such as the International Mathematics Olympiad. In 1985, Mainland China began participating in the Olympiad, then a quarter-century old. Over the past several years, Chinese participants have captured many gold medals and the team has often achieved first place. Similar results have occurred in other competitions, such as ones involving physics, chemistry, and information sciences.

These remarkable attainments are in need of explanation. What possible biological, familial, educational, and cultural factors may be involved in these high levels of academic performance? Vernon (1982) has summarized a large number of relevant studies in his discussion of the achievement of Asians in North America and many variables related to Asian children's achievement have been described in other volumes (Bond, 1986; Stevenson, Azuma, and Hakuta, 1986). Only the book edited by Bond focuses on Chinese children, and its chapters deal with many factors other than academic achievement. Rather than attempt to synthesize the analyses that have been made in these volumes, we will focus our attention in this chapter on a summary of the results of a series of large-scale studies conducted by our research group during the last decade in which we compared Chinese children with children from other countries (for detailed discussion of the studies, see Stevenson, Chen, and Lee, 1993; Stevenson, Lee, Chen, Lummis, Stigler, Fan, and Ge, 1990a; Stevenson, Lee, Chen, Stigler, Hsu, and Kitamura, 1990b; Stevenson and Stigler, 1992; Stigler, Lee, and Stevenson, 1990).

Our studies have involved students from kindergarten through eleventh grade in Taipei and in Beijing. They have been tested with curriculum-based tests of reading and mathematics, and they and their parents and teachers have been interviewed. We have replicated the studies in two American cities (Chicago and Minneapolis) and in Sendai, Japan.

This chapter is organized in three main sections. First, we describe the studies we have conducted. We then present information about the relative achievement status of Chinese students in comparison to their Japanese and American counterparts. Finally, we discuss factors that we believe can account for some of the reasons why Chinese students display such outstanding academic achievement.

Our Studies

Our studies have been conducted in large cities. It was not feasible to include students living in rural areas. Our discussion is valid, therefore, only for urban Chinese children. The two cities we selected, Taipei and Beijing, are among the more advanced cities in Taiwan and Mainland China. For comparison groups, we selected schools in the Minneapolis and Chicago metropolitan areas. Students in Minnesota have consistently been among the top performers in the National Assessment of Educational Progress (Educational Testing Service, 1993) and some of the suburban Chicago schools are reputed to be among the top schools in the nation. Within each metropolitan area, we included large, representative samples of students from a wide range of schools. In all, around 20,000 students have been studied. Because it was impossible to interview all these students and their parents, subsamples of students were selected for more intensive study. We conducted six studies between 1980 and 1992. The procedures used in these studies are summarized in the following paragraphs.

Study 1

The first study, conducted in 1980, included 1440 children, selected as representative samples of first and fifth graders from Taipei, and Minneapolis. These children were selected from ten schools in each city. In addition to tests of mathematics and reading achievement, a battery of cognitive tests was also given to the children. Children and their mothers and teachers were interviewed, and extensive time-sampling observations were made in each classroom for a total of 1600 hours in Taipei and 1353 in Minneapolis.

Study 2

After completing the study of elementary school children, we conducted a parallel study in 1984 of kindergarten children in Taipei and Minneapolis. The sample in each city consisted of 288 children, selected from twenty four kindergartens in each city as representative samples of five-year-olds. The children were given tests of mathematics, reading, and cognitive ability, and their mothers and teachers were interviewed. We conducted a formal observational study of four hours of classroom activity in each classroom.

Study 3

In 1986–1987, we conducted a more thorough exploration of achievement in mathematics. In this study we visited ten schools in Taipei, eleven in Beijing, and twenty in the Chicago metropolitan area. From each school we randomly selected two classrooms each for first and fifth grades. All children in these classrooms were given a group-administered mathematics test. A battery of individual mathematics tests was given to a random sample of twelve children (six boys and six girls) from each classroom. This subsample of children and their mothers and teachers were interviewed. In addition, we observed four hours of mathematics classes in each classroom.

Study 4

We also conducted a study of children's adaptation to school in Beijing and in Chicago in 1986. We gave tests of mathematics and reading to over 2400 first, third, and fifth grade students in Beijing and to nearly 3000 in Chicago. We later replicated portions of the study in 1990 in Beijing, including the administration of the mathematics test.

Study 5

We replicated part of Study 1 in 1984 and again in 1990 with approximately 240 fifth graders from each city we visited in 1980: Taipei and Minneapolis. We visited the same schools that we had visited in 1980, tested children with the same tests, and interviewed students and their mothers about the same topics included in the earlier study.

Study 6

In 1990–1992, we completed a large study of eleventh graders in Taipei and Minneapolis. One part of the study included representative samples of 1475 Chinese eleventh graders from Taipei and 1120 American eleventh graders. We gave them tests of mathematics, reading, and general information, and asked them to answer items in a long questionnaire dealing with their attitudes, beliefs, and current life situations. In a follow-up study conducted at the same time, we located as many of the first graders from our 1980 study (now eleventh graders) as we could find. This included 169 Chinese and 212 American students.

In addition to the Chinese and American students, Japanese students were included in several studies. The procedures for their selection followed those for the Chinese and American students.

Achievement Tests

Mathematics

All mathematics tests were constructed on the basis of analyses of the textbooks used in the schools where we conducted the studies. Detailed information from the textbooks made it possible to determine the skills and concepts taught in all locations and the semester and grade in which they were first introduced. In order to ensure fair comparisons, the test items tapped skills and concepts that were common to the textbooks used in all of the locations being studied. This guaranteed that all students had the same chance to be exposed to the information necessary to solve the problems and eliminated the possibility of a differential match between curricula and test items in the different cities.

Test items were arranged in order of difficulty. Kindergarten and first-grade children started with kindergarten items; third graders with first-grade items; fifth graders with third-grade items; and eleventh graders with fifth-grade items. The reliability was high for these tests.

In addition to the tests administered to all children, we gave a battery of individual tests tapping specific domains of mathematical knowledge to a

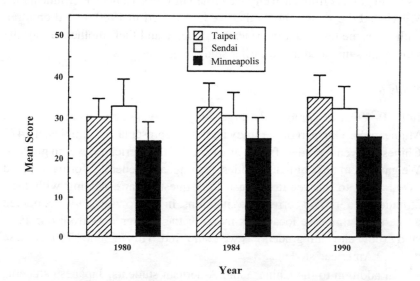

Figure 4.1: The Mean Mathematics Scores (+ 1 SD) of Fifth Graders at Three Different Testing Periods

subsample of first and fifth graders. The tests covered the areas that mathematics educators agreed to be the major ones included in elementary school mathematics. The reliability of all tests was satisfactory, but tended to vary according to the number of items included in the tests.

Reading

Reading tests usually consist of two parts: reading vocabulary and comprehension. The content of the reading tests was based on analyses of children's reading textbooks. All words were entered into a computer along with the semester in which they were first introduced. Tests for the first three grades contained mostly words that were common to all textbooks, and those for grades four to six contained either common words or equivalent words as judged by the semester of their first appearance in textbooks and by the frequency of occurrence based on word frequency counts.

Mathematics and Reading Performance

Mathematics

Chinese students in Taipei demonstrated great skill in mathematics. Their scores improved steadily during the last decade and they have outperformed Japanese students since 1984. They also greatly outperformed their American peers. For example, for all three groups of fifth graders tested in 1980, 1984, and 1990, the differences in mathematics scores between Taipei and Minneapolis children were 6.0 points, 7.5 points, 9.0 points — all larger than one standard deviation unit (see Figure 4.1).

Chinese children in Beijing also received high scores in mathematics. As Figure 4.2 shows, there was little overlap between the distributions of scores for Chinese and American students in each city for each grade. Only 2.2% of Chinese first graders, none of the third graders, and 1.4% of Chinese fifth graders performed at or below the average level of the American children.

Chinese students' improvement in mathematics achievement was not only evident in comparisons of the three groups of fifth graders, but also in comparisons made according to grade level. Figure 4.3 presents the mathematics scores for kindergarten, first, fifth and eleventh grades. The scores were standardized for each grade for purposes of comparison. It

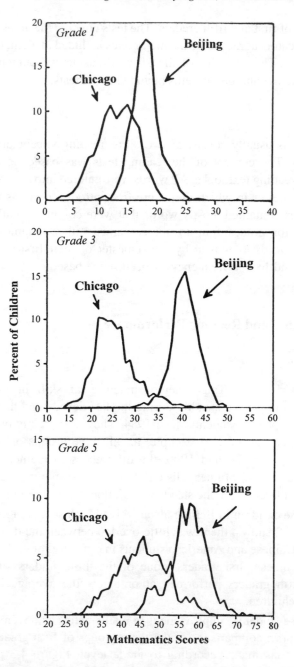

Figure 4.2: The Distributions of Mathematics Scores of First-, Third-, and Fifth-grade Children in Beijing and Chicago

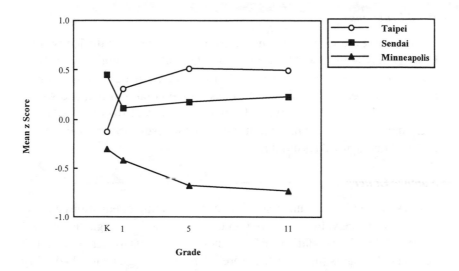

Figure 4.3:   The Standardized Mathematics Scores of Kindergarten, First-, Fifth-, and Eleventh-grade Students

is obvious that the Chinese students' scores improved between kindergarten and fifth grade and remained at a high level through the eleventh grade.

One common concern about results such as those reported above is that the test items focused too much on calculation and computation and too little on understanding and discovery of mathematical concepts. Would the Chinese advantage remain if they were tested on other domains of mathematics knowledge? Our 1986 study was designed to answer this question. Students were given a battery of tests administered in one-on-one sessions that tapped various domains and levels of mathematics knowledge. The tests tapped both problems of the types found in the elementary school curricula and ones that were indirectly related to the goals of the curricula. They included word problems, number concepts, measurement and scaling, estimation, operations, graphs and tables, spatial visualization, spatial relations, oral problems, geometry, and mental calculation.

We can illustrate the performance of the Chinese students by describing the results for three of the tests: word problems, number concepts, and mathematical operations.

Word Problems

The twenty seven word problems were arranged in order of difficulty from kindergarten items (e.g., "Joey had 3 marbles and then found 2 more. How many marbles does Joey have now?") to seventh-grade items (e.g., "A lake resort owner rented a cabin for 14 days on the condition that she would receive 40 dollars a day for every day it did not rain and 10 dollars a day for every day it did rain. At the end of 2 weeks, the resort owner received 380 dollars. How many days did it rain?").

Number Concepts

This test taps children's understanding of the meaning of equations and the concepts of place value, negative numbers, and fractions (e.g., "Here are 3 digits, 3, 6, 1. How could you arrange these three digits to form the biggest number?" "What is the number before 0?"). The first-grade test had thirty four items, and the fifth-grade test had thirty one items.

Operations

This eight-item test assesses children's abilities to map arithmetic operations onto the world and to verbalize the uses of arithmetic operations. For example, children were given an equation and asked to make up word problems, or children were asked to explain the uses of addition or division.

These three tests clearly required an understanding of mathematical concepts and of how to apply them in new problems. Chinese children performed well on these as well as on all the other tests (see Table 4.1). [For a detailed discussion of the other tests, see Stevenson et al. 1990a; Stigler, Lee, and Stevenson, 1990.] They displayed high levels of ability not only in computation, but also in very different types of items that required the

Table 4.1: Mean Scores on Three Individual Mathematics Tests

	Beijing	Taipei	Sendai	Chicago
Grade 1				
Word problems	9.2	5.1	6.6	3.6
Number concepts	20.4	14.8	19.7	15.0
Operations	11.5	6.1	9.2	5.8
Grade 5				
Word problems	18.3	17.2	18.5	12.7
Number concepts	28.2	26.6	29.3	21.1
Operations	13.4	11.4	11.9	8.9

application of their knowledge of mathematics to problems requiring novel, creative solutions. They displayed no indication of weakness that might be interpreted as excessive reliance on repetitive use of knowledge and skills learned on the basis of drill and memorization.

Reading Performance

Although cross-cultural differences in reading achievement were small, children in Taipei seemed to have an advantage when compared to other groups. For example, in 1980 first- and fifth-grade children in Taipei received higher scores on reading vocabulary and comprehension than Japanese and American children. In 1990, Japanese fifth graders surpassed Chinese children in reading vocabulary. By eleventh grade, however, reading scores of the Chinese students were once again slightly higher than those of the Japanese eleventh graders.

On the other hand, Beijing children performed at a lower level in reading than their Chicago counterparts. At first grade, the mean percentages of correct responses were 15.3 (Beijing) and 27.4 (Chicago), $p < .001$. The corresponding percentages at third grade were 57.3 and 63.3, $p < .001$. At fifth grade, there was no significant difference between the scores (76.9 versus 77.6).

Overall means may not be the most effective representation of the children's levels of performance, especially when children are learning to read writing systems that place different demands on the learner. For example, different conclusions are reached about children's reading ability when one looks at data for each semester and each grade. When we look at the scores for items that appeared in the children's textbooks at or below the children's grade level, Chinese children displayed superior reading ability. We can see in Figure 4.4 that the high overall scores obtained by the American children was derived from their advantage on items that were beyond their own grade level. Similar results were found with comprehension tests and with third and fifth graders.

Our interpretation of this phenomenon relies on a critical difference in reading written English and written Chinese. English is spelled phonetically so that a child who is able to sound out a word is able to "read" words well beyond the child's grade level. This is nearly impossible in reading Chinese. The sound and meaning of nearly all characters must be learned, for there is no obvious way to deduce either attribute from the form or structure of the character. Among words that had been taught in school,

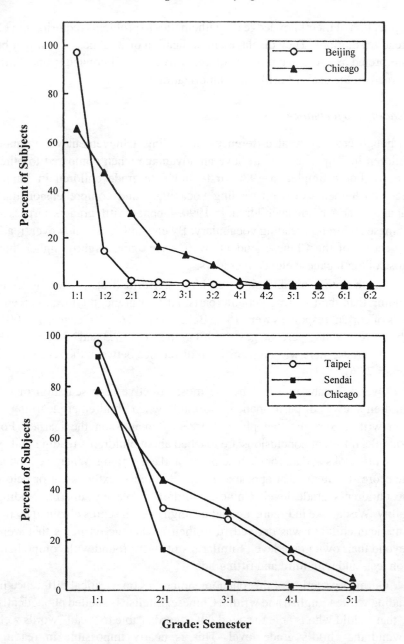

Figure 4.4: Percentage of First Graders Who Could Read Vocabulary Items at Various Grade and Semester Levels (The two studies referred to in the panels involved different vocabulary tests)

Chinese children did well. Their performance declined precipitously on words that had not yet appeared in their readers.

This pattern of achievement may be further strengthened by two other factors. First, Chinese children are taught to follow the curriculum, master what should be learned, but to wait before studying materials that will be covered later. Second, there is a tendency for Chinese schools to give somewhat less emphasis to reading than the American schools. For example, Chicago first grade teachers were found to allocate an average of 13.7 hours a week to reading and language arts, 5.7 hours more than the average of Chinese teachers.

Accounting for Chinese Children's High Achievement

Intellectual Abilities

A common explanation for the performance in mathematics of Chinese (as well as other Asian groups) is that they possess superior intellectual ability. This explanation has been very controversial, but we have found no convincing evidence, either in the literatuare or in our own studies, to support such a claim. [For extensive discussions on this topic we refer the reader to Flynn (1991), Sue and Okazaki (1990, 1991); Yee (1992).]

The Chinese children in our 1980 were given a battery of ten cognitive tests composed of items of the types found in traditional tests of intelligence, such as coding, spatial relations, perceptual speed, auditory memory, serial memory for words, serial memory for numbers, verbal-spatial representation, verbal memory, vocabulary, and general information.

There was no clear advantage in favor of Chinese children (see Fig. 4.5). In fact, the scores of American first-grade children tended to exceed those of their Chinese counterparts. By fifth grade, the overall means for the three cultures did not differ significantly from each other. Chinese, Japanese, and American students did not receive identical scores on every test, but there was no pattern that represented special strength of one group over another. Chinese children displayed marked superiority in serial memory for numbers; Japanese children received the highest score on tests of spatial relations and auditory memory; and American children received the highest scores on the test of verbal memory.

The strengths in particular tests are hard to interpret. However, later research has strongly suggested that the Chinese children's remarkable

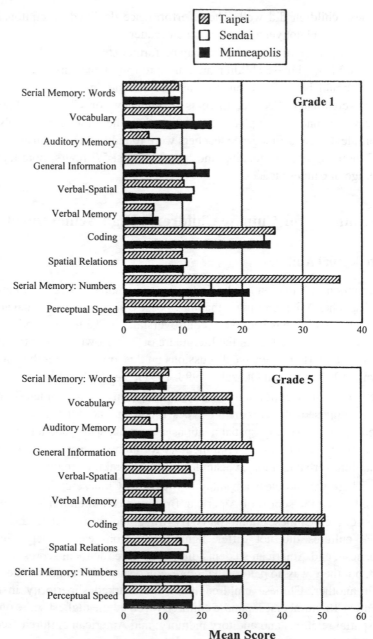

Figure 4.5:   Mean Scores on Ten Cognitive Tests.

memory for digits can be attributed to the shorter duration of pronunciation compared to digits in English or Japanese (see Chen and Stevenson, 1988; Stigler, Lee, and Stevenson, 1986).

Of special interest are the results of tests of general information that were given to Chinese children at four grade levels (kindergarten, first, fifth, and eleventh grades). Chinese children did not perform well on this test during kindergarten. Their average score was about 0.7 standard deviation units below the grand mean of students from all three cultures. Their scores rapidly rose, however, so that they were 0.4 standard deviation units below the grand mean by first grade; and by fifth grade their average was the same as the overall mean for all three groups of children. The mean score of Chinese eleventh graders remained near the overall mean (+0.1). From these data and from the results of the battery of cognitive tests, we find no evidence that enables us to account for the Chinese children's superior scores in mathematics on the basis of unusually high intelligence.

If it is not intelligence, how can we account for the high level of mathematics achievement among Chinese children? The answer must lie in children's experiences at home and at school. In the remainder of this chapter, we will discuss how cultural values, family involvement, and student motivation, play important roles in the Chinese children's high academic performance.

Cultural Values about Education

Value of Education

Chinese culture is known for its emphasis on education and learning. For centuries, Chinese people have believed in the value of education for the nation's well-being as well as for their own personal advancement.

The great importance placed on education has both historical and current significance. Education plays an important role in the life of the Chinese people as a ladder for upward mobility. Until the early twentieth century, selection of civil officials depended on competitive national examinations. Currently, admission to college in both Taiwan and Mainland China is very competitive. For example, although elementary schools enroll 98% of school-aged children in Mainland China, high school entrance has not been possible for every elementary school graduate. Only two-thirds go on to junior high. Of those who finish junior high school, fewer than 40% are able to continue their education in high school. Only about 20% of the high school graduates can hope to obtain some type of higher education. Thus, the chance that a Chinese child who has entered elementary school will be able to obtain a college education is less than one in twenty.

Inculcated with the value of education, Chinese children consider getting a good education as a central goal in their lives. Here is an example of the importance Chinese children give to education. We posed the following question to children in Beijing: "Let's say there is a wizard who will let you make a wish about anything that you want. What would you wish?" The majority (68%) of Chinese children proposed wishes related to education, such as "go to college," "have many books," "get many A's." Only 10% expressed wishes for material objects unrelated to education, such as a house or a toy; 5% had unrealistic fantasies such as wanting to live forever.

Similarly, when asked whether they wanted to go to college, almost all (96%) Chinese children gave an affirmative answer, despite what they must realize is an extremely unlikely possibility. Mothers also held high aspirations for their children: 91% wanted their children to obtain a college or post-graduate degree.

Value of Hard Work

Another cultural value that may account for Chinese children's achievement is the importance placed on hard work. In line with Confucian teachings, Chinese people place great emphasis on the malleability of human beings. They believe that achievement is possible if they work hard — regardless of their current level of ability. They do not deny the existence of differences in innate endowment among human beings, but they de-emphasize its importance as a controlling factor in people's lives. Innate abilities may determine the rate at which one acquires knowledge, but effort is believed to be responsible for the ultimate level of achievement.

A series of questions in our interviews tapped this emphasis on effort. Children and their parents and teachers were all asked how they perceived the importance of ability versus effort in children's achievement. The results were consistent: among the Chinese, effort was valued to a greater degree than innate abilities. For example, mothers in Taipei were asked to distribute 10 points among four factors (effort, innate ability, task difficulty, and luck) in terms of their importance for academic performance. They were instructed to give one point to the least important factor and then to distribute the remaining nine points to the other three factors. Chinese mothers assigned an average of 4.4 points to effort, 2.6 to innate ability, 1.9

to difficulty of the task, and 1.1 to luck. Chinese and Japanese mothers assigned more points, on the average, to effort (4.4 and 5.1 points) than did American mothers (3.9). On the other hand, American mothers assigned greater importance to ability (3.9 points) than the Chinese or Japanese mothers (2.5 and 2.4 points, respectively).

Chinese children displayed beliefs similar to those of their parents. Fifth graders in Beijing were asked to rate the importance of working hard, innate ability, task difficulty, and luck in school performance. They gave higher ratings to effort than to the three other factors. Their mean ratings on a 5-point scale were 4.8 (hard work), 2.5 (ability), 2.6 (task difficulty), and 1.4 (luck), where 1 was "not important at all" and 5 was "very important."

Chinese children in Taipei also placed great emphasis on the role of effort. Fifth graders were asked how strongly they agreed or disagreed with the following statements: (a) "The best students in the class always work harder than the other students." (b) "Everyone in my class has the same amount of ability in math." and (c) "The tests you take can show how much or how little natural ability you have." Chinese children agreed that the best students study harder and that their classmates had similar levels of ability in mathematics. They expressed some disagreement with the belief that tests reveal a student's natural ability.

Belief in the importance of hard work persists through high school, despite the fact that some students must have found that some classmates did well without studying hard and others maintained a mediocre record in spite of studying hard. Eleventh graders were asked which of four factors was most important for doing well in mathematics: a good teacher, studying hard, home environment, or intelligence. A majority (60%) of the Chinese eleventh graders picked "studying hard." Among the other alternatives, 18% choose "a good teacher," another 18% choose "intelligence," and 4% selected "the home environment." American students were less likely to pick "studying hard" as the most important factor, and Japanese students were most likely to make this choice (27% and 72%, respectively).

Family Involvement

Related to their belief in the importance of effort is the high degree to which Chinese parents and other family members are involved in their children's learning. Parents set high standards for their children and spend a large amount of time supervising and assisting their children with school work.

We sought information about parents' standards for academic achievement by asking them several questions about their expectations concerning their children's performance. We asked them how satisfied they were with their children's academic performance (or in some cases, performance in mathematics). Responses were consistent. Fewer than 10% of the Chinese parents said they were "very satisfied." From three to four times as many said they were not satisfied.

Their high standards were revealed vividly in their responses to another set of questions. Parents were asked to predict the score their child would get and the score they would be satisfied with on a hypothetical test of mathematics, where the average score was 70 out of a total of 100 possible points. Chinese mothers and fathers had high regard for their children's abilities. On the average, they said they expected their child would get a score of around 80 points, much above the "average." Of even greater interest here is the fact that they said they would not be satisfied unless their child scored 90 points or higher. The results were the same whether the question concerned reading or mathematics.

Children were aware of their parents' standards. When they were asked whether they thought they were doing as well as their parents wanted them to, the results were in accord with the parents' responses. Chinese children agreed that their parents were not satisfied with their school performance and would be satisfied only if they continued to improve.

Chinese parents frequently help their children with school work. Beijing mothers of first graders said they spent an average of 7 hours a week helping their children. The average for Taipei mothers of first graders was even higher: 7.5 hours. Such intense involvement did not continue through elementary school, but remained high. Mothers of fifth graders in Beijing and Taipei said they spent 4.5 and 5 hours a week, respectively, assisting their children. This degree of parental involvement in their children's academic success is high; for example, American and Japanese parents spent half as much time helping their children as did the Chinese parents.

Homework

A large amount of Chinese children's after-school time is taken up by homework (Chen and Stevenson, 1989). For example, mothers of Beijing first-graders estimated that their children spent an average of 65 minutes on homework each school day. This was more time than was spent playing with friends (57 minutes) or watching television (45 minutes). The corresponding amounts of time were very similar for fifth graders: averages of 70, 54, and 48 minutes, respectively. Similar results were found with children in Taipei.

Self-Evaluations

Chinese children were realistic in their self-evaluations of their academic performance. They considered themselves to be average or slightly above average compared to their peers; few believed they were either outstanding or extremely bad. These reasonably accurate levels of self-evaluation are different from those made by American children, whose self-evaluations often describe an above-average child (see Table 4.2). Chinese children appear to have the more accurate self-perceptions because frequent, explicit evaluations occur both at the levels of the classroom and the school. These evaluations — usually results of important tests to which numerical grades are assigned — are posted and are open to everyone's view.

Adjustment to School

Western visitors to schools in cities such as Beijing and Taipei come away with stories about the remarkable attentiveness and responsiveness of Chinese children, their apparent lack of psychological disturbance, and their generally calm demeanor. They are then surprised when they see the same children become vigorous, boisterous, and noisy when class is over and recess begins.

Table 4.2: Students' Self-evaluations of Academic Performance (Mean Ratings)

	Taipei	Sendai	Minneapolis	Scheffé
General Academic Performance				
Grade 5	4.3	3.9	4.6	M>T>S
Grade 11	4.0	3.4	4.4	M>T>S
Mathematics				
Grade 5	4.3	4.2	5.0	M>T, S
Grade 11	4.0	3.2	4.4	M>T>S
Reading				
Grade 5	5.1	4.2	4.8	M, T>S
Grade 11	4.5	4.1	4.7	M, T>S

Note: N's = 119-225 for each group. All differences were significant at least at $p < .01$. All scales were 7-point, 1 = "the worst" or "not at all good," 4 = "average," and 7 = "the best" or "very good."

Visitors are especially impressed by the lack of indications of tension. On the basis of reports in the Western media, they are led to expect that the pressure placed on Chinese students for academic achievement would be especially stressful. But these are impressions gained through casual, informal observations. Would more formal measures support these impressions? We sought to answer this question by asking elementary school teachers about the frequency with which their students displayed various symptoms of tension. Their responses supported the Western observers' impressions. On a 5-point scale, where 1 was "seldom" and 5, "often," the children were seldom rated as being fidgety (2.0), inattentive (2.2), complaining of headaches (1.0), stomach aches (1.1), and fatigue (1.3). Few children ever sought physical contact with teachers (1.1) or said that they wanted to leave school (1.1). All these ratings were notably below those made by American teachers; their ratings in every category reflected frequencies at least one level higher than was the case for the Chinese children.

Another approach to the question about the adjustment of Chinese children was taken in our study of eleventh graders. We asked over a thousand students in Taipei to rate the frequency with which they experienced stress, depression, anxiety, aggression, and various complaints of possible psychosomatic origin. The frequencies were low. Nevertheless, there were differences among the Chinese, Japanese, and American students. American students' ratings indicated that they experienced the most frequent feelings of stress, anxiety, aggression, and had headaches most often. Chinese students were somewhat more frequently depressed than the American and Japanese students and they also complained of more frequent problems in sleeping, loss of appetite, overeating, and diarrhea (see Table 3). These particular difficulties, it should be noted, are among the most common sources of disturbance reported in discussions of Chinese mental health (Cheung, 1986). Japanese students were the least likely to experience any of these feelings or problems.

Conclusions

The picture we have described of the academic achievement among Chinese students is very positive. They display high levels of achievement, not only in routine tasks in mathematics and reading, but also in aspects that require creative, novel solutions to problems in mathematics or deductions about the content of what they are reading.

The high levels of academic achievement are related to broad cultural

Table 4.3:   Indices of Maladjustment (Mean Ratings)

	Taipei	Sendai	Minneapolis	Scheffé
Stress	3.5	3.2	3.9	M>T>S
Depression	3.5	3.0	3.1	T>M, S
Academic Anxiety	4.1	3.8	4.2	M, T>S
Aggression	2.0	1.9	2.1	n.s.
Somatic Complaints				
Tired	3.1	2.7	3.1	M, T>S
Headache	2.0	1.9	2.5	M, T>S
Stomach ache	2.1	1.8	2.0	M, T>S
Can't sleep	2.4	1.5	2.8	I>M>S
Lost appetite	2.2	1.5	1.8	T>M>S
Overeating	2.4	1.9	2.1	T>M>S
Diarrhea	1.8	1.6	1.3	T>S>M
Urination	1.6	1.2	1.8	M>T>S

Note: All scales were 5-point (1 = "never", 3 = "once a week", 5 = "almost everyday", with the exception of academic anxiety which was a 7-point scale (1 = "not at all nervous / worried", 7 = "very nervous / worried). Due to the large sample size, N's = 1610–1615 (Chinese), 1216–1219 (American), 1141–1154 (Japanese), only differences that were significant at 0.001 level were indicated.

factors derived from traditional Chinese beliefs about human beings. Bolstered by a firm belief in the attainability of goals through hard work and aided by the involvement of the family in promoting children's progress in school, Chinese children devote themselves with great dedication to their school work. They study hard and are optimistic about their future. Their success in school does not appear to occur at great psycho-logical cost.

Of special importance is the rapid improvement in performance demonstrated by Chinese children after they enter school. Once they enter first grade their performance improves very rapidly over their more mediocre performance during the preschool years. These remarkable changes make the developmental study of the academic achievement of Chinese children not only of interest in its own right, but also of interest to others who seek an understanding of how the academic achievement of children elsewhere can be raised to more effective levels.

References

Bond, M. H. (Ed.). (1986). *The psychology of the Chinese people.* Hong Kong: Oxford University Press.

Chen, C., and Stevenson, H. W. (1988). Cross-linguistic differences in digit span of preschool children. *Journal of Experimental Child Psychology*, 46: 150–158.

———. (1989). Homework: A cross-cultural examination. *Child Development*, 60: 551–561.

Cheung, F.M.C. (1986). Psychopathology among Chinese people. In M. H. Bond (Ed.), *The psychology of the Chinese people* (pp. 171–212). Hong Kong: Oxford University Press.

Comber, L. C., and Keeves, J. (1973). *Science achievement in nineteen countries*. New York: Wiley.

Educational Testing Service. (1993). *Data compendium for the NAEP 1992 mathematics assessment of the nation and the states* (Report No. 23–ST04). National Center for Education Statistics, Office of Educational Research and Improvement, U.S. Department of Education.

Flynn, J. R. (1991). *Asian Americans: Achievement beyond IQ*. Hillsdale, NJ: Erlbaum.

Garden, R. A. (1987). The second IEA mathematics study. *Comparative Education Review*, 31: 47–68.

Husen, T. (Ed.). (1967). *International study of achievement in mathematics* (Vols. 1–2). Stockholm: Almqvist & Wiksell.

Lapointe, A. E., Mead, N. A., and Askew, J. M. (1992). *Learning mathematics*. Princeton, NJ: Educational Testing Service.

Lord, L., and Linnon, N. (1988, March 14). What puts the whiz in whiz kids. *U.S. News and World Report*, pp. 48–57.

Needham, J. (1954–1988). *Science and civilisation in China* (Vols. 1–6). New York: Cambridge University Press.

Ramirez, A. (1986, November 24). America's super minority. *Fortune*, pp. 148–161.

Stevenson, H. W., Azuma, H., and Hakuta, K. (Eds.). (1986). *Education and child development in Japan*. New York: W. H. Freeman.

Stevenson, H. W., Chen, C., and Lee, S. (1993). Mathematics achievement of Chinese, Japanese, and American children: Ten years later. *Science*, 259: 53–58

Stevenson, H. W., Lee, S., Chen, C., Lummis, M., Stigler, J. W., Fan, L., and Ge, F. (1990a). Mathematics achievement of children in China and the United States. *Child Development*, 61: 1053–1066.

Stevenson, H. W., Lee, S., Chen, C., Stigler, J. W., Hsu, C., and Kitamura, S. (1990b). Contexts of achievement: A study of American, Chinese, and Japanese children. *Monographs of the Society for Research in Child Development*, *Vol. 55*. (Serial No. 221).

Stevenson, H. W., Lee, S., and Stigler, J. W. (1986). Mathematics achievement of Chinese, Japanese, and American children. *Science*, 231: 693–699.

Stevenson, H. W., and Stigler, J. W. (1992). *The learning gap*. New York: Summit Books.

Stigler, J. W., Lee, S., Lucker, G. W., and Stevenson, H. W. (1982). Curriculum and achievement in mathematics: A study of elementary school children in Japan, Taiwan, and the United States. *Journal of Educational Psychology*, 74: 315–322.

Stigler, J. W., Lee, S., and Stevenson, H. W. (1986). Digit memory in Chinese and English: Evidence for a temporally limited store. *Cognition*, 23: 1–20.

———. (1990). *Mathematical knowledge of Japanese, Chinese, and American elementary school children*. Reston: VA: National Council of Teachers of Mathematics.

Sue, S., and Okazaki, S. (1990). Asian-American educational achievements: A phenomenon in search of an explanation. *American Psychologist*, 45: 913–920.

———. (1991). Explanations for Asian-American achievements: A reply. *American Psychologist*, 46: 878–880.

Vernon, P. E. (1982). *The abilities and achievements of orientals in North America*. New York: Academic Press.

Walker, D. A. (1976). *The IEA six subject survey: An empirical study of education in twenty-one countries*. New York: Wiley.

Yee, A. H. (1992). Asians as stereotypes and students: Misperceptions that persist. *Educational Psychology Review*, 4: 95–132.

5

Chinese Parental Influence and Their Children's School Success: A Paradox in the Literature on Parenting Styles

Ruth K. Chao and Stanley Sue

The Chinese in the United States have clearly achieved school success above the other ethnic groups, including Caucasian Americans. So striking is the superiority of Asians, especially Chinese, in school performance that many investigators have examined biological, cultural, familial, and other variables as possible explanatory factors. In this chapter, we primarily discuss the role of parenting and family in the academic achievement of Chinese Americans. While the focus is on Chinese Americans, we have broadened our review of research to include studies of Chinese in different parts of the world, and studies of other Asians in the United States. Chinese in the United States may share some of the values and practices exercised by Chinese in other parts of the world; they also have certain commonalities with Japanese, Koreans, Vietnamese, etc. in the United States (e.g., minority group status, stereotypes, etc.). Thus we judiciously refer to research on these other groups, if it furthers our understanding of Chinese Americans.

This chapter will attempt to address an apparent paradox in the literature involving Chinese parenting. Studies of Chinese parenting have often described the parents as being very controlling or restrictive. More recent research found that Asian-American parents, in general, are more authoritarian in their parenting style, and that among Caucasian-American samples this parenting style is not predictive of school achievement. However, Asian Americans, particularly the Chinese, are achieving quite well in school, often above the Caucasian Americans.

Baumrind's Parenting Styles

Baumrind (1971) had proposed three different parenting styles — namely, authoritative, authoritarian, and permissive, with authoritative as the style predictive of achievements. These parenting styles have been incorporated in much of the thinking and research done on parenting, and more specifically on the issue of parental control in the United States. Previously many researchers (Baldwin, Kalhorn, and Breese, 1945) and experts on parenting believed that less control and more "democratic" parenting (i.e., supporting the child's autonomy) were optimal for the child. Later, however, Baumrind (1971) argued for the importance of what she called "firm control," along with a democratic style of decision-making, and warmth. She found four child rearing dimensions — parental control, maturity demands, parent-child communication, and nurturance — from which the three different patterns of parenting emerged (i.e., authoritative, authoritarian, and permissive).

The authoritative mother exerts high parental control along with warmth. This mother would attempt to direct the child's activities, but in a rational, issue-oriented manner, encouraging verbal give-and-take, and sharing with the child the reasoning behind her policy. She values both autonomous self-will and expressive conformity. This pattern of authoritative parenting was found to be most related to the outcome of the child's competence.

The authoritarian mother, on the other hand, attempts to shape, control, and evaluate the behavior and attitudes of the child in accordance with a set standard of conduct, usually an absolute standard. She also values obedience as a virtue, believes in inculcating such instrumental values as respect for authority, respect for work, and the preservation of order and traditional structure. This mother does not encourage verbal give-and-take, believing that the child should accept her word for what is right. Similar to the authoritative style, the authoritarian style of parenting includes high control but, in contrast to the authoritative style, does not include warmth or support; also with the authoritarian style, the handling of power and decision-making is not performed in a democratic manner.

Dornbusch et al. as an Explicit Example of the Paradox

Dornbusch et al. (1987) investigated the relationship between parenting style and adolescents' school grades. Because these researchers did not make distinctions among the different Asian groups, specific findings for the Chinese cannot be made. However, their findings do pose an interesting paradox that very directly concerns the Chinese. In their study, they asked high-school students from four different ethnic groups, African American, Mexican American, Caucasian American, and Asian American, to rate their own parents according to the three parenting styles defined by Baumrind (1971).

Dornbusch et al. (1987) were attempting to show a relationship between the type of parenting reported (i.e., authoritarian, authoritative, or permissive) and the school performance of the adolescents. They predicted that the authoritarian and permissive patterns would be negatively associated with grades and the authoritative would be positively associated. Just as they had predicted, these researchers found that although the authoritative was associated with higher academic achievement levels among Caucasian Americans, this relationship was weak for Asian Americans and African Americans. In fact, Asian Americans were the highest on the *authoritarian* style *and* their adolescents had the highest achievement. The researchers themselves concluded that "Asian children in our public schools cannot be adequately explained in terms of the parenting styles we have studied" (p. 1256). This study is an explicit example of the paradox of the authoritarian parenting style as it is applied to Asians: Although the authoritative parenting style is supposed to be related to promoting higher school achievement in the children, Asians are found to be more authoritarian in their parenting style, and yet their children are performing quite well in school.

As a resolution to this paradox, Steinberg, Dornbusch, and Brown (1992) argued that the lack of a strong relationship between Asian parenting style and overall school achievement is due to the fact that the parental influence is not as important as the peer influence. In fact, Steinberg et al. (1992, p. 728) claim, "Asian youngsters report the highest level of peer support for academic achievement. Interestingly, and in contrast to popular belief, our survey data indicate that Asian American parents are less involved in their children's schooling than any other group."

On the other hand, Chao (1994) proposes other alternative explanations for this paradox regarding Chinese parenting: The concepts of authoritarian and authoritative do not capture what is most important about the child rearing style of the Chinese especially for predicting school success. Indeed, "authoritarian" is an incomplete and even misleading characterization of Chinese parenting.

Chinese School Performance

Chinese and other Asian Americans have been characterized in the media as academic success stories. In 1990, among persons 25 years of age and older, over 40% of Asian Americans had completed four or more years of college compared with 23% of Caucasian (non-Hispanic) Americans (O'Hare and Felt, 1991).

Sue and Abe (1988) in the *College Board Report* provided mean Scholastic Aptitude Test (SAT) scores, Achievement Test scores (ACT), high-school grades, and university grades for University of California Asian-American and Caucasian-American freshman students. They found that, "Consistent with previous studies …. Asian Americans achieved higher average SAT-mathematical scores than did Caucasian Americans …. They received lower average scores than did Caucasian Americans on SAT-verbal sections" (p. 4). In particular, the average score for the Chinese Americans was 473.4 on verbal and 611.8 on math and for the Caucasian Americans, 512.4 on verbal, and 576.9 on math. Large differences were found for the different Asian groups. Based on a 4-point scale where 4.00 is the maximum, high school grades were also higher for the Chinese (M = 3.73) than for the Caucasian Americans (M = 3.59); the Chinese also received higher university grades (i.e., 2.89 compared to 2.75 for Caucasians).

Suzuki (1988) provided percentages for (1) enrollment in school and college by age and race/ethnicity, (2) schooling completed by sex and race/ethnicity for persons 25 years or older, and (3) the average units (for college credit) earned by high school graduates by race/ethnicity and area of study. At all age levels beginning from the 3–4 age group through the 25–34 age group (with the exception of the 7–13 age group in which the difference was 0.6%), Asians had higher percentages of enrollment in schools or colleges. By the 16–17 year group the difference in percentages between the Asians and Caucasian Americans was substantial (Chinese 96%, and Caucasian Americans 89%). The differences were even greater in the older groups (18–19 year-old Chinese 84% and Caucasian Americans 53%; 20–21 year-old Chinese 74%, and Caucasian Americans 33%; 22–24 year-old Chinese 51% and Caucasian Americans 17%; 25–34 year-old Chinese 22% and Caucasian Americans 9%). For completion of high school, the percentages of Chinese males and females were 75 and 67, respectively, and the percentages of Caucasian males and females were 70 and 68, respectively. The percentage differences between the Chinese and Caucasian Americans completing four or more years of college were striking (Chinese males 44% and females 30%; Caucasian-American males 21% and females 13%). In addition, Asian students, especially the Chinese, earned more units in the core subjects preparatory to college than any other racial/ethnic group. Suzuki points out that Asians earned considerably more units in a number of areas including foreign languages, mathematics, and natural sciences than other students.

Cheung (1982) reviewed other studies that have found that Asians are superior to Caucasian Americans in school performance: In one study, regardless of social class differences, the Asian Americans had higher grade-point averages than Caucasian Americans or Blacks; also, Asian students from various community colleges in Arizona had higher college grade-point averages than all other minority groups; in addition, Asian-American students completed more years of schooling than Caucasian-American students and other ethnics, although Asian-American families had lower income levels than Caucasian-American families; Cheung reported another study that also found that although Asian college students had parents with less education and family income than Caucasian Americans, they had higher grade-point averages. From these analyses provided on the different Asian groups, Asian Americans and especially the Chinese, clearly seem to be performing at least at the same level as Caucasian Americans, and in most cases, above Caucasian Americans on a variety of measures related to school performance, particularly for high school and college.

There is very little literature on the performance of elementary school-aged children by racial/ethnic group. Stevenson and Lee (1990) have reported on *international* data regarding school performance from Chinese children in Taipei (Taiwan), Japanese children in Sendai (Japan), and American children in the United States (Minneapolis, Minnesota). They have shown that Chinese children obtained the highest scores on all three parts of a reading test at grade one, and on the vocabulary and comprehension sections at grade five. In mathematics the Chinese and Japanese both scored higher than the Americans on the applications of mathematical principles to the solution of word problems and on items requiring only calculation. Stevenson and Lee (1990, p. 18) stress that "Asian children's superiority in mathematics was not limited, therefore, to facility in mathematical computation; they also were more successful in using their knowledge about mathematics in solving problems."

The Literature Review on Parental Control with the Chinese

In order to examine the relationship between Chinese parenting style and the achievements of their children, it is important to establish that Chinese have parenting patterns that are distinct from other groups. There is evidence that Chinese are high in parental control and restrictiveness (Ho, 1986).

Lin and Fu (1990) investigated four specific child-rearing variables — parental control, encouragement of independence, expression of affection, and emphasis on achievement — taken from Block's Child-Rearing Practices Report (1981). They compared the Chinese in Taiwan, immigrant Chinese in the United States, and Caucasian-American parents on these four child-rearing variables. Lin and Fu (1990) found that the Chinese in Taiwan and the immigrant Chinese were higher in parental control, emphasis on achievement, and encouragement of independence than the Caucasian-American parents. They argued that the higher parental control of both Chinese samples is explained within the Chinese tradition of "parental authority and filial piety and the Confucian dictum that 'parents are always right'" (p. 430). However, the Chinese immigrants were found to be lower on parental control than the Chinese in Taiwan. The researchers felt that this finding reflected a gradual change in these immigrants due to acculturation in the United States.

Chiu (1987) reviewed literature on the child-rearing attitudes between Chinese-American and Caucasian-American mothers. He summarized the focus of this literature: "Traditional Chinese socialization practices appear to be more restrictive and controlling compared to American socialization practices which are more liberal and permissive" (p. 411). Most of the studies in his review have depicted child rearing according to the restrictive-permissive dichotomy, equating the Chinese with restrictiveness and the Americans with permissiveness. Specifically, Sollenberger (1968) found that a sample of mothers in Chinatown, New York had imposed rigid demands for conformity after the age of six, but they provided an abundance of nurturance and protection during early childhood. In addition, Kriger and Kroes (1972) administered a questionnaire on child-rearing attitudes to Chinese, Jewish, and Protestant mothers and found the Chinese mothers were the most restrictive, but not more hostile or rejecting than the other two groups. Yee (1983) looked at parenting and acculturation in Chinese-American parents and claimed that they expressed more control over the child's impulses, lower reciprocity, and less closeness. Law (1973) also argued that foreign-born Chinese mothers had more restrictive attitudes toward child rearing and higher acceptance toward their child- rearing and maternal roles than American-born Chinese mothers.

In Chiu's (1987) study, he also examined dimensions of "restrictiveness", "expression of hostility and rejection", and "democratic behaviors" using the Parental Attitude Research Instrument (PARI) with Chinese-American mothers, Chinese living in Taiwan, and Caucasian-American mothers. Similar to the other studies reviewed, Chiu found that the Chinese living in Taiwan were the most restrictive with the Chinese Americans in the middle. However, Chiu stresses that this strictness and restriction is meant more to protect than inhibit. Chiu also found that the Chinese-American mothers were the highest on the hostility-rejection scale (with the Chinese and Caucasian-American mothers the same), and surprisingly the highest in democratic behaviors. Chiu explained that the Chinese-American mothers were perhaps highest in hostility because most of them were separated from their families and did not have the same familial support that the Chinese and the Caucasian Americans had. This lack of familial support created more frustration for the Chinese American mothers, and thus this frustration may have caused them to show more approval of hostility toward the child. In reference to the high democratic behaviors, Chiu (1987, p. 417) concluded, "Chinese-American parents may no longer expect unquestioning obedience from their children and relationships within the family have become more democratic." This conclusion explains why the Chinese in America are higher on the democratic scale than the Chinese in Taiwan, but it does not explain why they are also higher than the Caucasian Americans, particularly on a scale that Caucasian Americans typically have scored quite high on.

In the psychology literature, many studies with the Chinese have depicted their global parenting style as being restrictive or controlling. Many investigations with Caucasian Americans conclude that high levels of restriction and control are responsible for lower education in those groups. However, the relationship between parental control or restrictiveness and lower school achievement is very different for Asian Americans (Dornbusch et al., 1987).

Differences in Attitudes and Expectations for School Performance

Other studies have demonstrated differences in parenting for Asians, as well as for Chinese, in terms of their attitudes and expectations for school performance. Yao (1985) very richly described findings involving the family characteristics of Asian-Americans (i.e., Chinese, Korean, Filipino, Vietnamese, and Asian Indian) and Caucasian-American high-achieving students selected from grades five through eleven. In her interviews, Yao

(1985) found the family life of the Asian Americans more structured and focused on formal educational experiences for the children. Overall, Asian Americans held education to be more important for their children's overall future success. Asian- American parents, in comparison to the Caucasian-American parents, (1) expected the child to get A's more often, (2) were less satisfied with the child's performance, (3) directed the child more toward certain occupations, (4) were more involved in the child's homework and projects, (5) were more regular, rigid, and task-oriented in weekend activities (i.e., involved in cultural activities, music lessons, and language school), (6) promoted after-school activities that were more individualized (i.e., music lessons) versus group-oriented ventures (i.e., sports), and (7) provided more stable home environments (i.e., less divorce, fewer family moves, and a more regular lifestyle with consistent weekday and weekend schedules).

Interestingly, Yao also asked the parents whether there were any areas in which they felt the child's peers had more influence than the parents. Almost half of the Asian parents claimed none. Yao (1985) concluded:

> These parents still had influence upon their children's social development, and maintained more control than did the child's peers in the areas of clothes, courses of study, food preference, extra-curricular activities, etc. In general, Asian parents seem to maintain more 'control' over their children than Anglo parents. (p. 204)

Slaughter-Defoe, et al. (1990) provided a review of studies on Asian-American parental influences, including Yao's (1985). Specifically, Mordkowitz and Ginsburg (1987) interviewed 15 successful Chinese-, Korean-, and Japanese-American children and found in their family backgrounds, (1) a strong home environment involving a monitoring of the child's free time, an investment in educational opportunities, and intact families; (2) parental values involving a respect for education, including teacher authority; and (3) parental expectations for achievement. In addition, Lee (1987) looked at a number of different factors to explain the academic success of 42 sixth- and seventh-grade Chinese-, Japanese-, and Korean-American students and found that the high parental expectations were more responsible for achievement than the effects of socioeconomic level and teacher/peer relations.

Stevenson and Lee (1990) summarized the findings from their major international study involving children from Taipei (Taiwan), Sendai (Japan), and Minneapolis (United States). As mentioned in the previous section, this was a longitudinal study with data first collected when the children were in the first grade and then again in the fifth grade. They found differences across the three cultures in terms of the parent's interest in the child's academic achievement, involvement of the family in the child's education, standards and expectations of parents concerning the child's academic achievement, and both the parent's and the child's beliefs about the relative influence of effort and ability on academic achievement.

Stevenson and Lee (1990) emphasized the vast differences in school achievement, described earlier, between the American children versus the Chinese and Japanese children in both math and reading. These differences in achievement had become even more striking from the first-grade level to the fifth-grade level. As Stevenson and Lee (1990) stressed, in light of the fact that kindergarten education is not universal in Taiwan, the Chinese children then seem to be making spectacular gains in achievement, even though they enter the first grade with fewer academic skills than American or Japanese children. Although these researchers claimed large differences in the school environments and curricula of each country, they also highlighted the importance of the attitudes and beliefs of the parents and family, and the involvement of both the parents and the children in schoolwork. Stevenson and Lee explained that with the Chinese, the whole family assisted the child with his/her schoolwork, unlike the American and Japanese families where the mother assumed the primary role. In the Chinese families, even mothers with little education effectively performed their role in supervising the child's homework, and between both parents, siblings, and other relatives there was usually someone available in Chinese families to assist children when they encountered problems in schoolwork.

Stevenson and Lee (1990) described many aspects of Chinese and Japanese parental influences that differ greatly from American parental influences. Overall, both the Chinese and Japanese parents, in comparison to the American parents, stressed the importance of academic achievement. As early as the first grade, Chinese and Japanese parents were structuring their child's day so they not only spent more time on homework than the American children, but their after-school and weekend time were around academically-related activities. Also, the Chinese parents were spending more time helping their children with school work.

Another important difference found in both Chinese and Japanese mothers versus American mothers was that they do not express what Stevenson and Lee (1990) called an "overly optimistic evaluation of their child's performance". American mothers gave their children the highest ratings in the areas of ability to learn, intellectual ability, general academic performance, and motivation. However, in the area of motivation, Chinese and Japanese mothers believed that their child's motivation to do well in school increased as the child progressed from first to fifth grade, and American mothers did not. Instead, American mothers perceived their children as having lower motivation at the fifth than at the first grade. Also, unlike American parents, both Chinese and Japanese parents were not as easily satisfied with lower levels of school performance — the child must perform at least above average. Less than 5% of the Chinese and Japanese mothers, in contrast to 40% of the American mothers, said they were very satisfied with the child's performance. The majority of Chinese and Japanese mothers were satisfied as opposed to not satisfied or very satisfied.

Stevenson and Lee (1990) also believed that the importance the Chinese and Japanese parents placed on hard work encouraged their children to also endorse this value, and to therefore apply themselves much more in their school work than American children. Other international studies also supported many of these findings. Chen and Uttal (1988) looked at the relationship of the parental beliefs among Americans and Chinese to their children's math and reading abilities. These researchers interviewed 580 American parents and 390 Chinese parents from Beijing, and they tested 720 American and 396 Chinese students from the first, third, and fifth grades in math and reading achievement. They found that the Chinese children received higher math and reading scores at all grades. These researchers attributed the Chinese children's school success to the fact that the Chinese parents were found to set higher standards for their children and to work more often with their children on homework than American parents. Specifically, Chinese mothers were generally not as satisfied with the child's current school performance as the American mothers (i.e., 76% of the American mothers were satisfied or very satisfied as compared to 36% of the Chinese). The differences were even larger for the fathers. The researchers also asked the parents what score they thought their child would get on a math test, and then what score they would be satisfied with. Both the American and Chinese mothers expected the child to get 80 to 85 points. However, the American mothers were satisfied with a math score that was an average of 7 points lower than the score they actually expected the child to receive. The Chinese mothers were satisfied with a score that was an average of 10 points *higher* than what they expected the child to receive.

Au and Harackiewicz (1986) looked at the influence of perceived-parental expectations upon children's math performance with 64 Chinese elementary school students from Hong Kong. The Chinese students were first asked to complete a questionnaire on their parents' expectations of their school performance. Then later, they were given an arithmetic test that was accompanied either by a parental evaluation condition or a peer evaluation condition (i.e., students were told to either have their parents or a peer sign a note that was attached to the test). They found that, overall, higher perceived-parental expectations were related to higher math performance. However, the positive influence of higher perceived-parental expectations was stronger when children anticipated that their parents would evaluate their performance rather than their peers. These findings revealed that parents' expectations for their children may have the most influence upon performance when children anticipate that their parents will find out how well they do.

In accounting for why Asian children succeed in school, and why they work so diligently, many researchers claimed that, overall, it was because their parents valued education, and had a strong respect for scholarship. Most of the studies just cited found that Asian parents, and in some studies Chinese parents, showed an extremely high involvement in the child's schooling, from spending a great deal of time with the child on homework (Chen and Uttal, 1988; Stevenson and Lee, 1990; Yao, 1985) to structuring both the child's after-school activities and weekend activities around academically-related things (Stevenson and Lee, 1990; Yao, 1985). Chinese parents were found to stress the importance of hard work in determining school achievement, and concomitantly, this belief was then passed on to the child (Chen and Uttal, 1988; Slaughter-Defoe et al., 1990; Stevenson and Lee, 1990). The high standards for performance that Chinese parents held, in terms of not being easily satisfied with low or average school performance, also was found to promote high achievement in the children (Au and Harackiewicz, 1986; Chen and Uttal, 1988; Stevenson and Lee, 1990; Yao, 1985). Overall, the results from these studies seemed to indicate the extent to which Chinese or Asian parents exhibited a great deal of input and influence on their children's school achievement.

To a large extent, these studies are only suggestive of a causal relationship between parenting style and achievements. While some studies show that Asians differ from other ethnic groups in emphasis on variables such as achievements, control, supervision, etc., many fail to not only show

between-group differences, but also within-group differences on the variables. That is, if children do well because of high parental expectations,
then we should investigate if (1) Chinese differ from Caucasians in having
higher expectations and higher achievements, and (2) within the Chinese
group, children from families that have high parental expectations will
outperform those from families that have low parental expectations. Simultaneous demonstration of the two points would be important.

Attempts to Resolve the Paradox

The inability to find a strong and consistent relationship between child-
rearing practices and achievement for different groups has lead Sue and
Okazaki (1990) to speculate that other factors may account for the academic
success of Asian Americans. They propose that perceptions of discrimination against ethnic-minority groups in the United States may enhance the
value of educational achievements as a means for upward mobility. If
this is the case, the relationship between achievements and child-rearing
practices may be low. Therefore, motivation to achieve and fears over the
consequences of school failure may be better predictors of achievement.
Other recent researchers have also claimed that for many minority groups,
particularly the Asians, parental influences, including parenting style, upon
school achievement are not as important as previously thought.

Steinberg's Work

After rigorously trying to operationally define Baumrind's parenting
styles, Steinberg et al. (1992) examined factors associated with achievements among Asian Americans as a follow-up to Dornbusch et al. (1987).
Steinberg et al. (1991) summarized the central findings of Dornbusch et al.
(1987):

> Across the sample as a whole, as hypothesized, parental authoritativeness was
> associated with higher grades .... When the sample was disaggregated into
> ethnic groups, however, the index of authoritativeness was significantly
> predictive of achievement only among the white adolescents; the index was
> marginally predictive among Hispanic-American adolescents, and not at all
> predictive in the Asian-American or African-American subsamples. (p. 21)

Similar to Dornbusch et al. (1987), Steinberg et al. (1991) also found Asian
parents were nonauthoritative, in general, and they were also less involved

in their children's schooling, and yet their children were doing very well in school.

Steinberg et al. (1992) concluded that the school achievement of the Asian students cannot be attributed to the parental practices. Instead, they argued that the distinguishing factors for Asian school achievement, relative to other ethnic groups, involve (1) the tremendous and consistent support that Asian students receive from their peer group, and (2) their strong belief in the negative occupational repercussions of educational mediocrity (i.e., their fear of the consequences of school failure).

With this second factor, Steinberg et al. (1992) explained that the Asian students so strongly fear the consequences of school failure because of the homogeneity of influences they encounter with their peers, and not because of the parental influences. Consequently, this peer influence, according to Steinberg and his colleagues, tended to offset the costs of nonauthoritative parenting practices. The Asian sample also showed very little parental involvement in school. According to Steinberg and his colleagues, Asian children are succeeding in school *despite* their parents' practices not *because of* their parents. Therefore, the question arises again, just as with the Dornbusch et al. (1987) study, can we conclude from this study that Asian parenting practices are not contributing to their children's school success?

Review of Specific Findings

The findings reported by Steinberg et al. (1992) revealed important and interesting ethnic differences for the Asians that should be highlighted. In general, the Asian sample was found to be the most successful in school, and the most likely to endorse both the belief in the value of getting a good education for enhancing their labor market success *as well as* the belief in the negative repercussions of not getting a good education. Students from all the ethnic groups endorsed the belief that getting a good education will enhance their labor market success. However, the belief in the *negative* consequences of school failure (i.e., that *not* getting a good education *hurts* their chances) was endorsed more by Asians than by any of the other ethnic groups, including the Caucasians. In other words, Asians were distinguished from the other ethnic groups not so much in their stronger belief that educational success pays off, but in their stronger fear that educational failure will have negative consequences. Therefore, this belief in the negative consequences of school failure was a better predictor of adolescent school performance than was the belief that doing well in school pays off.

Although Steinberg and his colleagues reported that Asian parents do tend to have higher expectations for their children's school performance, they again concluded that the parents' practices are not the influential factors to Asian students receiving higher grades. In effect, the Asian parents, as well as the parents from the other minority groups, are relatively less potent sources on the students, than the Caucasian parents, and their peers are more potent sources. Steinberg et al. (1992) explain:

> This is not to say the *mean* levels of parental encouragement are necessarily lower in minority homes than in majority homes. Rather, the relative magnitude of the correlations between parental encouragement and academic success and between peer encouragement and academic success is different for minority than for majority youth. (p. 727)

For all the minority groups, there was a higher correlation between peer encouragement and academic success in comparison to the correlations between *parental* encouragement and academic success. However, Steinberg and his colleagues do not specify what is meant by "parental encouragement". Therefore, it is unclear whether they are referring to the parenting styles, parental expectations, or another parental variable such as parental involvement in school.

The peer group of the Asians was found to differ from the peer group of the other minority groups in their "encouragement of academic achievement". Asian American students seemed to have peer support for academics that involved studying together, explaining difficult assignments, and so on. However, again, Steinberg et al. (1992, p. 728) point out there is a lack of relationship between the peer crowd membership and parenting practices in that "authoritatively raised minority youngsters do not necessarily belong to peer groups that encourage academic success." In addition, these researchers (p. 728) also stress that Asian-American parents are the least involved in their children's schooling: "In contrast to popular belief, Asian-American parents are less involved in their children's schooling than any other group of parents." This claim certainly does seem in direct contradiction to what past research has shown.

In the studies cited earlier, parental expectations or performance standards have been extensively discussed and found to be an important parental influence upon school achievement. In other cross-cultural studies involving Asian samples, parental involvement with child's schoolwork, and other aspects of Asian parental practices and beliefs were found to be very influential in predicting the children's school achievement (Au and

Harackiewicz, 1986; Chen and Uttal, 1988; Stevenson and Lee, 1990; Yao, 1985).

Chao's Alternative Argument to the Paradox

Chao (1994) argues that the concepts of authoritative and authoritarian are not capturing the aspects of Asian parenting that explain school success. More importantly, these concepts are somewhat ambiguous for Asians, and do not capture what is most important about their child-rearing or parenting style, particularly with the area of parental control.

Chao (1992) had interviewed 50 immigrant Chinese mothers primarily from Taipei (Taiwan) and 50 Caucasian American mothers all with pre-school-aged children, and of higher socio-economic status (i.e., both samples were well-educated). The mothers were first asked three open-ended questions involving (1) their view of child rearing, (2) how they feel they are similar to or different from other mothers, and (3) how they feel their parenting may impact their children's school achievement.

All the mothers were also administered two standard measures that have been used in the past by Lin and Fu (1990), and Kochanska (1990). As mentioned earlier, Lin and Fu (1990) had used the parental control factor taken from Block's (1981) Child Rearing Practices Report (CRPR) as their measure of parental control. They had found in their study that Chinese mothers score significantly higher than Caucasian-American mothers on the parental control factor as well as significantly lower on the expression of affection factor. Kochanska (1990) had also used factors taken from Block's CRPR to derive authoritarian and authoritative parenting-style dimensions.

Then all the mothers were administered a series of questionnaire items that were intended to bring out aspects of Chinese parenting and thought that might be missing in other standard instruments. This questionnaire covered four topic areas, aims of parental control, parental expectations for high school and career, child development ideologies, and mother-child relationship ideologies. Within these four topic areas were different types of items capturing Chinese views. The aims of control items reflected the notion of training, particularly around self-discipline in study skills, and in parental respect. The parental expectations items reflected high expectations for school success and career mobility. The child development ideology items reflected the importance of early training by exposing young children to explicit examples of proper behavior, and exposing and involving children as much as possible in the adult world. The items for the mother-child relationship ideologies stressed the importance of a high maternal involvement and sacrifice.

Many of the items designed to depict Chinese child rearing above were derived from the literature of East-Asian scholars that specifically discussed "child training" instead of "child rearing". The parent's training of the child can be captured by the Chinese term, "chiao shun", which indicates "training" (i.e., educating, or inculcating) children in the appropriate, culturally approved behaviors, particularly in performing well in school.

Thus, as one resolution to this paradox evident in Dornbusch et al. (1987) and Steinberg et al. (1992), Chao (1992 and 1994) has offered a new, indigenous parenting style concept, captured by this notion of "jiao shun" or "training". Because studies such as Lin and Fu (1990), Dornbusch et al. (1987), and Steinberg and his colleagues (1992) had found that the Chinese or Asians were significantly higher on parental control and authoritarian parenting style, these measures were then controlled for in order to test whether differences still exist between both groups of mothers on the Chinese child-rearing items reflecting the notion of "training". In other words, both groups of mothers were in a sense "statistically matched" on these standard measures to determine whether there would still be important differences on these "training" items that would, in effect, better explain the parenting or child-rearing style of the Chinese.

Interestingly, just looking at their scores on these standard measures, the Chinese were indeed significantly higher on Block's parental control factor (used by Lin and Fu, 1990), and the authoritarian dimension (used by Kochanska, 1990). However, the Chinese mothers were also just as high as the Caucasian Americans on the authoritative dimension, and the expression of affection factor. Thus, existing instruments continue to assess Chinese parents as more authoritarian than Caucasian-American parents, but the high authoritative parenting scores of the Chinese begin to suggest that authoritarian is an incomplete, or even misleading characterization of the Chinese.

Similar results were also found with mothers from Japan: Power, Kobayashi-Winata, and Kelley (1992, p. 202) had found in their study of mothers of 3- to 6-year old children from Japan and the United States that the Japanese shared some aspects of the permissive and authoritative styles, but that "the authoritarian style appears to be uniquely associated with the United States." Therefore, the authoritarian parenting style does not at all capture or describe Japanese parenting either.

In addition, even after accounting for their level of control, Baumrind's parenting styles, and their education, the Chinese still scored higher than the Caucasian Americans on the Chinese items involving the three other topic areas, parental expectations for high school and career, child development ideologies, and mother-child relationship ideologies. Two of the Chinese parental expectations items replicated results found by Yao (1985) and Stevenson and Lee (1990) — Chinese parents expect their children to get good grades and go to a good university. There were also two other items that suggest the reasons behind these expectations — the importance of education for bringing honor to the family, and for assuring future success such as getting a good job and earning a good income.

The Chinese items for the areas, child development ideologies and mother-child relationship ideologies, especially explain a great deal about Chinese parental control, and its impact on school achievement. Specifically, parental control for the Chinese is primarily motivated around their intense concern for their children to be successful, particularly in school. Sometimes this may involve driving the child when the child's own motivation is not adequate. Oftentimes training children fairly early on to work very hard and be disciplined (as depicted in the child development ideology items) would for the Chinese be one way to foster the child's self-motivation. Other times this control may look much like guiding the child to the level of performance that is desired. Specifically, Chinese children are given very extensive experiences of what's expected of their behavior in general. Chinese children are from a young age exposed to explicit models or examples of proper behavior, and to many aspects of the adult world (as captured in the Chinese child development ideology items). In conjunction with their expectations for school achievement and proper behavior, the mothers also offer immense support to the child through their high sacrifice and involvement (as reflected in the items for the mother-child relationship ideologies). This type of mother-child relationship may have just as important or influential effect on the child as the type of control they exert.

In addition, the Chinese mothers' responses to the interviews reflected the type of "training" they felt contributed to their children's school success. They stressed that (1) they expect more in a variety of different ways (i.e., they believe they can do more; they assign extra work and outside music or language lessons as well as study groups or tutoring; and they encourage the child to have specific career aspirations early on); (2) they invest much more in education (i.e., they stressed the sacrifices they make, and the necessity of having both parents working in order to save money for the child's schooling); (3) they value education specifying that Chinese culture has had a historical respect for scholars; (4) they endorse beliefs about the repercussions of not getting a good education (i.e. one cannot be successful in life without an education); (5) they believe that foreigners have to be better to have access to more opportunities; and (6) they feel that getting a good education is a means of bringing honor to the family.

Therefore, the concepts of authoritative and authoritarian do not capture what is most important about Chinese child rearing especially for predicting school success. Chao (1992 and 1994) has demonstrated that even after accounting for their level of parental control, Baumrind's parenting styles, and their education, there were still important differences on the Chinese child rearing items, captured by the general notion of "training" or "chiao shun".

The concept of "training" may more clearly capture the parenting style of the Chinese than the authoritarian concept, because the latter concept may be somewhat ambiguous for the Chinese. On the one hand, the Chinese do share some aspects of the authoritarian parenting style in their child training approaches. As indicated in Chao's (1994) study, the Chinese mothers did endorse many qualities of Baumrind's authoritarian parenting style, such as obedience, respect for work and the traditional order, and a set standard of conduct emphasizing parental authority. Hence, this endorsement is why they end up scoring high on authoritarian. However, on the other hand, the parenting style of the Chinese (i.e., captured by the notion of "training") has distinct differences from the authoritarian notion because the authoritarian notion is embedded in a socio-cultural tradition that Chinese do not necessarily share.

According to Smuts and Hagen (1985), this notion of authoritarian has evolved from a long cultural tradition beginning with the evangelical and Puritan religious movements. These movements have been quite preoccupied with stressing "domination" of the child, or the "breaking of the child's will", because of the belief in "original sin" (i.e., the concept of guilt attached to the infant by reason of deprivation of his/her original nature). This very harsh, ambivalent view of the child dominated both the advisory literature for parents as well as children's own reading for up to two centuries. Even though after World War II there was an extreme shift from this harsh, ambivalent treatment of the child to a more "democratic", "child-centered", and permissive approach, nonetheless the authoritarian concept received even more "notoriety" as the antithesis to this more "modern", "democratic" approach.

The Chinese, both in the U.S. and especially in East Asia, may not have experienced the extensiveness of this American socio-cultural tradition. This concept, therefore, may imply something entirely different for the Chinese than for those more immersed in American mainstream culture. Although they may share some aspects of this concept, as discussed in the previous paragraph, parental control for the Chinese may also be associated with a great deal of maternal involvement and support, less domination per se of the child, and thus a more positive approach than the more authoritarian type of control. Therefore, another argument was proposed that authoritarian parenting is predictive of school achievement in the Chinese specifically because (1) for the Chinese, authoritarian control is related to a high level of maternal involvement and sacrifice; and (2) Chinese children may be deriving very "positive" effects from the type of parental control exhibited by Chinese parents.

Specifically, among Caucasian Americans authoritarian control has tended to correlate with parental rejection, hostility, and lack of support (Rohner and Pettengill, 1985), whereas among the Chinese, authoritarian control may be related to a very different mother-child relationship. This relationship involves both a very high maternal involvement and sacrifice in addition to some of the emotional support and intimacy most often associated with Caucasian-American parenting. Indeed, Rohner and Pettengill (1985) had shown that Korean adolescents that had perceived their parents as more controlling had also perceived them as being more accepting and warm. However, Lau and Cheung (1987) had argued that their findings were due to the fact that two types of high parental control must be distinguished for Asians (i.e., the domineering versus the organizing type of control). They found that many Chinese parents scored quite high on the organizational pattern of control, and that only this type of parental control correlated with parental warmth. Lau and Cheung pointed out that this organizational control was for the purpose of keeping the family running more smoothly and for fostering family harmony. In addition, their finding that the organizational pattern of control was predominant among Chinese may also indicate another aspect of Chinese parental control that the authoritative and authoritarian parenting styles are not capturing. Specifically, a different type of more family-based control along with a very supportive relationship with the child may be the parenting aspects that contribute to Asian-American school success.

Second, Chinese children in comparison to Caucasian-American children may be deriving an entirely different meaning from this type of control. Authoritarian control may be regarded as domineering by Caucasian-American children. However, Chinese children may experience this control as simply a clearer message of what's expected of them, not as something entirely negative. Because Chinese parents often exert control in conjunction with high involvement and support, their children may find these control behaviors more acceptable. For instance, Steward and Steward (1973) had conducted an observational study of Caucasian-American, Mexican-American, and Chinese-American mothers with their preschool-aged children during a teaching task. They found that Chinese mothers' teaching styles were distinctive in terms of "their selective use of specificity of instructions" and in terms of "providing a high proportion of enthusiastic positive feedback" (p. 336). Their specificity of instructions was "selective" in the sense that the instructions were most often given after the child had demanded or asked for help. These researchers also had found that both the Mexican-American and Chinese-American children gave more "accepting responses" than the Caucasian-American children. Therefore, these results seem to indicate that Chinese mothers offer their directions or expectations based on the child's needs. In conjunction with these directives, Chinese mothers also offer a high level of support, and thus the children are more often accepting of these directives.

In addition, the Rohner and Pettengill (1985) study seems to indicate that Korean adolescents do not perceive their parents' controlling behaviors in a negative way. Chao (1994) also argues that the type of more organization or family-based control found by Lau and Cheung (1987) resembles her idea of clearer parental expectations or messages; this type of control may be interpreted by the Chinese, or perhaps even Asian, children as such, rather than as harmful domination.

Therefore, although Dornbusch et al. (1987), and Steinberg et al. (1991 and 1992) had found that Asian children's school success could not be explained by Baumrind's parenting styles, there are a number of different explanations for this finding: (1) these parents in some aspects are less authoritarian than previously thought; (2) those authoritarian aspects they do endorse also, however, go along with a very supportive mother-child relationship; (3) some aspects of parental control are quite different from the socio-cultural traditions of the authoritarian concept, and may not involve domination per se, but rather the "organizational" or "family-based" control found by Lau and Cheung (1987); and (4) the children may be interpreting their parents' control behaviors as more positive, clearer expectations or messages, rather than as parental domination. We propose that in order to resolve this paradox, more relevant and therefore indigenous concepts for describing the parenting style of the Chinese must be derived that incorporate not only the more family-based type of control relevant to the Chinese, but also the high involvement and devotion of the Chinese mother.

Methodological and Measurement Issues

The previous sections have provided a cross-cultural analysis of the parenting style *concepts* originally captured by Baumrind (1971). However, the findings on the relationship between parenting style and school achievement must also be considered in light of the actual *measures* that were used by Dornbusch et al (1987), and Steinberg et al. (1992). Specifically, the measures used to depict Baumrind's concepts contain items that are more relevant and meaningful to Caucasian Americans and much less so to individuals from other socio-cultural backgrounds. In addition, because the Dornbusch et al. (1987) and Steinberg et al. (1991 and 1992) studies focused on a different age group, high school students, this may also explain ethnic-group differences on the parental involvement measure used by Steinberg et al. (1992). Therefore, this last section will also review the specific items that comprised the measure, "parental involvement in school". There are important cultural implications apparent in this measure that suggest future lines of investigation.

Measure of Parenting Style

Conceptual Meaning of the Items Differ for Asians

For instance, in the Dornbusch et al. (1987) study, the items they used to capture Baumrind's parenting styles of authoritative, authoritarian, and permissive appear to be more relevant and discriminating for the Caucasian-American sample, but much less so for the Asian-American sample. The items used to discriminate the three parenting styles included family communication, parent's response to good grades, and parent's response to bad grades. The items that comprised the authoritative family-communication style were: Parents tell the youth to look at both sides of issues, they admit that the youth sometimes knows more, they talk about

politics within the family, and they emphasize that everyone should help
with decisions within the family.

The meaning of these items may reflect a type of family interchange
that is more central to American culture rather than other cultures. This
authoritative style of family interchange emphasizes that every individual,
as well as every opinion has equal weight, and should be voiced in an open
forum, rather like the democratic form of government in the United States.
However, this may not be the communication styles that families from
other cultures, especially many of the Asian cultures, are accustomed to.
Many Asian cultures, including the Chinese, have an imperative respect for
the word and opinion of elders (Bond and Hwang, 1986; Liu, 1986), and
more importantly, not every opinion, or even every issue related to the
family needs to be discussed by the family as a whole. Because these items
reflect ideas or values more central to Caucasian-American culture, the
Asian students then (depending on how acculturated they are to mainstream
American values) may not be interpreting these items in the same manner
as the Caucasian students.

Parenting Measures Too Circumscribed to Education

To measure authoritarian parenting (i.e., high control, and lack of warmth
and democratic decision-making) according to parents' responses to good
or bad grades may also be misleading. Instead of measuring parental
warmth or control, these items may simply reflect how much Asians, in
comparison to Caucasian Americans, emphasize educational success for
their children. For example, according to this authoritarian measure, these
parents, in response to poor grades, would get upset, reduce the youth's
allowance, or ground the youth; in response to good grades, parents would
ask the child to do even better, and that the other grades should be as good.
With this singular focus on academic or educationally-related issues, these
items may be especially loaded for Asians. Because many of the Asian
groups emphasize education very strongly, including the Chinese, these
parents have high expectations for their children's school performance.
Therefore, when a child is doing well, the Asian parent may encourage the
child by telling him/her to do even better, and when the child gets a bad
grade this will greatly concern the Asian parent. If the parent feels the child
is not applying himself/herself, the Asian parent may try to punish the child.
To the Asian parent the educational performance of the child is imperative
and is the basis for the child's overall future success. Therefore, any

problems that the child has in school would be taken very seriously. In addition, rather than indicating negative parental intervention, these parental control behaviors would indicate parental concern, involvement, and even love.

Age Differences in the Studies

One very important difference between the studies that have found the parental influences to be significant versus those that claim the peer group is most important focus on different age groups of students. The other studies that found parental factors to be significant focused on younger children (i.e., preschool through elementary-school age). In addition, Lee's (1987) study included both sixth and seventh grade students (cited in Slaughter-Defoe et al., 1990), and Yao's study (1985) included a range of students from the fifth to the eleventh grades (with the average grade level as 7.4). However, student samples from Dornbusch et al. (1987), and Steinberg et al. (1991 and 1992) were from the tenth, eleventh, and twelfth grades, in other words, high school only. Therefore, the peer group would be very salient for the high-school students in these studies, and for these researchers to stress the peer-group influence is most important and informative. However, to conclude that the school success of Chinese and other Asians is explainable largely in terms of their peer crowd — to the *exclusion* of the parental influences — is perhaps too hasty. Particularly with the measure of "parental involvement in school", the results for Asian parents do not indicate that the parents have somewhat *less* of an influence in comparison to the peer crowd, but rather that Asian parents simply do not exhibit involvement in their children's schooling.

Measure of Parental Involvement in School

Cultural Differences as a Function of Age

The way that "parental involvement in school" was measured may not have captured the type of things that Asian parents are doing with their children at the high-school level. Closer inspection of the items from the measure, "parental involvement in school", indeed, seemed to indicate that these items may not be assessing the type of involvement that Asian parents are providing for their *high-school aged* children. The items that comprised "parental involvement in school" consisted of "makes sure I do my homework", "checks my homework over", "knows how I am doing in school", "goes to school programs for parents", "watches me in sports or activities", and "helps me in choosing my courses".

Specifically, the items regarding homework and courses (i.e., "makes sure I do my homework", "checks my homework over", and "helps me in choosing my courses") reflect a type of parental involvement in which parents act as managers of the child's schooling and school work — making sure the child takes the right courses, does his/her homework, and does it correctly. This type of "management" role would not be part of what the Chinese parents are most focused on for their *high school-aged* children. By the time their children are in high school, they would already expect the children to know what courses to take and to do their homework and do it well, or with maximum effort. Chinese parents who still needed to remind their children to do their work, and to check the quality of their work would more likely represent parents having difficulties with their children, rather than being "involved or conscientious" parents. This may be especially true with Asians. Also, some of the Chinese parents may be immigrants and may not be capable of helping and checking over high-school level homework, as well as knowing what courses their adolescents should take. Immigrant status is also an important factor for the items "goes to school programs for parents", and "watches me in sports or activities". Immigrant parents are less likely to attend parent-teacher conferences, and other school activities, especially at the high school level, because of language and cultural differences or difficulties. Therefore, the relevancy of these items for the Chinese may be quite different when compared to the Caucasians.

Chinese parents in East Asia as well as in the United States may show vast cultural differences from Caucasian-American parents as to the type of involvement they manifest with their children across the different grade levels in school. They may show changes in their goals and practices in a completely different manner or direction than the changes found in Caucasian parents regarding their goals and practices. Chinese parents as well as other Asians may be focusing their children much earlier than Caucasian parents on schoolwork and on applying themselves to their schoolwork; whereas Caucasian-American parents may think that parental pressure should be applied only as the child gets older, more during high school, and not so much in elementary school. Indeed, Song and Park (1993) found that among Korean parents in Korea, direct teaching and supply of reference materials were quite high at the second-grade level, but began to significantly decrease by the sixth grade. Also, Steward and Steward (1973) found that the Chinese-American mother considered teaching to be an important component of her maternal role, and regular formal instruction began in the home as early as preschool.

By the time their children are in high school, Chinese parents would already have established that their children are focused on their schoolwork. Instead, the Asian or Chinese parent might be discussing preparation for college with the child — very specifically focusing the child on what university they should apply to, what their major should be, and accordingly, what type of job they should try to attain when they finish college. According to this measure of parental involvement in school, Asian-American parents would not appear to be as involved in their adolescent's schooling when in fact they may be very highly involved and supportive.

Conclusion

The studies discussed in this chapter have raised some interesting questions as to the type of parental involvement and practices that Chinese or Asian parents may be exhibiting with their children in school. Many of the findings summarized in Steinberg et al. (1992) on the influence of the Asian student's peer group are very informative. However, investigating the relationship between parental behavior and high school achievement may be more complicated than supposed. It is premature to claim that Chinese parents, as well as Asian parents in general, exert no influence over their adolescent's school achievement, and play no role in producing the higher achievement levels of students. Chao (1992 and 1994) has suggested that the lack of relationship found between authoritative parenting style and school achievement may be due to the fact that these parenting style concepts may not be adequate for capturing Chinese parenting. Therefore, Chao (1992 and 1994) had proposed a more relevant, indigenous concept for capturing Chinese parenting style that perhaps may better explain their school success. Particularly with the area of parental control, the Chinese may be exhibiting a type of high control that is more organizational in quality rather than strictly dominating. Also this chapter has suggested that the specific measures for parenting style as well as Steinberg and colleagues' "parental involvement in school" may not be capturing just what the Chinese and other Asian parents are doing with their children. Specifically with parental involvement in school, parents of the Chinese as well or Asian students do not exhibit the same type of involvement in school and the same type of parental practices as the Caucasian-American parents. This chapter has raised some possibilities for investigating whether Asian parents, in comparison to Caucasian parents, are focusing their children much earlier, and much more intensely on their school work; and whether by the time their children are in high school the Asian parents are shifting some of their children's focus to applying for college, and eventually entering the job market. There is an urgent need for longitudinal studies, that focus on changes in schooling concerns that may more fully capture Asian-American parental involvement.

References

Au, T.K.F., and Harackiewicz, J. M. (1986). The effects of perceived parental expectations on Chinese children's mathematics performance. *Merrill-Palmer Quarterly*, 32 (4): 383–392.

Baldwin, A., Kalhorn, J., and Breese, F. (1945). Patterns of parent behavior. *Psychological Monographs*, 58 (3, Serial No. 268).

Baumrind, D. (1971). Current patterns of parental authority. *Developmental Psychology Monographs*, 4 (1, Part 2).

Block, J. (1981). *The child-rearing practices report (CRPR): A set of Q items for the description of parental socialization attitudes and values*. Berkeley: University of California, Institute of Human Development.

Bond, M., and Hwang, K. K. (1986). The social psychology of the Chinese people. In M. Bond (Ed.), *The psychology of the Chinese people* (pp. 213–266). Hong Kong: Oxford University Press.

Chao, R. (1992). *Immigrant Chinese mothers and European–American mothers: Their aims of control and other child rearing aspects related to school*. Unpublished doctoral dissertation, University of California, Los Angeles.

————. (1994). Beyond parental control and authoritarian parenting style: Understanding Chinese parenting through the cultural notion of training. *Child Development*, 65: 1111–1120.

Chen, C. S., and Uttal, D. (1988). Cultural values, parents' beliefs, and children's achievement in the United States and China. *Human Development*, 31: 351–358.

Cheung, C. P. (1982). Student perceptions of parental practices and effort — A comparison of Chinese, Anglo, and Hispanic students. *Dissertation Abstracts International*, 43: 6A.

Chiu, L. H. (1987). Child-rearing attitudes of Chinese, Chinese–American, and Anglo–American mothers. *International Journal of Psychology*, 22: 409–419.

Dornbusch, S., Ritter, P., Leiderman, P., Roberts, D., and Fraleigh, M. (1987). The relation of parenting style to adolescent school performance. *Child Development*, 58: 1244–1257.

Ho, D. (1986). Chinese patterns of socialization: A critical review. In M. Bond (Ed.), *The psychology of the Chinese people* (pp. 1–37). Hong Kong: Oxford University Press.

Kochanska, G. (1990). Maternal beliefs as long-term predictors of mother–child interaction and report. *Child Development*, 61: 1934–1943.

Kriger, S. F., and Kroes, W. H. (1972). Child-rearing attitudes of Chinese, Jewish, and Protestant mothers. *The Journal of Social Psychology*, 86: 205–210.

Lau, S., and Cheung, P. C. (1987). Relation between Chinese adolescents' perception of parental control and organization and their perception of parental warmth. *Developmental Psychology*, 23: 726–729.

Law, T. T. (1973). Differential child-rearing attitudes and practices of Chinese–American mothers. *Dissertation Abstracts International*, 34: 4406A.

Lee, Y. (1987). *Academic success of East–Asian Americans: An ethnographic comparative study of East–Asian–American and Anglo–American academic achievement*. Seoul: American Studies Institute, Seoul National University Press.

Lin, C. Y., and Fu, V. (1990). A comparison of child-rearing practices among Chinese, immigrant Chinese, and Caucasian–American parents. *Child Development*, 61: 429–433.

Liu, I. M. (1986). Chinese cognition. In M. Bond (Ed.), *The psychology of the Chinese people* (pp. 73–105). Hong Kong: Oxford University Press.

Mordkowitz, E., and Ginsburg, H. (1987). Early academic socialization of successful Asian–American college students. *The Quarterly Newsletter of the Laboratory of Comparative Human Cognition*, 9 (2): 85–91.

O'Hare, W. P., and Felt, J. C. (1991). *Asian Americans: America's fastest growing minority group*. Washington, D.C. : Population Reference Bureau.

Power, T., Kobayashi-Winata, H., and Kelley, M. (1992). Child-rearing patterns in Japan and the United States: A cluster analytic study. *International Journal of Behavioral Development*, 15 (2): 185–205.

Rohner, R., and Pettengill, S. (1985). Perceived parental acceptance–rejection and parental control among Korean adolescents. *Child Development*, 56: 524–528.

Slaughter-Defoe, D., Nakagawa, K., Takanishi, R., and Johnson, D. (1990). Toward cultural / ecological perspectives on schooling and achievement in African– and Asian–American children. *Child Development*, 61: 363–383.

Smuts, A. B., and Hagen, J. W. (1985). *History of the family and of childhood*: *Monographs of the Society for Research in Child Development*, 50 (4–5, Serial No. 211).

Sollenberger, R. (1968). Chinese–American child-rearing practices and juvenile delinquency. *Journal of Social Psychology*, 74: 13–23.

Song, M. J., and Park, Y. T. (1993, March). *Learning style and perceived parental academic socialization in Korean children.* Paper presented at the 60th Anniversary Meeting of the Society for Research in Child Development, New Orleans, LA.

Steinberg, L. (1990, August). *Adolescent development in ecological perspective.* Paper presented at The Annual Meeting of the American Psychological Association, Boston, MA.

Steinberg, L., Dornbusch, S., and Brown, B. (1992). Ethnic differences in adolescent achievement: An ecological perspective. *American Psychologist*, 47: 723–729.

Steinberg, L., Mounts, N., Lamborn, S., and Dornbusch, S. (1991). Authoritative parenting and adolescent adjustment across varied ecological niches. *Journal of Research on Adolescence*, 1: 19–36.

Stevenson, H., and Lee, S. Y. (1990). *Contexts of achievement. Monographs of the Society for Research in Child Development*, 55 (1–2, Serial No. 221).

Steward, M., and Steward, D. (1973). The observation of Anglo–, Mexican–, and Chinese–American mothers teaching their young sons. *Child Development*, 44: 329–337.

Sue, S., and Abe, J. (1988). *Predictors of academic achievement among Asian–American and White students* (Report No. 88–11). New York: College Entrance and Exam Board.

Sue, S., and Okazaki, S. (1990). Asian–American educational achievements: A phenomenon in search of an explanation. *American Psychologist*, 45: 913–920.

Suzuki, B. (1988, April). *Asian–Americans in higher education: Impact of changing demographics and other social forces.* Paper presented at the meeting of the National Symposium on the Changing Demographics of Higher Education, New York, NY.

Yao, E. (1985). A comparison of family characteristics of Asian–American and Anglo–American high achievers. *International Journal of Comparative Sociology*, 26 (34): 198–208.

Yee, J.H.Y. (1983). Parenting attitudes, acculturation and social competence in the Chinese–American children. *Dissertation Abstracts International*, 43: 4166B.

6

Achievement Goals and Causal Attributions of Chinese Students*

Kit-tai Hau and Farideh Salili

In recent years, cross-cultural research on motivation and achievement has focused more on the role of culture in mediating achievement cognition. It is suggested that disparities in cultural experiences can lead to the development of different concerns for achievement, different domains of action and different criteria for success (De Vos, 1973). Hence, people from different cultures may hold different meanings, goals and perception of causes of achievement and they may pursue their achievement goals in different ways.

The present chapter aims at investigating the cultural variations in causal attributions and goals of achievement. More specifically, in this chapter, we will review studies on the achievement goals and causal attributions of Chinese students and compare the findings with those reported in the Western cultures. It is hypothesized that cultural values of collectivism, emphasis placed on diligence, and importance of education among Chinese have major influence on causal attributions and achievement goal orientations of the Chinese students. In the following sections a brief review of literature on these two areas will be presented first.

Achievement Goals and Causal Attributions

Achievement Goals

It has been suggested that achievement goal orientation is an important

* Preparation of this chapter was supported in part by a grant made available by the Hong Kong Institute of Educational Research at the Chinese University of Hong Kong.

determinant of motivation and achievement (Dweck, 1986; Elliott and Dweck, 1988). Two contrasting goals have been identified and received substantial research interest. In one, the performance goal, individuals seek to maintain a positive judgment of their own ability and avoid negative judgments by trying to prove their superiority and competence. In the other, the learning goal, individuals tend to increase their competence, to understand or master new tasks. Other labels such as task- vs. ego- (Nicholls, Cheung, Lauer, and Patashnick, 1989), task- vs. competitive- (Covington and Omelich, 1984), or mastery- vs. performance-orientation (Ames and Archer, 1987) have also been used interchangeably to describe these two types of contrasting goals.

Students' goals are influenced by a variety of personal, sociocultural and contextual factors. For example, Ames and Archer (1987) examined mothers' belief about the role of ability and effort in school learning. They found that those mothers preferring mastery (i.e., learning) goals placed stronger emphasis on the child's effort and active participation in learning. On the other hand, mothers with stronger performance goals placed greater emphasis on normative standards to define school learning. It was argued that whether students could focus on the efficacy of their effort (e.g., in cognition retraining) depended largely on the goal orientation of their parents. Ames and Archer's findings also suggested that a performance goal priority might have negative consequences for students who had doubts about their ability or who did not compare favorably with others.

Causal Attributions

Since 1970's studies on achievement motivation have focused on analyzing "how children construe the situation, interpret events in the situation, and process information about the situation" (Dweck, 1986, p. 1040).

In an achievement event, such as a school examination, questions like "why did I succeed or fail?" or "why does Peter get a higher mark than me?" may invoke many causes. Weiner (1979, 1990) has proposed a three dimensional classification of such causes (see Table 6.1).

In the first dimension, locus of causality, causes are said to be either internal (within) or external (outside) to the individual. The most frequently cited internal causes in a school setting are ability and effort, and external causes are luck and task difficulty. The second dimension, stability, contrasts stable (invariant) and unstable (variant) causes. Examples of relatively

Table 6.1: **Causes of Success and Failure, Classified According to Locus, Stability, and Controllability**

	Internal		External	
Controllability	Stable	Unstable	Stable	Unstable
Uncontrollable	Ability	Mood	Task Difficulty	Luck
Controllable	Typical effort	Immediate effort	Teacher bias	Unusual help from others

Note: From "A Theory of Motivation for Some Classroom Experiences" by B. Weiner, 1986, *Journal of Educational Psychology*, 71 (1): pp. 3–25.

stable causes are ability, typical effort, and socioeconomic status, whereas those of instability include immediate effort, attention and mood.

Things that are internal are not necessarily controllable (e.g., sickness). Similarly, external causes can be uncontrollable (e.g., incurable disease) or controllable by an external agent (e.g., help from a friend). Consequently, a third dimension, controllability, has been proposed. A fourth dimension, globality (Abramson, Seligman, and Teasdale, 1978), has also been widely used to distinguish the causes that affect a wide range of situations (e.g., general intelligence) from those that influence only a limited scope of events (e.g., specific skills).

Causal attributions and their dimensions have been linked to expectancy of future success and affective reactions. The stability of a cause (rather than its locus), for example, will determine the expectancy change. An outcome is expected to recur if the cause is stable. Success due to good luck produces surprise, whereas that due to great effort results in calmness (Weiner, 1985).

Some attributional styles are considered to be more undesirable than the others. Research on learned helplessness suggest that attributions of failure to global, stable and internal factors will lead to low self-esteem and general and chronic helpless depression (Abramson et al., 1978; Brewin and Furnham, 1986; Peterson and Seligman, 1984). The depression-prone individuals overgeneralize in failures and constrict in successes.

Similar results were revealed with students in mainland China. Zhang and Wang (1989) examined the relationship between attributional style and depression among 105 university students in Beijing. The former was measured by the Attributional Style Questionnaire (Peterson, Semmel, von Baeyer, Abramson, Metalsky, and Seligman, 1982) while the latter was assessed with the Beck Depression Inventory (Beck, 1967). The findings were also supportive of learned helplessness theory — depression was more serious with those students who attributed success to specific and unstable causes and failure to global and stable causes.

Consistent with Western findings, Lin (1979) found that among Taiwan high school students, internal (ability and effort) attributions for positive events were correlated with positive personal and social adjustment, whereas internal attribution for negative events were negatively related to adjustment. On the other hand, external attributions for positive or negative events are negatively correlated with personal and social adjustments. In another study with 510 Taiwan university students, Huang, Hwang, and Ko (1983) also found that students who tended to attribute negative life events to internal, stable, and global factors were more depressive.

Relations Between Achievement Goals and Attributions

People with different goals will perceive and attribute their (as well as others') performance in accordance with their own goals (Nicholls et al., 1989, p. 69). Such differences in causal attributions have been examined by manipulating the salience and values of learning and performance goals in experimental tasks (e.g., Ames, 1984; Ames and Ames, 1981, 1984, Ames and Felker, 1979). Ames (1984) using line drawing puzzles, compared children's performance in individualistic (i.e., performance evaluation is based on the child's own past performance) and competitive (i.e., performance is evaluated in comparison with performance of another child) conditions. In the former, children worked alone and were told to solve as many puzzles as they could and try to improve their performance on the second task. In the latter, children worked in pairs and were exhorted to solve more puzzles than their partners. Ames found that effort attributions were dominant in the learning involved condition, whereas ability attributions were stronger in the performance involved condition.

Similar results were also obtained in a study using a questionnaire. Ames and Archer (1988) asked high school students to indicate their perceptions of classroom goals, use of learning strategies, task choices, attitudes, and causal attributions. Results showed that students who perceived an emphasis on performance goals made more ability attributions, whereas, those perceiving mastery (i.e., learning) goals had a stronger belief in the importance of their own effort.

In summarizing the relation between achievement goals and attribution to ability, Nicholls et al. (1989) pointed out that performance goal (ego orientation) was associated with the belief in the importance of ability. He explained, 'This is rational in that if onets criterion of success is to out-perform one's peers, it will be much easier to do this with superior ability' (Nicholls, 1989, p. 72). On the other hand, people with a strong learning goal believe that to guarantee success, deep understanding through one's effort is more important than superior ability.

Cultural Factors Affecting Attributions and Goals

The meaning of achievement is culturally specific, and closely related to people's achievement goals (Agarwal and Misra, 1986; Bond, 1983; Fyans, Salili, Maehr, and Desai, 1983; Maehr, 1974; Maehr and Nicholls, 1980). That is, achievement concerns many be different in different cultures. As an example, 'if a culture values family loyalty or cooperation, outcomes demonstrating these qualities would be considered as achievement' (Agarwal and Misra, 1986, p. 718).

In this section, important cultural characteristics (e.g., collectivism, emphasis of diligence and education) which may affect the achievement orientations and attribution patterns of Chinese students are examined.

Collectivism

Chinese is often described as a culture where collectivism is emphasized (e.g., Hofstede, 1980). This collectivistic orientation has far reaching im-plications in shaping achievement orientations of the Chinese. In a study Li, Cheung, and Kau (1979) examined the competitive and cooperative behavior of Chinese children in Taiwan and Hong Kong by asking them to participate in the Madsen Cooperative Board experiment (Madsen, 1971). It was shown that older Chinese students were more cooperative than younger ones under both competitive and cooperative reward structures. The results were contradictory to those obtained in the U.S.A. (Madsen, 1971) which showed more competition among older students.

In another study, Bond, Leung, and Wan (1982a) (see also Leung and Bond, 1984) asked United States and Hong Kong university students to rate their perception of and behavioral intentions towards a hypothetical student who made various degree of contributions towards a course project. They found that the collectivistic Chinese in Hong Kong were more egalitarian in their allocation of rewards than the individualistic Americans.

It was suggested that Chinese more egalitarian distribution was to promote the group cohesiveness valued by collectivistic cultures.

The collectivistic orientation also leads to greater effort under group (vs. individual) condition. Gabrenya, Wang, and Latane (1985) compared social loafing among Chinese and American Grade 6 and 9 students, the phenomenon in which people usually exert greater effort when they work individually than when they do so in a group, where identifiability of members' individual outputs is obscured. It was found that Americans evidenced social loafing whereas Chinese exhibited the opposite (social striving). That is, Chinese students performed better in pairs than alone.

Similar findings that Chinese performed better in cooperative conditions were also reported by Yu (1980). Yu compared students' performance under individual failure and collective situations. In the former, the task was structured as if it were an established test of creativity and ability to organize, which was similar to the competitive orientation. In the latter situation, the task was said to be one which compared the subjects with students in other countries. It was found that the individual failure situation was not particularly salient in arousing the need for achievement. Rather, Chinese responded more favorably under the collective situation when the demand for individual's achievement was less overt.

Yu (1980) argued that aspirations solely for individualistic purposes was relatively less important in the Chinese context. This is because traditionally Chinese place great emphasis on inter-dependence and affiliation. This is in contrast with the highly valued independence and individualism in the American and Western cultures. All these findings suggest stronger learning and weaker performance goals among Chinese students.

Emphasis on Diligence

Though it is difficult to give a detailed account of Chinese child rearing practices here, Ho (1989b) has pointed out two important characteristics in his review of the socialization in contemporary China, namely, authoritarian moralism (vs. democratic-psychological orientation) and collectivism (vs. individualism). The former involves impulse control (vs. expression) whereas the latter involves interdependence (vs. autonomy) and conformism (vs. unique individuation) (Ho, 1989b, p. 144).

Demand and expectation of Chinese parents are high. In a study which compared the child-rearing practices among Chinese living in Taiwan, Chinese-Americans immigrated from Taiwan, and Anglo-American parents,

Chiu (1987) found that Chinese parents tended to have higher ratings than American parents on parental control and emphasis on achievement. Chinese mothers were also more restrictive and controlling than Chinese-American or AngloAmerican mothers.

Similar attitudes towards education was also displayed by overseas Chinese. Ghuman and Wong (1989) interviewed 34 Chinese families in Manchester (U.K.) to ascertain their views on various aspects of their children's education and schooling. Most of them had been living in the U.K. for more than ten years. It was found that these parents valued education highly, liked more homework for their children and preferred a stricter regime in schools.

Chinese parents are harsh with their children, especially when they feel that their children are old enough to be responsible for their own behavior (Ho, 1981, 1989a). Nevertheless, Chinese children are left independent at an age comparatively older than those in the West. Feldman and Rosenthal (1991) asked Grade 10 and 11 students from Hong Kong, Australia and the U.S.A. to complete questionnaires about the age at which they expected to achieve behavioral autonomy. In general, they found that Chinese youths in Hong Kong had later expectations for autonomy, placed less value on individualism, outward success, and individual competence. However, Chinese students placed higher value on tradition and prosocial behaviors.

The stronger social orientation of Chinese children was also revealed in Domino and Hannah's (1987) content analyses of a set of 701 stories generated by Chinese and American children. They found that Chinese stories evidenced greater social orientation, concern with authority and moral-ethical rectitude, and greater salience of the role of natural forces and chance, fewer instances of physical aggression, and less economic orientation. It is interesting to note that in a number of American stories, the story plot was resolved by the child protagonist paying for the damage, with no recognition of the moral misconduct involved. The mentioning of making compensation by monetary means (e.g., the child's allowance being restricted as a punishment) was rare in Chinese stories.

Chinese children are reared in an environment where effort, endurance, and hard work are emphasized (Yang, 1986). They are taught to work hard even when the probability of success is very low. There are many Chinese proverbs such as "if one keeps on grinding, one can turn an iron pillar into a needle" (*tiezhu mo cheng zhen* 鐵柱磨成針) and "if one has the perseverance, one can even remove a hill, the symbolic obstacle, by carrying away the sand with baskets" (*yugong yi shan* 愚公移山) (for other similar

Chinese legends, see Hess et al., 1987), which emphasize the importance of effort rather than ability. People who attempt tasks beyond their ability are admired and commended rather than being laughed at. "Knowing the impossibility of accomplishment but still working hard" (*zhi qi buke wei er wei zhi* 知其不可爲而爲之 is a highly praised virtue.

As a last note to the harsh child rearing, high demand and control among Chinese parents, one may wonder whether such behavior may lead to negative parent-child relationship. Particularly since parents especially the fathers, are detached and demand great respect from their children. However, the study by Lau and Cheung (1987) is illuminating. In their study with Grade 10 Chinese students in Hong Kong, two kinds of parental control, namely, control (dysfunctional) and organization (functional) were distinguished. The former was primarily restrictive, dominating, and interfering in nature, whereas the latter was functional in maintaining coordination and order in the family. The former was related to less cohesion and more conflict with parents, whereas the opposite was true for the organizational control. This study suggests that the high demand and control of Chinese parents may not necessarily lead to worse parent-child relationships. On the contrary, organizational control may lead to greater cohesion and harmony within the family. However, negative attitudes of the Chinese children towards their parents may be reflected in a different way. For example, passive aggressive behaviour, and a detached attitudes have been commonly observed among the Chinese. More studies are necessary in order to shed light on this issue.

Importance of Education

Education has a high status among Chinese traditional values, children are taught that "all jobs are low in status, except study which is the highest" (*wan ban jie xia pin, wei you du shu gao* 萬般皆下品，唯有讀書高). Education is believed to be important not so much because of its being a social ladder in the social hierarchy, but as an intrinsic training towards the better development of the whole person (Ho, 1981; Mordkowitz and Ginsburg, 1987).

The importance of education among Chinese is also reflected in empirical cross-cultural studies on students' attitudes. In Chen's (1989) comparison study of Grade 1 to 5 students in China and the U.S.A., it was found that Chinese students at all grades liked school in general more than their American counterparts did. Chinese students mentioned education-related wishes (e.g., books stationery, grades, future educational aspirations, and knowledge), whereas the Americans were more fond of materialistic wishes (e.g., money, toys, pets, fantasies). As reflected by their wish, Chinese perceived education as their central task. Chen (1989) concluded that Chinese children had incorporated traditional beliefs in the value of education. As compared with the American children, Chinese children were more concerned about their school work and education.

To a certain extent, Chinese students consider school work as their duty towards their parents. In Mordkowitz and Ginsburg's (1987) interview with 15 Asian-American (Chinese, Japanese, and Korean) students, they found a reciprocity of parents' love and children's hard work in school. The parents showed their love by providing the best possible opportunities for learning while the children tried to return love by doing their best in school. Children's academic striving was driven by a strong sense of guilt about the sacrifices made by their parents.

Chinese Achievement Orientations

Learning Goals and Effort Attributions

Cultural values of collectivism and emphasis on hard work, effort and perseverance have important implications on Chinese achievement orientations. There is some converging empirical evidence from a number of researches suggesting that Chinese are learning orientated and attribute their performance more to their effort than to their ability. Hess et al. (1987) compared the family beliefs of children's performance in China and America. In their interviews with mothers and children, they found a gradual change in attributional patterns among Chinese living in China, Chinese living in America and American Caucasians. Chinese mothers in China attributed their children's failure predominantly to lack of effort, whereas Chinese mothers in America viewed effort as important but assigned considerable responsibility to other sources. In contrast with Chinese, Caucasian Americans attributed least to effort.

Studies with Chinese students in Hong Kong also supported the above findings. Hau and Salili (1990) examined the causal attributions and achievement goals of 603 primary school students in Hong Kong. Twelve specific causes (e.g., effort, ability) were provided, and the students were asked to rate the importance of each of them as related to their performance in an actual examination. Results showed that as compared to the younger students, the older students were more learning oriented and they attributed their performance more to internal causes (e.g., effort) and study at home.

In another study using the antecedent-consequent method (Triandis, 1972), Salili and Mak (1988) found that "effort" was perceived by Hong Kong students as the most important antecedent for "academic achievement", "being wealthy", and "career success". Chinese students are taught to be responsible for their own academic performance; if they fail, they must have been lazy, if they succeed, it is because of their hard work. Nevertheless, the achievement event in Salili and Mak's (1988) study was hypothetical. The attributions students made might reflect more the traditional Chinese values rather than students' beliefs about real situations.

A mathematical model, the information integration method (Anderson, 1981, 1982), has also been used to examine whether Chinese children actually believe that effort can compensate for the lack of ability in academic performance. In the study, Hau and Salili (1991b) asked 711 Chinese primary school, high school, and university students in Hong Kong to predict the academic performance of hypothetical students whose effort and ability levels are known (e.g., Predict the examination performance of a student who is "very high in ability" and "very hardworking.")

The main concern of the study was the students' integration process. Specifically, the data obtained were tested with the goodness of fit for different integration rules. Results showed that Chinese students predominantly used the adding rather than the multiplying rule in their prediction of academic performance. The use of the adding rule indicated that the Chinese believe effort always adds on to performance irrespective of the subjectts ability level. This is contradictory to the multiplying rule users who believe that the effect of effort on performance is smaller when ability is low.

The above studies showed a convergence in findings that effort and task orientation are strongly emphasized among Chinese children. However, in Yang's (1982) and Stipek, Weiner, and Li's (1989) studies, no evidence was found for the characterization of Chinese students as emphasizing effort over ability as a cause of achievement outcomes. In Yang's study, the relationships between causal attributions and affective consequences among 415 university students in Taiwan were examined with 48 hypothetical situations. It should be noted that his questions assessing students' attributions were problematic because students were asked to indicate their desired causes ('If you obtain a good result in an examination, what is the cause that you hope your performance is due to?') rather than their perceived actual causes. Students might perceive that their success was due to effort, but they might hope that it was due to ability.

In Stipek et al.'s (1989) study, the generality of attribution-emotion relations was tested with 101 and 78 university students in mainland China and the U.S.A. respectively. As pointed out by Stipek et al., the findings that their Chinese subjects did not particularly emphasize effort over ability is probably because "the educated Chinese [i.e. the subjects in that study] may be thinking very much like young, educated Americans, whereas older Chinese and their school-age children, who are still dominated by parental and teacher socialization, maintain a different set of perceptions and beliefs" (1989, p. 115). Further research is needed to explore changes in academic causal attributions in different educational levels. Research exploring these changes throughout elementary, high-school, and tertiary level would help to discern Chinese culturally specific values or education systems.

Self-Effacing Attributions

In many attributional studies, it has been well demonstrated that there is a tendency for subjects to attribute their success to internal factors and failure to external causes (e.g., Marsh, 1986; Miller and Ross, 1975; Zuckerman, 1979; for cultural differences, see Fletcher and Ward, 1988). This has been called egoistic attributions, self-serving effect, or self-serving bias. For example, in Arkin and Maruyama's (1979) study with 240 university students, the successful students attributed their psychology examination performance more to internal and stable factors than unsuccessful or average students did. Chandler and Spies (1981) also found that students with below average performance attributed their failure more to external factors (e.g., luck, teacher's skill), whereas high performance students attributed their success more to effort, ability, and control.

The socialization process among Chinese which emphasizes collectivism, group-serving (vs. self-serving), and modesty suggests that self-effacing rather than egoistic attributions might be expected among Chinese. This phenomenon has been investigated among the Chinese. In an experimental competitive matrix game, Chinese students were asked to attribute under public (attributions made known to competitors) and anonymous (attributions not known by competitors) conditions (Wan and Bond, 1982). It was found that under both conditions, the self-serving bias was observed for both the attributions of ability and effort. In luck attributions, however, an egoistic bias was found under the anonymous condition, whereas a self-effacing bias was revealed under the public condition.

Bond, Leung, and Wan (1982b) argued that among Chinese, people making self-effacing attributions were better liked because such acts maintained harmonious interpersonal relationships. In their experiment, confederates working on an intellectual task made either self-effacing or egoistic (self-enhancing) attributions for their performance. Their results showed that a self-effacing confederate, though rated as less competent, was better liked than a self-enhancing one. This was in contradiction with the U.S. finding that competent persons were better liked. However, the results supported the notion that the need to maintain group harmony might sometimes override the need to show one's competence.

In another study, using the Intellectual Achievement Responsibility (IAR) Questionnaire, Chiu (1986) found that Chinese students (Grades 6, 8) in Taiwan attributed their success less to internal controllable causes and their failure more to internal factors than their American counterparts. That is, Chinese students assumed more personal responsibility for failures than American students. The above findings with young children were replicated again with another group of adolescents in America and Taiwan (Chiu, 1988).

Generally, the above studies showed that Chinese students take less credit for their achievement, especially in public situations. Such self-effacing (rather than egoistic) behavior is in accordance with the Chinese socialization ("modesty is a great virtue") and may reflect students' tendency to maintain group harmony and cooperation.

Effort as an Extremely Internal, Controllable, Stable, and Global Cause

In many studies subjects' attributional dimension scores were derived from their response to specific causes (e.g., internality score was the sum of ratings on effort and ability). It is assumed that the test constructors can accurately interpret and classify the causes into dimensions. However, such prior classification of causes into dimensions has been challenged. Ronis, Hansen, and O'Leary (1983) asked subjects to rate scenarios with scales on both causes (luck, ability, difficulty, and effort) and attribution dimensions (locus and stability). Results only partially supported the common sense classification.

In another similar study, Chandler and Spies (1984) examined the dimensional meaning of 11 causes along five causal dimensions (locus, globality, controllability, tability, and predictability). They found that the subjects' dimensional assignments differed greatly from Weiner's original proposed meaning. Five of the eight specific causes had dimensional meaning different from Weiner's original classification. Agreements with theoretical assignments were found in only 62% of the possible instances.

Similar challenge to the a priori classification of causes was also raised by Bar-Tal, Goldberg, and Knaani (1984) in their study with Israeli Grade 7 students. The subjects were asked to rate 24 specific causes along the locus, stability, and controllability dimensions. As Weiner (1983; 1986, p. 112) warned, a basic error often found in attributional researches was the acceptance of a priori categorization of causes without considering the situation as perceived by the subjects.

The assignment of dimensional meaning to specific causes is even more equivocal in cross-cultural studies. It is because, as challenged by Fletcher and Ward (1988, p. 235), "It implies that the attribution categories are given the same meanings across cultures, ... and that the underlying attributional dimensions are the same." Thus, it is important to compare the perception of the dimensional meaning of specific causes among subjects from different cultures.

Betancourt and Weiner (1982) carried out one of the first attempts in such a cross-cultural comparison. They asked university students from Chile and the U.S.A. to rate eight causes in separate hypothetical situations along the locus, stability, and controllability dimensions. Prior classifications were supported (e.g., causes theoretically classified as external were found to be significantly more external). However, it was found that Chilean students perceived external causes as more external, stable causes as less stable, and controllable causes as less controllable than U.S. students.

Schuster, Forsterlung, and Weiner (1989) also examined the dimensional meaning of specific causes in five nations (Belgium, West Germany, Indian, South Korea, and England). Their study included 22 specific causes and 4 causal dimensions (locus, stability, controllability, and globality). High agreement among four of the nations was found. However, Indians perceived all causes to be more external, variable, and uncontrollable as compared with subjects from other cultures. Except for the Indian data, results generally supported the prior theoretical dimensional classifications of specific causes.

In spite of the good agreement to prior classifications as reported by Betancourt and Weiner (1982), and by Schuster et al. (1989), it should be pointed out that Betancourt and Weiner studied the overall effects of the classification system (e.g., "Are the external causes as a whole external?") rather than examining causes one by one to see if a certain cause was classified correctly (e.g., "Is luck external ?"). On the other hand, in Schuster et al.'s study, only four causes, effort, ability, luck and task difficulty were examined, and merely according to the locus and stability dimensions. More studies in different cultures using a broader range of causes and in more dimensions are needed.

The causal dimensional meaning of specific causes as perceived by Chinese students has been examined by Hau and Salili (1991a, 1992). In their studies, Chinese high school and university students in Hong Kong were asked to rate the meaning of 13 specific causes along four causal dimensions (locus, controllability, stability, and globality). It was found that specific causes :effort, interest in study, study skill, and ability in study shared many common characteristics. They were perceived as the most internal, controllable, stable and global causes among the 13 causes presented to the subjects. However, comparison of the dimensional ratings revealed that these causes, with the exception of effort, were more internal than stable or controllable. Effort was more internal, controllable, global than stable. On the other hand, teachers' bias and luck were generally perceived to be relatively external, uncontrollable, unstable, and specific, and were the least important factors in determining performance.

Contrary to Harari and Covington's (1981) findings in the U.S.A., effort was the most important cause and had very salient characteristics in that it was in the extreme of ,every dimension scale rated by the Chinese students. Ability was, however, considered relatively unimportant and ranked only fourth after, effort, interest in study, and study skills. These results are congruent with other studies among the Chinese (e.g., Hess et al., 1987; Salili and Mak, 1988) and Iranian students (Salili, Maehr, and Gillmore, 1976).

This emphasis on internal and controllable causes by the Chinese students in the studies may also reflect strong moral responsibility for achievement through studying and working hard in the Chinese culture (Yang, 1986). Students are taught by teachers and parents at a very early age that one can learn study skills by working hard; and in so doing they will develop higher ability. Furthermore, they are encouraged to learn by drill because it is believed that their interest in study, which initially may be totally lacking, will be cultivated later through their repetitive work.

Weiner et al.'s (1971) four classic specific causes, namely, effort, ability, luck, and difficulty, have been adopted in many attributional studies. They are supposed to differ along the locus of causality and controllability dimensions. However, results among the Chinese students (Hau and Salili, 1991a, 1992) showed that effort and ability were not as distinctive as proposed by Weiner (see Hau and Salili, 1991c for similar findings). Indeed, the dimensional meaning of specific causes showed great similarity among effort, interest in study, study skill and ability. These specific causes were perceived as the most internal, controllable, stable and global causes. Such perception was particularly strong among older students.

The resemblance among effort, ability, interest, and skill may again originate from Chinese strong belief in the power of hard work. Chinese parents strongly emphasize to their children that if one works hard, one will slowly build up one's interest and study skills. The learning of study skills and the cultivation of interest will subsequently lead to an improvement in ability. Thus, in the mind of Chinese parents, interest and ability are equally controllable just as study skills and effort. This is in contrast with the Western philosophy which stresses individualism and states that interest should come naturally.

Studies in other Oriental Cultures

There have been quite a number of studies which examined the validity of the attribution theory in non-Western countries, or compared the attribution patterns across different cultures (see Fletcher and Ward, 1988, for a discussion of various cross-cultural issues). Evidence suggests that some characteristics among Chinese (e.g., strong emphasis on effort) are common to people in other Asian or oriental countries as well.

Academic attributions of six Asian-American ethnic groups (2511 Grades 4 to 11 Chinese, Filipino, Japanese, Korean, Vietnamese, and other Southeast Asian students) were compared in Mizokawa and Ryckman's (1990) study. Results showed that Koreans attributed the most, while, Southeast Asians (other than Vietnamese) the least to effort (Chinese in the middle). All groups (except Japanese) attributed to effort more for their success than for failure. Furthermore, effort was perceived as more important than ability in explaining academic performance.

Sun (1991) has also examined how foreign students studying in the University of California attributed for their language test (similar to TOEFL). There were totally 126 students from six different geographic regions (China, Japan, Korea, South Asia, America, and Europe). He found that Americans and Europeans attributed their performance more to ability than Koreans did; whereas Chinese and South Asians (Filipino, Indian, Indonesian) attributed more to effort than their American and European counterparts.

In another study, Fry and Ghosh (1980) compared Canadian Caucasian and Asian Indian children's attributions for performance in experimental tasks. They found that Caucasians took greater personal credit for success and attributed their failure to luck whereas Indians assumed more personal responsibility (effort and ability.) for failure and attributed their success to luck. They argued that it might be because Asian children have a lesser need to protect their ego and they are ready to take more personal responsibility for their failures.

In a longitudinal study with students in Japan and the U.S.A., Holloway, Kashiwagi, Hess, and Azuma (1986) attempted to explain the superior mathematics performance of Japanese elementary and high school students by interviewing the children and their mothers. They found that Japanese mothers and children attributed students' mathematics performance more to effort, and less to ability than their American counterparts. Japanese mothers were less likely to blame the school, children's ability, luck, or the task difficulty for students' bad performance. On the other hand, mothers in the U.S.A. did not use any one overriding explanation.

It is interesting to note that in Holloway et al.'s (1986) study, no strong correlation was found between mothers' and children's attributions. Holloway et al. suggested that the transmission is not from one agent (the mother) to one or few children. Rather it is a many-to-many (many parents to many children) process transmitted through the mass media, teachers, and peers as well as parents. Thus, the cultural setting (vs. family environment) may be more important in transmitting such values or goal orientations. Holloway et al. further suggested that some beliefs such as religion and politics may be transmitted one-to-one, while others are socialized in more diffused ways.

Coping strategies have also been used to explain the cross-cultural differences. Kashima and Triandis (1986) argued that as self-serving bias could be interpreted as a consequence of individual coping, it would be significant in societies in which self-reliance was emphasized (e.g., the

U.S.A.). Self-serving bias would be less salient in cultures in which social support was strong (e.g., Japan). Such a hypothesis was supported in their study with university students in the two countries, especially in their ability attributions. As regards attributions to other factors, the students made more realistic attributions which reflected the obvious situational information.

Indians are also shown to have characteristics similar to Chinese. In Agarwal and Misra's (1986) study of the goals and means of achievement of rural and urban Indian students, they found that achievement goals were multidimensional in nature (composed of ten factors). Furthermore, Indians indicated a number of noncompetitive, family-related, and societal goals (e.g., approval, cultural achievement, progress of family and social acceptance, social harmony and development). Contrary to individualistic and competitive striving, social concern was relatively quite important among the Indians.

General Discussion

From the above review of literature, there seems to be convergent evidences that Chinese students are learning oriented and attribute their performance more to their effort as compared with their Western counterparts. These may originate from collectivism, the emphasis on diligence, and the high value placed on education within the Chinese culture. Furthermore, the tendency to maintain group harmony and cooperation within the Chinese culture may also lead to self-effacing rather than egoistic attributions, especially when the attributions are made publicly.

It was also noted that effort and ability are perceived as internal, controllable, stable, and global causes. The close resemblance between effort and ability as perceived by Chinese children can be due to the achievement goal orientations of the students. As pointed out by Nicholls (1984), the compensatory relationship between effort and ability may become less important when the students are learning (or task) oriented. Ability, effort, and difficulty are less differentiated under learning involvement situations.

In the present review, a parallel, rather than compensatory, relationship between effort and ability has been found among the Chinese. That is, effort and ability are not very distinctive, which gives further credence that effort and learning goals are stressed in the Chinese culture.

Evidence also suggests that learning orientation is a more desirable goal for education. This goal is associated with attributions to interest, effort, seeking to understand (rather than memorization), and collaborative work. Nicholls, Patashnick, and Nolen (1985) found that it was the only orientation that was related to satisfaction with school learning.

From the above findings, Nicholls et al. alerted people who emphasized the role of schools in the advancement of one's wealth and social status. They cautioned, "[The emphasis] that education should increase one's status and income was the most likely to be associated with academic alienation and the least likely to be accompanied by commitment to learning, and satisfaction with learning in school" (1985, p. 691). Parents and teachers who emphasize the socioeconomic gains of education and the importance of outperforming peers have to reconsider such possible harmful consequence.

If learning goals are so desirable, teachers may like to know ways to induce and provide such an orientation in their classes. This is actually possible. Nicholls, Cobb, Wood, Yackel, and Patashnick (1990) were able to demonstrate experimentally that students' achievement orientations could be changed with the class structure. In their experiment, the class was marked by an atmosphere of dialogue and collaborative problem solving. Students' mathematical interpretations were taken seriously, and teachers took care not to steer the students to predetermined solutions. It was found that these methods could raise students' task orientation and beliefs that success depended on attempts to understand and cooperation with peers. The class was also found to be lower on the desire for superiority over one's friends, desire to avoid work, and beliefs that success depends on superior ability.

In this chapter we have concentrated on studies which used students as subjects and academic performance as the achievement event. It would be interesting to see whether Chinese students' tendency to attribute performance to effort is generalized to other non-academic achievement domains (e.g., achievement in social relations) as well. Further research is needed to shed light on this issue.

In the cross-cultural study of attributions, the spontaneity of attributions and the variety of specific causes being used in a culture are also important research areas to be explored. In the former area, researchers (Bond, 1983; Fletcher and Ward, 1988) have argued that as people make attributions because of their need to explain and control their environment, then people in cultures differing in such need (i.e., control-adaptiveness subjugation dimension) may engage themselves in attributions to different extent. Those from a culture with stronger belief in dominating control over nature would engage themselves more in attributional activities than those from a more compliant culture. Future studies should examine whether Chinese have strong belief in self dominating control over nature and whether such belief is domain specific (e.g., one can control achievement in academic performance but not in social relation).

In the second area of research, it would be meaningful to explore the different categories of specific causes (other than the four classic causes — effort, ability, luck, difficulty) being used in different cultures. There is a need for in-depth open-ended interviews with Chinese subjects to assemble a list of specific causes being used by the Chinese. Fletcher and Ward (1988) further suggested that there should be more studies focusing on the comparisons of underlying causal dimensions across cultures. They also suggested closer examination of the linkages between cultural variables (e.g., beliefs, values, or behavioral patterns) and subsequent attributions. In this respect, the concurrent measurement of these intervening cultural variables and attributions in the same study is necessary.

All in all, though there are not many actual cross-cultural studies directly comparing Chinese students with those in other cultures, a convergence in findings from various studies suggests that Chinese students are learning oriented. Chinese students also attribute their performance more to their effort than to their ability. Noteworthily, Chinese students' learning orientation and stronger attributions to effort (than to ability) are believed to be positive characteristics to be sustained. Future research should examine more closely how these achievement orientations are transmitted and cultivated in the family and the school. It is important to identify those cultural values that foster the development of these desirable achievement orientations.

References

Abramson, L. Y., Seligman, M.E.P., and Teasdale, J. D. (1978). Learned helplessness in humans: Critique and reformulation. *Journal of Abnormal Psychology*, 87 (1): 49–74.

Agarwal, R., and Misra, G. (1986). A factor analytic study of achievement goals and means: An Indian view. *International Journal of Psychology*, 21: 717–731.

Ames, C. (1984). Achievement attributions and self-instructions under competitive and individualistic goal structures. *Journal of Educational Psychology*, 76 (3): 478–487.

Ames, C., and Ames, R. (1981). Competitive versus individualistic goal structures: The salience of past performance information for causal attributions and affect. *Journal of Educational Psychology*, 73 (3): 411–418.

——— . (1984). Systems of student and teacher motivation: Toward a qualitative definition. *Journal of Educational Psychology*, 76 (4): 535–556.

Ames, C., and Archer, J. (1987). Mothers' beliefs about the role of ability and effort in school learning. *Journal of Educational Psychology*, 79 (4): 409–414.

——— . (1988). Achievement goals in the classroom: Students' learning strategies and motivation processes. *Journal of Educational Psychology*, 80 (3): 260–267.

Ames, C., and Felker, D. W. (1979). An examination of children's attributions and achievement-related evaluations in competitive, cooperative, and individualistic reward structures. *Journal of Educational Psychology*, 71 (4): 413–420.

Anderson, N. H. (1981). *Foundations of information integration theory*. New York: Academic Press.

——— . (1982). *Methods of information integration theory*. New York: Academic Press.

Arkin, R. M., and Maruyama, G. M. (1979). Affection, affect, and college exam performance. *Journal of Educational Psychology*, 71 (1): 85–93.

Bar-Tal, D., Goldberg, M., and Knaani, A. (1984). Causes of success and failure and their dimensions as a function of SES and gender: A phenomenological analysis. *British Journal of Educational Psychology*, 54: 51–61.

Beck, A. T. (1967). *Depression: Clinical, experimental, and theoretical aspects.* New York: International Universities Press.

Betancourt, H., and Weiner, B. (1982). Attributions for achievement-related events, expectancy, and sentiments: A study of success and failure in Chile and USA. *Journal of Cross-Cultural Psychology*, 13 (3): 362–374.

Bond, M. C., Leung, K., and Wan, K. C. (1982a). How does cultural collectivism operate? The impact of task and maintenance contributions on reward distribution. *Journal of Cross-cultural Psychology*, 13 (2): 186–200.

——— . (1982b). The social impact of self-effacing attributions: The Chinese case. *The Journal of Social Psychology*, 118: 157–166.

Bond, M. H. (1983). A proposal for cross-cultural studies of attribution. In M. Hewstone (Ed.), *Attribution theory: Social and functional extensions* (pp. 144 –157). Oxford: Blackwell.

Brewin, C. R., and Furnham, A. (1986). Attributional versus preattributional variables in self-esteem and depression: A comparison and test of learned helplessness theory. *Journal of Personality and Social Psychology*, 50 (5): 1013–120.

Chandler, T. A., and Spies, C. J. (1981). Attribution as predictor of expectancy in several three component exams. *Teaching of Psychology*, 8 (3): 174–175.

——— . (1984). Semantic differential placement of attributions and dimensions in four different groups. *Journal of Educational Psychology*, 76 (6): 1119–1127.

Chen, C. (1989). *A study of Chinese and American children's attitude towards schooling.* Unpublished manuscript, University of Michigan. (ERIC Document Reproduction Service No. ED 305 165).

Chiu, L. H. (1986). Locus of control in intellectual situations in American and Chinese school children. *International Journal of Psychology*, 21: 167–176.

———. (1987). Child-rearing attitudes of Chinese, Chinese–American, and Anglo–American mothers. *International Journal of Psychology*, 22: 409–419.

———. (1988). Locus of control differences between American and Chinese adolescents. *The Journal of Social Psychology*, 128 (3): 411–413.

Covington, M. V., and Omelich, C. L. (1984). Task-oriented versus competitive learning structures: Motivational and performance consequences. *Journal of Educational Psychology*, 76 (6): 1038–1050.

De Vos, G. A. (1973). *Socialization for achievement.* CA: University of California Press.

Domino, G., and Hannah, M. T. (1987). A comparative analyses of social values of Chinese and American children. *Journal of Cross-Cultural Psychology*, 18 (1): 58–77.

Dweck, C. S. (1986). Motivation processes affecting learning. *American Psychologist*, 41 (10): 1040–1048.

Elliott, E. S., and Dweck, C. S. (1988). Goals: An approach to motivation and achievement. *Journal of Personality and Social Psychology*, 54 (1): 5–12.

Feldman, S. S., and Rosenthal, D. A. (1991). Age expectations of behavioural autonomy in Hong Kong, Australian and American youth: The influence of family variables and adolescents' values. *International Journal of Psychology*, 26 (1): 1–23.

Fletcher, G. J. O., and Ward, C. (1988). Attribution theory and processes: A cross-cultural perspective. In M. H. Bond (Ed.), *The cross-cultural challenge to social psychology* (pp. 230–244). Beverly Hill, CA: Sage.

Fry, P. S., and Ghosh, R. (1980). Attributions of success and failure — Comparison of cultural differences between Asian and Caucasian children. *Journal of Cross-Cultural Psychology*, 11 (3): 343–363.

Fyans, L. J., Salili, F., Maehr, M. L., and Desai, K. A. (1983). A cross-cultural exploration into the meaning of achievement. *Journal of Personality and Social Psychology*, 44 (5): 1000–1013.

Gabrenya, W. K., Jr., Wang, Y. E., and Latane, B. (1985). Social loafing on an optimizing task: Cross-cultural differences among Chinese and Americans. *Journal of Cross-Cultural Psychology*, 16 (2): 223–242.

Ghuman, P., and Wong, R. (1989). Chinese parents and English education. *Educational Research (NFER)*, 31 (2): 134–140.

Harari, O., and Covington, M. V. (1981). Reactions to achievement behavior from a teacher and student perspective: A developmental analysis. *American Educational Research Journal*, 18 (1): 15–28.

Hau, K. T., and Salili, F. (1990). Examination result attribution, expectancy and achievement goals among Chinese students in Hong Kong. *Educational Studies*, 16 (1): 17–31.

——— . (1991a). Structure and semantic differential placement of specific causes: Academic causal attributions by Chinese students in Hong Kong. *International Journal of Psychology*, 26 (2): 175–193.

——— . (1991b, April). *Inferences of academic performance among Chinese students: Integration of ability and effort Information*. Paper presented at the American Educational Research Association Annual Conference, Chicago, IL.

——— . (1991c, April). *Informational value of teachers' evaluative behavior on perceived ability and effort*. Paper presented at the American Educational Research Association Annual Conference, Chicago, IL.

——— . (1992). *Causal dimensional meaning of specific causes among Chinese students in Hong Kong*. Unpublished manuscript. The Chinese University of Hong Kong, Hong Kong.

Hess, R. D., Chang, C. M., and McDevitt, T. M. (1987). Cultural variations in family beliefs about children's performance in Mathematics: Comparisons among People's Republic of China, Chinese–American, and Caucasian–American Families. *Journal of Educational Psychology*, 79 (2): 179–188.

Ho, D.Y.F. (1981). Traditional patterns of socialization in Chinese society. *Acta Psychologica Taiwanica*, 23 (2): 81–95.

——— . (1989a). Continuity and variation in Chinese patterns of socialization. *Journal of Marriage and the Family*, 51 (1): 149–163.

——— . (1989b). Socialization in contemporary mainland China. *Asian Thought and Society*, 14 (41–42): 136–149.

Hofstede, G. (1980). *Culture's consequences: International differences in work-related values*. Beverly Hills, CA: Sage.

Holloway, S. D., Kashiwagi, K., Hess, R. D., and Azuma, H. (1986). Causal attributions by Japanese and American mothers and children about performance in Mathematics. *International Journal of Psychology*, 21: 269–286.

Huang, H. C., Hwang, K. K., and Ko, Y. H. (1983). Life stress, attribution style, social support, and depression among university students. *Acta Psychologica Taiwanica*, 25 (1): 31–47.

Kashima, Y., and Triandis, H. C. (1986). The self-serving bias in attributions as a coping strategy — A cross-cultural study. *Journal of Cross-Cultural Psychology*, 17 (1): 83–97.

Lau, S., and Cheung, P. C. (1987). Relations between Chinese adolescents' perception of parental control and organization and their perception of parental warmth. *Developmental Psychology*, 23 (5): 726–729.

Leung, K., and Bond, M. H. (1984). The impact of cultural collectivism on reward allocation. *Journal of Personality and Social Psychology*, 47 (4): 793–804.

Li, M. C., Cheung, S. F., and Kau, S. M. (1979). Competitive and cooperative behavior of Chinese children in Taiwan and Hong Kong. *Acta Psychologica Taiwanica*, 21: 27–33.

Lin, P. C. (1979). Relationship between attribution and adjustment in junior high school students (In Chinese). *Acta Psychologica Taiwanica*, 21 (2): 61–74.

Madsen, M. C. (1971). Developmental and cross-cultural differences in the cooperative and competitive behavior of young children. *Journal of Cross-Cultural Psychology*, 2: 365–371.

Maehr, M. (1974). Culture and achievement motivation. *American Psychologist*, 29 (12): 887–896.

Maehr, M. L., and Nicholls, J. G. (1980). Culture and achievement motivation: A second look. In N. Warren (Ed.), *Studies in cross-cultural psychology*. New York: Academic Press.

Marsh, H. W. (1986). Self-serving effect (bias?) in academic attributions: Its relation to academic achievement and self-concept. *Journal of Educational Psychology*, 78 (3): 190–200.

Miller, D. T., Ross, M. (1975). Self-serving biases in attribution of causality: Fact or fiction? *Psycholoqical Bulletin*, 82 (2): 213–225.

Mizokawa, D. T., and Ryckman, D. B. (1990). Attributions of academic success and failure: A comparison of six Asian–American ethnic groups. *Journal of Cross-Cultural Psychology*, 21 (4): 434–451.

Mordkowitz, E. R., and Ginsburg, H. P. (1987). Early academic socialization of successful Asian–American college students. *The Quarterly Newsletter of the Laboratory of Comparative Human Cognition*, 9 (2): 85 91.

Nicholls, J. G. (1984). Achievement motivation: Conceptions of ability, subjective experience, task choice, and performance. *Psychological Review*, 91 (3): 328–346.

———. (1989). *The competitive ethos and democratic education*. Cambridge, MA: Harvard University.

Nicholls, J. G., Cheung, P. C., Lauer, J., and Patashnick, M. (1989). Individual differences in academic motivation: Perceived ability, goals, beliefs, and values. *Learning and Individual Differences*, 1 (1): 63–84.

Nicholls, J. G., Cobb, P., Wood, T., Yackel, E., and Patashnick, M. (1990). Assessing students' theories of success in mathematics: Individual and classroom differences. *Journal for Research in Mathematics Education*, 21 (2): 109–122.

Nicholls, J. G., Patashnick, M., and Nolen, S. B. (1985). Adolescents' theories of education. *Journal of Educational Psychology*, 77 (6): 683–692.

Peterson, C., and Seligman, M.E.P. (1984). Causal explanations as a risk factor for depression: Theory and evidence. *Psychological Review*, 91 (3): 347–374.

Peterson, C., Semmel, A., von Baeyer, C., Abramson, L. Y., Metalsky, G. I., and Seligman, M.E.P. (1982). The attributional style questionnaire. *Cognitive Therapy and Research*, 6: 287–299.

Ronis, D. L., Hansen, R. D., and O'Leary, R. D. (1983). Understanding the meaning of achievement attributions: A test of derived locus and stability scores. *Journal of Personality and Social Psychology*, 44 (4): 702–711.

Salili, F., Maehr, M. L., and Gillmore, G. (1976). Achievement and morality: A cross-cultural analysis of causal attribution and evaluation. *Journal of Personality and Social Psychology*, 33 (3): 327–337.

Salili, F., and Mak, P.H.T. (1988). Subjective meaning of success in high and low achievers. *International Journal of Intercultural Relations*, 12: 125–138.

Schuster, B., Forsterlung, F., and Weiner, B. (1989). Perceiving the causes of success and failure: A cross-cultural examination of attribution concepts. *Journal of Cross-Cultural Psychology*, 20 (2): 191–213.

Stipek, D., Weiner, B., and Li, K. (1989). Testing some attribution–emotion relations in the People's Republic of China. *Journal of Personality and Social Psychology*, 56 (1): 109–116.

Sun, Y. (1991). Analysis of the students' successful exam results — A cross-cultural study of attributional theory (In Chinese). *Acta Psychologica Sinica*, 23 (2): 178–187.

Triandis, H. C. (1972). *The analysis of subjective culture*. New York: Wiley.

Wan, K. C., and Bond, M. H. (1982). Chinese attributions for success and failure under public and anonymous conditions of rating. *Acta Psychologica Taiwanica*, 24 (1): 23–31.

Weiner, B. (1979). A theory of motivation for some classroom experiences. *Journal of Educational Psychology*, 71 (1): 3–25.

———. (1983). Some methodological pitfalls in attributional research. *Journal of Educational Psychology*, 75 (4): 530–543.

———. (1985). An attributional theory of achievement motivation and emotion. *Psychological Review*, 92 (4): 548–573.

———. (1986). *An attributional theory of motivation and emotion*. New York: Springer-Verlag.

———. (1990). History of motivational research in education. *Journal of Educational Psychology*, 82 (4): 616–622.

Weiner, B., Frieze, I. H., Kukla, A., Reed, L., Rest, S., and Rosenbaum, R. M. (1971). *Perceiving the causes of success and failure*. Morristown, NJ: General Learning Press.

Yang, K. S. (1982). Causal attributions of academic success and failure and their affective consequences. *Acta Psychologica Taiwanica*, 24 (2): 65–83.

———. (1986). Chinese personality and its change. In M. H. Bond (Ed.), *The psychology of the Chinese people* (pp. 106–170). Hong Kong: Oxford University Press.

Yu, S. H. (1980). Chinese collective orientation and need for achievement. *The International Journal of Social Psychiatry*, 26 (3): 184–189.

Zhang, Y. X., and Wang, Y. (1989). Attributional style and depression (In Chinese). *Acta Psychologica Sinica*, 21 (2): 141–148.

Zuckerman, M. (1979). Attribution of success and failure revisited, or: The motivational bias is alive and well in attribution theory. *Journal of Personality*, 47: 245–287.

Learning, Schooling, and Socialization: A Chinese Solution to a Western Problem

John B. Biggs

Context and Quality of Learning: An Apparent Contradiction

Western research into learning and teaching seems to have firmly established several propositions about the conditions under which good learning takes place. However, studies of students from what Ho (1991) calls "Confucian heritage" cultures, which would include Mainland China, Taiwan, Hong Kong, Singapore, and Japan, appear to challenge this conventional wisdom. This "paradox of the Chinese learner", as I have referred to it elsewhere (Biggs, 1994), provides an interesting challenge to researchers into learning and teaching. My concern here is to examine this so-called paradox from the point of view of the "fit" of schooling into Confucian heritage cultures, or "CHCs", as they are referred to from now on.

First, I outline the nature of the paradox.

The Teaching / Learning Context and Learning Quality

The type of teaching context prevailing in many Asian countries is typically characterized as unvarying and expository, taking place in what seem to be highly authoritarian classrooms, where the main thrust of teaching and learning is focused on preparation for external examinations, which tend to address low level cognitive goals, and to exert excessive pressure on teachers and exam stress on students (Beeby, 1966; Biggs, 1991a; Ho, 1991; Morris, 1985). Even in prosperous systems such as those in Hong Kong and Singapore, public funding per student capita is a fraction of what it is in USA, Canada, Great Britain, or Australia; class sizes are correspondingly larger, and support services such as guidance and counselling much lower. Such conditions of teaching have been associated empirically, at least in Western contexts, with low cognitive level learning strategies and with poor learning outcomes (Biggs, 1979, 1987; Bourke, 1986; Crooks, 1988; Ramsden, 1985; Ramsden, Martin, and Bowden, 1989).

In keeping with this pattern, Western observers have noted that Asian students use predominantly rote-based, low level, cognitive strategies, both in their own culture (Hong Kong) (Murphy, 1987), and overseas (Ballard and Clanchy, 1984; Bradley and Bradley, 1984; Samuelowicz, 1987). External examiners' comments on the examination papers submitted from one Hong Kong tertiary institution include the following: "regurgitative, with little insight and understanding of the subject in question", "… differences between better and poorer students being reflected in more effective recall than in qualitative factors." One tertiary educator in Hong Kong remarks:

> Hong Kong students display almost unquestioning acceptance of the knowledge of the teacher or lecturer. This may be explained in terms of an extension or transfer of the Confucian ethic of filial piety. Coupled with this is an emphasis on strictness of discipline and proper behavior, rather than an expression of opinion, independence, self-mastery, creativity and all-round personal development.
>
> (Murphy, 1987: 43)

As for students studying abroad, Samuelowicz (1987) sought staff and students' perceptions of problems facing overseas students in Australia. Staff comments heavily endorsed a common stereotype of Asian students:

> In my discipline they all want to rote learn material rather than think. (Animal Science and Production)

> Students from Malaysia, Singapore, Hong Kong appear to be much more inclined to rote learning. Such an approach does not help problem solving. (Dentistry)

> (Asian students) tend to look on lecturers as close to gods. Often they are very reluctant to question statements or textbooks. (Parasitology)

> … it can be difficult to cope, in small (graduate) classes, with overseas students who are reluctant to discuss, criticize reading and express an opinion. (Commerce)
>
> (Samuelowicz, 1987: 123–25)

The picture is thus a coherent one to Western eyes; Asian students are brought up in a restrictive teaching/learning environment, which commits them to a passive, uncritical, and reproductive mode of learning.

Comparative Studies of Academic Achievement

This neat picture is, however, flatly contradicted by the hard evidence. The kind of reproductive approach that is attributed to many Asian students is widely associated with low levels of achievement (Biggs, 1979, 1987; Marton and Saljo, 1976; Watkins, 1983), yet CHC students typically achieve significantly *higher* than Western students. The superior achievement of CHC students, particularly but not exclusively in the areas of mathematics and science, has been documented both for Asians abroad, as overseas students or as newly arrived immigrants (Flynn, 1992; Sue and Okazaki, 1990), and in their own countries (Chen, Lee and Stevenson, this volume; International Association for the Evaluation of Educational Achievement, 1988; Robitaille and Garden, 1989; Stevenson, Stigler, Lee, Lucker, Kitamura, and Hsu, 1985).

Let us first consider the high achievement of overseas Asians. The academic attainment of Chinese American students is estimated as that expected on the basis of an IQ 21 points higher than it actually is (Flynn, 1992). The University of California recently imposed quotas negatively discriminating against ethnic Chinese applicants, requiring them to score higher than other groups on the GRE to gain admission, in order to avoid hugely disproportionate numbers of Chinese on campus. New Zealand's top medical school, also on finding much higher proportions of students of Asian descent, abruptly changed their selection system from one based solely on examination marks to include "personal qualities, ... and awareness of community issues and New Zealand society" (*South China Morning Post*, 25 May, 1992). The exceptional performance of overseas students, and of children of immigrants, might readily be explained on grounds of selectivity or pressures for upward mobility through education (Sue and Okazaki, 1990), respectively; such "East v. West" comparisons may not then be comparing like with like. Rather more impressive is the evidence that *locally* educated CHC students outperform Westerners.

Several major studies have compared academic achievement in different countries. The largest in scale are those carried out under the auspices of the International Association for the Evaluation of Educational Achievement (IEA) (IEA, 1988; Robitaille and Garden, 1989), while the careful studies of Stevenson and his Michigan colleagues have focused on qualitative aspects of the teaching and learning of mathematics and reading, and on the actual conditions under which teaching takes place in selected schools from Mainland China, Taiwan, Japan, and the USA (Stevenson and Stigler, 1992).

Medrich and Griffith (1992) recently subjected three IEA surveys conducted over the last 25 years in each of science and of mathematics to considerable critical scrutiny, and after allowing for retention rates and sampling error, and for different patterns at different age levels and in different subjects and subtests, Hong Kong, Korea, Japan, and Singapore were amongst the highest scoring countries, and nearly always higher than the US. One notable exception to the latter was Hong Kong's highly variable performance in science in the Second International Science Study conducted in 1984, which was extremely poor at ages 10 and 14, but better than any other country in the last year of secondary school; a pattern which is regrettably explicable in terms of that system's curriculum design and resourcing.

The pattern is similar, if less pronounced, in subjects other than science and mathematics. Preliminary results from an IEA study of reading literacy (Johnson and Cheung, 1991) show that at Grade 4, Hong Kong students score slightly above the international average reading score in their mother tongue (Chinese), and well below when tested in English, a second language, although still above the lowest country tested. By Grade 9, Hong Kong students read in Chinese at well above the international average, and while their performance in English is still below the international mean for (mother tongue) reading, it is twice as good as the lowest country. These data are not startling, but they do show that in verbal skills Hong Kong students are as good or better than students from other countries. Their success at science and mathematics, in other words, does not appear to be bought at the expense of either mother tongue or second language literacy.

The question of relative performance in reading raises interesting questions about the cognitive demands of written English and written Chinese which are discussed by Chen et al. in Chapter Four of this volume. Their data also demonstrate that irrespective of subject, the *rate of improvement* over the grades in Asian schools is consistently higher than it is in American schools.

The general pattern is thus clear. The CHC countries mentioned are not only holding their own against better resourced Western educational systems, but typically outperform them. It cannot reasonably be argued that such performance is attributable to excessive rote learning skills. The superior performance of Chen et al.'s Chinese students is not restricted to "the more routine" tasks in mathematics and reading, but also embraces creative and high level aspects as well (see also Stevenson and Stigler,

1992, for further details).

High Cognitive Level Learning Strategies

Also in contradiction to expectations deriving from the teaching/learning context, and especially to the observations (not to say stereotyping) of Asian students by Westerners, is the hard data, as opposed to observation, on ethnic Chinese students' approaches to learning. Despite the examination pressures and associated reproductive teaching/learning strategies, and the almost exclusive reliance on expository teaching in large classes, with their low level cognitive goals, the teaching methods, and the large classes, Hong Kong and Singapore students students typically report a preference for high level, meaning-based, learning strategies, both in their own culture (Biggs, 1989a; 1991a; Kember and Gow, 1989), and overseas in Australian institutions (Biggs, 1987; Volet and Kee, 1993).

Such meaning-based learning strategies are associated with high quality performance (Biggs, 1979, 1987; Marton and Saljo, 1976; Watkins, 1983), which is of course in keeping with the superior academic achievement of CHC students noted above. However, this explanation leaves the problem of explaining how CHC students acquire these or other strategies in such apparently unpromising teaching/learning contexts, whereas Western students tend not to acquire them, when circumstances for doing so are more favorable.

Two Incompatible Pictures

In sum, then, we have two pictures. Each is internally consistent, but each quite contradicts the other:
1. The first picture is that poor teaching/learning contexts prevail in many Asian countries, and that Asian students are perceived as syllabus-dependent, passive, and prone to rote learning.
2. The second picture is that Asian students achieve extraordinarily well in high level academic tasks, and that they are prone to adopting highly adaptive learning strategies.

Approaches to Learning

A convenient way of conceptualizing relationships involving the student, the teaching context, student learning processes, and the learning outcome, is the presage-process-product model of teaching and learning, which in one form or another underlies much, possibly most, Western classroom research (Dunkin and Biddle, 1974). In more recent and more powerful versions of that model, the components involving student charactistics, the teaching/learning context, and the like are in dynamic equilibrium, forming a *system* (Biggs, 1993b; von Bertalanffy, 1968).

This basic model, called "3P" for short, conceptualizes individual difference and contextual factors as "presage", co-existing prior to task engagement; "process" as on-line handling of the task; and "product" as the outcome, usually expressed as achievement. Student presage factors are relatively stable, learning-related, characteristics of the student, which would include prior knowledge, abilities, values and expectations concerning achievement, and of immediate relevance, approaches to learning as predispositions to engage in academic activities in certain ways (see below). Teaching presage factors are contextual, including the superstructure set by the teacher and the institution, such as the course structure, curriculum content, methods of teaching and assessment, and classroom climate.

Students' perceptions of the teaching context directly affect their motives and predispositions, and their immediate decisions for action. This last metacognitive activity focuses on process, how to go about the task. Such task processing can be in terms of high or low level strategies.

The product of learning is usually expressed as achievement in terms of grades. Cognitively, outcomes may be described as quantitative, as amount of relevant detail they contain, or qualitative, in terms of how well the detail is structured. Affective outcomes refer to the students' feelings about the learning experience.

There are two kinds of effect produced in the model, direct and indirect. The direct effects result from the linear progression from presage to process to product, as in the classical model; the systems property produces the indirect effects. The direct effects of presage factors on student learning processes, and of processes on the learning product have been heavily researched. Thus, both student and teaching presage variables have been found to relate to ways in which the learning task is processed (Biggs, 1987; Ramsden, 1985), which in turn relate to the quantity and quality of outcomes (Biggs, 1979, 1987; Marton and Saljo, 1976; Watkins, 1983). Thus, for example, excessive examination pressure leads to low level processing strategies, which lead in turn to low level outcomes (Ramsden, Martin, and Bowden, 1989).

The indirect effects result from the systems property, namely that these relationships take place in a context of a steady state of mutual inter-relationships. Thus, students develop preferences for stable ways of handling school tasks on the assumption that the existing system is on-going, as in the same way teachers develop stable teaching styles. This notion of a steady state is critical for indexing the quality of the learning that goes on in the classroom (Biggs, 1993a). This is most relevant to the present issue of quality learning, because *culture* provides an important underlay to the specifics of what goes on in the classroom, as elaborated below.

For the present, the model suggests that the joint effects of individual student differences and the teaching context on the learning outcome are mediated in large part by the students' approaches to learning. This is the sticking point in the present argument. If Asian students achieve so well, they must be using appropriate strategies. Such strategies do not come from simplistic or impoverished teaching contexts. So where do they come from?

Approaches to Learning in CHC Students

An important key to the puzzle thus lies in the way in which students approach learning tasks. The concept of "approach to learning" has been around for several years. Originally, Marton and Saljo (1976) referred to two such approaches, surface and deep. A student adopting a surface approach to a set task would have the intention of "satisficing" rather than satisfying the task demands, or in other words getting the task out of the way with minimum effort but giving the appearance of having completed the task satisfactorily. Rote learning with the intention of reproducing key aspects of the task rather than of understanding them is a common way of sweeping under the academic carpet. A student using a deep approach, on the other hand, would have the intention of understanding the task demands and completing it is as well or as appropriately as possible, and is therefore concerned essentially with meaning.

Biggs (1979) later added a third approach, achieving, which is con-cerned with maximizing grades, and students adopting this approach dis-play what are usually called good study skills with respect to self- and time-management. While it may seem that deep oriented students would be likely to achieve well, this does not necessarily follow, as the question of maximizing grades is separate from that of achieving one or a few tasks in depth; clearly the nature of the assessment is crucial. In fact, good or academically oriented students display both deep and achieving approaches, while low achieving students are oriented towards a surface approach (Biggs, 1987).

Approaches to learning may refer to the *process* level in the 3P model, that is to the learning strategies adopted prior to the outcome of learning, or to *predispositions* to adopt particular processes, which is what is meant when students are asked by questionnaire how they usually go about learning (Biggs, 1993a). The latter is what is meant in the present context, as our focus is on how students are predisposed to learn.

The *Learning Process Questionnaire* (LPQ) (at secondary level) and the *Study Process Questionnaire* (SPQ) (at tertiary level) were originally developed and normed for Australian samples, but both instruments have been translated into Chinese and adapted for use in Hong Kong, with comprehensive Hong Kong norms being available (Biggs, 1992). Since questionnaire assessment of students' learning approaches reflects the contexts in which they have been taught (Biggs, 1993a), the classroom environments in Hong Kong Government schools and in Australian schools would lead one to expect, for the reasons suggested earlier, that Hong Kong schools would in comparison to Australian schools predispose students towards a surface approach, and away from a deep approach. The achieving approach would expected to be higher in Hong Kong, by virtue of the higher competition for many fewer tertiary places, and the much higher general upward mobility in Hong Kong.

Expectations were confirmed in the case of achieving, but precisely the opposite occurred on deep and surface (Biggs, 1989a, 1991a). With minor exceptions in some small subgroups, the great majority of Chinese students, at middle and senior secondary levels, and at university and in polytechnics, reported themselves as higher on deep, and lower on surface approach than comparable Australian students. Similar results were found comparing Singaporean and Australian students (op. cit.).

The only major exception to this very strong and highly significant set of differences was a comparison between medical students, where the differences were even more strongly pronounced, but in the *opposite* direction, with Hong Kong students now much higher on surface, and lower on deep and achieving, than Australian students. Here, however, the Australian students came from a medical faculty using a problem-based approach to teaching school, which is associated with low surface, and high deep and achieving, scores (Newble and Clarke, 1986).

This finding is important as it establishes the validity of the instruments in the Hong Kong context; if surface scores had been higher, and deep lower, in the problem-based group then the validity of local applications of the SPQ would have been thrown seriously into question.

The nonmedical data thus suggest quite strongly and contrary to common stereotypes that, at least at the level of self-report, Chinese students tend to rely *less* on an approach involving uncritical rote learning than do Western students, and more on a deep approach emphasizing understanding of meaning.

Given the Western research, how can this be? We seem so far to be missing something. The argument to date has simplistically relied on applying relationships found in Western educational settings to students used not only to different teaching/learning contexts, but who are raised from birth, and socialized, according to different cultural traditions. Thus, two major questions need to be addressed:

1. What other cultural differences have been found in learning-related factors in ethnic Chinese students as compared to Western students?
2. What differences might exist between Western and ethnic Chinese relationships between culture and schooling?

These questions are addressed in the following sections.

Other Cultural Differences in Learning-Related Factors

Several characteristics conducive to good learning appear to have been internalized through socialization practices to a greater extent by CHC Asians than by Westerners. These characteristics may include the following:

Understanding through Memorizing

As noted, ethnic Chinese report a stronger concern with meaning in rating their approaches to study than do Australian students. On the other hand, Westerners perceive a much higher incidence of repetitive learning amongst CHC students (Samuelowicz, 1987); in this perception itself, they are probably right. They are wrong, however, in their interpretation: that repetitive learning preempts understanding.

Marton, Tse, and Dall'Alba (1992) studied Mainland Chinese teachers' conceptions of learning and understanding and found a belief that understanding came about through memorization. Thus a text would be studied many times, understanding being enhanced by each reading. Hess and

Azuma (1991) found that Japanese teachers use a similar strategy, which is not used by US teachers: "repetition as a route to understanding" (p. 6).

It is possible that this strategy arises from the nature of learning characters, and interpreting written characters. Learning the thousands of characters in common use obviously requires a good deal of repetitive learning, rather more than learning an alphabet system. Characters are traditionally learned by the Two Principles. The First Principle involves much intertwined activity using the Five Organs: the eyes to see the shape, the ears to hear the sound, the hand to write the shape, the mouth to speak the sound, the mind to think about the meaning. The Second Principle is to contextualise; each character as it is learned is formed with another into a word, and each word is formed into a sentence. Repetitive certainly, rigid maybe, but embedded in meaning always (at least that is the intention), with much use of learner activity in widely different modes. Meaning and activity are key ingredients in quality learning anywhere.

The limited number of characters means that new meanings are created according to which characters are juxtaposed with each other. Text thus becomes multi-layered, with shifts and shades of meaning being revealed on repeated readings. Repetition thus has an important role in the acquisition of meaning at the text level as well as at the word and sentence levels. An interesting question is whether repetition *creates* understanding, or is an important *precondition* for establishing understanding by other means. Marton et al. found that Chinese teachers may hold both beliefs, the more sophisticated belief being that repetition is a useful strategy for mastering detail or lower order task components in order that the bigger picture becomes clearer. That view of course is highly compatible with modern cognitive psychology. In discussing the teaching of reading alphabetized texts, Kirby (1988) stresses that it is only when the lower level functions of decoding have been automated (by dint of much repetition) that the working memory space necessary for processing meaning can become available. This view is perfectly compatible with Chinese and Japanese beliefs about the acquisition of meaning.

Repetition may also be used to provide access to material that is already meaningfully learned. Tang (1991) found that Hong Kong tertiary students (taught in English) used an approach to learning she called "deep memorizing", which students adopted specifically as an exam-taking strategy. They first ensured that they understood the point or concept in focus, and then committed it to memory in order to ensure it was later accessible in the exam. Likewise, Kember and Gow (1989) found that tertiary students in Hong

Kong used the sequence: "understand — memorize — understand — memorize....", which they attribute to the fact that the students are taught in English and this is a way of reducing working memory load in a second language.

This use of rote memorizing is not confined to Hong Kong, or to learning in L2. Thomas and Bain (1984) found that Australian tertiary students used the same strategy in preparing for examinations. The strategy is universal. Actors learn their lines by rote to ensure they will be able to reproduce them reliably. Indeed, it is only then that they can afford to concentrate on meaning and interpretation.

In the West, the misconception has arisen that rote and meaningful are not complementary but mutually exclusive, a conception possibly sharpened by overgeneralizing Ausubel's (1968) classic distinction. However, it is only in the particular circumstance of the surface approach to learning that rote learning preempts meaning. Otherwise, as we have seen, rote and meaningful learning may be complementary processes, in any culture.

To return to the incompatible pictures, when Westerners perceive Chinese students indulging in much repetition, they are mistaking the use of a contextually useful strategy for a learning pathology. For various reasons, such as the nature of the Sino-Japanese writing systems, and Confucian beliefs in perseverence (see below), the strategy of repetition is highly adaptive and sensible, and in no way preempts understanding. It would seem that these Western commentators have never participated in amateur dramatics, or have forgotten their own examination preparation strategies.

Attributions for Success and Failure

Numerous studies have drawn attention to the fact that people in Asian cultures attribute success to effort, and failure to lack of effort, rather than to ability, while Westerners see ability as primarily responsible for success and failure to lack of ability (Chen et al., this volume; Hau and Salili, this volume; Hess and Azuma, 1991; Holloway, 1988). Hau and Salili (1991) found that Hong Kong secondary students attribute their academic success to, in order: effort, interest in study, study skill, mood, and ability. The first four attributions are more or less controllable; the fifth, which Western students see as most important for success, is not. Strategy attributions, such as study skill, are particularly valuable in redeeming poor performance (Clifford, 1986).

In other words, Asian students tend normally to see ways in which they can improve their performance; Western students tend to attribute past performance to things they can't do anything about. Such a pattern of attributions must make a huge difference to reactions to formal instruction (Stevenson and Stigler, 1992).

Motivation

To say that Asian, and particularly Chinese, students are highly motivated may be true, but the assertion needs examining. In the West, motivation is categorized as extrinsic, intrinsic, and achievement, which reflect ways in which other people (and particularly students) can be induced to undertake tasks that otherwise they would not feel any need to perform.

A more general way of conceptualizing motivation is in terms of the expectancy-value motivational model, which states that if anyone is to engage an activity, they need to expect some valued outcome (Feather, 1982). To feel the need to carry out a task, in other words, one needs to perceive that the act has some kind of *value*, and that one is *likely to succeed*. Few are moved by the pot of gold at the end of an impossible rainbow: few by the easy capture of the paltry. If the student does not value success, or does not expect to be successful however much success is valued, then the student remains unmotivated. Both value and expectancy need to be high.

The value of academic learning to the student has traditionally been enhanced by associating learning with the categories of motivation: to make the consequences salient in extrinsic or achievement motivation, or to select already valued or interesting content. In this there are undoubted cultural differences. Hess and Azuma (1991) say of Japanese students that they possess "a sense of diligence and receptiveness (that) fits uncomfortably into the more familiar American concepts of intrinsic and extrinsic motivation." (p. 7). This "sense of diligence" they say is absent in Western school students, who need to be motivated extrinsically by making classrooms and tasks, which are intrinsically unpleasant, more attractive. According to Hess and Azuma, that strategy they say is simply unnecessary in Japan; Japanese students climb the academic peaks because they are there, and they are expected to climb them. A Chinese proverb reminds students that "In books there are golden houses and beautiful girls". The scholar's rewards may be of the body as much as of the soul. Not so in the puritannical West, where scholars devote much effort to find evidence that extrinsic reward destroys intrinsic motivation (e.g. Deci, 1975).

In Hong Kong, a mix of motives and pressures forces people to operate well into redline; social, familial and personal factors (see Chao and Sue, this volume) combine to create a powerful motivational complex that produces very effective task engagement, not all necessarily in a surface way. This also makes it difficult to disentangle extrinsic from intrinsic or achieving motives. The specific motive is then not so much the issue in determing the level at which a student engages a task, as how the student perceives the value of successfully completing the task, and on the chances of doing so. Ethnic Chinese expect success, by virtue of attributing success to effort and to instrumental skills that may readily be acquired, such as study skills. Bright Westerners, attributing success to ability, may also expect success, but only the bright. The less than bright see school as the place where disengagement is the logical strategy.

Cue-seeking and Time on Task

Attributions to effort and strategy rather than to ability would tend to make students adept at "cue-seeking", that is being on the watch for signs that particular content or certain activities are likely to be more productive in terms of marks than other activities (Miller and Parlett, 1974).

In studying Hong Kong tertiary students' adaptation to different modes of assessment, Tang (1991) found that while student predispositions to use particular study processes exerted little effect on actual approach used in preparing for different modes of assessment, their perceptions of task-appropriate preparation strategies had strong relations to their on-line processing, and to their performance in the test format in question. Most students saw test and assignment as assessing different things, broad coverage and study in depth respectively, and so adapted their approach to the format, not to their predispositions. In interview, they showed themselves to be very alert to cues supplied (often unwittingly) by teachers, and would often share their perceptions collaboratively.

It is therefore likely that, with their attribution system emphasizing coping and strategy and the high value placed on institutional success in learning, CHC students would be particularly alert for ways in which they can cue the focus of the content of their learning, and their learning-related activities, to its perceived value in attracting marks. Volet and Kee (1993) asked Singaporean students studying in Australia what were the twelve most important ways of studying in each country, they found that the students were extremely rapid in adjusting to Australian as opposed to their habitual task demands. "Being able to read and understand main ideas" was the foremost demand in both countries, but in Singapore second and third most important were: "Always aim to get the correct answer" and "Learn lecture material by heart", respectively. After one year in Australia, these became least important, and "Evaluate different ideas and give own opinion" became second most important. "Always acknowledge source of information" was of least importance in Singapore, but became of middling importance after a year in Australia. Such prompt and adaptive shifting to the context lead Volet and Kee to conclude that these students' study approaches were "highly responsive to the demands of a specific learning situation rather than determined by inherent characteristics of individual or cultural groups" (p. 3).

Diligence in the sense of time spent on task likewise follows from effort attributions for success, and correspondingly, CHC Asians are prepared to spend much more time on task than Western students, both formal or timetabled time and informal time spent on either homework, or voluntarily in studying (Stevenson and Stigler, 1992).

Collaborative Learning

Tang (1993) found that 87% of 38 students interviewed about their assessment preparation strategies prepared for the assignment in spontaneously formed groups. Participants' comments emphasized that groupwork was preliminary to individual elaboration; there was little evidence of cloned or plagiarized assignments. Collaboration focused on preliminary reading and interpretation of background knowledge, and students who did so adopted deep-related strategies such as analyzing, relating, and applying, very much more than did students preparing individually. Collaborating students did not get higher marks than the latter, but they did write better structured essays.

The seemingly easy success of cooperative groupwork (Lai, 1991; Leung, 1992) in the Hong Kong system, which is otherwise strongly expository and competitive, possibly indicates a collectivistic mode of interaction that through socialization procedures is easily accessible in Chinese culture (Ho, 1986), but which the formal school system, based on an outdated Western model, all but ignores.

In CHC systems other than Hong Kong, however, both formal and informal peer interaction on academic tasks is widespread (Stevenson and Stigler, 1992). Hess and Azuma (1991) draw attention to a particular method of group work as a means of problem and error analysis, which they call "sticky probing". A single problem is discussed by students, with teacher adjudicating, for hours until a consensus acceptable to the teacher and group is reached. Such a method, boring though it may appear to be, must enhance a deep understanding of the focus problem.

Culture and Schooling

There are then considerable differences between Western and Confucian heritage cultures in ways that would bear upon learning, especially in an institutionalized context. If, as suggested earlier, the components of classroom learning form a system striving towards equilibrium, we are left with the question as to what it is in the Confucian heritage cultural context that supports a deep approach to learning more than is the case in the West. What, in short, are the differences in the relationships between culture and schooling in East as opposed to the West?

This question prompts another: What is it that schools require of students that is different from their extracurricular life? There are several conditions that are required for learning in school, as opposed to everyday learning (Resnick, 1987; Biggs, 1991b). The most important of these focus on the question we have already examined at some length: motivation.

Everyday learning is mostly concerned with personally valued content, experienced first hand, and situated functionally in context. This situated nature of everyday learning solves many other problems, particularly of motivation and of acquiring skills of self-management. The content learned in school, on the other hand, is mostly declarative knowledge; statements about what *other* people experience or think to be important. The former situations are interesting and self-involving, but the latter are not.

Schools generally are not "user friendly", as Hess and Azuma (1991) put it. However, they are made much less so by Western socialization methods. Schools the world over require children to be obedient, to conform to group norms, and to persist at what seem to them to be pointless tasks, values that are incorporated into CHC methods of socialization, but are actually discouraged in Western child rearing (Hess and Azuma, 1991). Western children are raised to be assertive and independent, to be curious and to explore on their own terms, only to be forced into the collectivistic forced labor of grade school. Hence the need for motivation, intrinsic, extrinsic or achieving, to make such an asystematic system work; classroom activities need to be made attractive or elaborate systems of negative reinforcement created, which makes Western classrooms highly externally controlled (Hess and Azuma, 1991). The contrasts between everyday and school learning in the West have the odd consequence that students would prefer physically or psychologically to "goof off", when reason suggests, in times of high youth unemployment, that an education taken seriously would provide a more attractive alternative to the dole queue.

That gap, between culture and schooling, appears less traumatic in Confucian heritage cultures. Hess and Azuma (1991) specifically suggest that Japanese socializing practices create "internal dispositions" that predispose students to accept the requirements of obedience, conformity, and persistence put upon them by schooling. It seems likely that the same argument could be used of ethnic Chinese students, both in their general orientation towards learning and in their academic performance, and independently of whether they study at home or overseas. Traditional Chinese practices (see Sue and Chao; Wu, this volume) would appear to be much more successful in predisposing students to accept the conditions that formal schooling impose on them if they are to learn satisfactorily. The evidence reviewed here would implicate several such learning-related activities, arising mostly from socialization practices rather than from school itself. Such activities would include: beliefs in the effectiveness of repetitive and boring activity, attributions for success and failure that encourage not only further effort after failure but the acquisition and use of improved self-management strategies, certain cultural beliefs about learning and teaching, ability to read cues, and willingness to undertake group problem solving, spontaneously if necessary.

Conclusions

Of the two pictures that have been painted here of the ethnic Chinese learner, the second, indicating that CHC students typically perform well and use learning strategies of a high cognitive level, is the one that stands up to close examination. In trying to explain this, given that Asian classrooms do not represent what Western research would define as exemplary learning environments, it would be possible to marshall several arguments. The genetic argument, that Asians are genetically more able and that this inherited ability over-rides the effects of schooling, has already been examined and rejected (Chen et al., this volume; Sue and Okazaki, 1990). Other arguments would be that conventional liberal-progressive wisdom about what constitutes a good learning environment is either wrong, or may be correct in Western cultures, but does not transfer to Confucian heritage cultures.

It is however not necessary to reject Western research establishing relationships between learning contexts, deep approaches to learning, and high level outcomes, or even to question its relevance to Confucian heritage cultures. Rather, elaborating and generalizing an argument put forward by Hess and Azuma (1991), it is suggested that cultural factors to do with values, attributions for success and failure, and the genesis of motivation, prepare ethnic Chinese more readily for the demands made by schooling than do Western patterns of socialization. Such factors provide Chinese children with the predispositions (1) that help them to cope with the affective and cognitive demands of schooling more effectively than those internalized by the generality of Western students, and (2) that lead them to develop more adaptive learning strategies than the latter.

Further, the nature of schooling in many CHC systems is in fact quite responsive to cultural values and priorities to do with the value of education, the ordering of the curriculum, and teacher-student and student-student interaction (Stevenson and Stigler, 1992), so that a context for learning is provided that is in the end compatible with Western beliefs about contexts for good learning (Biggs, 1994).

What all this tells us is that what appear to Western eyes to be negative indicators with regard to the quality of learning are not so when viewed against a cultural backdrop. Specifically, the learning-related values and activities acquired *out* of school, through socialization, may be more important for effective learning *in* school than the particular motives and strategies engendered by the school context itself. This is not to say that the immediate context is unimportant — the CHC students studied by Volet and Kee (1993) were remarkably sensitive to context — but the nature of their sensitivity, and what it was they were sensitive to in their school context, were socially or culturally determined.

That is an important conclusion, and would suggest that the problems of lack of motivation and commitment found in so many Western schools may have an origin beyond school, so that changing teaching methods and curricula may only be tinkering with the problem. However, the point of the present contribution is not to diagnose the problems of Western schooling, but rather to point to the strong relationship between socialization and schooling that exists in Confucian heritage cultures, which seems to add enormously to the effectiveness of schooling in these cultures.

References

Ausubel, D. P. (1968). *Educational psychology: A cognitive view*. New York: Holt, Rinehart and Winston.

Ballard, B., and Clanchy, J. (1984). *Study abroad: A manual for Asian students*. Kuala Lumpur: Longman.

Beeby, C. (1966). *The quality of education in developing countries*. Cambridge, MA: Harvard University Press.

Biggs, J. B. (1979). Individual differences in study processes and the quality of learning outcomes. *Higher Education*, 8: 381–394.

————. (1987). *Student approaches to learning and studying*. Hawthorn, Vic: Australian Council for Educational Research.

————. (1989a). Approaches to learning in two cultures. In V. Bickley (Ed.), *Teaching and learning styles within and across cultures: Implications for language pedagogy*. Hong Kong: Education Department, Institute of Language in Education.

————. (1989b). Students' approaches to learning in Anglo–Chinese schools. *Educational Research Journal*, 4: 8–17.

————. (1991a). Approaches to learning in secondary and tertiary students in Hong Kong: Some comparative studies. *Educational Research Journal*, 6: 27–39.

————. (1991b). Student learning and the context of school. In J. Biggs (Ed.), *Teaching for learning: The view from cognitive psychology* (pp. 7–26). Hawthorn, Vic: Australian Council for Educational Research.

————. (1992). *Learning processes in Hong Kong students: Using the learning and study process questionnaires* (Occasional Papers No. 14). Hong Kong: University of Hong Kong, Faculty of Education.

————. (1993a). What do inventories of students' learning processes really measure? A theoretical review and clarification. *British Journal of Educational Psychology*, 63: 3–19.

————. (1993b). From theory of practice: A cognitive systems approach. *Higher Education Research and Development*, 12: 73–86.

————. (1994). What are effective schools? Lessons from East and West. *The Australian Educational Researcher*, 21: 19–39.

Bourke, S. (1986). How smaller is better: Some relationships between class size, teaching practices, and student achievement. *American Educational Research Journal*, 23: 558–571.

Bradley, D., and Bradley, M. (1984). *Problems of Asian students in Australia: Language, culture and education*. Canberra: Australian Government Printing Service.

Clifford, M. M. (1986). The comparative effects of strategy and effort attributions. *British Journal of Educational Psychology*, 56: 75–83.

Crooks, T. J. (1988). The impact of classroom evaluation practices on students. *Review of Educational Research*, 58: 438–481.

Deci, E. L. (1975). *Intrinsic motivation*. New York: Plenum.

Dunkin, M. J., and Biddle, B. J. (1974). *The study of teaching*. New York: Holt, Rinehart and Winston.

Feather, N. (Ed.). (1982). *Expectations and actions*. Hillsdale, NJ: Erlbaum.

Flynn, J. F. (1992). *Asian Americans: Achievement beyond IQ*. Hillsdale, NJ: Erlbaum.

Hau, K. T., and Salili, F. (1991). Structure and semantic differential placement of specific causes: Academic causal attributions by Chinese students in Hong Kong. *International Journal of Psychology*, 26: 175–193.

Hess, R. D., and Azuma, M. (1991). Cultural support for schooling: Contrasts between Japan and the United States. *Educational Researcher*, 20 (9): 2–8.

Ho, D. Y. F. (1986). Chinese patterns of socialization: A critical review. In M. H. Bond (Ed.), *The psychology of the Chinese people* (pp. 1–37). Hong Kong: Oxford University Press.

———. (1991, June). *Cognitive socialization in Confucian heritage cultures*. Paper presented to Workshop on Continuities and Discontinuities in the Cognitive Socialization of Minority Children. US Department of Health and Human Services, Washington, DC.

Holloway, S. D. (1988). Concepts of ability and effort in Japan and the US. *Review of Educational Research*, 58: 327–345.

International Association for the Evaluation of Educational Achievement. (1988). *Science achievement in seventeen countries: A preliminary report*. Oxford: Pergamon Press.

Johnson, R. K., and Cheung, Y. S. (1991, December). *Reading literacy in Hong Kong in Chinese and English: A preliminary report on the IEA study*. Paper read to Annual Conference, Institute of Language in Education, Hong Kong.

Kember, D., and Gow, L. (1989). Cultural specificity of approaches to study. *British Journal of Educational Psychology*, 60: 356–363.

Kirby, J. R. (1988). Style, strategy, and skill in reading. In R. R. Schmeck (Ed.), *Learning strategies and learning styles*. New York: Plenum.

Lai, E. (1991). Effects of cooperative learning on student learning outcomes and approaches to learning in Sixth Form Geography. Unpublished master's thesis, University of Hong Kong, Hong Kong.

Leung, W. Y. (1992). Effects of student–student interaction on approaches to learning and on academic performance. Unpublished master's thesis, University of Hong Kong, Hong Kong.

Marton, F., and Saljo, R. (1976) On qualitative differences in learning: Outcome and process. *British Journal of Educational Psychology*, 46: 4–11.

Marton, F., Tse, L. K., and Dall'Alba, G. (1992). *Solving the paradox of the Asian learner*? Paper given to 4th Asian Regional Conference, International Association for Cross-Cultural Psychology, Kathmandu.

Medrich, E., and Griffith, J. (1992). *International mathematics and science assessments: What have we learned*? Washington, DC: US Department of Education, National Center for Education Statistics.

Miller, C.M.L., and Parlett, M. (1974). *Up to the mark: A study of the examination game*. London: Society for Research into Higher Education.

Morris, P. (1985). Teachers' perceptions of the barriers to the implementation of a pedagogic innovation: A South East Asian case study. *International Review of Education*, 31: 3–18.

Murphy, D. (1987). Offshore education: A Hong Kong perspective. *Australian Universities Review*, 30 (2): 43–44.

Newble, D., and Clarke, R. M. (1986). The approaches to learning of students in a traditional and in an innovative problem-based medical school. *Medical Education*, 20: 267–273.

Ramsden, P. (1985). Student learning research: Retrospect and prospect. *Higher Education Research and Development*, 5(1): 51–70.

Ramsden, P., Martin, E., and Bowden, J. (1989). School environment and sixth form pupils' approaches to learning. *British Journal of Educational Psychology*, 59: 129–142.

Resnick, L. B. (1987). Learning in school and out. *Educational Researcher*, 16 (9): 13–20.

Robitaille, D., and Garden, R. (1989). *The IEA study of mathematics II: Contexts and outcomes of school mathematics*. Oxford: Pergamon Press.

Salili, F., Hwang, C. E., and Choi, N. F. (1989). Teachers' evaluative behavior: The relationship between teachers' comments and perceived ability in Hong Kong. *Journal of Cross-Cultural Psychology*, 20: 115–132.

Samuelowicz, K. (1987). Learning problems of overseas students: Two sides of a story. *Higher Education Research and Development*, 6: 121–134.

Sue, S., and Okazaki, S. (1990). Asian–American educational achievements: A phenomenon in search of an explanation. *American Psychologist*, 44: 349–359.

Stevenson, H. W., and Stigler, J. (1992). *The learning gap: Why our schools are failing and what we can learn from Japanese and Chinese education*. New York: Summit Books.

Stevenson, H. W., Stigler, J., Lee, S., Lucker, G., Kitamura, S., and Hsu, C. (1985). Cognitive performance and academic achievement of Japanese, Chinese and American children. *Child Development*, 56: 718–734.

Tang, K. C. C. (1991). *Effects of different assessment procedures on tertiary students' approaches to learning*. Unpublished doctoral dissertation, University of Hong Kong, Hong Kong.

————. (1993). Spontaneous collaborative learning: A new dimension in student learning experience? *Higher Education Research and Development*, 12: 115–130.

Thomas, P., and Bain, J. (1984). The contextual dependence of learning approaches: The effects of assessment. *Human Learning*, 3: 227–240.

Volet, S. E., and Kee, J. P. P. (1993). *Studying in Singapore — Studying in Australia: A student perspective* (Occasional Paper No. 1). Murdoch University Teaching Excellence Committee.

von Bertalanffy, L. (1968). *General systems theory*. New York: Braziller.

Watkins, D. A. (1983). Depth of processing and the quality of learning outcomes. *Instructional Science*, 12: 49–58.

8

Mental Health of Chinese Adolescents: A Critical Review*

Daniel T. L. Shek

Introduction

In Western societies, adolescence has been conceived of as a period of "storm and stress" and there are theories suggesting that adolescence is necessarily tumultuous (Erikson, 1968; Freud, 1958). However, the "turmoil" hypothesis in connection with adolescent development (Schechter and Wright, 1977) has received equivocal support and there is increasing evidence suggesting that the majority of adolescents do not have much emotional stress and mental health problems during this period of life (Offer and Schonert-Reichl, 1992; Petersen, 1988; Powers, Hauser, and Kilner, 1989). From a cross-cultural perspective, it is obviously interesting and important to ask whether the "tumultuous" portrait of adolescence and the related findings also emerge in other cultures. In particular, these questions should be asked with reference to Chinese culture (and different Chinese societies) since Chinese adolescents constitute roughly one-fifth of the world's adolescent population. Based on a comprehensive review of the literature in psychology, psychiatry and the related disciplines, Ho, Spinks, and Yeung (1989) listed 3,548 bibliographic citations pertinent to Chinese patterns of behavior. However, an analysis of the book's Subject Index reveals that there are only 226 citations (6.4%) related to the subject "adolescents". Amongst these 226 citations, only 6 references (2.7%) are

* This work was supported in part by RGC Earmarked Grant (CUHK 155/94H). Portions of the data reported in this chapter were based on a research project which was financially supported by The Research Committee, The Chinese University of Hong Kong and Madam Tan Jen Chiu Fund.

related to "adolescent mental health" and none of the work is devoted to "adolescent mental disorders".

A major aim of this chapter is to bring together the relevant yet diverse research materials on Chinese adolescent mental health in China, Hong Kong and Taiwan. Specifically, the following questions will be addressed: (1) What phenomena can be observed with respect to the mental health status of Chinese adolescents, particularly with reference to the "turmoil" hypothesis? (2) Based on the existing studies, what correlates of Chinese adolescent mental health can be identified and what related conceptual models can be formulated? (3) What is the scientific status of the existing studies of Chinese adolescent mental health?

In this review, empirical studies of Chinese adolescent mental health based on both the "privative" sense (i.e., absence of mental problems, impairments, or disorders: Freeman, 1984) and the "positive" sense of mental health (Jahoda, 1958) are included. As far as the privative sense of the concept is concerned, adolescent psychopathology (including psychiatric morbidity and psychological symptoms) will be examined. Concerning positive mental health, studies of self-concept, self-esteem, meaning in life and life satisfaction among Chinese adolescents will be focused upon.

Psychopathology among Chinese Adolescents

The epidemiology, symptomatology and etiology of mental disorders among people in Mainland China were reviewed in Cheung (1986), Kleinman and Lin (1981), and Lin (1985). In the past fifteen years, a number of community epidemiological studies have been carried out in China based on which information concerning psychopathology amongst Chinese adolescents may be extracted. For example, Liu J. Q. et al. (1980) found that the overall prevalence rates for all forms of mental disorders in the 10–14, 15–19, and 20–24 age groups were 0.5, 2.7 and 16.2 per 1,000 respectively, with the prevalence rate in the 20–24 age group ranking the second highest amongst all age groups. It was also reported that the mean incidence rates of schizophrenia and all forms of mental disorder began to rise in the 10–14 age group, reaching a peak in the 15–19 age bracket in the period between 1964 to 1978. Besides, an analysis of the onset age of different forms of psychiatric illness in some of the epidemiological studies showed that a significant proportion of the patients had their onset of symptoms during age 15 to age 24 (Chen et al., 1984; Chen et al., 1986a, 1986b; Liu X. H. et al., 1980; Yang et al., 1980).

A survey of the statistics on the proportion of adolescent mental patients in the total psychiatric population also revealed that amongst those who were diagnosed as having mental illnesses, a significant proportion of them were adolescents (Ma, 1980; Nanjing Neuropsychiatric Institute, 1980; The Teaching and Research Group of Psychiatry of Beijing Medical College et al., 1980; Yang et al., 1980). For example, Kleinman (1982) reported that 25% of the out-patients seeking psychiatric consultation were in the 15–25 age bracket. The data arising from some of the review studies also suggest a similar pattern on the proportion of adolescent patients in the psychiatric population (e.g., Chen et al., 1984; Jiang et al., 1986).

Apart from the above-mentioned epidemiological studies which were conducted with reference to the general population, there are also a limited number of studies which directly examine psychopathology in the adolescent population (Hu, 1994). Based on the responses of 500 senior secondary school students to the Symptoms Checklist, Hu (1994) found that 49.6% of the students could be regarded as "mild" psychiatric cases and 10.8% of them could be regarded as "severe" psychiatric cases. In an attempt to investigate neurasthenia in 1,693 students, Wei et al. (1993) found that the morbidity rate was 5.13%. Based on the statistics compiled by the World Health Organization (1991), Shek (1993b) found that adolescent suicide rates in China were comparatively higher than those in Hong Kong and in other Western countries.

Although the age brackets used in the above-mentioned epidemiological studies are not the same across studies, the findings generally suggest that adolescents in the 15–24 age bracket might be vulnerable. However, there are other epidemiological studies with smaller samples suggesting that adolescents might not be particularly vulnerable (Shandong Province Mental Hospital et al., 1984) and that rates of neuroses (Chen, 1986; Xiang et al., 1986) and affective psychoses (Ou et al., 1986; Zhao Y. H. et al., 1986a, 1986b) were low in the 15–24 age bracket as compared to other age groups. However, if it is reasonable to assume that studies with larger sample sizes are more valid, it can be inferred from the existing data that the period between age 15 and the mid-twenties might be a vulnerable period for adolescents in Mainland China.

Besides epidemiological data, adjustment problems in adolescents in China have been reported. Yu (1985) examined the adjustment of Nanjing children and adolescents and found that high rates existed in some of the items. Shen, Wang, and Yang (1985) showed that the prevalence rates of minimal brain dysfunction in children in Beijing were higher than those reported in the Western literature. Zhao K. Y. et al. (1986) analyzed 1,500 cases seeking psychological consultation in a general hospital setting (1,000 cases in person and 500 cases via post) and found that 50.6% of those seeking help in person were between 16–25 and 68.4% of those seeking help via letter were within the same age bracket. In a community survey conducted in Shanghai, it was found that one-third of the adolescent respondents had adjustment problems ("One-third," 1991). In contrast, Yie and Rocklin (1988) studied the patterns of test anxiety amongst secondary school and university students and reported that Chinese students in general had lower levels of worrying, emotionality and overall test anxiety than American students.

In Hong Kong, while some epidemiological studies have been conducted (Lee, 1985; Millar, 1979; Mitchell, 1969; Shek and Mak, 1987), such studies were not primarily designed to investigate adolescent mental health, and attempts to examine adolescent mental health directly are few (Chen, 1988; Khoo, 1986). In a study conducted by the Hong Kong Council of Social Service (1982) using the Mooney Problem Checklist, it was found that while the potential client rate for the age group 16 or below was 8.11%, the estimated percentage of secondary school students who were potential clients in the age group 17 or above was 7.06% and an average rate of potential clients (regardless of age) of 7.81% was reported. A similar attempt using the Mooney Problem Checklist showed that roughly 10% of adolescent students in Chai Wan needed case counselling (Chan, 1983). In another study, the revised Mooney Problem Checklist was employed by Leung, Salili and Baber (1986) to study problem behavior in Hong Kong adolescents. Their results showed that the subjects expressed concern over schooling and examinations, and that fear of failure in examinations and poor academic performance were repeatedly indicated.

Psychiatric morbidity and symptoms amongst adolescents in Hong Kong have been examined in a number of studies. In a large-scale epidemiological study of the mental health of secondary school students in Hong Kong, Shek (1988) found, based on the responses of the subjects to the General Health Questionnaire (GHQ), that while 23.7% of the students could be regarded as probable cases based on the Likert scoring method, 63.7% of the subjects could be considered as psychologically "at risk" using the GHQ scoring method. The Research Team on Youth Development (1989) carried out a similar investigation by administering the modified Chinese version of the GHQ-12 to 1,500 Hong Kong secondary school students. Although the researchers stated that it was not the primary objective of the study to detect "probable psychiatric cases", they reported that the prevalence rate based on the Likert scoring procedure was 13.6%. The results of this study also revealed that a significant proportion of the respondents felt stressful and unhappy. Shek (1992a) further showed that 33.6% of the college respondents had GHQ scores above the morbidity cutoff point.

Utilizing the Chinese Somatic Scale, Shek and Mak (1992) and Shek (1994) found that 9.9% and 13.3% of the subjects respectively could be classified as "psychologically at risk" based on their responses to the chronic and acute sub-scales. In a similar attempt to study stress and mental health amongst 544 Hong Kong adolescents, Choy, Lam, and Ngai (1990a) used a modified version of the Chinese Somatic Scale and reported that the "potential prevalence rates" of mental disorders were 12.1% and 10.4% based on the chronic and acute sub-scales respectively.

In their study of anxiety in Hong Kong adolescents, Cheung and Lee (1984) administered the Taylor Manifest Anxiety Scale (MAS) and the Achievement Anxiety Test (AAT) to secondary school students. Their results showed that the overall anxiety scores on the MAS and the Debilitating Anxiety Sub-scale of the AAT amongst Hong Kong students were higher than students in the United States. Utilizing the Chinese version of the State-Trait Anxiety Inventory, Shek (1991b) found that the mean trait anxiety and state anxiety scores of Hong Kong students were higher than the mean scores of high school students reported in the Western literature (Spielberger, Gorsuch, and Lushene, 1970). Shek (1992a) found that the mean trait anxiety score in college students was higher than those reported in the Western literature.

Concerning depressive problems in Hong Kong adolescents, Shek (1991a) found that based on the subjects' responses to the Chinese Beck Depression Inventory, 53% of the respondents had either mild, moderate or severe levels of depression and the mean total BDI score for this sample was higher than those reported in the West. It was also found that while the percentage of respondents who could be considered as non-depressive was similar to the figures reported in the Western literature (e.g., Carlson and Cantwell, 1979; Kaplan, Hong, and Weinhold, 1984; Rutter, Graham, Chadwick, and Yule, 1976; Teri, 1982), the proportion of students who could be classified as severely depressed was higher than in previous studies. Shek (1992a) showed that 36.4% of university students in Hong Kong could be classified as mildly, moderately or severely depressed. In another study of depression among Primary 4 to Form 2 students in Hong

Kong, it was found that 31% (if a liberal cutoff score was used) or 19% (if a conservative cutoff score was used) of the respondents could be classified as severely depressed (The Boys' and Girls' Clubs Association of Hong Kong, 1993). In a study of suicidal ideation and attempted suicide in 316 secondary school students, Fong (1993) found that 3.8% of the respondents had attempted suicide in the past and 41.8% of the subjects once had or were having suicide ideation.

Concerning adolescent suicide and attempted suicide in Hong Kong, Lo (1985) reviewed the related statistics and noticed that amongst those who died from all causes, 16.8% in the 15–24 age bracket and 18.3% in the 25–34 age bracket were suicide cases and that these two figures were highest when all age brackets were under comparison. He also found that attempted suicide was most prevalent in the 15–24 age group (42% of all attempted suicide cases). However, Hau (1985) compared statistics on adolescent suicide in Hong Kong, Japan and Singapore and found that adolescent suicide rates in Hong Kong were lower than those in Japan and Singapore. In a study of the case notes of 67 adolescents aged below 16 who had attempted suicide, Chung, Luk, and Lieh-Mak (1987) reported that the mean incidence of attempted suicide in the five year period was 4.4 per 100,000 and suggested that this rate was very low in comparison with other Western countries.

In an attempt to compare youth suicide in Hong Kong, the developed world and the People's Republic of China in the period 1973 to 1988, Pritchard (1993) concluded that adolescent suicide in Hong Kong was not prevalent and the data did not support the claim that there was an "epidemic" of youth suicide in Hong Kong. In a review of adolescent suicide statistics during the period 1980 to 1991, Shek (1995) found that adolescent suicide rates in Hong Kong have been relatively stable for the period under study and suicide rates in the 10–24 age bracket for the period under study were the lowest when compared with other adult age groups. Shek (1995) also observed that adolescent suicide rates in Hong Kong appear to be lower than those reported in the Western contexts and in China.

The patterns of stress amongst Hong Kong adolescents were examined by Choy, Lam, and Ngai (1990a). Using a modified Social Readjustment Rating Scale, they found that the most frequently reported life change events experienced by adolescents included "worrying about finding jobs after graduation" and "change in social activities". They also observed that "relatives' emigration", "conflict with siblings" and "friends' emigration" were assessed to have the greatest impact on the respondents.

In a review of the statistics on psychiatric problems amongst university students, Singer (1985) showed that roughly 1.5% to 2% of the total student population of the University of Hong Kong had severe psychiatric disorders and 10 to 20% had milder psychological problems, and he concluded that the results obtained were broadly similar to those reported in other countries. Based on the author's own observations, Law (1979) stated that the common psychiatric problems expressed by Hong Kong students included school phobia, psychosomatic disorders, neurotic disorders, conduct disorders, and childhood psychoses.

The prevalence of mental disorders in Taiwan is indicated in the studies by Cheung (1986), Kleinman and Lin (1981), and Yeh (1985). In such reviews, it can be seen that few epidemiological studies have been conducted to examine psychiatric morbidity in Taiwanese adolescents. For example, in a discussion of student mental health in Taiwan, only four studies are mentioned in Yeh (1985). Based on the findings of an epidemiological study on Taiwanese university students, Yeh, Chu, Ko, Lin, and Lee (1972) found that 5.1% of the students could definitely be regarded as psychiatric cases and 25.6% showed milder psychological symptoms which could be regarded as "highly probable psychiatric cases". Their results also showed that a majority of the manifested psychiatric symptoms were related to psychophysiologic reactions and psycho-neuroses. On the basis of college students' responses to the Ko Mental Health Questionnaire, Ko, Yang, Cheng, and Li (1975) reported that 4% of Taiwanese students under study had severe psychological impairment problems, 12% had medium psychological impairment problems and 32% to 38% had slight psychological risk problems. Utilizing a two-stage case identification method in a community study of mental disorders in the Kaohsiung district of Taiwan, Cheng (1985) found that the unstandardized case rates for the male and female respondents in the 15–24 age bracket were 5.3% and 31.3% respectively.

In their study of psychophysiological disorders in Taiwan, Rin, Chu, and Lin (1966) showed that 27% of the respondents in the 15–24 age bracket had such disorders. Miao (1976) employed the Zung's Self-Rating Depression Scale (SDS), Zung's Self-Rating Anxiety Scale (SAS) and Ko's Mental Health Questionnaire (KMHQ) to examine the mental health status of Taiwanese college freshmen. Her results showed that the percentages of subjects above the morbidity cutoff scores in the SDS, SAS and KMHQ were 23.5%, 17%, and 41% respectively. Both the SDS and SAS were again used by Miao (1977) to study the mental health status of college seniors, and similar findings on the percentages of subjects above the morbidity cutoff score in the SDS (21%) and SAS (16%) were obtained. Based on the ratings of teachers, Hsu (1966, 1973) examined the prevalence rates of behavior problems in primary and junior high school students in Taiwan and reported that 10–13% of the students had excessive behavioral problems.

With respect to adolescent suicide in Taiwan, Chieuh (1982) examined the standardized death rates on suicide and self-inflicted injuries in Taiwan from 1960 to 1979 and found that 37.7% of the males and 49.2% of the females were in the 10–29 age bracket. Rin, Cheng, and Chen (1974) examined the trend found in suicides reported in selected Taiwan news-papers and observed that 49% of the published suicide cases were aged 29 or below. Yeh (1985) also noticed that the suicide rate for Taiwanese adolescents began to rise after the age of 15, with the first peak appearing in the 20–24 age group.

Besides research in China, Hong Kong, and Taiwan, other studies have also been conducted to examine the psychopathology and adjustment of Chinese adolescents in overseas contexts. In their study of culture patterns and adolescent behavior, Hsu, Watrous, and Lord (1961) compared the mental health of Chinese adolescents in Hawaii and White adolescents in Chicago based on the data derived from projective techniques. Their results showed that although the quantity of affective energy in the two groups was similar, adolescents in Hawaii exhibited less emotional immaturity. In contrast, Chang (1985) compared Black, White and overseas Chinese college students in terms of their responses to the Zung's Self-Rating Depression Scale and found that there was no difference in depression scores across these ethnic groups.

Several studies have also been conducted on the mental health of Chinese students studying abroad. In one such study, Chu, Yeh, Klein, Alexander, and Miller (1971) found that students studying in the United States had poorer mental health than Taiwanese students studying in the United States. Bourne (1975) examined the psychological problems of Chinese students and reported that several problem areas, including the demand for excellence and the conflict generated from the ethnic identity, created many difficulties for the students around which psychiatric impair-ments would later emerge. Based on her clinical experiences, Cheung (1979) pointed out the problems and difficulties experienced by Chinese students studying in the United States. Ko (1979) studied the adjustment of overseas Chinese students in Taiwan and observed that their mental health was poorer than that of local students. Similar findings were obtained in the study of Yeh et al. (1972) which showed that those who came from outside Taipei had more mental health problems.

In a review of the mental health of Asian American teenagers, Liu, Yu, Chang, and Fernandez (1990) observed that the commitment rates for Asian youth aged between 15 to 24 in mental hospitals and correctional institutions were lower than the rates reported for the White American, Black, and the Spanish-speaking populations. However, they also demonstrated that although the age-specific suicide rates in the 15–24 age group amongst Chinese were lower than those for White Americans and Japanese Americans, data on the proportional mortality for selected deaths showed two interesting observations: (1) suicide accounted for 16.8% of deaths amongst Chinese Americans, as compared to 11.9% and 19.0% in White Americans and Japanese Americans respectively; (2) the change of proportional mortality rates for suicide amongst Chinese Americans in 1970 and 1980 was 200%, as compared to 52.6% in White Americans and 32.9% in Japanese Americans.

Several observations can be extracted from the above review on Chinese adolescent psychopathology and adjustment problems. Firstly, in terms of the number of studies conducted exclusively on adolescent psychopathology, more studies have been carried out in Hong Kong and Taiwan than in Mainland China. There is also a paucity of research findings on the mental health and adjustment of overseas Chinese adolescents. Secondly, the magnitude of the prevalence rates and the extent of psychiatric or adjustment problems reported are observed to vary considerably both within and across different Chinese communities under focus.

Thirdly, the reported data in general indicate that adjustment and mental health problems exist in Chinese adolescents. Although few studies have been conducted exclusively on adolescent samples in China (Hu, 1994), an examination of those epidemiological surveys and other related studies suggests that adolescence might be a vulnerable period as compared to other life stages. In Hong Kong and Taiwan, most of the studies show that a significant proportion of adolescents (ranging from roughly 10% to 30%) might be psychologically at risk, and adjustment problems in Chinese adolescents have been reported.

Fourthly, in terms of the magnitude of mental health and adjustment problems amongst Chinese adolescents, the reported data (particularly those related to prevalence rates) seem to suggest that adolescents in Hong Kong and Taiwan are more tumultuous than those in Mainland China.

Fifthly, when the findings are compared with those obtained in the West, it can be observed that the extent of mental health and adjustment problems amongst adolescents in Hong Kong and Taiwan is roughly similar to, or slightly higher than, the reported rates and figures in the West (e.g., Kandel and Davis, 1986; Kaplan, Hong, and Weinhod, 1984; Paton and Kandel, 1978; Rutter, Graham, Chadwick, and Yule, 1976; Teri, 1982). However, consistent with the data based on adults, impairment rates for adolescent mental disorders in Mainland China are observed to be lower than those reported in the West.

To what extent can the above review enable us to discover whether Chinese adolescents are tumultuous? A major thesis of the "turmoil" hypothesis is that psychological problems in adolescents are common and that adolescence is necessarily a time of intense stress. A logical deduction of this assertion is that a majority of adolescents should display mental health problems. This argument was held by Offer and Schonert-Reichl (1992) who concluded that "the majority of recent research findings suggest adolescence should not be characterized as a time of severe emotional upheaval and turmoil because the majority (80%) of adolescents manage this transition quite well. Nevertheless, a sizable proportion of youth (20%) do not fare so well, with many not receiving the help they may need" (p. 1003).

Assuming that the studies under review are methodologically acceptable (this will be discussed later) and bearing in mind the problems involved in comparing data across different epidemiological studies, it can be seen that most of the reported prevalence rates for the various kinds of psychological disorders and problems do not exceed 50% and that such rates are not particularly high when compared with other adult samples. In other words, the general picture that can be derived from the present review is that a majority of Chinese adolescents do not show signs of psychological disturbance and that the "storm and stress" notion does not receive strong support from the present review. This picture is in fact consistent with the observation of Powers, Hauser, and Kilner (1989) who noted that epidemiological data in the past 20 years (e.g., Offer and Offer, 1975) revealed that severe emotional disturbances appeared in only 10–20% of adolescents. However, when using epidemiological findings to dismiss the "turmoil" hypothesis, it should be realized that there are problems asso-ciated with this interpretation (Petersen, 1988). In addition, the observation that most of the adolescents in the studies under review are not psychologically "at risk" does not mean that adolescence as a transitional period is automatically a smooth one and the need for helping those who are psychologically at risk should not be undermined (Offer and Schonert-Reichl, 1992).

Positive Mental Health among Chinese Adolescents

Regarding research on positive mental health amongst adolescents in Mainland China, a review of the literature shows that related studies are almost non-existent. Although Zhang and Dong (1990) carried out a study on the relationship between distinctiveness and spontaneous self-concept in Chinese students, there was unfortunately no discussion on the question of whether the subjects had favourable perceptions about themselves.

In Hong Kong, self-concept in adolescents has been examined in several studies. Based on their argument that self-concept might more profitably be assessed by a free response approach, Bond and Cheung (1983) administered the Twenty-Statements Test to university students in Hong Kong, Japan and the United States to examine their spontaneous self-concept. They found that in terms of the ratio of positive to negative statements in the protocols of the subjects, the Hong Kong ratio was in-between the Japanese and American ratios.

In an attempt to study crisis and vulnerability in adolescents, Lau (1990) found that the self-concept of academic ability increased with age whereas the self-concept of appearance decreased with age: such findings were taken as an indication that "adolescence is a period quite susceptible and vulnerable to disturbance" (p. 125). In a study in which the construction of self amongst university students was examined using the repertory grid test, Shek (1992a) found that 6.6% of the subjects construed their real self as being far away from their ideal self.

Self-esteem in Hong Kong adolescents has also been examined in a number of studies. In a study in which the Chinese version of the Rosenberg Self-esteem Scale was used (Young Women's Christian Association, 1984), it was found that 19% of the respondents had a low level of self-esteem. Unfortunately, the frequency of responses to the various items is not described in the report. The Rosenberg Self-esteem Scale was again employed by The Research Team on Youth Development (1989) and it was found that 33.7% of the subjects could be regarded as having a "negative" sense of self-esteem; 17% of them required counselling services. The data also showed that 70% of the respondents felt that they were unsuccessful and 52% of the subjects claimed that they did not have any good qualities. In an attempt to study the subjects' global self-esteem using 9 items formulated in a way similar to the Rosenberg Self-esteem Scale, Cheung and Tam (1984) suggested that there were two aspects in the configuration of self-esteem (positivity and negativity) and concluded that the self-esteem of the subjects leaned slightly toward the positive pole.

Besides self-concept and self-esteem, some studies have been conducted to study the meaning of life for Hong Kong adolescents. Based on the subjects' responses to the Chinese Purpose in Life Questionnaire (PIL), Shek (1986) reported that the mean total score of Chinese students was comparatively lower than that of the Western subjects (e.g., Crumbaugh, 1968). A similar finding was obtained in a sample of post-secondary school students by Shek, Hong, and Cheung (1987) who noted that more than one-fifth of the subjects felt bored and confused about life and had seriously thought about suicide. In an attempt to understand the purpose in life of university students, Shek (1992a) showed that while the mean total PIL score was higher than that derived from secondary school students, it was still lower than that of Western subjects reported in the literature.

In Taiwan, studies of the self-concept of adolescents have been carried out and these are exclusively based on the fixed response format approach. Lu (1979) investigated the self-concept of Taiwanese children and adolescents using a scale based on the Tennessee Self-Concept Scale and concluded that the self-concept of the subjects was high. Lu (1981) examined the self-concept amongst 309 male and 339 female Taiwanese students in elementary and junior high school using the Tennessee Self-Concept Scale and suggested that the subjects had positive self-concept.

In a study of the ego identity and sub-cultural changes amongst Taiwanese university students, Ho (1985) found that two-fifths of the subjects were having ego identity crisis, and Ho (1990) further showed that the degree of identity crisis in the subjects over a 5 year period had increased. Ho (1987) examined the meaning of life among 873 Taiwanese students in colleges and junior colleges using the Chinese Purpose in Life Questionnaire and concluded that a quarter of the students lacked purpose and meaning in their lives.

Utilizing the Offer Self-Image Questionnaire for Adolescents, Turner and Mo (1984) found that while Taiwanese adolescents had significantly lower scores (compared with norms for Americans) in several areas (including Impulse Control, Emotional Tone, and Body and Self-Image on

Psychological Self; Social Relationships and Vocational-Educational Goals on Social Self; Sexual Self; Mastery of External World and Psychopathology on Coping Self), Chinese subjects scored slightly higher on Morals (Social Self) and Superior Adjustment (Coping Self). Offer, Ostrov, Howard, and Atkinson (1988) further reported that while Taiwanese adolescents were negative in their appraisal of their physical well-being and attractiveness (Personal Self) and had conservative sexual attitudes (Sexual Self) and poor mastery of external world (Coping Self), they showed signs of good adjustment (Coping Self).

A number of observations can be extracted from the preceding review of the positive mental health of Chinese adolescents. Firstly, more studies on adolescent positive mental health have been carried out in Hong Kong and Taiwan than in Mainland China. Secondly, the existing findings are piecemeal and equivocal. For example, while there are findings indicating that Chinese adolescents have a similar or more positive self-concept and self-esteem than adolescents in other cultures, there is evidence showing that Chinese adolescents have a lower sense of purpose and existential well-being.

How far do the findings in the area of positive mental health support the "turmoil" hypothesis ? Since there is no sign in the existing studies that a majority of adolescents lack positive mental health, it may be inferred that the tumultuous portrait of adolescent development does not receive strong support from the present review. However, this inference should be qualified: there are few studies in this area (hence no definitive conclusions can be reached) and there is evidence suggesting that adolescents have more problems with their self-concept compared to preadolescent children (Lau, 1990).

Offer and Sabshin (1974) suggested that mental health could possibly be defined in terms of four perspectives — mental health as health (i.e., absence of psychological symptoms), mental health as average, mental health as utopia, and mental health as transactional systems. A survey of the literature shows that Chinese adolescent mental health has been defined predominately in terms of the first perspective and that few studies have been conducted with respect to adolescent positive mental health. A similar observation with reference to the Western culture was also highlighted by Powers, Hauser, and Kilner (1989) who warned that the psychological community was relatively ignorant about positive mental health and optimal functioning in adolescents.

Correlates of Chinese Adolescent Mental Health

Personal and Psychological Factors

While few studies have been conducted in China to examine sex differences in adolescent mental health, studies in Hong Kong tend to show that female adolescents have more psychiatric symptoms (Choy, Lam, and Ngai, 1990a; Shek, 1989b; The Boys' and Girls' Clubs Association of Hong Kong, 1993; The Research Team on Youth Development, 1989) and a lower sense of self-esteem than male adolescents (Cheung and Tam, 1984). As far as adolescent suicide and attempted suicide are concerned, Hau (1985) and Pritchard (1993) noted the comparatively higher suicide rate amongst female adolescents, and Chung, Luk, and Lieh-Mak (1987) observed the female predominance in attempted suicide in children and adolescents in Hong Kong. Sex differences in help-seeking behavior have also been reported (Cheung, 1984). By contrast, there are some studies in which sex differences in mental health were not found (e.g., Hong Kong Council of Social Service, 1982; Shek, 1992a; Shek, Hong and Cheung, 1987) or in which the obtained data were inconclusive (e.g., Cheung and Lee, 1984). However, when the existing data are taken as a whole, one develops the impression that female adolescents in general have poorer mental health as compared to male adolescents in Hong Kong, and that this phenomenon is particularly pronounced in younger adolescents.

In the case of Taiwan, the picture of sex differences in adolescent mental health is less clear. While there are studies showing the existence of sex differences (Cheng, 1985; Ho, 1987; Rin, Cheng, Chen, 1974), there are also studies showing either no sex differences in mental health (e.g., Miao, 1977; Turner and Mo, 1984) or mixed results (Miao, 1976; Yeh et al., 1972).

Concerning the effect of age, studies conducted in China generally show that adolescent psychopathology and problems begin to rise in early adolescence, reaching a peak in late adolescence and early adulthood (e.g., Wei et al., 1993). Similarly, adolescent mental health has been found to vary with age in several studies in Hong Kong, with adolescents of a higher age showing poorer mental health (Shek, 1988, 1989a; The Boys' and Girls' Clubs Association of Hong Kong, 1993; The Research Team on Youth Development, 1989). For example, Shek (1995) showed that suicide rates among teenagers in early adolescence were lower than those among adolescents in late adolescence. However, Ko, Yang, Cheng, and Li (1975) showed that the mental health of older university students was better than of younger ones in Taiwan, and inconsistent findings on the differences between older and younger Taiwanese adolescents on their self-image have also been reported (Offer, Ostrov, Howard, and Atkinson, 1988).

Finally, relationships between adolescent mental health and psychological factors, including intelligence (Cheung and Tam, 1984), values (Ho, 1987), personality (Chang, Tseng, and Yeh, 1987; Hu, 1994; Yang and Yang, 1974), and attribution styles as well as cognitive factors (Chan and Tsoi, 1984), have been reported. For example, Huang, Hwang, and Ko (1983) examined life stress, attribution style, and social support in college students. They found that subjects who attributed negative events to internal, stable and global factors tended to be more depressive, and those who were classified as depressive tended to attribute the events to uncontrollable factors. Their data also showed that while normal subjects tended to attribute events which are negative in nature to *yuan* more than depressive subjects, both normal and depressive subjects were equally likely to attribute positive events to *yuan*. Similar data on the link between attributional style and depression were reported by Zhang and Wang (1989).

In an attempt to examine the impact of "actual-ideal" discrepancies in the representation of self and significant-others, self-consciousness and locus of control on adolescent mental health within the control theory's framework, Shek (1992a) found that while these factors were related to adolescent mental health, subjects with high "actual-ideal" discrepancy in self-representation, coupled with a high sense of consciousness and an externality of control, had the poorest mental health.

There are also research findings showing that there is a substantial relationship between psychiatric symptoms and existential functioning in Chinese adolescents. Shek (1992b, 1993a) showed that adolescents with a high sense of purpose in life had fewer psychiatric symptoms and better positive mental health, and such findings were interpreted in the light of Victor Frankl's theory. Shek (1993c) found that those who had a high sense of hopelessness had poorer mental health in terms of psychiatric morbidity and positive mental health criteria. There are also data demonstrating that adolescent depression is linked to loneliness (The Boys' and Girls' Clubs Association of Hong Kong, 1993).

Stressors and Moderating Factors

There is evidence suggesting that adolescent mental health is related to life stress (e.g., Yeh, Ko, and Hwang, 1981). In their study of the relationship between attribution styles, coping and depression, Huang, Hwang, and Ko (1983) showed that depressive scores were positively correlated with objective as well as subjective life event scores, and that depressive subjects conceived negative events as more uncontrollable, stable and undesirable. Choy, Lam, and Ngai (1990a) similarly showed that objective as well as subjective stress levels were weakly related to both chronic and acute somatic symptoms. In a follow-up study on the impact of examination stress on the health of adolescents in Taiwan, Chang (1987) showed that an individual who perceived the University Entrance Examination as more stressful displayed more psychological symptoms.

Concerning the relationship between social support and mental health, Huang, Hwang, and Ko (1983) found that social support scores were correlated negatively with depression scores. They also showed that when social support was treated as ego strength, the ego strength index was positively related to depressive scores. Similar results concerning the beneficial impact of social support were also found by other researchers (Chang, Tseng, and Yeh, 1987; Choy, Lam, and Ngai, 1990b). There is also evidence showing that college students who used unadaptive coping strategies tended to show more depression, somatization, and phobic anxiety symptoms (Zhang and Fang, 1990).

Socialization and Family-related Factors

With reference to Mainland China, it was found that there have been few empirical studies in this area, although the characteristic features of Chinese socialization patterns in China and their possible impacts have been described and discussed (e.g., Ho, 1986; Li, 1985). However, there have been some recent attempts to study related issues (e.g., Guo et al., 1989; Hu, 1994; Huang et al., 1990; Tseng, Tao, Jing, Chiu, Yu, and Velma, 1988) and the role of parental education in minimal brain dysfunction of children has also been discussed (Shen, Wang, and Yang, 1985).

The data arising from several studies in Hong Kong show that parenting styles are related to adolescent mental health. By administering the Parent Image Differentials to Hong Kong students, it was found that parenting styles were related to the personality of children (Chan, 1978) and their cognitive abilities (Chan, 1981). In a similar attempt in which the relationship between recalled parental treatment styles and mental health in Chinese secondary school students was examined, Shek (1989c, 1992a, 1993d) showed that recalled paternal treatment and maternal treatment styles correlated significantly with measures of psychiatric symptoms and indices of positive mental health. Other research findings on the impact of family variables or the quality of parent-child relations on psychiatric morbidity (Shek, 1990a; The Boys' and Girls' Clubs Association of Hong Kong, 1993; The Research Team on Youth Development, 1989), self-esteem (Cheung and Tam, 1984; The Research Team on Youth Development, 1989), problem behavior (Leung, Salili, and Baber, 1986) and mental health knowledge (Shek, 1990b) among Chinese adolescents have been reported.

In a review of the relationship between family factors and behavior in children and adolescents in Taiwan, Yang (1986) examined more than 50 empirical studies. Concerning the impact of family composition, ordinal position, socioeconomic status and maternal employment status, he noticed that children in nuclear and stem families were more close-minded than those in extended families and that those children experiencing father absence tended to exhibit over-masculinity and maladjustment. While no definite conclusion could be drawn with regard to the role of ordinal position on psychological development, only children were found to have a higher chance of being sent by their parents for psychological consultation. Furthermore, children and adolescents with a lower socio-economic status tended to have more delinquent and problem behavior and lower self-esteem; and children with working mothers seemed to be more insecure, with more aggressiveness and dependency, and displaying more mother-child relationship problems.

Regarding the impact of parenting styles and child-rearing practices on the development of Taiwanese children and adolescents, Yang (1986) concluded that parenting styles with the attributes of acceptance, positive regard, proper restraint, love, reward and reasoning tend to induce positive social and emotional development in children and adolescents (including the cultivation of positive self-concept, self-assertion, and internal locus of control) and the inhibition of delinquent behavior. Observations on the relationship between family factors and test anxiety (Chang, Tseng, and Yeh, 1987) or examination stress amongst adolescents in Taiwan (Chang, 1987) have also been reported.

Education-related Factors

Few studies have been conducted in China to examine the role of education-related factors in adolescent mental health. Yie and Rocklin (1988) showed that while senior secondary school students had higher test anxiety than full-time university students, those studying in evening universities (i.e., part-time students) had the highest level of test anxiety. Students in different forms were also observed to have different levels of growth-related needs (Huang, Zhang, and Zhang, 1988). Hu (1994) found that education-related factors (such as examination pressure) were highly related to adolescent psychological problems.

In Hong Kong, there are findings suggesting that students with different levels of educational attainment might have different mental health, and there are studies suggesting that students in higher forms have poorer mental health (e.g., Cheung and Lee, 1984; Shek, 1988; Shek and Mak, 1992; The Boys' and Girls' Clubs Association of Hong Kong, 1993; The Research Team on Youth Development, 1989). In Taiwan, Ko (1976) found that when comparing junior high school male students, senior high school male students and university male students, the mental health of the senior high school group was the worst, and there was no significant difference between the junior high school group and the university group. In her study of the mental health of university students, Miao (1977) found that university seniors were less depressive than juniors.

The mental health of adolescents has also been shown to be differentially related to the different characteristics associated with schools, including school type (Cheung and Tam, 1984; Shek, 1988; Shek and Mak, 1992), school mode (Shek, 1988; Shek and Mak, 1992), and school environment (Ko, Yang, Cheng, and Li, 1975). The mental health of students was also shown to be related to their specialization (Miao, 1976; Miao, 1977), their perceived relationship with the school (Cheung and Tam, 1984), and their participation in school activities (Yeh et al., 1972).

With regard to the impact of examination, Law (1978) studied examination stress in fifth formers in Hong Kong and found that urban boys and rural girls showed an increase in GHQ scores; this finding was explained in terms of different parental expectations of academic achievement of boys and girls. In a follow-up study of the influence of examination stress on the health of Taiwanese adolescents, Chang (1987) examined the health and behavior of students who were going to attend the University Entrance Examination (UEE Group) versus those who were not going to take this examination (non-UEE Group). It was revealed from the findings that the UEE group showed more symptoms related to social dysfunctioning and there was an increase in the self-report physical and somatic symptoms in this group. Research findings on the relationship between actual or perceived academic performance and student mental health have also been reported (Chang, Tseng and Yeh, 1987; Cheung and Tam, 1984; Miao, 1977).

Societal Factors

There is evidence suggesting that the degree of urbanization (Yang, 1980) and mass media (Hu, 1994) are related to adolescent mental health. Ko (1975) examined student mental health problems in two differently in-dustrialized cities based on the Ko's Mental Health Questionnaire. He found that the mental health of females in the large city was poorer than that of females in the small city and that it was easier for female dwellers in the large city to feel depressed and hostile. Research findings on the relation-ship between living density and mental health (Shek, 1988) and the possible influence of housing type on children's well-being (Ekblad and Werne, 1990) have also been reported.

Summary

The preceding review shows that a number of personal, psychological, familial, education-related and societal factors have been found to be re-lated to the mental health of Chinese adolescents, although the existing data are not conclusive and the reported effect sizes are not strong. Concerning the number of studies on the correlates of Chinese adolescent mental health, more studies have been conducted in Hong Kong and Taiwan than in China. The observation that a wide range of factors are related to Chinese adoles-cent mental health clearly implies the futility of understanding adolescent mental health on any one single level and the importance of utilizing a multivariate and systemic approach. This implication is consistent with the view of Powers, Hauser, and Kilner (1989) which suggests that models on adolescent mental health should involve the integration of biological, psychological, social and cultural variables.

It can be seen that most of the existing studies have been conducted within the framework of descriptive epidemiology (where prevalence rates and correlates of adolescent mental health were the basic foci) and, with a few exceptions (Huang, Hwang, and Ko, 1983; Shek, 1990a, 1992a), there is a severe lack of conceptual models on the causal mechanisms involved in Chinese adolescent mental health. This situation is in fact similar to that in the West. For example, with specific reference to adolescent depression, Simons and Miller (1987) remarked that "compared with the abundance of research investigating the causes of adult depression, few studies have been completed on the etiology of depression among adolescents" (p. 326).

Methodological Problems of the Studies under Review

With specific reference to the scientific status of studies on Chinese adolescent mental health, it has been noticed that a number of methodological problems are intrinsic to most of the studies under review. The primary problem is related to the assessment of Chinese adolescent mental health, and there are two related issues which constitute this problem of assessment, one on the philosophical and the other on the operational level. Philosophically, the basic question is whether there are any cultural variations in the manifestations and definitions of psychopathology and positive mental health. If the answer is affirmative, tools developed in the Western culture might not be so applicable in the Chinese context. In addition, if the conception of mental disorders is different in the Chinese culture, the reported prevalence rates would also be different. For example, Kleinman and Mechanic (1979) argued that the report of a low rate of mental illness in China appeared to reflect the narrow definition of disorders and somatic and physical expression of the illnesses. Lin, Kleinman, and Lin (1981) also remarked that the implementation of epidemiological surveys in the Chinese culture might be superficial and naive.

Even if it is assumed that there is a cultural similarity in the manifestation and definition of psychopathology and positive mental health and that Western tools can be used in Chinese culture, there is still a series of related questions on the operational level, including the problems of translation, adaptation, and the scientific status of the translated and adapted tools. On the question of translation, some of the researchers translated the English version without reporting the measures used to ascertain the objectivity of the translation procedures (e.g., Young Women's Christian Association, 1984). In addition, the validity of some of the scales and the related cutoff points in adolescent samples were unclear (e.g., Choy, Lam and Ngai, 1990a; The Research Team on Youth Development, 1989; Young Women's Christian Association, 1984). Some researchers even used tests in a manner inconsistent with the philosophy of the test. For example, the "modified" GHQ-12, which is not consistent with the original test logic of the GHQ, was used to detect cases by The Research Team on Youth Development (1989). Some of the existing studies also show limitations on the research implementation level. In some of the studies carried out in China, "barefoot doctors" were commonly employed to conduct the interviews. Although data on the reliability of the diagnostic interviews were reported in such studies, the question of the validity of the data collected can still be raised. It was also pointed out by Lin and Kleinman (1981) that the employment of neighbourhood cadres in identifying those who had mental problems might result in an under-estimation of the false-negative rates.

The results of this review also show that the degree of sophistication of the statistical analyses conducted in the existing studies varies a lot and that analyses in some of the studies are not thorough enough so that interpretations of the data might therefore be blurred. For example, the norm of the samples and the psychometric properties of the measures of mental health are not described in most of the studies (e.g., Leung, Salili and Baber, 1986; Miao, 1976, 1977; The Research Team on Youth Development, 1989; Yie and Rocklin, 1988; Young Women's Christian Association, 1984) and efforts to ascertain the psychometric properties of the measuring tools in adolescent samples are seldom carried out.

It was also noticed that some researchers even performed statistical analyses in an inappropriate manner (e.g., Choy, Lam and Ngai, 1990a; The Research Team on Youth Development, 1989; Yang, 1980). For example, based on the results of analyses of variance, The Research Team on Youth Development (1989) concluded that adolescent mental health was related to grade without removing the possible confounding effect of age. In many other studies in which multiple pairs of correlations amongst the variables were studied (Choy, Lam, and Ngai, 1990a; Miao, 1976, 1977; The Research Team on Youth Development, 1989), few attempts have been made to guard against the occurrence of Type 1 error.

Another problem concerns the fairness of the conclusions and inferences drawn from the data reported. It was found that in some of the studies, the inferences and interpretations drawn are far-fetched and unjustified. For example, Choy, Lam, and Ngai (1990b) concluded that their study on adolescent stress "strongly shows that Hong Kong still falls short of meeting the needs of youth. Rapid change has thrown out major social institutions such as the family, the school and work creating stress on youths while failing to guide and support them" (p. 78). This conclusion is obviously unjustified since the question of whether Hong Kong has failed to meet the needs of young people and whether they are without guidance was not examined in the study. Similarly, while the data showed that there were no overall sex differences in test anxiety, Yie and Rocklin (1988) still concluded that there was a need to give more counselling to female students. In many other studies, difficulties intrinsic to the interpretation of the data are not stated and readers are not cautioned on the possible limitations of the studies (e.g., The Research Team on Youth Development, 1989; Turner and Mo, 1984).

The final methodological problem that can be seen is that most of the existing studies are cross-sectional in nature and longitudinal attempts to examine changes are almost non-existent. One consequence of this situation is that causal mechanisms involved in Chinese adolescent mental health cannot be properly identified and the related developmental phenomena cannot be adequately described. According to Powers, Hauser, and Kilner (1989), longitudinal research is the "royal road" for the understanding of adolescent mental health and the related research is linked to the conception that mental health is a result of a changing time and culture (Offer and Sabshin, 1974).

Conclusions

The present chapter attempts to review and integrate existing studies on Chinese adolescent mental health. With reference to the questions posed at the beginning of this chapter, several conclusions can be drawn: a) most of the studies on Chinese adolescent mental health have been geared toward the study of adolescent psychopathology and they were seldom guided by well-articulated theoretical models; b) the data arising from the existing epidemiological studies and research on positive mental health generally do not lend strong support to the "turmoil" hypothesis; c) while Chinese adolescent mental health has been found to be related to a number of personal, psychological, stress-related, family-related, education-related and societal factors, there is a severe lack of integrative models to accommodate the observed relationships; and d) most of the existing studies on Chinese adolescent mental health are plagued by methodological problems. In view of the paucity of research data and the methodological problems intrinsic to most of the existing studies in this field, there is an obvious need to conduct further studies (particularly longitudinal studies) with more methodological vigor, to replicate the existing findings, and to build up a more solid database with theoretical insights. However, in an attempt to accomplish these tasks, there is an urgent need for researchers to re-conceptualize the meaning of adolescent mental health and to re-consider the related conceptual and methodological issues involved (Offer and Schonert-Reichl, 1992; Powers, Hauser, and Kilner, 1989).

References

Bond, M. H., and Cheung, T. S. (1983). College students' spontaneous self-concept: The effect of culture among respondents in Hong Kong, Japan, and the United States. *Journal of Cross-Cultural Psychology*, 14 (2): 153–171.

Bourne, P. G. (1975). The Chinese student — Acculturation and mental illness. *Psychiatry*, 38: 269–277.

The Boys' and Girls' Clubs Association of Hong Kong (1993). *Report on the study of adolescent depression*. The Boys' and Girls' Clubs Association of Hong Kong.

Carlson, G. A., and Cantwell, D. P. (1979). A survey of depressive symptoms in a child and psychiatric population. *Journal of the American Academy of Child Psychiatry*, 18: 587–599.

Chan, C. M., and Tsoi, M. M. (1984). The BDI and stimulus determinants of cognitive-related depression among Chinese college students. *Cognitive Therapy and Research*, 8: 501–508.

Chan, J. (1978). Parent–child interaction and personality. *New Horizons*, 19: 44–52.

———. (1981). Correlates of parent–child interaction and certain psychological variables among adolescents in Hong Kong. In J.L.M. Binnie-Dawson, G. H. Blowers, and R. Hoosain (Eds.), *Perspectives in Asian cross-cultural psychology* (pp. 112–131). Lisse, Netherlands: Swets and Zeitlinger.

Chan, S. L. (1983). *The adolescents' mental health and social support in Chaiwan* (In Chinese). Unpublished master's thesis, The Chinese University of Hong Kong, Hong Kong.

Chang, C. (1987). Follow-up study of examination stress on health of adolescents in Taiwan (In Chinese). *Acta Psychologica Taiwanica*, 29 (2): 93–112.

Chang, C., Tseng, C. C., and Yeh, L. W. (1987). Risk factors on children's test anxiety (In Chinese). *Acta Psychologica Taiwanica*, 29 (2): 83–92.

Chang, W. C. (1985). A cross-cultural study of depressive symptomatology. *Culture, Medicine and Psychiatry*, 9: 295–317.

Chen, C. H. et al. (1984). Incidence and prevalence rate of schizophrenia in community mental health service from 1975–1981 (In Chinese). *Chinese Journal of Neurology and Psychiatry*, 17 (6): 321–324.

———. (1986a). Data analysis of an epidemiological study on mental disorders, drug and alcoholic dependences and personality disorders (In Chinese). *Chinese Journal of Neurology and Psychiatry*, 19 (2): 70–72.

———. (1986b). Analysis of epidemiological data of schizophrenia (In Chinese). *Chinese Journal of Neurology and Psychiatry*, 19 (2): 73–76.

Chen, F. P. (1986). An epidemiologic investigation on neuroses (In Chinese). *Chinese Journal of Neurology and Psychiatry*, 19 (5): 301–305.

Chen, S. (Ed.). (1988). *Mental health in adolescence*. Hong Kong: Mental Health Association of Hong Kong.

Cheng, T. A. (1985). A pilot study of mental disorders in Taiwan. *Psychological Medicine*, 15: 195–203.

Cheung, F. K. (1979). Mental health problems and adjustment of Chinese students in the United States. *Hong Kong Journal of Mental Health*, 8 (1): 47–55.

Cheung, F.M.C. (1984). Preferences in help-seeking among Chinese students. *Culture, Medicine and Psychiatry*, 8: 371–380.

———. (1986). Psychopathology among Chinese people. In M. H. Bond (Ed.), *The psychology of the Chinese people* (pp. 171–212). Hong Kong: Oxford University Press.

Cheung, F.M.C., and Lee, P.L.M. (1984). Anxiety among secondary school students in Hong Kong and its relationship to academic performance. *Education Journal*, 12 (1): 56–63.

Cheung, T. S., and Tam, S. Y. (1984). *An analysis of the self-esteem of adolescents in Hong Kong: Configurations and determinants*. Hong Kong: The Chinese University of Hong Kong, Centre for Hong Kong Studies.

Chieuh, C. M. (1982). An analysis of the statistical data on death by suicide and self-inflicted injury in Taiwan (In Chinese). *Chinese Medical Journal*, 29: 36–45.

Choy, B. K., Lam, C. M., and Ngai, S.S.Y. (1990a). *Stress and social support among young people*. Hong Kong: The Friends of Scouting.

———. (1990b). Stress and social support among young people: Community responses to youth needs. In *Proceedings of 1989 International Conference on Youth* (pp. 75–80). Hong Kong: Hong Kong Council of Social Service.

Chu, H. M., Yeh, E. K., Klein, M. H., Alexander, A. A., and Miller, M. H. (1971). A study of Chinese students' adjustment in the U.S.A. *Acta Psychologica Taiwanica*, 13: 206–218.

Chung, S. Y., Luk, S. L., and Lieh-Mak, F. (1987). Attempted suicide in children and adolescents in Hong Kong. *Social Psychiatry*, 22: 102–106.

Crumbaugh, J. C. (1968). Cross-validation of purpose in life test based on Frankl's concepts. *Journal of Individual Psychology*, 24: 74–81.

Ekblad, S., and Werne, F. (1990). Housing and health in Beijing: Implications of high-rise housing on children and the aged. *Journal of Sociology and Social Welfare*, 17 (1): 51–77.

Erikson, E. H. (1968). *Identity: Youth and crisis*. New York: Norton.

Fong, S.Y.Y. (1993). A study on suicidal ideation and attempted suicide in 316 secondary school students. *Hong Kong Journal of Mental Health*, 22: 43–49.

Freeman, H. (Ed.). (1984). *Mental health and the environment*. London: Churchill Livingstone.

Freud, A. (1958). Adolescence. In *Psychoanalytic study of the child* (Vol. 13). New York: International Universities Press.

Guo, L. T. et al. (1989). Family life events and behavior problems in children (In Chinese). *Chinese Journal of Neurology and Psychiatry*, 22 (4): 242–245.

Hau, K. T. (1985). Adolescent suicide and remedial counselling methods (In Chinese). *Education Journal*, 13 (1): 28–36.

Ho, D.Y.F. (1986). Chinese patterns of socialization: A critical review. In M. H. Bond (Ed.), *The psychology of the Chinese people* (pp. 1–37). Hong Kong: Oxford University Press.

Ho, D.Y.F., Spinks, J. A., and Yeung, C.S.H. (Eds.). (1989). *Chinese patterns of behavior: A sourcebook of psychological and psychiatric studies*. New York: Praeger.

Ho, Y. C. (1985). *A study of the subculture and related determinants in Chinese University students*. Unpublished doctoral dissertation. (In Chinese). Taiwan: National Normal University.

———. (1987). College students' meaning of life and its correlates: An empirical study of the concept of logotherapy (In Chinese). *Bulletin of Educational Psychology*, 20: 87–106.

———. (1990). Ego identity and subculture changes over a five-year period: A case of students from two teachers' universities (In Chinese). *Bulletin of Educational Psychology*, 23: 119–142.

Hong Kong Council of Social Service. (1982). *Estimating the size of the potential clientele of school social work service*. Hong Kong: Hong Kong Council of Social Service.

Hsu, C. C. (1966). A study on "problem children" reported by teachers. *Japanese Journal of Child Psychiatry*, 7: 91–108.

———. (1973). A comparative study of well-adjusted and maladjusted junior high school students. *Journal of the Formosan Medical Association*, 72: 167–183.

Hsu, F.L.K., Watrous, B. G., and Lord, E. M. (1961). Culture pattern and adolescent behavior: A comparison of Hawaii Chinese and Chicago White adolescents. *International Journal of Social Psychiatry*, 7: 33–53.

Hu, S. L. (1994). A study on the mental health level and its influencing factors of senior middle school students (In Chinese). *Acta Psychologica Sinica*, 26 (2): 153–160.

Huang, H. C., Hwang, K. K., and Ko, Y. H. (1983). Life stress, attribution style, social support and depression among university students (In Chinese). *Acta Psychologica Taiwanica*, 25 (1): 31–47.

Huang, S. K. et al. (1990). A preliminary exploration for the factors of some early family environment of schizophrenia (In Chinese). *Chinese Journal of Neurology and Psychiatry*, 23 (4): 198–199.

Huang, X. T., Zhang, J. F., and Zhang, S. L. (1988). Investigation on the structure of Chinese university student's needs (In Chinese). *Information on Psychological Sciences*, 52 (2): 7–12.

Jahoda, M. (1958). *Current concepts of positive mental health*. New York: Basic Books.

Jiang, Z. N. et al. (1986). Changes in the admission rate and episodic features of hysteria in the past 25 years (In Chinese). *Chinese Journal of Neurology and Psychiatry*, 19 (5): 268–271.

Kandel, D., and Davies, M. (1986). Adult sequelae of adolescent symptoms. *Archives of General Psychiatry*, 43: 255–262.

Kaplan, S. L., Hong, G. K., and Weinhold, C. (1984). Epidemiology of depressive symptomatology in adolescents. *Journal of the American Academy of Child Psychiatry*, 23: 91–98.

Khoo, T. P. (Ed.). (1986). *Mental health in Hong Kong*. Hong Kong: Mental Health Association of Hong Kong.

Kleinman, A. (1982). Neurasthenia and depression: A study of somatization and culture in China. *Culture, Medicine and Psychiatry*, 6: 117–190.

Kleinman, A., and Lin, T. Y. (Eds.). (1981). *Normal and abnormal behavior in Chinese culture*. Dordrecht, Netherlands: Reidel.

Kleinman, A., and Mechanic, D. (1979). Some observations of mental illness and its treatment in the People's Republic of China. *Journal of Nervous and Mental Disease*, 167 (5): 267–274.

Ko, Y. H. (1975). Student mental health problems in two different industrialized cities. *Acta Psychologica Taiwanica*, 17: 25–38.

———. (1976). The mental health of junior and senior high school boys. *Acta Psychologica Taiwanica*, 18: 37–52.

———. (1979). The mental health of the overseas Chinese students in the new environment. *Acta Psychologica Taiwanica*, 21: 1–7.

Ko, Y. H., Yang, K. S., Cheng, H. H., and Li, P. H. (1975). The relationship between school environment and college student mental health (In Chinese). *Bulletin of the Institute of Ethnology*, 39: 125–149.

Lau, S. (1990). Crisis and vulnerability in adolescent development. *Journal of Youth and Adolescence*, 19 (2): 111–131.

Law, S. K. (1978). Urban-rural differences in student mental health: The Hong Kong scene. *Australian and New Zealand Journal of Psychiatry*, 12: 277–281.

———. (1979). Common child psychiatric problems in the school setting. *Hong Kong Journal of Mental Health*, 8 (1): 25–27.

Lee, R.P.L. (1985). Social stress and coping behavior in Hong Kong. In W. S. Tseng and D.Y.H. Wu (Eds.), *Chinese culture and mental health* (pp. 193–214). New York: Academic Press.

Leung, P.W.L., Salili, F., and Baber, F. M. (1986). Common adolescent problems in Hong Kong: Their relationship with self-esteem, locus of control, intelligence and family environment. *Psychologia*, 24: 91–100.

Li, X. T. (1985). The effect of family on the mental health of the Chinese people. In W. S. Tseng and D.Y.H. Wu (Eds.), *Chinese culture and mental health* (pp. 85–94). New York: Academic Press.

Lin, K. M., and Kleinman, A. (1981). Recent development of psychiatric epidemiology in China. *Culture, Medicine and Psychiatry*, 5: 135–143.

Lin, K. M., Kleinman, A., and Lin, T. Y. (1981). Overview of mental disorders in Chinese cultures: Review of epidemiological and clinical studies. In A. Kleinman and T. Y. Lin (Eds.), *Normal and abnormal behavior in Chinese culture* (pp. 237–272). Holland: D. Reidel Publishing Company.

Lin, T. Y. (1985). Mental disorders and psychiatry in Chinese culture: Characteristic features and major issues. In W. S. Tseng and D.Y.H. Wu (Eds.), *Chinese culture and mental health* (pp. 367–393). New York: Academic Press.

Liu, J. Q. et al. (1980). An epidemiologic investigation of mental disorders in Xuhui district of Shanghai (In Chinese). *Chinese Journal of Neurology and Psychiatry*, 13 (1): 1–6.

Liu, W. T., Yu, E.S.H., Chang, C. F., and Fernandez, M. (1990). The mental health of Asian American teenagers: A research challenge. In A. R. Stiffman and L. E. Davis (Eds.), *Ethnic issues in adolescent mental health* (pp. 92–112). Beverly Hills, CA: Sage Publications.

Liu, X. H. et al. (1980). An epidemiologic survey of psychoses in Sizhuan province (In Chinese). *Chinese Journal of Neurology and Psychiatry*, 13 (1): 7–9.

Lo, W. H. (1985). Suicide and attempted suicide in Hong Kong — With a note on prevention. *Hong Kong Journal of Mental Health*, 14: 64–72.

Lu, C. M. (1979). Self concept characteristics of Chinese children and adolescents (In Chinese). *Bulletin of Educational Psychology*, 12: 123–132.

———. (1981). A three year follow-up of the self concept of Chinese children and adolescents (In Chinese). *Bulletin of Educational Psychology*, 14: 115–124.

Ma, S. P. (1980). An epidemiologic investigation of psychoses in Laoshan county of Qingdao (In Chinese). *Chinese Journal of Neurology and Psychiatry*, 13 (1): 22–23.

Miao, E. (1976). An exploratory study on college freshmen mental health status. *Acta Psychologica Taiwanica*, 18: 129–147.

———. (1977). A study on college seniors' mental health status: A sub-cultural and cross-cultural approach to anxiety and depression. *Acta Psychologica Taiwanica*, 19: 97–110.

Millar, S. E. (1979). *The biosocial survey in Hong Kong*. Canberra: The Australian National University, Centre for Resource and Environmental Studies.

Mitchell, R. E. (1969). *Levels of emotional strain on Southeast Asian cities* (Vol. 1). Taipei: Orient Cultural Service.

Nanjing Neuropsychiatric Institute. (1980). An epidemiologic mass survey of mental disorders in Nanjing (In Chinese). *Chinese Journal of Neurology and Psychiatry*, 13 (1): 13–14.

Offer, D., and Offer, J. (1975). *From teenage to young manhood: A psychological study*. New York: Basic Books.

Offer, D., and Sabshin, M. (1974). *Normality: Theoretical and clinical concepts of mental health*. New York: Basic Books.

Offer, D., Ostrov, E., Howard, K. I., and Atkinson, R. (1988). *The teenage world: Adolescents' self-image in ten countries.* New York: Plenum Medical Book Company.

Offer, D., and Schonert-Reichl, K. A. (1992). Debunking the myths of adolescence: Findings from recent research. *Journal of the American Academy of Child and Adolescent Psychiatry,* 31 (6): 1003–1014.

One-third of young people in Shanghai were mentally unsound. (In Chinese). (1991, July). *Oriental Daily,* p. 8.

Ou, L. H. et al. (1986). Epidemiological survey of affective psychosis in Jieyang county, Guangdong province (In Chinese). *Chinese Journal of Neurology and Psychiatry,* 19 (2): 99–102.

Paton, S. M., and Kandel, G. (1978). Psychological factors and adolescent drug use: Ethnicity and sex differences. *Adolescence,* 13: 187–200.

Petersen, A. C. (1988). Adolescent development. *Annual Review of Psychology,* 39: 583–607.

Powers, S. I., Hauser, S. T., and Kilner, L. A. (1989). Adolescent mental health. *American Psychologist,* 44 (2): 200–208.

Pritchard, C. (1993). A comparison of youth suicide in Hong Kong, the developed world and the People's Republic of China 1973–1988: Grounds for optimism or concern ? *Hong Kong Journal of Mental Health,* 22: 6–16.

The Research Team on Youth Development. (1989). *A report on the mental health and family systems among secondary school students in Hong Kong* (In Chinese). Hong Kong: Hong Kong Baptist College, Department of Social Work.

Rin, H., Cheng, L. T., and Chen, T. (1974). Some trends found among suicides reported on a newspaper (In Chinese). *Acta Psychologica Taiwanica,* 16: 7–24.

Rin, H., Chu, H. M., and Lin, T. Y. (1966). Psychophysiological reactions of a rural and suburban population in Taiwan. *Acta Psychiatrica Scandinavica,* 42: 410–473.

Rutter, M., Graham, P., Chadwick, O.F.D., and Yule, W. (1976). Adolescent turmoil: Fact or fiction? *Journal of Child Psychology and Psychiatry,* 17: 35–56.

Schechter, M. D., and Wright, D. M. (1977). Adolescence: Psychopathology. In B. B. Wolman (Ed.), *International encyclopedia of psychiatry, psychology, psychoanalysis and neurology* (pp. 250–254). New York: Van Nostrand Reinhold.

Shandong Province Mental Hospital et al. (1984). A psychiatric epidemiologic survey on the Chang Shan Islands (In Chinese). *Chinese Journal of Neurology and Psychiatry,* 17 (1): 48–52.

Shek, D.T.L. (1986). The purpose in life questionnaire in a Chinese context: Some psychometric and normative data. *Chinese Journal of Psychology,* 28 (1): 51–60.

————. (1988). Mental health of secondary school students in Hong Kong: An epidemiological study using the General Health Questionnaire. *International Journal of Adolescent Medicine and Health*, 3 (3): 191–215.

————. (1989a). Prevalence and correlates of psychological morbidity in secondary school students in Hong Kong: An epidemiological study using the General Health Questionnaire. In A.M.C. Ng and F.M.C. Cheung (Eds.), *Selected papers on youth studies in Hong Kong 1984–87* (pp. 98–126). Hong Kong: The Chinese University of Hong Kong, Centre for Hong Kong Studies.

————. (1989b). Sex differences in the psychological well-being of Chinese adolescents. *Journal of Psychology*, 123 (4): 405–412.

————. (1989c). Perception of parental treatment styles and psychological well-being in a sample of Chinese secondary school students. *Journal of Genetic Psychology*, 150 (4): 403–415.

————. (1990a). Depressive symptoms in Chinese adolescents: A study of the impact of parental treatment styles, mental health attributes and chronic anxiety. In *Proceedings of the 1989 International Conference on Youth* (pp. 65–74). Hong Kong: Hong Kong Council of Social Service.

————. (1990b). Mental health knowledge of Chinese secondary school students in Hong Kong. *Education Journal*, 18 (2): 143–152.

————. (1991a). Depressive symptoms in a sample of Chinese adolescents: An empirical study using the Chinese version of the Beck Depression Inventory. *International Journal of Adolescent Medicine and Health*, 5 (1): 1–16.

————. (1991b). *The Chinese version of the State-Trait Anxiety Inventory: Some normative data*. Unpublished manuscript.

————. (1992a). Actual-ideal discrepancies in the representation of self and significant-others and psychological well-being of Chinese adolescents. *International Journal of Psychology*, 27 (3): 229.

————. (1992b). Meaning in life and psychological well-being: An empirical study using the Chinese version of the Purpose in Life Questionnaire. *Journal of Genetic Psychology*, 153 (2): 185–200.

————. (1993a). The Chinese Purpose in Life Test and psychological well-being in Chinese college students. *International Forum for Logotherapy*, 16: 1–10.

————. (1993b, August). *Adolescent suicide in Hong Kong*. Paper presented at the 1993 World Congress of the World Federation for Mental Health, Tokyo, Japan.

————. (1993c). Measurement of pessimism in Chinese adolescents: The Chinese Hopelessness Scale. *Social Behavior and Personality*, 21 (2): 107–120.

————. (1993d). Perception of parental treatment styles and psychological well-being of Chinese college students. *Psychologia*, 36: 159–166.

————. (1994). Somatic symptoms in Chinese secondary school students in Hong Kong: Observations and service implications. *Therapeutic Care and Education*, 3 (1): 27–38.

————. (1995). Adolescent suicide in Hong Kong (1980–1991). *International Journal of Adolescent Medicine and Health*, 8(1), 65–86.

Shek, D.T.L., Hong, W., and Cheung, M.Y.P. (1987). The Purpose in Life Questionnaire in a Chinese context. *Journal of Psychology*, 12 (1): 77–83.

Shek, D.T.L., and Mak, J.W.K. (1987). *Psychological well-being of working parents in Hong Kong: Mental health, stress and coping responses*. Hong Kong: Hong Kong Christian Service.

————. (1992). The mental health of secondary school students in Hong Kong: An epidemiological study using the Chinese Somatic Scale. *Research in Education*, 48: 12–25.

Shen, Y. C., Wang, Y. F., and Yang, X. L. (1985). An epidemiological investigation of minimal brain dysfunction in six elementary schools in Beijing. *Journal of Child Psychology and Psychiatry*, 26 (5): 777–787.

Simons, R. L., and Miller, M. G. (1987). The role of negative cognitions and socio-environmental stress in the etiology of adolescent depression. *Social Work*, 32: 326–330.

Singer, K. (1985). Psychiatric morbidity in university students in Hong Kong: Prevalence, sociocultural and clinical aspects. *Journal of Hong Kong Medical Association*, 37: 117–120.

Spielberger, C. D., Gorsuch, R. C., and Lushene, R. F. (1970). *Manual for the State-Trait Anxiety Inventory*. Palo Alto, CA: Consulting Psychologists Press.

The Teaching and Research Group of Psychiatry of Beijing Medical College et al. (1980). An investigation of psychiatric disorders in Haidian district of Beijing (In Chinese). *Chinese Journal of Neurology and Psychiatry*, 13 (1): 10–12.

Teri, L. (1982). The use of the Beck Depression Inventory with adolescents. *Journal of Abnormal Child Psychology*, 10 (2): 277–284.

Tseng, W. S., Tao, K. T., Jing, H., Chiu, J. H., Yu, L., and Velma, K. (1988). Family planning and child mental health in China: The Nanjing survey. *American Journal of Psychiatry*, 145: 1396–1403.

Turner, S. M., and Mo, L. L. (1984). Chinese adolescents' self-concept as measured by the Offer Self-Image Questionnaire. *Journal of Youth and Adolescence*, 13 (2): 131–143.

Wei, X. B. et al. (1993). The study on neurasthenia in students at university (In Chinese). *Chinese Journal of Nervous and Mental Diseases*, 19 (2): 80–82.

World Health Organization. (1991). *World health statistics*. Geneva: World Health Organization.

Xiang, M. Z. et al. (1986). An epidemiological investigation of neurosis in 12 districts of China (In Chinese). *Chinese Journal of Neurology and Psychiatry*, 19 (2): 87–91.

Yang, D. et al. (1980). An investigation of psychoses in Hunan province (In Chinese). *Chinese Journal of Neurology and Psychiatry*, 13 (1): 15–18.

Yang, H. L. (1980). The mental health of junior high school students in the urban, county and city areas (In Chinese). *Acta Psychologica Taiwanica*, 21: 35–39.

Yang, K. S. (1986). Effects of family factors on child behavior: A review of empirical studies in Taiwan (In Chinese). *Acta Psychologica Taiwanica*, 28 (1): 7–28.

Yang, K. S., and Yang, P. H. (1974). Relationship of repression-sensitization to self-evaluation, neuroticism, and extraversion among Chinese senior high-school boys. *Acta Psychologica Taiwanica*, 16: 111–118.

Yeh, E. K. (1985). Sociocultural changes and prevalence of mental disorders in Taiwan. In W. S. Tseng and D.Y.H. Wu (Eds.), *Chinese culture and mental health* (pp. 265–286). New York: Academic Press.

Yeh, E. K., Chu, H. M., Ko, Y. H., Lin, T. Y., and Lee, S. P. (1972). Student mental health: An epidemiological study in Taiwan. *Acta Psychologica Taiwanica*, 14: 1–25.

Yeh, E. K., Ko, Y. H., and Hwang, K. K. (1981). Life stress and mental health (In Chinese). *Bulletin of the Institute of Ethnology*, 52: 173–210.

Yie, R. M., and Rocklin, T. (1988). Cross-cultural research on anxiety testing (In Chinese). *Information on Psychological Sciences*, 53: 25–29.

Young Women's Christian Association. (1984). *A survey of the emotions of young people in Ngau Tau Kok* (In Chinese). Hong Kong: Young Women's Christian Association.

Yu, L. (1985). An epidemiologic study of child's mental health problems in Nanjing district. In W. S. Tseng and D.Y.H. Wu (Eds.), (1985). *Chinese culture and mental health* (pp. 305–314). New York: Academic Press.

Zhang, Y. X., and Dong, L. (1990). Can the distinctiveness theory explain the spontaneous self-concept of Chinese students? (In Chinese). *Information on Psychological Sciences*, 65: 10–16.

Zhang, Y. X., and Fang, X. (1990). The adaptability of coping strategies and psychological symptoms. *Acta Psychologica Sinica*, 22 (2): 217–223.

Zhang, Y. X., and Wang, Y. (1989). Attribution style and depression. (In Chinese). *Acta Psychologica Sinica*, 21 (2): 141–148.

Zhao, K. Y. et al. (1986). Analysis of 1,500 cases of psycho-counselling psychology in a general hospital (In Chinese). *Chinese Journal of Neurology and Psychiatry*, 19 (6): 325–328.

Zhao, Y. H. et al. (1986a). The analysis of epidemiological data of psychosis other than schizophrenia (In Chinese). *Chinese Journal of Neurology and Psychiatry*, 19 (2): 77–79.

———. (1986b). An epidemiological investigation of affective psychosis (In Chinese). *Chinese Journal of Neurology and Psychiatry*, 19 (2): 97–98.

9

Attention Deficit-Hyperactivity Disorder in Chinese Children*

Jin-pang Leung

Introduction

Children who consistently exhibit inattention, overactivity, and impulsivity are often known as hyperactive. A host of terms have been used more-or-less interchangeably for labeling such symptoms, including hyper-kinesis, hyperkinetic impulse disorder, hyperkinetic syndrome, and brain damage syndrome (Ayllon and Milan, 1983). Although researchers from Mainland China (e.g., Zhang and Huang, 1990) often refer to this disorder as minimal brain dysfunction (MBD), in this chapter the term Attention Deficit-Hyperactivity Disorder (ADHD) has been adopted for general reference for reasons to be explained later. Other synonymous terms will be introduced wherever required in the context of discussion.

ADHD as a common childhood disorder has raised concern from parents and teachers for an obvious reason: the symptoms hinder the normal functioning of affected children in both social and academic milieus. The high energy output and short attention span on any task invariably annoy adults as well as peers while simultaneously causing learning problems in school. Systematic description of this disorder can be found in western medical literature as early as the middle 1800s (see Ross and Ross, 1982). One of the first attempts to conceptualize childhood hyperactivity was presented by George Still (1902) in a series of published lectures delivered to the Royal College of Physicians in England. However, this topic did not

* Preparation of this chapter has been supported by an earmarked research project grant (CUHK 7/91) awarded by the Hong Kong University and Polytechnics Grants Committee. The author would like to thank Dr. John Sachs for his assistance in proofreading the first draft of this chapter.

attract too much attention from health professionals until after the Second World War. Widespread interest did not emerge until the late 1960s (see Levy, 1966), and hyperactivity is now a common and highly studied phenomenon in western societies (e.g., O'Leary, Vivian, and Nisi, 1985; Ross and Ross, 1982; Taylor and Sandberg, 1984).

There are many literature reviews (e.g., Barkley, 1987, 1989; Douglas, 1983; Rutter, 1977; Whalen, 1989; Zentall and Zentall, 1983) which have been conducted by British and North American scholars on the various aspects of hyperactivity observed with Caucasian children. These reviews have been useful in clarifying important issues, promoting understanding of the disorder, and earmarking progress achieved in the field. In addition, such information forms the basis of remedial measures in rehabilitation work for affected children. Unfortunately, a comparable documentation of ADHD research on Chinese children has not been done. The present chapter is an initial attempt to examine the literature related to hyperactivity in Chinese children.

The existence of the hyperactivity syndrome among Chinese children has been reported in a number of articles (e.g., Salili and Hoosain, 1985; Shen, Wang, and Yang, 1985; Wang, Chong, Chou, and Yang, 1993; X. L. Yang, 1985), but there are issues of both academic and practical interest that are yet to be explored. One prominent issue to be addressed is the validity of the concept of hyperactivity in the context of Chinese culture. If the answer is positive, then do cross-cultural differences exist? In other words, do Chinese children behave in the same way as Caucasian children? There are also questions concerning the similarities and differences between Chinese hyperactives and their western counterparts in terms of causes/etiologies and treatment of this disorder. At a general level, clinical researchers are more concerned with the universality of childhood hyperactivity (Henker and Whalen, 1989; Ho, 1980). Is this a universal or a cultural phenomenon? In layman's terms, does hyperactivity vary in the eyes of the beholder? The answer to this question carries important theoretical and practical implications for the study of psychopathology in general, and of hyperactivity in particular. For if hyperactivity is culture-specific, then it provides support for the notion that the conceptualization, identification, and intervention of psychopathology are ultimately rooted in the belief systems of the given culture. That is to say, the study of abnormal behavior makes better sense within the culture concerned and the findings from one culture may not be directly transferable to another culture.

It is difficult, if not impossible, to resolve all the above questions at this stage given the dearth of research on Chinese children. The present chapter can only be regarded as an initial effort to throw some light on a number of important issues and to delineate the range of research being done on the subject. These goals are achieved by reviewing studies on childhood hyperactive disorders conducted in major Chinese societies including China, Taiwan, and Hong Kong. Literatures relevant to the etiology, prevalence, assessment, and treatment of ethnic Chinese children with hyperactivity are searched; available findings are analysed. Points of interest and concern are raised. Observations regarding research procedures, methodologies, limitations, and contributions of the Chinese studies are also discussed. Finally, directions and possibilities for future research are discussed.

During the process of conducting the present review, a number of difficulties have been encountered. One major problem emerged during the process of locating research articles and reports written by authors from Mainland China. The bulk of relevant studies are published in local periodicals instead of international ones and are invariably written in Mandarin Chinese. For these reasons and others, the Chinese literature is less accessible to scholars outside China. Hence, it is quite possible that I have unknowingly missed relevant information and data on the topic. To provide as complete a representation as possible, I have also included reports published in international journals by Chinese and/or non-Chinese authors.

Readers should also note that available empirical research studies are mainly conducted with children living in China, Taiwan, and Hong Kong, though studies involving Taiwanese children are relatively scarce. In addition, very little relevant data have been collected on Chinese children outside these three major Chinese societies (e.g., Yao, Solanto, and Wender, 1988). For example, there are no identifiable records on Singaporean children suffering from ADHD.

Hyperactivity among Chinese Children

The noxious symptoms and widespread nature of ADHD has continued to perplex and intrigue health professionals and education workers. In the 1960s, the hyperactivity phenomenon increasingly captured the attention of North American and European child-health experts. Since then, numerous investigations on the disorder have been conducted (Whalen, 1989). Current indications show that western countries continue to invest more resources into this area resulting in many research projects with hyperactive children being planned and implemented. In contrast, comparable research efforts with children of Chinese descent are lacking. Fortunately, some Chinese societies under direct western influence, such as Hong Kong and Taiwan, have already begun developing their data bases on childhood hyperactivity disorder. In Mainland China, however, hyperactivity is a relatively new concept due to a long period of self-imposed isolation from outside influences.

Since the inauguration of the People's Republic in October 1949, Chinese leaders considered accepting foreign assistance a disgrace for the country. As they believed, the communist ideology and the hard working nature of the Chinese people would bring technological, economical, social, and cultural independence to China without foreign aid. This closed-door policy based on the "self-sufficient" philosophy effectively prohibited scientific exchanges between Chinese scholars and their Western counterparts. The isolation continued until recently when the Chinese government realized the importance of international contact in the country's drive for modernization. Since 1978, China has gradually opened up her door to foreign investments and technological know-how. At the same time, social and cultural exchanges have been slowly re-established. One direct consequence of the "open-door policy" is the re-exposure of Chinese clinicians to contemporary research findings on childhood psychopathology. Among the variety of disorders, hyperactivity has captured the attention of many people, including health professionals, teachers, parents and others (X. L. Yang, 1985).

Heightened Awareness of ADHD in China

Records of mental illness in the classic Chinese scripts and writings are scarce (Cheung, 1986) let alone writings on childhood hyperactivity. As Lin (1985) observed, the commonly held view by Chinese parents is that children suffer little from poor mental health. Traditionally, deviant behaviors such as overactivity were considered conduct problems or naughtiness (*wan pi*) due to lack of control on the part of the child. Misbehaviors from younger children were usually tolerated but wrongdoing by school-aged children would be sanctioned by verbal and physical punishment (Ho, 1986). These beliefs have been challenged in recent years. Hyperactivity disorder began to arouse great concern in China in the early 1980s (Shen et al., 1985; Tao, 1992; X. L. Yang, 1985). Suddenly, there was a surge of attention on ADHD and the scale of public interest was unprecedented. By observation, there are at least two reasons for this abrupt change of attitude toward hyperactivity.

Influence of Western Child Psychopathological Concepts

The influx of western ideas constitutes one of the major factors. The open-door policy implemented since the downfall of the "Gang of Four" has allowed the importation of western perspectives into China more freely than before. Chinese psychologists and clinicians thus gained access to western research findings on psychopathological disorders. Since then they have become aware of the possibility of ADHD in children and the behavioral symptoms associated with the disorder. Fascinated by the concept of hyperactivity, Chinese child care workers have begun to observe children more closely for symptoms similar to those described in the western literature. Large scale surveys have been conducted for assessing the prevalence of the disorder among Chinese children (e.g., Shen et al., 1985; X. L. Yang, 1985). Most importantly, Chinese researchers have begun to publicize their findings in national magazines and newspapers. Some enthusiastic educationists even include information on ADHD in mental health education programs. The effect on the general public is dramatic. An incident described by Xu (1985) serves to demonstrate the reaction of the people. As observed in Shanghai, the phenomenon of hyperactivity was introduced in one issue of the popular scientific magazine *Science Pictorial* (*Kexue huabao*) and the content immediately aroused great interest and concern among school teachers. They asked parents to send children with behavioral problems for psychiatric assessment. Parents also became really worried and observed their children very closely for any sign of hyperactivity. Before too long, health clinics were flooded with suspected cases and the number of hyperactive children diagnosed increased sharply within a few months!

Traditional Value Placed on Education

Parental concern about academic achievement in children has been the major thrust behind the heightened interest in hyperactivity among Mainland Chinese (X. L. Yang, 1985). Traditional cultural heritage puts much emphasis on education and academic achievement (Ho, 1986). Chinese parents try very hard to provide educational opportunities for their children (especially sons) because education has always been considered the best way of achieving success in future careers. Most parents wish that their children will out-race their peers in school and subsequently gain university entrance. The high demand for, but very limited supply of, university places in China has created hot competition among schools and children alike. Outstanding academic results in public examinations have become the prerequisite for higher education admission. Understandably, parents became highly concerned over ADHD the first time they heard about the possible adverse effects of this disorder on the academic performance of younger children. Symptoms of hyperactivity in their children were being anxiously sought (Xu, 1985). Some even hastily attributed their children's unsatisfactory school performance to the affliction of ADHD. In modern China, the implementation of the "one-child family" policy (for population control) has generated more parental anxiety on academic achievement of children than ever before (Tao and Chiu, 1985). Unlike the old days when a family could have many children, single-child Chinese parents nowadays can only hope that their child demonstrates academic excellence and thus gains respect for the family.

Common Diagnostic Systems and Labels

Since a Chinese system of childhood psychopathology has not been clearly established thus far, hyperactivity research with Chinese children relies heavily on findings from their western counterparts. To provide a framework against which the Chinese studies can be meaningfully discussed, the diagnostic systems for hyperactive disorder adopted by western researchers are presented next.

Western researchers have been working on hyperactivity for a long time but they have yet to arrive at an agreement as to the exact nature of this dysfunction (Whalen, 1989). Hence, many terms have been adopted for labeling children suffering from this behavioral disorder. Nomenclature has changed according to the theoretical emphasis researchers have adopted for interpreting the nature of hyperactivity. Strauss and Lehtinen (1947) postulated the existence of a relationship between children's hyperactivity and brain damage. It was hypothesized that restlessness and inattention could be caused by minor brain injury during perinatal and postnatal traumas. Hence the term "Minimal Brain Damage" and later "Minimal Brain Dysfunction" (Wender, 1971) was coined accordingly. Since many children exhibiting inattention, overactivity, and impulsivity had experienced no obvious assault to their brains or nervous systems, MBD has gradually lost its popularity among child mental health workers.

In 1980 when the American Psychiatric Association (APA) published the third edition of *Diagnostic and Statistical Manual of Mental Disorders* (DSM-III), the term "hyperactivity" was divided into two separate categories, namely, Attention Deficit Disorder "with Hyperactivity" and "without Hyperactivity". In a later revision (DSM-III-R) published in 1987, the label was amended to "Attention Deficit-Hyperactivity Disorder" (ADHD). The changing label reflects a growing concern among American clinicians on the attentional, activity, and impulsivity problems of these children labelled hyperactive. They argue that the attentional problem of these children tends to persist even up to adulthood while the overactivity generally disappears in adolescence. So in the long run, attention deficit is probably the more basic symptom affecting the overall development of a child (see Barkley, 1989). (Interestingly, in the most updated 4th version of the DSM [APA, 1994], ADHD is divided up into three subtypes once again.)

According to the tenth edition of *International Classification of Disease* (ICD-10) published by the World Health Organization in 1990, the condition is referred to as "Hyperkinetic Syndrome of Childhood". However, the ICD-10 diagnostic criteria differs somewhat from the DSM-III. The most notable difference is that the American system tends to define ADHD as a broader concept while the ICD system requires "pervasiveness of hyperactivity" to be an important criterion (Luk, 1986; Luk, Leung, and Yuen, 1991c; Rutter, 1989). Hence a child is more likely to be labelled hyperactive when a clinician adopts the DSM rather than the ICD for diagnostic purposes. Although each system has its inherent advantages and disadvantages, the APA diagnostic system is influential and widely accepted among psychologists and health professionals. For this reason and others, the term ADHD as suggested by DSM-III-R (APA, 1987) has been adopted here for referring to the group of symptoms related to hyperactivity and attention. However, terms used by other authors will not be excluded and are treated as synonyms.

In the following sections, the etiology, prevalence, assessment, and treatment of ethnic Chinese children with hyperactivity will be examined. For comparison purposes, western findings will be introduced wherever appropriate.

Etiologies

The list of causes proposed for ADHD are numerous, and some of them will be examined here because of their relevance to Chinese research. Generally speaking, the causes of the disorder have been attributed to two groups of factors, namely, biological and environmental.

Biological Factors

Research generally cannot establish a logical connection between hyperactive symptoms and brain damage (Rutter, 1982) and even neurological research has found little sign of cortical injury in these children. However, investigations conducted in Mainland China have established evidence for brain damage as a cause of childhood hyperactivity. For example, Li, Zhu, Su, Zheng, Hua, Li, and Li (1985) found that among the hyperactive children from Changsha and Liuzhou, 19.7% had suffered from perinatal brain injuries while 76.6% had a history of possible infancy brain injury due to diseases, intoxication, and accidents. Yang, Pan, Gu, Hu, Li, Zhang, and Su (1987) observed some neurological soft signs of brain dysfunction in 68.8% of those affected children in Chengdou. It was concluded that ADHD could be related to the delayed development of the central nervous system. A study conducted in Taiwan (Soong, 1984) also found evidence of early brain assaults in attention-deficit children. As compared to the 18% of the normal control, 66% of the identified children had one or more perinatal risk factors. In addition, a greater proportion of the affected group had neurological soft signs and other disabilities including short attention, mirror writing, motor incoordination, poor memory, poor number concept, and speech delay during early stages of development. Hence at least part of the evidence is in line with the notion of neurological dysfunction in hyperactivity (e.g., Hertzig, Bortner, and Birch, 1969; Wender, 1971).

However, there are also studies with Chinese children (Wang, 1981; Xu, 1985; X. L. Yang, 1985) which have not found evidence of brain damage. For example, from a large scale survey (Wang, 1981) involving 11 primary schools in Guangzhou, Guangdong province, only a small proportion of the 85 identified ADHD children had birth complications (11.8%) and infantile disease (20.0%) which could have led to neurological assaults. Based on these cases, there was no obvious evidence of brain damage nor structural injury of the central nervous system. As Li et al. (1985) cautioned, infantile illnesses and accidents might not affect the nervous system of children, although certain diseases (e.g., meningitis) tend to infect neurological structures.

Hence, investigations conducted with Chinese children have been equivocal on the issue of brain dysfunction as a cause of ADHD. Such discrepancies among Chinese studies cannot be easily explained. These surveys were based largely on parent and teacher interviews which relied on retrospective recalls. The reliability of information would be low when parents had to remember past events way back in their children's infancy and even perinatal periods. However, even the unreliability of the informants cannot explain the vast differences reported. Luk et al. (1991c) conducted clinical observations in addition to traditional assessments on 61 Hong Kong children diagnosed as ADHD according to the DSM-III-R and as hyperkinetic syndrome according to the ICD-9. Data show that the association between neurocognitive impairment and hyperactivity is very strong when clinicians narrowly define this disorder. Hence the inconsistency could have resulted from the variety of diagnostic systems and the level of stringency adopted by the researchers.

Another hypothesized biological factor causing ADHD is a genetic one. This has attracted increasing attention from researchers dealing with childhood hyperactivity of Chinese children. Similar to findings based on western cohorts (Biederman, Munir, Knee, Armentano, Autor, Waternaux, and Tsuang, 1987; Cantwell, 1977; Deutsch, Swanson, and Bruell, 1982; Morrison and Stewart, 1973; O'Connor, Foch, Sherry, and Plomin, 1980; Willerman, 1973), Chinese children born into families with alcoholism, psychopathy, and hyperactivity are more likely to be affected (Li et al., 1985; Yang et al., 1987). Among the 184 cases reported by Li et al. (1985), some parents had either been labeled "naughty" (36.4%) or attention deficit (27.1%) when young, while other children had siblings suffering from the same disorder (29.1%). A substantial proportion (40.5%) had relatives with psychopathologies.

Additional data has demonstrated the importance of biological factors in ADHD. Shen and Wang (1984) found MHPG excretion in the urine of ADHD children to be significantly different from that in controls. These results suggest that there may well be a genetic predisposition to the disorder which leads to the excessive excretion of certain types of chemicals in these children.

In sum, the notion that biological and hereditary factors determine the formation of hyperactivity among Chinese children has remained a plausible hypothesis. Since people from different ethnic groups are genetically dissimilar, differences in ADHD prevalence rates can be attributed to hereditary influences if other confounding factors are controlled. Thus cross-national data will be useful for unravelling the secret of heredity in the formation of ADHD. Although there are a lot of data available from

Caucasian children (Whalen, 1989), information gathered from Chinese children is meagre and scattered. Consequently, a meaningful comparison, at this stage, between ADHD Chinese children and their western counterparts is not possible. To unravel the effect of genetic factors, cross-national comparisons are indispensable. Hence much more systematic, empirical research is needed in this area.

Environmental Factors

Efforts have been made by western researchers (Block, 1977; Willis and Lovaas, 1977) to establish the external causes of ADHD. Environmental factors are particularly relevant to a cross-cultural perspective of psychopathology as the Chinese socialization pattern creates a family milieu very different from those found in the West and other oriental cultures (Cheung, 1986; Ho, 1980, 1986). In the present context, the environment of a child is construed as having physical as well as psychosocial components.

In China, the degree of urbanization appears to be connected with the identification of ADHD. Generally speaking, children from cities are less likely to be diagnosed as suffering from attention deficit and hyperactivity than those from suburban areas and rural areas. For example, Shen et al. (1985) reported 3.1%, 7.8%, and 7.0% of MBD children from urban schools, suburban schools and schools in mountain areas respectively. X. L. Yang (1985) also observed a similar geographic distribution of MBD affected children in urban (4.1%), suburban (7.3%), and rural mountain (7.3%) areas. The reported rates are highly compatible between the two studies probably due to the fact that both surveys were conducted in Beijing, the capital city of China. The urbanization factor reflects socioeconomic differences and the availability of educational facilities in favor of urban over rural areas.

Research conducted in China also provides much evidence for the importance of family and school in affecting the occurrence of ADHD. In one study reported by Wang (1981), parental over-control, lack of control, and over-indulgence were found in about 72% of the ADHD children! The disorder is also found to be correlated negatively with other variables such as social economic status and educational level of parents (Li et al., 1985; Yang et al., 1987; X. L. Yang, 1985). For example, in a Beijing study, X. L. Yang (1985) found that the higher the level of the father's education, the less likely was his child to be diagnosed as MBD. For fathers whose education reached college level, high school, or primary school/no formal education, the rates of their children diagnosed as MBD were 3.6%, 8.3%, and 10.9% respectively. Not unrelated to the education level is the occupation of parents in association with ADHD children. Also in Beijing, Shen et al. (1985) found that hyperactivity affected children were more likely to come from worker and peasant parents and less likely to come from professional (scientific and technical) or administrative personnel parents.

However, counter evidence can be found in a mental health survey carried out in Nanjing by Tseng, Tao, Jing, Chiu, Yu, and Kameoka (1988). Part of their study compared behavior patterns between only children and children with siblings. If family environment is related to behavioral disorder such as hyperactivity, then differences should be identified between the two groups. It was found that only children were not having more behavioral difficulties than their multi-sibling counterparts. In conclusion, Tseng et al. (1988) do not agree with speculations that "the one-child-per-couple policy in China may result in problematic behavior among only children" (p. 1403).

In a more systematic investigation by Zhang, Song, and Cui (1986), a group of 200 ADHD children were compared with normal children in a series of psychological tests. The results show that family influence constitutes one important factor in the occurrence and development of problems in a child and that parental attitude toward a hyperactive child and the kind of home education have a close bearing on the development of cognitive and social skills.

Since the likelihood of ADHD diagnosis relates to the socio-economic status of the family and the education level of parents, people tend to ascribe a causal relationship between the etiology of ADHD and these factors. However, given the biological evidence delineated earlier, a complete environmental explanation of hyperactivity is premature.

Prevalence

Data on prevalence rates mainly come from epidemiological studies and there are two major accessible sources. The first consists of large-scale surveys on mental health or behavior problems of a general nature, usually conducted at the national or provincial level (Chuang and Cheng, 1987; Ekblad, 1990; Leung, Luk, and Lee, 1989; Liu, 1988; Luk, Lee, and Yu, 1986; Tseng et al. 1988; Wang, Shen, Gu, Jia, and Zhang, 1989; Xu, 1985; K. S. Yang, 1981). Results obtained from this kind of study are less informative and of a relatively low reliability. Diagnoses were often based on global measures which tended to encompass more than one disorder or overlapped with other disorders. Hence prevalence rates estimated from such surveys were easily under- or over-estimated. Furthermore, these studies provide relatively little information pertinent to the characteristics, distribution, and identification of ADHD. However, given the dearth of research conducted on hyperactivity in Chinese children, these survey reports inevitably become an important source of information.

For the purpose of the present review, more emphasis has been put on a second source of information which consists of epidemiological studies specifically designed to gain data on ADHD (e.g., Guizhou Mental Hospital, 1981; Jin, 1982; Li et al., 1985; Luk, Leung, Bacon-Shone, Chung, Lee, Chen, Ng, Lieh-Mak, Ko, Wong, and Yeung 1991a; Salili and Hoosain, 1985; Shanghai Mental Hospital, 1981; Shen et al., 1985; Wang, 1981; Wang, Yang, and Shen, 1983; Yan, Chu, Sing, Tang, Fong, and Li, 1981; X. L. Yang, 1985; Yang et al., 1987). It is worth noting that the majority of these studies were conducted in Mainland China. Epidemiological investigations on children are relatively scarce in other more westernized Chinese societies such as Hong Kong, Taiwan, and Singapore. These areas outside China tend to focus more on other aspects of ADHD research, such as assessment and standardization of instruments, which will be covered in a later section.

General Prevalence Rate

When figures and numbers are compared, prevalence rates reported by different studies vary greatly. According to some reports (Guizhou Mental Hospital, 1981; Jin, 1982; Shanghai Mental Hospital, 1981; Wang, 1981; Wang et al., 1993), about 1.9 to 13.0% of children have been identified as MBD in various districts of China. In terms of variation, the range is somewhat narrower than that observed with non-Chinese children. Estimates made in the U.S. show between 1% and 20% of the school-age population are hyperactive depending on the rigor or strictness of the criteria used to define the disorder (Cantwell, 1977; Eisenberg, 1973; Ross and Ross, 1982; Safer and Allen, 1976; Wender, 1971; Whalen and Henker, 1976) and the degree of agreement required among different raters (Lambert, Sandoval, and Sassone, 1978). However, despite claims of comparability (e.g., Salili and Hoosain, 1985; Wang et al., 1993; X. L. Yang,

1985), prevalence rates in Chinese societies are generally lower than those observed in western ones. One of the extreme examples (Wang, 1981) comes from a study in Guangzhou, the capital city of a southern province known as Guangdong. Guangzhou is one of the most densely populated cities in China and there are frequent trade and cultural exchanges between Guangzhou and Hong Kong. Given the influences from highly westernized Hong Kong, researchers were only able to find a very low occurrence of ADHD averaging 1.53%, with 1.34% among high school students and 1.90% among primary school pupils. Although the rate observed in Beijing was higher, Shen et al. (1985) diagnosed only 5.8% of the children surveyed in six elementary schools in Beijing as MBD. Generally speaking, these rates tend to be lower than those reported by western researchers. This discrepancy in prevalence rates between Chinese and Caucasians may reflect differences on the perception of hyperactivity.

Sex Ratio

As a rule, more boys than girls are diagnosed as ADHD or MBD independent of the criteria adopted or the screening instrument used (Barkley, 1989). Even changes in diagnostic labels and shifts in symptomatic emphasis during the past few decades would not alter this differential sex distribution. Western studies have found the proportion of males versus females to be from 2:1 to 10:1 (APA, 1980; Ross and Ross, 1982; Wender, 1987). Although a recent study in Taiwan reported only a 3.3:1 ratio, many more boys than girls are diagnosed within Chinese societies with the ratios varying from 5:1 (Li et al., 1985; Yan et al., 1981) to 9:1 (Wang, 1981). Even with newly immigrated Chinese-American children (grades 1 to 6), the boy:girl ratio was 5.1:1 (Yao et al., 1988). Interestingly, a study by Salili and Hoosain (1985) found 8.9% of hyperactive boys but no hyperactive girls in a Hong Kong sample if the U.S. cutoff criterion of two standard deviations above the mean was used. This drastic sexual difference cannot be easily explained. The authors suggested that sex role differences are much more exaggerated in a Chinese society such as Hong Kong. Girls are trained to be quiet, obedient, attentive, and reserved from an early age and they are expected to display these behaviors. As data were based on teachers' observations, Hong Kong girls would have a smaller chance to score high on the ratings if they managed to play the sex role well in the school setting.

Age Differences

The prevalence rate by age is another variable usually reported in epidemiological studies. In western samples, the number of ADHD children usually increases from five years old, peaks at around 8 years old, and declines thereafter (APA, 1980; O'Malley and Eisenberg, 1973; Safer and Allen, 1976; Werry and Quay, 1968). Hence an inverted-U or -V shaped curve will be formed when the prevalence is plotted against age. However, some countries like West Germany and New Zealand showed a different age pattern in that steady declines were observed with increasing age (see Salili and Hoosain, 1985). Among Chinese children, the distribution of hyperactivity symptoms is more or less an inverted-U, but the peak age depends on where the sample was selected. In the southern province of Guangdong (Wang, 1981), for example, ADHD occurs most frequently in children of relatively young age (5–6 years old). Hong Kong is a highly westernized city at the edge of Guangdong province but the highest rate of ADHD has been observed in older children, 9–10 years for boys and 7–8 years for girls (Salili and Hoosain, 1985). Compatible with this pattern is the ratio reported by Shen et al. (1985) from a Beijing sample. In sum, the peak age of prevalence varies over a large range and extends from early childhood through to middle-late childhood.

Based on these epidemiological studies on Chinese children, it can be shown that the manifestation and/or perception of attention problems and hyperactivity could be determined by a number of factors. Apart from the afore-illustrated age and sex variables, the prevalence of ADHD also depended on the degree of urbanization, parental education level and social economic status (Shen et al., 1985; X. L. Yang, 1985). These factors and others appeared to play important roles in the positive identification of ADHD.

Assessment

There are basically three major types of instruments for assessing ADHD, namely, psychiatric interviews, behavior rating scales, and objective laboratory tests (Barkley, 1987). Each type of instrument reveals a different facet of hyperactivity. Depending on the kind of information required, an instrument can be used independently or in conjunction with others. Studies conducted with Chinese also make use of these measures for diagnosis.

Psychiatric Interviews

Psychiatric interviews are useful for collecting a wide range of information about a child (Edelbrock and Costello, 1984). There exists a handful of studies with Chinese children employing psychiatric interviews designed for parents, and sometimes teachers, as respondents. Some researchers used the interview as the sole assessment instrument (e.g., Li et al., 1985; Shen et al., 1985; Tao, 1992; Wang, 1981; Yang et al., 1987) while others used it to complement other measures (e.g., Luk et al., 1991c). Many of the interviews employed were developed from diagnostic systems such as the DSM-III and the ICD-10. But seldom have relevant psychometric properties of these instruments been reported when used with Chinese, and hence their qualities are somewhat questionable. However, this situation is not unlike research conducted in other countries using psychiatric interviews (Whalen, 1989). In a Hong Kong study on the assessment of ADHD, Luk et al. (1991c) adopted a better developed psychiatric interview by Rutter and Graham (1968). According to a factor analytic study (Taylor, Schachar, Thorley, Wieselberg, and Rutter, 1986), relevant factors on overactivity, short attention span, distractability, fidgetiness and social disinhibition emerged. However, even this semi-structured interview has not been validated with the Chinese population. Since proper psychometric information (e.g., reliability, validity, and normative data) is essential for clinical diagnosis and assessment, perhaps psychiatric interviews presently adopted from the western literature are more suited for preliminary screening purposes.

Recently, a quantitative diagnostic system based on DSM-III has been developed by applying the Bayesian probability theory. A mathematical formula of diagnosis was derived and a rating scale for the quantitative measurement of MBD was designed. A pilot study was carried out in China by Qu and Sun (1987) who analyzed and compared comprehensive clinical data of MBD and non-MBD children. Results were most encouraging as the concordant rate between clinical and quantitative diagnoses reached 98.5%. However, this finding must be accepted with caution because the clinical diagnosis could have been based on a similar diagnostic system from which the quantitative model was derived. Without detailed information, data obtained by Qu and Sun (1987) cannot be unequivocally interpreted. Nevertheless, this new approach to assessment is an innovative one which deserves further empirical enquiry. If the reliability and validity of this model can be established, then it could simplify the diagnostic processes of ADHD.

Behavior Rating Scales

Chinese research employs rating scales extensively for diagnostic purposes. Among the numerous scales listed in the literature, Conners Teacher Rating Scales or CTRS (Conners, 1969; Goyette, Conners, and Ulrich, 1978) is the most extensively used assessment tool by investigators from both China and Hong Kong (Leung et al., 1989; Luk et al., 1991c; Salili and Hoosain, 1985; Wang et al., 1993; X. L. Yang, 1985; Yao et al., 1988; Zan, 1989; Zhang et al., 1986). Other commonly adopted rating scales include Rutter's (Rutter, 1967; Rutter, Tizard, and Whitmore, 1970) Parent Scale A and Teacher Scale B (Ekblad, 1990; Luk et al., 1991c; Wang et al., 1989; X. L. Yang, 1985), Achenbach and Edelbrock's (1983) Child Behavior Checklist (Chuang and Cheng, 1987; Li, Su, Townes, and Varley, 1989; Tseng et al., 1988), Achenbach and Edelbrock's (1983) Child Behavior Checklist — Teacher Report Form (Chuang and Cheng, 1987; Li et al., 1989), Werry and Sprague's (1970) Werry-Weiss-Peters Activity Rating Scale (Soong, 1984; Wang et al., 1993; Zhang et al., 1986), Richman and Graham's (1971) Behavior Screening Questionnaire (Luk et al., 1986), and McQuire and Richman's (1986) Preschool Behavior Checklist (Luk, Leung, Bacon-Shone, and Lieh-Mak, 1991b).

From the above brief survey, it is clear that a great variety of rating scales and behavior checklists have been adopted for assessing ADHD among Chinese children. Unfortunately, these scales were imported indiscriminately from the West and were often directly translated into Chinese with minor alterations or without any modification before administration. Any changes effected were based on the researchers' judgement. In the majority of cases, proper validations of the translated tests were lacking.

A few exceptions do exist, however. For the Child Behavior Checklist (Achenbach and Edelbrock, 1983), the only validation study with Chinese that the author is aware of was done in Taiwan. Chuang and Cheng (1987) applied the checklist to a sample of 6-12-year-old boys selected from three elementary schools in the Taipei area. Factor analysis extracted seven narrow-band behavior problem syndromes from parents' ratings and eight narrow-band behavior problem syndromes from teachers' ratings. Comparisons based on scale scores indicated that the clinical group was rated significantly higher on most behavior problems than the normal group.

Luk, Leung, and Lee (1988a) conducted a factor-analytical study on the CTRS with over 2000 Hong Kong school children and found factors resembling those obtained from American, British, and New Zealand children. However, here Hyperactivity and Conduct Problem were ex-tracted as one single factor instead of two separate factors. In a subsequent study, Luk and Leung (1989) validated the CTRS by comparing the scores between a group of normal children and a group of clinically identified ADHD children. It was found that with the factors extracted, the CTRS was successful in discriminating between these two groups. In another study (Leung et al., 1989), the same scale was also validated among 1746 special school pupils (aged from 6 to 12 years old) of both sexes. Children with various handicaps such as mental retardation, behavioral problems, and physical disabilities were included in the study. Factor structures obtained were more or less the same as those from previous studies. It was concluded that factors in the CTRS are useful in classifying behavior in both normal and handicapped Hong Kong Chinese children. Furthermore, normative data on the CTRS were collected with Chinese children in Hong Kong (Luk, Leung, and Lee, 1988b). A sample of 914 children with 495 boys and 419 girls, aged between 6 and 12 years, was included.

Despite the fact that a great deal of work on the standardization and evaluation of the CTRS has been done in Hong Kong, researchers in other Chinese societies (e.g., China and Taiwan) have not yet made any reference to the Hong Kong data. Since the Hong Kong normative and stand-ardization data have been published only recently, it may take some time before they find their way into other Chinese studies. Furthermore, as these data were published in local psychiatric journals that enjoy a circulation limited to health professionals working in Hong Kong, researchers outside Hong Kong are unlikely to be familiar with these results.

Objective Laboratory Tests

Unlike interviews and rating scales, laboratory tests provide objective measures of vigilance sustained attention, ability of impulse control, and activity level in children. Up to now, research with Chinese children has under-utilized laboratory measures. Only a small number of studies have employed objective type tests (Leung, 1989; Leung and Luk, 1988; Luk et al., 1991c; Zhang et al., 1986). For a comprehensive assessment of child-hood hyperactivity, Luk et al. (1991c) included a few objective tests in addition to the psychiatric interview and common behavioral ratings scales. These were the Continuous Performance Test (CPT; Rosvold, Mirsky, Sarason, Bransome, and Beck, 1965) to assess attention, the Matching Familiar Figures Test (MFFT; Cairns and Crammock, 1978) to gauge impulsivity, and the actometer in the form of a wrist watch (Schulman and Reisman, 1959) to measure the activity level of subjects. The majority of these laboratory type tests are simple to administer, less time consuming, and relatively inexpensive when compared with interview and rating scales. Given the lack of health professionals and the large population in Mainland China, objective tests should have great potential for development in assessing ADHD.

Treatment

Data on the efficacy of treatment regiments are largely collected from non-Chinese children, and only fragmented records involving Chinese children have been found in the literature. Western research has attempted numerous treatment approaches with ADHD children but most methods proved to be effective only in specific problem areas (Ross and Ross, 1982). For example, medication is useful in reducing activity level but may not affect aggressive behavior (Taylor, 1986). Treatment regiments with some proven efficacy include drug therapy, behavior therapy (at home and in the classroom), and cognitive-behavioral training. As pointed out by Barkley (1989), at present none of the treatment methods actually "cures" the disorder and their value lies in the temporary release or reduction of behavioral and/or emotional symptoms. Based on the research reports available on Chinese children, very few authors commented on or mentioned treatment issues while the actual research conducted on intervention techniques was minimal. Consequently, only limited and fragmented information on a small number of treatment methods which have been applied to Chinese children are available. The neglect of therapy is not unexpected, however, given the lack of under-standing on the hyperactivity phenomenon.

Drug Therapy

In western countries such as the United States, drug therapy is the most popular approach being used. According to some surveys (Godow, 1981; Safer and Krager, 1983), about 1% to 2.6% of school children in the United States are receiving medication for controlling ADHD symptoms. Stimulants and antidepressants are two classes of psychotropic drugs which have proven effective for this purpose. Commonly prescribed stimulants include methylphenidate (Ritalin), d-amphetamine (Dexedrine), and pemoline (Cylert). Apparently, the use of drugs is also very common with Chinese children according to some reports. For example, in the 814 ADHD children examined by Li et al. (1985), 525 cases were prescribed Ritalin (10–40 mg per day). Among them, 503 cases were found effective and 472 cases showed therapeutic effects after a month of medication. According to adults' reports, children demonstrated improved attention span, reduced activity level, and better academic performance. However, medication was associated with certain side effects: 13.1% of the children had reduced appetite, and individual cases had amnesia, irritation, fatigue, sweating, skin rash, and others. Another drug prescribed was caffeine (48 cases), and 66.7% of the treated children showed positive effects. Compared with Ritalin, caffeine was not as effective, but it also had fewer side effects.

Some interesting results have been reported by Wang (1981) who observed ADHD children being "cured" by drug treatments. The author cited a "typical case" of a 7-year-old hyperactive boy. The doctor initially put him on a trial of various drugs including sedatives and sleeping pills without any success. Finally, Ritalin was prescribed to the child. This drug helped to calm him down and to control other inappropriate behaviors (e.g., eye blinking). Medication was cut by the parents after 5 months of treatment when the child's behavior became manageable. No relapse was observed at a 4-month followup. This curative effect of Ritalin has not been observed in other drug reports and it deserves further investigation. Unfortunately, few details concerning these cured cases (e.g., proportion of children, family background, etc.) have been provided by Wang (1981). Thus further analysis and replication of these results by other researchers is denied.

Due to the relatively fast action of medication in suppressing children's hyperactivity and defiance, an enormous amount of research has been conducted on Caucasian children to reveal the underlying processes and the educational implications of drug treatments (Brown, Ebert, and Minichiello, 1985). With the large population and the growing identification of ADHD in China, Chinese psychiatrists are more inclined to prescribe medication to children of concerned parents (Li et al., 1985). However, our existing knowledge on the nature of most of the drugs and their long term side effects is too limited. Large scale applications are not warranted.

Behavior Modification

There is only one study with Chinese hyperactive children which attempted a behavioral approach to treatment. Zan (1989) reported such a program in

China using the technique of behavioral and contingency management as a means of intervention. Forty hyperactive children (30 boys and 10 girls, age 4–5 years) were selected from two kindergartens according to their CTRS (short version) scores. They were randomly divided into two groups. The treatment group was given extra activities on top of the regular program provided by the schools while the control group was not. The intervention included two 20-minute sessions of daily music listening (one in the morning and one in the afternoon), one 30-minute drawing and singing session in the afternoon, token reinforcement on appropriate behaviors, and parental consultation. The results showed that the treatment group improved significantly in terms of CTRS and IQ scores when compared with the control group.

Based on the positive findings, the treatment program reported by Zan (1989) appeared promising. It was simple and it required no professional personnel to run. But at this stage researchers cannot be too optimistic about the treatment outcome because the study suffers from some methodological faults in sampling and design. First of all, diagnostic errors could have been made since only one assessment instrument (i.e. CTRS) was used. The sample selected could have been contaminated by children with other disorders. For instance, some of the children receiving treatment might have had problems other than hyperactivity (e.g., conduct disorder) and thus a different school setting plus contingency management techniques were sufficient to change their behavior. Secondly, even if all the children were ADHD, the intervention effects might have been confounded by a bias effect. Teachers and staff knew about the program and they might have paid special attention to the treatment group but not the control group. Hence differential improvements between the two groups could be the result of treatment or the artifact of procedural errors. Thirdly, all the tests and instruments employed had not been validated and standardized on the Chinese population. Dependent measures might not have been reliably assessed. Given these limitations, Zan's (1989) findings must be viewed with caution.

Other Methods

At least three unconventional treatment approaches, which could have important implications for ADHD, deserve a special mention here. The first one is reported in a study by Matsumoto, Tsujimoto, Morishita, Ueeda, and Kaneko (1975). Although no Chinese children were involved, these authors investigated the sedation of hyperactive children using acupuncture, an ancient Chinese therapeutic approach. Twenty hyperactive children were randomly divided into two equal groups. The control group took a sleep inducing drug while the treatment group underwent acupuncture therapy in addition to medication. It was found that the acupuncture group took significantly less time than the control group to fall asleep. In conclusion, acupuncture may be used as a principle technique or an adjunct to drugs for controlling hyperactivity in ADHD children. Acupuncture is considered a relatively simple and inexpensive intervention which has been successfully applied to treat other problematic behavior such as smoking (see Leung, 1991). Hence the observation made by Matsumoto et al. (1975) holds promise for ADHD therapy but much more research is needed before its clinical application can be established.

The second treatment approach worth noting is the application of group therapy to maladjusted children (Chen, 1984). Children from a Taiwan elementary school were selected based on their problematic behaviors in school, including restlessness, truancy, disobedience, fighting, lying, and asocialness. They went through 50 sessions of group therapy which consisted of the therapist's storytelling and group members' puppet playing followed by structured discussion. Children receiving therapy showed significant improvement in their behavior when compared with the respective controls. Apparently, these groups consisted of hyperactive children whose behavior also improved, as reported by the teachers. It would be interesting to explore further the effectiveness of group therapy designed specifically for ADHD. If its usefulness can be established, then group therapy should make a great contribution to the rehabilitation of affected children.

More recently, traditional Chinese medicine (TCM) was used for experimental treatment of ADHD children in China. According to some reports (Ding, 1992; Zhang and Huang, 1990), the results of such treatment were comparable or better than those with western medicine (WM). For example, a study reported by Ding (1992) assessed the effectiveness of TCM using a control group design. Sixty hyperactives were randomly assigned to either the TCM treatment group or the WM group. For the TCM group, children were given a Chinese herb known as "qianxining" while for the WM group children were prescribed stimulant drugs. When results were compared with the WM control group, the TCM group showed improvements in a number of physiological measures in the autonomic nervous system. It was concluded that "qianxining" was a satisfactory hypotensive remedy for children affected by ADHD. Unfortunately, Ding (1992) did not report any behavioral measure of hyperactivity. It was hard to determine whether physiological differences between the two groups could be translated into behavioral performance improvement. Obviously, in order to reveal the remedial effects of TCM on ADHD, more systematic research with rigorous designs is needed. Since TCM has a long history in China and is acceptable to the public at large, it has many advantages over other treatments if its clinical utility can be successfully established.

Methodological Limitations

Having considered research data on Chinese children, there are also methodological issues concerning the reviewed studies which might have direct implications on the validity and reliability of the findings. Some problems raised in this section are particularly pertinent to the reports published in periodicals and magazines within Mainland China. I will consider these issues in turn.

One major problem observed in the articles reviewed is the lack of sufficient details for interpretation since clear methodologies were not often provided. Apart from a few exceptions (e.g., Salili and Hoosain, 1985; Shen et al., 1985), many studies did not report clearly their sampling procedures. This throws some doubts on the representativeness of the samples used and thus hampers the generalizability of the data so collected. A small number of studies (e.g., Qu and Sun, 1987; Tseng and Soong, 1983) did not even have a clearly defined methodology and the findings were suggestive rather than definitive. For the data collected from Chinese children to be more valuable, researchers must attempt to refine their research tools by employing more rigorous experimental designs and appropriate statistical techniques. Among the limitations noted, assessment problems are most prominent due to the fact that all studies must first deal with diagnosis of the disorder.

For an accurate and meaningful determination of ADHD prevalence rates, valid and appropriate assessment instruments are needed. At present, researchers working with Chinese children tend to import instruments mainly developed for Caucasian children. Obviously, it is convenient and economical to adopt existing tests and scales, but caution must also be exercised when using them. A direct, unmodified transfer has obvious problems such as cultural relevance (Ho, 1980). Hence validation studies should be carried out first to assure the discriminative power of the adopted instruments. Then, this should be followed by the establishment of Chinese norms.

With the standardization results, data collected in the Chinese context would be more compatible with those collected elsewhere.

In addition to the lack of standardization of imported tests and scales, some difficulties have been encountered when comparing results across Chinese studies due to the dissimilar definitions adopted by researchers for hyperactivity. Western researchers often employ different diagnostic systems — the broad DSM-III-R criteria or the narrow ICD-9 and -10 criteria — but implications for diagnosis are always discussed in relation to how broadly the disorder of childhood hyperactivity is defined (Prendergast, Taylor, Rapoport, Bartko, Donnelly, Zametkin, Ahearn, Dunn, and Wieselberg, 1988; Rutter, 1989). Hence, using a broader criteria (DSM) will label more children as hyperactive than using a narrow criteria (ICD) (Luk et al., 1991c). However, studies with Chinese seldom explicitly clarify the rationale for selecting a given diagnostic criterion. The choice of tests and scales appears to depend on the individual researcher's preference and previous exposure to these instruments. Consequently, the data presented in different reports are not often directly comparable. To resolve this problem, future studies with Chinese children should endeavour to arrive at common diagnostic criteria which will make cross comparisons more interpretable.

In a number of studies on Chinese children (e.g., Chuang and Cheng, 1987; Salili and Hoosain, 1985; Zan, 1989), only a single measure was used for identifying ADHD symptoms. The validity of this practice is somewhat questionable as far as psychiatric diagnosis is concerned. Nowadays, serious researchers in this field do not trust a diagnosis based on one measure alone. An accurate assessment of ADHD must include multiple sources of information for two good reasons (Barkley, 1987). First of all, hyperactivity has been confused often with other childhood disorders such as conduct problems, oppositional behavior, or learning disabilities. Secondly, manifestations of symptomatic behavior vary in different situations as some children rated as ADHD at school by teachers can be rated as normal at home by parents (Schachar et al., 1981). This case can be best illustrated by a Hong Kong study on "clinic-observable" and "reported" hyperactivity (Leung and Luk, 1988). Using a series of attention tasks, Leung and Luk (1988) showed that "reported-clinically observable" hyperactive children had significant attentional difficulties in comparison with children with only "reported" hyperactivity and with normal control children. Similar results were obtained by Luk et al. (1991c) with another sample of ADHD Hong Kong children. This finding suggests that more than one source of information is needed to avoid mis-diagnosis. Taken

together, the modern assessment of ADHD "should rely on several informants, employ multiple settings, and use a variety of assessment methods that
focus on not only the primary symptoms of ADHD, but also the child's
academic and social functioning, as well as the integrity of his or her family
environment" (Barkley, 1989, p. 47).

Discussion

In the present chapter, research on ADHD of Chinese children has been
examined. Data on the etiology, epidemiology, assessment, and treatment
are considered in the light of findings from non-Chinese populations.
According to the literature reviewed, it appears that hyperactivity is not
unique to western cultures and that ADHD can also be found among
Chinese children. However, the sudden surge of ADHD cases all over
China suggests that the phenomenon could have been an artifact unknowingly fabricated by Chinese psychopathologists when they came into direct
contact with the concept of childhood hyperactivity for the first time.
Among the issues noted, the most controversial one is whether ADHD is
created in the eye of the beholder. At present, it appears that the Chinese
experience cannot help to resolve this issue, but it does highlight the
intriguing nature of the disorder and the difficulties in the accurate identification of ADHD. Next we will consider this issue in more detail.

Factors Related to Positive Identification

Does cultural bias influence the understanding and perception of childhood
hyperactivity among Chinese people? The answer to this question appears
to be affirmative. A number of authors (Cheung, 1985, 1986; Ho, 1980,
1986; K. M. Lin, 1981) have demonstrated that traditional cultural and
medical beliefs have a great effect on shaping the Chinese conception of
psychopathology in both adults and children.

Despite claims of compatibility of ADHD prevalence rates between
Chinese and western children (e.g., Li, et al., 1989), available evidence
suggests otherwise. Chinese children appear less likely to be diagnosed as
ADHD than their Western counterparts. This is true to the extent that
instruments developed in the west have been adopted for diagnostic
purposes. Another difference is found in the sex ratio between boys and
girls. Compared with western data, larger ratios are usually obtained from
Chinese samples (e.g., Salili and Hoosain, 1985). In other words, within

Chinese societies girls are less likely to be diagnosed as hyperactive than boys.

Epidemiological data from studies on Chinese children clearly show that there exists a whole host of factors which affect the occurrence and diagnosis of hyperactive children. These include geographical loca-tion, urbanization, social economic status, teachers' instructional approach, parents' education, and family background. Children from other non-Chinese societies are not exceptions to these physical, environmental, psychosocial influences (Whalen, 1989). However, Chinese children appear to be more prone to these effects as relatively large variations in prevalence rates have been obtained.

ADHD in the Eye of the Beholder

A behavioral deviation is a problem only to the extent that it disrupts the normal functioning of the sufferer and/or other people. In China hyper-activity was not a concern in the past. The sudden surge of hyperactive cases therefore serves as a good example for illustrating the influence of the subjective element on positive diagnosis. Lin (1984) suspected that the increase is a result of "category fallacy" whereby the availability of a concept for childhood hyperactivity has led to the application of the diag-nostic criteria indiscriminantly. Not only are new cases being affected but also past cases which were labelled as other disturbances of behavior might have been re-diagnosed as ADHD.

Apparently, not only laymen are vulnerable to the error of selective perception. In a recent study, Mann, Ikeda, Mueller, Takahashi, Tao, Humris, Li, and Chin (1992) have demonstrated that even experts can deviate from one another. Mental health professionals from China (N=8), Indonesia (N=12), Japan (N=9), and the United States (N=8) were asked to watch videotaped vignettes of four 8-year-old boys under both individual and group settings. The professionals then rated these children for the presence and degree of hyperactive-disruptive behaviors. Chinese and Indonesian clinicians scored significantly higher occurrences of the tar-geted behavior than their Japanese and American counterparts. The authors concluded that perceptions of hyperactivity across countries were deter-mined by clinicians' cultural background even if uniform rating criteria were applied. This finding further confirms the notion that hyperactivity varies, to a certain extent, in the eye of the beholder.

But this does not mean that hyperactivity is solely determined by subjective interpretation of children's behavior. As demonstrated in cross cultural studies (see Whalen, 1989), ADHD can be diagnosed in different ethnic groups given the symptoms specified. The seemingly widespread nature tends to support the universal notion of hyperactivity. Perhaps the most we can conclude at this stage is that ADHD is a universal phenomenon to the extent that it can be identified according to a given set of criteria but that its severity, range, and distribution are specific to the cultural practice of the society to which these criteria are applied.

Based on the Chinese data and those reviewed by western researchers (e.g., Barkley, 1989), it has become clear that (1) childhood hyperactivity can be found in many ethnic groups brought up in very different cultures, and (2) a number of factors can affect its rate of prevalence. Ho's (1980) question on whether ADHD is a universal or culturally determined phenomenon can be given an unsettling answer. Available evidence shows that hyperactivity is universal to the extent that it can be identified in different ethnic groups. However, it is also culturally bound in that its prevalence pattern is influenced by social and psychological factors pertinent to specific cultures. Perhaps the manifestation of attention problems and hyperactivity is another example of the nature-nurture interaction (Eisenberg, 1983; Henker and Whalen, 1989; Rutter, 1977; Schachar et al., 1981). This notion is coherent with the conclusion of Shen et al. (1985) who hypothesized that MBD children have the biological disposition toward hyperactivity while its form, severity, and modality is controlled by social factors.

Looking into the Future

The Chinese account for one-fifth of the population on earth and they constitute an economic and social power that cannot be ignored. Any psychological concepts and theorization would not be complete without taking into consideration the behavior of these people. Perhaps one major contribution that researchers working with Chinese can make is to conduct comparison studies on different groups of Chinese children of dissimilar cultural background. For instance, controlled studies could be conducted involving ethnic Chinese children brought up in families under different levels of western influences (e.g., United States, Hong Kong, and China). Having controlled for the heredity factor, the results from such studies would reveal the role of the cultural element in affecting the various aspects of hyperactivity. Such information would be useful for developing a theoretical model or paradigm for explaining differences in hyperactivity observed between Chinese children and their western counterparts. With data inside and outside Chinese culture, the role of genetic and biological factors in affecting ADHD can be determined.

Relative to the great variety of studies found in the western literature, the scope of ADHD research with Chinese children can be considered narrow and inadequate. The present review shows that the topics covered by Chinese studies are largely confined to epidemiology of the disorder. They account for over half of the reports available. However, epidemiological studies are mainly surveys and the knowledge so acquired remains at a descriptive level. When ADHD was still a relatively new phenomenon in China, epidemiological data was necessary for gauging the severity of the disorder among Chinese children. Now the foundation has been laid and the time is right for more studies devoted to the understanding of underlying processes of hyperactivity and attention problems, and how they interact with environmental factors. Researchers need to broaden their interests since the knowledge base on ADHD Chinese children lags far behind that of its non-Chinese counterparts. For example, some topics receiving great attention in western countries (Barkley, 1989), namely, basic deficit of ADHD (e.g., cognitive impairments) and the treatment of hyperativity (e.g., drug responses, long-term outcome, etc.), are rarely available from the Chinese context. Hence future works should endeavour to conduct cross-national studies in various aspects of childhood hyperactivity. Data from different perspectives will not only expand the knowledge base on ADHD but will also help to resolve issues relating to the nature, the assessment, and the intervention of this peculiar childhood disorder.

As shown in the present review, recent research has covered a lot of ground in epidemiology and assessment among Chinese children. With this foundation and the fast growing psychological data base on the Chinese (e.g., Bond, 1986; in press), perhaps it is time for researchers to look beyond existing western frameworks and develop new perspectives appropriate to the Chinese culture. In view of the uniqueness of the Chinese people and their value system, the study of ADHD in the Chinese context would help health professionals gain further insights toward understanding the hyperactivity phenomenon. At this juncture, attention should be given also to basic research for unraveling the underlying deficits associated with ADHD, and the data thus obtained would be useful for developing treatment techniques and rehabilitation programs of high efficacy. It would be advantageous if a unified diagnostic system based on the Chinese culture can be developed and adopted by all professionals working with Chinese children. Having such a system would facilitate comparisons of results across different studies. But in order to get there, contemporary researchers working with Chinese children have to be more innovative and systematic than their predecessors.

Given the groundwork already laid on Chinese ADHD research, some resolutions are in order as we move into the 21st century. Apart from utilizing vigorous and appropriate methodologies, the scope of research should be broadened to include topics other than epidemiology. In addition, future research with Chinese children should aim at developing indigenous assessment instruments that are culturally appropriate. In the beginning there was a need for adopting western perspectives, but scholars must gradually wean themselves from western dependence. With continuous efforts, an indigenous and coherent framework of Chinese childhood hyperactivity can be built from data collected within the Chinese culture.

References

Achenbach, T. M., and Edelbrock, C. (1983). *Manual for the child behavior checklist and revised child behavior profile.* Burlington: University of Vermont, Department of Psychiatry.

American Psychiatric Association. (1980). *Diagnostic and statistical manual of mental disorders* (3rd ed.). Washington DC: Author.

———. (1987). *Diagnostic and statistical manual of mental disorders* (3rd ed., rev.). Washington DC: Author.

———. (1994). *Diagnostic and statistical manual of mental disorders* (4th ed., rev.). Washington DC: Author.

Ayllon, T., and Milan, M. A. (1983). Hyperactivity and attention deficit disorders. In M. Hersen, V. B. van Hasselt, and J. L. Matson (Eds.), *Behavior therapy for the developmentally and physically disabled.* New York: Academic Press.

Barkley, R. A. (1981). Hyperactivity. In E. J. Mash and L. G. Terdal (Eds.), *Behavioral assessment of childhood disorders* (pp. 127–184). New York: Guilford Press.

———. (1987). The assessment of Attention Deficit-Hyperactivity Disorder. *Behavioral Assessment,* 9: 207–233.

———. (1989). Attention Deficit-Hyperactivity Disorder. In E. J. Mash and R. A. Barkley (Eds.), *Treatment of childhood disorders* (pp. 39–72). New York: Guilford Press.

Biederman, J., Munir, K., Knee, D., Armentano, M., Autor, S., Waternaux, C., and Tsuang, M. (1987). High rate of affective disorders in probands with attention deficit disorders and in their relatives: A controlled family study. *American Journal of Psychiatry*, 144: 330–333.

Block, G. H. (1977). Hyperactivity: A cultural perspective. *Journal of Learning Disability*, 110: 236–240.

Bond, M. H. (Ed.). (1986). *The psychology of the Chinese people*. Hong Kong: Oxford University Press.

———. (Ed.). (in press). *Handbook of Chinese psychology*. Hong Kong: Oxford University Press.

Brown, G. L., Ebert, M. H., and Minichiello, M. D. (1985). Biochemical and pharmacological aspects of attention deficit disorder. In L. M. Bloomingdale (Ed.), *Attention deficit disorder: Identification, course and treatment rationale*. New York: Spectrum Publications.

Cairns, E., and Cammock, T. (1978). Development of a more reliable version of the Matching Familiar Figures Test. *Developmental Psychology*, 11: 244–248.

Cantwell, D. (1977). Hyperkinetic syndrome. In M. Rutter and L. Hersov (Eds.), *Child psychiatry modern approaches* (pp. 524–555). London: Blackwell Scientific Publications.

Chen, C. C. (1984). Group therapy with Chinese school children. *International Journal of Group Psychotherapy*, 34: 485–501.

Cheung, F.M.C. (1985). An overview of psychopathology in Hong Kong with special reference to somatic presentation. In W. S. Tseng and D.Y.H. Wu (Eds.), *Chinese culture and mental health* (pp. 287–304). Orlando, FL: Academic Press.

———. (1986). Psychopathology among Chinese people. In M. H. Bond (Ed.), *The psychology of the Chinese people* (pp. 171–212). Hong Kong: Oxford University Press.

Chuang, S. F., and Cheng, S. W. (1987). Factor-based behavior problem syndromes among 6–12 year-old boys in Taiwan. *Proceedings from the Symposium on Study of Growth and Development* (pp. 143–66). Taipei: Group for Study of Growth and Development.

Conners, C. K. (1969). A teacher rating scale for use in drug studies with children. *American Journal of Psychiatry*, 126: 884–888.

Deutsch, C. K., Swanson, J. M., and Bruell, J. M. (1982). Over-representation of adoptees in children with the attention deficit disorder. *Behavioral Genetics*, 12: 231–238.

Ding, Q. (1992). Clinical study of qianxining in the treatment of 60 cases of *yang* hyperactivity due to *yin* deficiency type of hypertension (In Chinese). *Zhongguo zhongxiyi jiehe zazhi*, 12: 388–389.

Douglas, V. I. (1983). Attentional and cognitive problems. In M. Rutter (Ed.), *Developmental neuropsychiatry* (pp. 280–329). New York: Guilford Press.

Edelbrock, C. S., and Costello, A. (1984). Structured psychiatric interviews for children and adolescents. In G. Goldstein and M. Hersen (Eds.), *Handbook of psychological assessment* (pp. 276–290). New York: Pergamon Press.

Eisenberg, L. (1973). The overactive child. *Hospital Practice*, 8: 151–260.

———. (1983, April). *Minimal brain damage and disordered behavior*. Paper presented at WHO National Workshop on the Psychosocial Aspect of Primary Health Care, Beijing, China.

Ekblad, S. (1990). The children's behaviour questionnaire for completion by parents and teachers in a Chinese sample. *Journal of Child Psychology and Psychiatry*, 31: 775–791.

Godow, K. D. (1981). Prevalence of drug treatment for hyperactivity and other childhood behavior disorders. In K. D. Gowdow and J. Loney (Eds.), *Psychosocial aspects of drug treatment* (pp. 13–70). Boulder, CO: Westview Press.

Goyette, C. H., Conners, C. K., and Ulrich, R. F. (1978). Normative data for Revised Conners Parent and Teacher Rating Scales. *Journal of Abnormal Child Psychology*, 6: 221–236.

Guizhou Mental Hospital. (1981). Report on the investigation of MBD children in 5 elementary schools in Guiyang (In Chinese). *Guizhou Medicine*, 6: 47–50.

Henker, B., and Whalen, C. K. (1989). Hyperactivity and attention deficits. *American Psychologist*, 44: 216–223.

Hertzig, M. E., Bortner, M., and Birch, H. G. (1969). Neurologic findings in children educationally designated as "brain damaged." *American Journal of Orthopsychiatry*, 39: 437–446.

Ho, D.Y.F. (1980). Childhood psychopathology: A dialogue with special reference to Chinese and American cultures. In A. Kleinman and T. Y. Lin (Eds.), *Normal and abnormal behavior in Chinese culture* (pp. 137–55). Dordrecht, Netherlands: Reidel.

———. (1986). Chinese patterns of socialization: A critical review. In M. H. Bond (Ed.), *The psychology of the Chinese people* (pp. 1–37). Hong Kong: Oxford University Press.

Jin, F. Z. (1982). Report on the investigation of MBD children in 11 primary school in Yanbian District (In Chinese). *Chinese Journal of Nervous and Mental Disorders*, 8: 46.

Kessen, W. (Ed.). (1975). *Childhood in China*. New Haven: Yale University Press.

Lambert, N. M., Sandoval, J., and Sassone, D. (1978). Prevalence of hyperactivity in elementary school children as a function of social system definers. *American Journal of Orthopsychiatry*, 48: 446–463.

Leung, J. P. (1989). *Performance of Hong Kong school children on Computerized Continuous Performance Test and delay task*. Report submitted to the Hong Kong Institute of Asia–Pacific Studies, The Chinese University of Hong Kong.

———. (1991). Smoking cessation by auricular acupuncture and behavioral therapy. *Psychologia*, 34: 177–187.

Leung, P.W.L., and Luk, S. L. (1988). Differences in attention control between "clinic-observable" and "reported" hyperactivity: A preliminary report. *Child: Care, Health and Development*, 14: 199–211.

Leung, P.W.L., Luk, S. L., and Lee, P.L.M. (1989). Problem behaviour among special school children in Hong Kong: A factor-analytical study with Conners' Teacher Rating Scale. *Psychologia*, 32: 120–128.

Levy, S. (1966). The hyperkinetic child a forgotten entity, its diagnosis and treatment. *International Journal of Neuro-psychiatry*. 2: 330–336.

Li, X. R., Su, L. Y., Townes, B. D., and Varley, C. K. (1989). Diagnosis of attention deficit disorder with hyperactivity in Chinese boys. *Journal of American Academy of Child and Adolescent Psychiatry*, 28: 497–500.

Li, X. R., Zhu, S. L., Su, L. Y., Zheng, Z. S., Hua, X. X., Li, S. R., and Li, M. (1985). Child hyperactivity disorder: A clinical and neuropsychological study of 814 cases (In Chinese). *Chinese Journal of Neurology and Psychiatry*, 18: 382–385.

Lin, K. M. (1981). Traditional Chinese medical beliefs and their relevance for mental illness and psychiatry. In A. Kleinman and T. Y. Lin (Eds.), *Normal and abnormal behavior in Chinese culture* (pp. 95–111). Dordrecht, Netherlands: Reidel.

Lin, T. Y. (1984). *Mental health and family values*. Public lecture delivered at Chung Chi College, The Chinese University of Hong Kong, Hong Kong, 1 March.

———. (1985). Mental disorders and psychiatry in Chinese culture: Characteristic features and major issues. In W. S. Tseng and D.Y.H. Wu (Eds.), *Chinese culture and mental health* (pp. 367–393). Orlando, FL: Academic Press.

Liu, S. H. (1988). Child mental problems in Sichuan province. *International Journal of Mental Health*, 16: 67–74.

Luk, S. L. (1986). Diagnosis and treatment of hyperkinetic syndrome of childhood: Recent advances. *Journal of Hong Kong Psychiatry Association*, 6: 28–32.

Luk, S. L., Lee, P.W.H., and Yu, K. K. (1986). Behaviour problem in a group of preschool boys in Hong Kong. *The Hong Kong Journal of Pediatrics*, 1: 14–25.

Luk, S. L., and Leung, P.W.L. (1989). Conners' Teacher's Rating Scale — A validation study in Hong Kong. *Journal of Child Psychology and Psychiatry*, 30: 785–793.

Luk, S. L., Leung, P.W.L., Bacon-Shone, J., Chung, S. Y., Lee, P.W.H., Chen, S., Ng, R., Lieh-Mak, F., Ko, L., Wong, V.C.N., and Yeung, C. Y. (1991a). Behaviour disorder in pre-school children in Hong Kong: A two-stage epidemiological study. *British Journal of Psychiatry*, 158: 213–221.

Luk, S. L., Leung, P.W.L., Bacon-Shone, J., and Lieh-Mak, F. (1991b). The structure and prevalence of behavioral problems in Hong Kong preschool children. *Journal of Abnormal Child Psychology*, 19: 219–232.

Luk, S. L., Leung, P.W.L., and Lee, P.L.M. (1988a). Conners' Teacher Rating Scale in Chinese children in Hong Kong. *Journal of Child Psychology and Psychiatry*, 29: 165–174.

————. (1988b). Normative data of Conners' Teacher Rating Scale in Chinese children in Hong Kong. *Journal of Hong Kong Psychiatric Association*, 8: 41–44.

Luk, S. L., Leung, P.W.L., and Yuen, J. (1991c). Clinic observations in the assessment of pervasiveness of childhood hyperactivity. *Journal of Child Psychology and Psychiatry*, 32: 833–850.

Mann, E. M., Ikeda, Y., Mueller, C. W., Takahashi, A., Tao, K. T., Humris, E., Li, B. L., and Chin, D. (1992). Cross-cultural differences in rating hyperactive-disruptive behaviors in children. *American Journal of Psychiatry*, 149: 1539–1542.

Matsumoto, K., Tsujimoto, T., Morishita, H., Ueeda, K., and Kaneko, Z. (1975). A variation of acupuncture used in the sedation of hyperactive children. *American Journal of Acupuncture*, 3: 43–46.

McQuire, J., and Richman, N. (1986). Screening for behavior problems in nurseries: The reliability and validity of the Preschool Behaviour Checklist. *Journal of Child Psychology, Psychiatry and Allied Disciplines*, 27: 7–32.

Morrison, J. R., and Stewart, M. A. (1973). Evidence of polygenetic inheritance in the hyperactive child syndrome. *American Journal of Psychiatry*, 130: 791–792.

O'Connor, M., Foch, T., Sherry, T., and Plomin, R. (1980). A twin study of specific behavioral problems of socialization as viewed by parents. *Journal of Abnormal Child Psychology*, 8: 189–199.

O'Leary, K. D., Vivian, D., and Nisi, A. (1985). Hyperactivity in Italy. *Journal of Abnormal Child Psychology*, 13: 485–500.

O'Malley, J. E., and Eisenberg, L. (1973). The hyperkinetic syndrome. In S. Walzer and P. H. Wolff (Eds.), *Minimal cerebral dysfunction in children* (pp. 95–103). New York: Grune and Stratton.

Prendergast, M., Taylor, E., Rapoport, J. L., Bartko, J., Donnelly, M., Zametkin, A., Ahearn, M., Dunn, G., and Wieselberg, H. M. (1988). The diagnosis of childhood hyperactivity: A U.S.–U.K. cross-national study of DSM-III and ICD-9. *Journal of Child Psychology and Psychiatry*, 29: 289–300.

Qu, J. Y., and Sun, Y. W. (1987). A quantitative diagnostic study with hyperkinetic syndrome children (In Chinese). *Chinese Journal of Neurology and Psychiatry*, 20: 72–74.

Richman, N., and Graham, P. J. (1971). A behavioral screening questionnaire for use with three-year-old children: Preliminary findings. *Journal of Child Psychology and Psychiatry*, 12: 5–33.

Ross, D. M., and Ross, S. A. (1982). *Hyperactivity: Current issues, research, and theory*. New York: Wiley (Original work published 1976).

Rosvold, H. E., Mirsky, A. F., Sarason, L., Bransome, E. D., and Beck, L. D. (1965). A continuous performance test of brain damage. *Journal of Consulting Psychology*, 20: 343–350.

Rutter, M. (1967). A children's behavior questionnaire for completion by teachers: Preliminary findings. *Journal of Child Psychology and Psychiatry*, 8: 1–11.

———. (1977). Brain damage syndrome in childhood: Concepts and findings. *Journal of Child Psychology and Psychiatry*, 18: 1–21.

———. (1982). Syndromes attributed to "minimal brain dysfunction" in children. *American Journal of Psychiatry*, 139: 21–33.

———. (1989). Child psychiatric disorders in ICD-10. *Journal of Child Psychology and Psychiatry*, 30: 499–513.

Rutter, M., and Graham, P. J. (1968). The reliability and validity of the psychiatric assessment of the child: I. Interview with the child. *British Journal of Psychiatry*, 114: 563–579.

Rutter, M., Tizard, J., and Whitmore, K. (1970). *Education, health and behaviour*. London: Longman.

Safer, D. J., and Krager, J. M. (1983). Trends in medication treatment of hyperactive school children. *Clinical Pediatrics*, 22: 500–504.

Safer, R., and Allen, D. (1976). *Hyperactive children: Diagnosis and management*. Baltimore: University Park Press.

Salili, F., and Hoosain, R. (1985). Hyperactivity among Hong Kong Chinese children. *International Journal of Intercultural Relations*, 9: 177–185.

Schachar, R., Rutter, M., and Smith, A. (1981). The characteristics of situationally and pervasively hyperactive children, implication for syndrome definition. *Journal of Child Psychology and Psychology*, 22: 375–392.

Schulman, J. L., and Reisman, J. M. (1959). An objective measure of hyperactivity. *American Journal of Mental Deficiency*, 64: 455–456.

Shanghai Mental Hospital (1981). *Study on MBD children in Shanghai*. Paper presented at the WHO/Nanjing Workshop on Child Psychiatry, Nanjing, China.

Shen, Y. C., and Wang, Y. F. (1984). Urinary MHPG.SO4 excretion in 73 MBD school children. *Biological Psychiatry*, 19: 861–870.

Shen, Y. C., Wang, Y. F., and Yang, X. L. (1985). An epidemiological investigation of minimal brain dysfunction in six elementary schools in Beijing. *Journal of Child Psychology and Psychiatry*, 26: 777–787.

Soong, W. T. (1984). Attention deficit hyperkinetic syndrome: Clinical characteristics. *Bulletin of the Chinese Society of Neurology and Psychiatry*, 10: 104–113.

Still, G. F. (1902). Some abnormal psychial conditions in children. *Lancet*, i: 1008–1012, 1077–1082, 1163–1168.

Strauss, A. A., and Lehtinen, L. E. (1947). *Psychopathology and education of the brain-injured child*. New York: Grune and Stratton.

Tao, K. T. (1992). Hyperactivity and attention deficit disorder syndromes in China.

Journal of the American Academy of Child and Adolescent Psychiatry, 31: 1165–1166.

Tao, K. T., and Chiu, J. H. (1985). The one-child-per-family policy: A psychological perspective. In W. S. Tseng and D.Y.H. Wu (Eds.), *Chinese culture and mental health* (pp. 153–65). Orlando, FL: Academic Press.

Taylor, E. A. (1986). Childhood hyperactivity. *British Journal of Psychiatry*, 149: 562–573.

Taylor, E. A., and Sandberg, S. (1984). Hyperactive behavior in English school children: A questionnaire survey. *Journal of Abnormal Child Psychology*, 12: 143–155.

Taylor, E. A., Schachar, R., Thorley, G., Wieselberg, M., and Rutter, M. (1986). Conduct disorder and hyperactivity: II. A cluster analytic approach to the identification of a behavioural syndrome. *British Journal of Psychiatry*, 149: 760–767.

Tseng, C. C., and Soong, W. T. (1983). Diagnostic description of speech retardation (In Chinese). *Acta Psycholgica Taiwanica*, 25: 25–30.

Tseng, W. S., Tao, K. T., Jing, H., Chiu, J. H., Yu, L., and Kameoka, V. (1988). Family planning and child mental health in China: The Nanjing survey. *American Journal of Psychiatry*, 145: 1396–1403.

Wang, R. L. (1981). An investigation of hyperactive syndrome in eleven primary schools and kindergartens in Dongshan district of Guangzhou city (In Chinese). *Chinese Journal of Neurology and Psychiatry*, 14: 32–35.

Wang, Y. C., Chong, M. Y., Chou, W. J., and Yang, J. L. (1993). Prevalence of Attention Deficit-Hyperactivity Disorder in primary school children in Taiwan. *Journal of Formos Medical Association*, 92: 133–138.

Wang, Y. F., Shen, Y. C., Gu, B. M., Jia, M. X., and Zhang, A. L. (1989). An epidemiological study of behaviour problems in school children in urban areas of Beijing. *Journal of Child Psychology and Psychiatry*, 30: 907–912.

Wang, Y. F., Yang, X. L., and Shen, Y. C. (1983). An investigation of the prevalence of MBD children in 4 primary schools in Beijing. *Journal of the Beijing Medical College*, 1 (Suppl.): 69–71.

Wender, P. H. (1971). *Minimal brain dysfunction in children*. New York: Wiley.

———. (1987). *The hyperactive child, adolescent, and adults*. New York: Oxford University Press.

Werry, J. S., and Quay, H. (1968). Studies on the hyperactive child: An empirical analysis of the minimal brain dysfunction syndrome. *Archives of General Psychiatry*, 19: 9–16.

Werry, J. S., and Sprague, R. L. (1970). Hyperactivity. In C. G. Costello (Ed.), *Symptoms of psychopathology* (pp. 397–417). New York: Wiley.

Whalen, C. K. (1989). Attention deficit and hyperactivity disorders. In E. J. Mash and R. A. Barkley (Eds.), *Treatment of childhood disorders* (pp. 131–169). New York: Guilford Press.

Whalen, C. K., and Henker, B. (1976). Psychostimulants and children: A review and analysis. *Psychological Bulletin*, 83: 1113–1130.

Willerman, L. (1973). Activity level and hyperactivity in twins. *Child Development*, 44: 288–293.

Willis, T. J., and Lovaas, I. (1977). A behavioral approach to treating hyperactive children: The parent's role. In J. B. Millichap (Ed.), *Learning disabilities and related disorders* (pp. 119–140). Chicago: Year Book Medical.

World Health Organization. (1990). *International classification of disease* (10th ed.). United Nation: Author.

Xu, T. Y. (1985). Child mental health and elementary schools in Shanghai. In W. S. Tseng and D.Y.H. Wu (Eds.), *Chinese culture and mental health* (pp. 315–323). Orlando, FL: Academic Press.

Yan, W. W., Chu, C. W., Sing, C. W., Tang, Y. L., Fong, S. K., and Li, F. H. (1981). A survey of minimal brain dysfunction (In Chinese). *Information on Psychological Sciences*, 9: 28–33.

Yang, K. S. (1981). Problem behaviour in Chinese adolescents in Taiwan — A classificatory-factorial study. *Journal of Cross-Cultural Psychology*, 12: 179–193.

Yang, H. Q., Pan, Z. Y., Gu, D. M., Hu, S. H., Li, Q., Zhang, H. Q., and Su, L. C. (1987). A survey of hyperkinetic syndrome among 1027 primary school children in Chengdou city (In Chinese). *Chinese Journal of Neurology and Psychiatry*, 20: 120.

Yang, X. L. (1985). An investigation of minimal brain disorders among primary school students in the Beijing area. In W. S. Tseng and D.Y.H. Wu (Eds.), *Chinese culture and mental health* (pp. 315–324). Orlando, FL: Academic Press.

Yao, K. N., Solanto, M. V., and Wender, E. H. (1988). Prevalence of hyperactivity among newly immigrated Chinese–American children. *Journal of Developmental and Behavioral Pediatrics*, 9: 367–373.

Zan, S. L. (1989). *The intervention on hyperactive children*. A paper presented at the Childhood in the 21st Century: International Conference on Early Education and Development (0–6 years), Hong Kong.

Zentall, S. S., and Zentall, T. R. (1983). Optimal stimulation: A model of disordered activity and performance in normal and deviant children. *Psychological Bulletin*, 94: 446–471.

Zhang, H., and Huang, J. (1990). Preliminary study of traditional Chinese medicine treatment of minimal brain dysfunction: Analysis of 100 cases. (In Chinese). *Zhongguo zhongxiyi jiehe zazhi*, 10: 278–279.

Zhang, Y., Song, W. Z., and Cui, Q. C. (1986). The relation between psychological test and family factors in hyperactive children (In Chinese). *Acta Psychologica Sinica*, 18: 371–379.

10

Adolescent Delinquent Behavior in Chinese Societies

Kwok Leung and Ruth Mei-tai Fan

Delinquent behavior has been actively researched in several disciplines, such as psychology, sociology, and criminology, and many theories have been put forward to explain its occurrence (e.g., Johnson, 1979; Kaplan, 1980; Lemert, 1967). Despite the voluminous literature on delinquent behavior, most research is conducted in North America and Europe, and the amount of cross-cultural research is disappointingly small (Naroll, 1983). The absence of cross-cultural research in delinquent behavior is a major problem: as Triandis (1980) has clearly pointed out, the lack of cross-cultural verification poses a serious threat to the universality of theories. Without such cross-cultural data, it is uncertain whether the theories of delinquent behavior developed in the West are applicable to non-Western societies (DeFleur, 1969). The aim of the present chapter is to fill this gap by providing a review of major research on adolescent delinquent behavior in Chinese societies. The chapter begins with a comparison of the characteristics of juvenile delinquency in Chinese societies and those in the West. The applicability of Western theories of delinquent behavior in a Chinese context is then examined. Finally, with the aim of extending current theorization about delinquent behavior and of developing a truly universal theory of delinquent behavior, some directions for future research on juvenile delinquency in Chinese societies are proposed.

We would like to thank Kuo-shu Yang, Rance P. L. Lee, and Y. W. Cheung for their comments on earlier drafts of this chapter.

Underlying Structure of Delinquent Behavior

Considerable work has been done in the West on the classification of delinquent behavior (e.g., Quay and Werry, 1972). The general finding is that delinquent behavior can be viewed as a single dimension. For instance, Hindelang, Hirschi, and Weis (1981) have reviewed a number of studies which employed factor analysis and cluster analysis to examine the under-lying dimension of delinquent behavior, and they have concluded that the unidimensional conceptualization of delinquent behavior is consistent with the data available. A number of studies with Chinese subjects have shown that the unidimensional view of delinquent behavior is also tenable in Chinese societies. Yang (1981) has conducted a large-scale study to look into the underlying structure of delinquent behavior in Taiwanese adoles-cents. A list of 130 problem behaviors was derived from the problem behavior literature as well as from consultations with local school teachers and personality psychologists. A group of 2432 male and 2723 female adolescents within an age range of 13–15, who were drawn from junior high schools in Taipei with a stratified sampling scheme, were asked to indicate anonymously how often they enacted each of the problem be-haviors. The data were then factor analyzed: the results showed that delin-quent behaviors clustered together to form one factor, and also that they can be further grouped into two related sub-factors, namely, pleasure-seeking (e.g., drinking, gambling) and rule-violating (e.g., aggressive behavior, violations of school rules). Yang (1981) concluded that the underlying structure of problem behavior of Chinese adolescents is similar to that uncovered by American and European researchers.

In the cross-cultural study of delinquent behavior by Feldman, Rosenthal, Mont-Reynaud, Leung, and Lau (1991), delinquent behaviors were conceptually classified into three types, namely, school-based mis-conduct, anti-social behavior, and status offences, and each type showed reasonably high internal reliabilities across the Chinese, American, and Australian adolescents studied. Judging from the nature of the delinquent behaviors included in each type, school-based misconduct and anti-social behavior correspond to the rule-violation factor identified by Yang (1981), and status offences correspond to his pleasure-seeking factor. Furthermore, as in Yang's (1981) study and many other Western studies (e.g., Hindelang et al., 1981; Leung and Drasgow, 1986), the three delinquent factors are substantially correlated.

It may be concluded that there is considerable convergence in the underlying structure of delinquent behavior in Chinese and Western adolescents. Delinquent behavior is basically unidimensional, although it can be broken down into several related sub-groups.

Occurrence of Delinquent Behavior in Chinese Adolescents

Feldman et al. (1991) found that Chinese school children from the 10th and 11th grades in Hong Kong reported a significantly lower level of antisocial behavior (e.g., damaging school property, taking something without asking the owner), school misconduct (e.g., being late to school, cheating in tests), and status offences (e.g., smoking cigarettes, drinking alcohol) than their counterparts from the U.S. and Australia. To the best of our knowledge, this is the only study that provides a direct comparison between the frequency of delinquent behavior of Chinese adolescents with that of Western adolescents. Obviously, it is premature to draw a definite conclusion based on the results of a single study. In the absence of other empirical results, we have to turn to indirect evidence that pertains to the relative occurrence of delinquent behavior in Chinese societies as compared to the West.

One obvious indicator of the extent of juvenile delinquency in a society is the number of adolescents prosecuted in each year. Although it is sometimes difficult to compare crime statistics across nations (Wilkins, 1980), such cross-cultural comparisons would be informative if they yielded results consistent with those obtained from other types of comparisons. The statistics available suggest that the juvenile crime rate is much lower in Chinese than in Western societies. For instance, an average annual rate of 0.16% of the age group 7–15 in Hong Kong was prosecuted between the years 1966 to 1970, and the figure increased slightly to 0.27% in the years 1976 to 1980 (Y. W. Cheung, 1985). In contrast, the corresponding figure was 0.53% for the same age group in Canada in 1966 (Hagan, 1977). Based on data from the mid 1970s, Naroll (1983) ranked 42 countries according to the proportion of juvenile criminals among all criminals in each country, and Hong Kong ranked below all the Western nations in his sample. In other words, juvenile crime was much less serious in Hong Kong than in the West in the 1970s.

A second area that is able to shed some light on cultural differences in delinquent behavior is the substantial cross-cultural literature on aggression. A major subset of delinquent behavior is aggressive behavior, which includes damaging property, threatening people, and hurting people (e.g.,

Hindelang et al., 1981). As argued before, different subsets of delinquent behavior usually show high intercorrelations, and this legitimizes the use of the frequency of a subset to imply the frequency of the whole set. Thus, the frequency of aggressive behavior should be able to serve as an accurate surrogate for the frequency of delinquent behavior. In general, the cross-cultural results available suggest that, compared to the West, Chinese children show a higher level of cooperativeness and a lower level of aggressiveness (e.g., Bond and Wang, 1983; Ekblad, 1986; Ekblad and Olweus, 1986; Ho, 1986). For instance, Domino and Hannah (1987) analyzed the stories generated by Chinese children from Beijing and American children (11 to 13 years), and reported that stories produced by Chinese children contained fewer instances of physical aggression than those produced by American children. Ekblad (1988) found that Swedish primary and preschool children showed a higher level of aggressive behavior than their counterparts in Beijing, China.

Why Are Chinese Adolescents Less Delinquent?

Given the seriousness of juvenile crime in many societies and the urgent need to identify its causes for effective prevention, it is disappointing to note that the important question of why Chinese adolescents are generally less delinquent than Western adolescents has only been minimally explored. On top of the practical values of this line of work, it may also provide a new perspective to evaluate the validity of various theories of delinquent behavior. Unfortunately, to the best of our knowledge, there is no research that attempts to link this cultural difference to current theories of delinquent behavior. In the following sections, several rather ad hoc explanations for this intriguing cultural difference are reviewed. In the absence of direct empirical data, most of the arguments are based on indirect evidence and hence are speculative.

Suppression of Delinquent Behavior in Socialization

Cross-cultural researchers of aggressive behavior in general agree that, in line with Confucian philosophy, Chinese parents suppress aggressiveness and encourage impulse control in their children (for reviews, see Bond and Wang, 1983; Ho, 1986). For instance, Sollenberger (1968) reported that most Chinese–American mothers did not demand that their children behave aggressively and fight back under any circumstances, whereas most

American mothers encouraged their children to engage in aggressive behavior in "appropriate" situations. Ryback, Sanders, Lorentz, and Koestanblatt (1980) reported that Chinese parents from Taiwan were less likely to allow aggressive behavior in their children than were American and Israeli parents.

These studies suggest that Chinese parents are likely to suppress violent behavior in their children. The strong socialization pressure for impulse control and suppression of aggressiveness can explain why delinquent behaviors, at least the violent types, are less frequent in Chinese societies. This conclusion highlights the importance of socialization practices as an explanation for cultural differences in delinquent behavior.

Pressure to Conform

In a review of conformity behavior in the Chinese, Bond and Hwang (1986) concluded that, compared with Westerners, Chinese show a high level of conformity towards high-status targets. Some evidence also suggests that the behavior of the Chinese is more rule-driven. Wilson (1974) found that children's behavior is more governed by internalized rules in Hong Kong and Taiwan than in the U.S. Bloom (1977) reported that compared with American and French subjects, his sample of Hong Kong Chinese showed a lower level of social principle, reflecting a tendency of unanalytic adherence to the rules set by authority figures. It may be argued that because delinquent behavior always involves some degree of violation of rules set by authority figures such as parents, teachers, and government officials, the higher level of conformity towards authority figures and rule abidance in Chinese adolescents may partially explain why they are generally less delinquent than their Western counterparts.

Genetic Influence

It is possible that genetic influences may partly account for the lower level of delinquent behavior in Chinese adolescents. As argued before, a subset of delinquent behavior involves violence, hostility, and aggressiveness. Thus, if hereditary factors affect the occurrence of aggressive behavior, they will also have some bearing on delinquent behavior. It is well-known that individual differences in aggressiveness may be partly explainable by genetic factors (Hinde, 1974), and it is therefore possible that cultural differences in aggressiveness may also be partly attributable to genetic

influence. Freedman (1971) compared the behavior of Chinese–American
and European-American newborns, and found that Chinese newborns were
less emotionally reactive, habituated more rapidly to aversive stimuli, and
were easily consoled when upset. As these differences are found with
newborns, who have not yet been subjected to the influence of socialization, they are likely to be genetically determined. In addition, these characteristics seem to continue beyond infancy (e.g., Freedman, 1974; Kagan,
Kearsley, and Zelazo, 1978). In light of these findings, Bond and Hwang
(1986) speculated that these traits may partly explain why Chinese show a
lower level of aggressiveness than Westerners, and that such differences are
partly genetically determined. Obviously, this provocative hypothesis
awaits future empirical verification: some scientists express serious doubts
about the connection between genes and violence (The Seville Statement on
violence, 1990).

Gender Differences in Delinquent Behavior

Studies conducted in the West generally show that male adolescents display
more delinquent behavior than female adolescents (for a review, see
Duke, 1977). Consistent with the results from the West, studies in Chinese
societies have also confirmed such a gender difference. For instance, both
Lau and Leung (1992) and Feldman et al. (1991) reported that among
Chinese adolescents in Hong Kong, the frequency of delinquent behavior is
higher for males than for females. Similar gender differences in delinquent
behavior are also found in Taiwan (e.g., Lin, 1984a; Tsai, 1990). It now
seems quite certain that the gender difference in delinquent behavior is
universal. It should also be pointed out that this difference parallels the
gender difference in aggressive behavior (Segall, 1988), which provides
further support for using data on aggressiveness to derive conclusions about
delinquent behavior.

Personality Correlates of Delinquent Behavior

A number of studies have examined the relationship between personality
traits and delinquency behavior in Chinese societies. Generally speaking,
the results obtained are quite consistent with the results obtained in
the West. In Taiwan, both Lu and Chuang (1992) and Yang, Wu, and Yue
(1986) found that sensation-seeking, impulsivity and aggressiveness are
related to delinquent behavior. Lai (1988) found that juvenile delinquents

are lower in self-control but higher in extroversion. Hwang and Hwang (1982) administered the Edwards Personal Preference Schedule to a group of delinquent youths, and found that the delinquent group reported a lower need for achievement, deference, order, and succour, but a higher need for heterosexuality than normal youths. Chuang (1986) found that pleasure-seeking was related to delinquency. Multiple offenders were stronger in psychopathic pleasure-seeking and were more emotionally disturbed. Using the Minnesota Multiphasis Personality Inventory (MMPI) to contrast a delinquent group and a normal group, Ma (1978) found that the delinquent group showed a higher tendency of antisocial behavior. This pattern was also found by Leung (1992) and Cheung (1986) with a similar research design in Hong Kong.

Theories of Delinquency Behavior Examined in Chinese Societies

Although a variety of theories for delinquent behavior have been proposed in the West (e.g., Matza, 1964; Rutter and Giller, 1983), many studies on delinquent behavior conducted in Chinese societies are descriptive in nature and are not guided by theories. For instance, Chu and Yang (1978) found that adolescents were more likely to engage in delinquent behavior if their parents also displayed delinquent behavior. Lu and Chuang (1992) found that children from one-parent families are more likely to suffer from insufficient parental concern and care and to engage in delinquent behavior. Chang and Yang (1975, Chapter 3) have reviewed two studies in Taiwan that have provided a description of the demographic characteristics of juvenile delinquents. Consistent with the results obtained in the West, juvenile delinquents in Taiwan tended to be from poorer and larger families, to have parents with a lower education, and to be less educated themselves (Chen, 1966; Lo, 1966). Wang (1985) has reported a similar pattern among juvenile delinquents in Mainland China. Yu, Wei, and Hsu (1987) have reviewed two surveys conducted in Mainland China, and listed a number of family factors that are related to juvenile delinquency, such as poor conduct on the part of parents and conflict in the family. Similar factors were identified by Liu (1990) in his review of the juvenile crime statistics in Heilongjiang, China. Obviously, this sort of descriptive study is only useful in setting the stage for more theoretical work in the future.

A few studies, however, are explicitly guided by current theories of delinquent behavior. Y. W. Cheung (1985) has provided a review of the studies conducted in Hong Kong on juvenile delinquency up to the mid 1980s. The first systematic empirical study on juvenile delinquency in Hong Kong was undertaken by Ng (1975), and was guided by the control theory proposed by Hirschi (1969). According to Hirschi (1969), the occurrence of delinquent behavior is a result of the weakening of social control, which is conceptualized as social bonds. Hirschi (1969) further classifies social bonds into four types. *Attachment* refers to a heightened sense of importance placed upon the feelings and views and expectations of significant others, such as parents, siblings, and teachers. Individuals are likely to behave properly because they are concerned with the views, feelings, and expectations of significant others and as a result are reluctant to disappoint or frustrate them by engaging in delinquent behavior. *Commitment* refers to the pursuit of some widely valued goal in life, such as receiving a formal education, pursuing a career, building a family, and so on. Delinquent behavior is avoided because it will interfere with the attainment of these important goals. *Involvement* refers to a submergence into socially accepted activities with the result that there is simply no time and energy for delinquent behavior. Finally, *Belief* refers to the values and beliefs that individuals hold, which restrain them from engaging in delinquent behavior. In Ng's (1975) study, various factors assumed to be related to delinquent behavior were explored, including (1) family factors, such as family structure, demographic characteristics of parents, relationships in the family, and parental style, (2) school factors, such as academic performance, attitude toward school, and educational aspiration, (3) living conditions, (4) employment conditions, (5) relationships with peers, (6) leisure activities, and (7) social attitudes. The subjects of the study were divided into two groups. The delinquent group consisted of 479 randomly chosen juvenile offenders in the age range of 12 to 20. The control group consisted of a sample of 491 adolescents who did not have any criminal records. This sample was matched with the delinquent group in terms of age, sex, and living conditions, and was randomly selected from a list of youths included in the Household Expenditure Survey conducted by the Hong Kong Government in 1973. A comparison of these two groups provided substantial support for Hirschi's (1969) social control theory. With regard to attachment, non-delinquent subjects had better relationships with, and a more positive attitude toward, both family and school than delinquent subjects. With regard to commitment, non-delinquent student subjects were more confident of their academic ability, and had better academic performance and higher educational aspiration. For those who were working, non-delinquent subjects were more enthusiastic about their job and changed job less frequently. With regard to involvement, there was no difference between the two groups in their involvement in socially acceptable activities. On the other hand, the delinquent group was more involved with socially stigmatized activities, such as gambling and smoking. Finally, with regard to belief, the delinquent group was more negative about the police and less accepting of conventional moral standards. Thus, Ng's results (1975) are generally consistent with Western findings and supportive of the control theory of Hirschi (1969).

Ng (1980) has provided a more comprehensive test of the control theory of Hirschi (1969) in a follow-up study, the design of which was similar to the first study with two exceptions. First, parents were also interviewed so that it is possible to check whether the views of the respondents and their parents are consistent. Second, in the non-delinquent group, respondents who admitted to having committed criminal offenses were excluded. This procedure allowed a more precise and unconfounded comparison between the delinquent and non-delinquent groups. Her results basically corroborated the results of the first study. The two groups did not differ in terms of family structure (e.g., family size, education level of parents), but the delinquent group reported more negative relationships with parents, stronger associations with peers who were also delinquent, stronger involvement in socially unacceptable leisure activities, and stronger endorsement of unconventional moral beliefs and values. Results of a discriminant analysis indicated that the influence of peers was stronger than other variables. In short, this study also yielded strong support for control theory.

Mok (1985) has examined the impact of a set of variables similar to those examined by Ng on delinquent behavior, but with a different methodology. First, his respondents were students from 38 secondary schools in Hong Kong. Two classes of students from each school participated in his survey, resulting in a total of 1464 respondents. Second, Mok relied on self-report measures on 15 problem behaviors, such as stealing and damaging public property, rather than on official criminal records, to establish the delinquent and non-delinquent groups. A group of 149 students who admitted that they had committed 8 or more delinquent acts were classified as delinquent, and another group of 121 students who stated that they had never committed any of the delinquent acts were classified as non-delinquent. Despite these differences, Mok's results are very similar to those reported by Ng (1975, 1980). The delinquent group reported poorer relationships with their family, more delinquent friends, and fewer socially approved beliefs and values. In a re-analysis of the data collected by Mok (1985) using the technique of path analysis, M. K. Cheung (1985) reported that the influence of peers on delinquent behavior was more significant, confirming a similar finding reported by Ng (1980).

Yang et al. (1986) also employed a two-group design to assess the validity of control theory in Taiwan. The normal group consisted of 2912 youths and the delinquent group consisted of 802 institutionalized youths in the same age group. Again, the results are generally supportive of control theory. With regard to attachment, the delinquent group reported poorer relationships with parents and a lower attachment to family. With regard to commitment, the delinquent group expressed a lower desire for stability and security. With regard to belief, the delinquent group reported a lower endorsement of legal norms and a lower respect for the police. The only finding that is inconsistent with control theory is that the delinquent group did not differ much from the normal group with regard to attachment to school and teachers.

The studies reviewed above are based on control theory proposed by Hirschi (1969), and have ignored other theories of delinquent behavior. Cheung and Ng (1988) corrected this shortcoming and proposed an integrated model derived from control theory as well as several other major theories, including differential association theory, strain theory, and labeling theory. As control theory has been introduced above, only the other theories will be briefly described. Differential association theory argues that delinquent behavior occurs as a result of the acquisition of skills for committing crime as well as the motives and attitudes in support of criminal behavior through interacting with other people (Sutherland and Cressey, 1978). According to Cheung and Ng (1988), this theory implies that delinquent adolescents are more likely to be associated with delinquent friends and that because of the influence of such friends, they are more likely to uphold values in line with delinquent behavior. Strain theory argues that delinquent behavior occurs because individuals have no access to legitimate means for achieving their aspired goals (Cloward and Ohlin, 1960; Merton, 1938). According to Cheung and Ng (1988), this theory implies that delinquent adolescents are more likely to experience educational strain (i.e., the perception of a gap between their educational aspiration and the realistic educational level that they can attain), and that they are likely to be from families of low socio-economic status. Finally, labeling theory argues that the application of a delinquent label to adolescents will channel them to more delinquent behavior. According to Cheung and Ng (1988), this theory implies that parents evaluate delinquent adolescents less favorably. Based on these four theories, Cheung and Ng (1988) developed a model of delinquent behavior that takes into account all these implications. To test their model, a survey was conducted in 10 secondary schools in Hong Kong, with 1139 respondents drawn from forms 1 to 4 (grades 7 to 10). Self-report measures were used for all variables in the model, including delinquent behavior which was measured by an eight-item scale. Using path analytic techniques, Cheung and Ng (1988) were able to show that differential association theory received the strongest support. That is, association with delinquent friends showed the strongest effect on delinquent behavior. Control theory and labeling theory were also supported in that both attachment to parents and schools and negative labeling were related to delinquent behavior significantly. Finally, strain theory did not receive any support in the data. Both educational strain and family socio-economic status had no direct impact on delinquent behavior. The lack of support for strain theory was not surprising since many studies in the West have also failed to support this view (e.g., Akers and Cochran, 1985; Johnson, 1979). In general, the results of Cheung and Ng (1988) are consistent with findings in the West.

Tsai (1990) has evaluated social control theory and differential association theory in Taiwan with 573 adolescents in the 12 to 18 age group. Her results also provided general support for both theories. Delinquency was associated with a poorer attachment to school, a poorer family environment, a stronger association with delinquent peers, a higher involvement in socially unacceptable activities, a lower desire for education and achievement, a higher desire for money, negative beliefs about victims, and a lack of respect for traditional values and beliefs.

Wang (1987) has evaluated five theories in Taiwan: social control, strain, differential association, power-control, and conflict. The first three theories have already been described, and only the power-control and conflict theories need explanation. According to Turk (1971) and Quinney (1977), conflict theory states that the class structure of society affects the definition of delinquency. The ruling class (the class with power) has a stronger influence on the formulation of the law as well as when and to whom the law is applied. The prediction is that the lower class is more likely to be prosecuted and labeled as delinquent. According to Hagan, Gillis, and Simpson (1985) and Hagan, Simpson, and Gillis (1987), power-conflict theory states that delinquency occurs when individuals are given power in the absence of control (and the concomitant absence of punishment), and this argument has been used to explain the gender difference in delinquent behavior. Males are more likely to engage in delinquent behavior than females because males are given more power but are subject to less control and less punishment for delinquent behavior in society. In a two-group design, involving 801 students in the normal group and 527 youths in the delinquent group, Wang (1987) showed that only social control and conflict theories received some support. With regard to control theory, attachment to parents and school is related to a lower level of delinquency, while attachment to friends showed no relationship with delinquency. The involvement in conventional leisure activities was related to a lower level of delinquency. Putting a higher value on money was related to a higher level of delinquency, while commitment to good grades was related to a lower level of delinquency. A higher level of perceived seriousness and certainty of punishment for delinquent behavior was related to a lower level of delinquency. Finally, stronger endorsement of the law was related to a lower level of delinquency. With regard to conflict theory, it was found that a lower social status or a minority status was related to a higher level of delinquency.

Lin (1984b) has evaluated the relationships between delinquent behavior and some variables derived from social learning theory, control theory, differential association theory, symbolic interaction theory and the frustration- aggression hypothesis. In the study, a total of 2604 institutionalized juvenile delinquents in Taiwan were surveyed. An interesting feature of the study is that no control group was used. Instead, the delinquent youths were classified into three groups based on the crime they had committed: aggressive crime only, aggressive crime plus other crime, and non-aggressive crime. In the absence of a control group, it is difficult to evaluate the causes of delinquent behavior. However, Lin's (1984b) results do provide some insights about the causes of violent crime. He found that compared to non-violent delinquents, violent delinquents had parents who were more permissive, they were more influenced by peers who were also violent delinquents, they were more aggressive, and they were more likely to reject conventional beliefs about the law. In addition, the circumstances in which a crime was committed were different among different types of delinquents, and such differences included the time when the crime was committed, the characteristics of the victim, and the use of substances before the crime was committed. All in all, these findings can be loosely interpreted as consistent with the predictions of the theories upon which the variables of the study were based.

Hsi (1982) has tested an integrated model of delinquent behavior based on differential association, strain (or differential opportunity theory), and labeling theories in a two-group design in Taiwan. The delinquent group consisted of 256 male institutionalized delinquents, whereas the control group consisted of 235 male students in the same age group. Using the technique of path analysis, it was found that consistent with differential association theory, being from a family with delinquent members was predictive of cutting classes, dropping out of school, and delinquent behavior. Consistent with strain theory, being from a broken family was predictive of cutting classes, dropping out of school, and delinquent behavior. Consistent with labeling theory, cutting classes and dropping out of school were also predictive of delinquent behavior. It should be pointed out, however, that being from a broken family may be related to variables other than differential opportunity as stated in strain theory, such as relationship with parents. Thus, this finding cannot be regarded as providing firm support for strain theory.

A recent theory of delinquent proposed by Kaplan (1972; 1982) deserves attention since its validity is also confirmed by data obtained in Chinese societies. According to Kaplan (1972; 1982), with the motive of enhancing self-esteem, people tend to maximize the experience of positive self attitudes and minimize the experience of negative self attitudes. Attitudes of self rejection may develop if individuals are unable to defend themselves against, adapt to, or cope with circumstances that may threaten their self-esteem. Such situations include parental and peer rejection, lack of competence, and failure at school. If such situations occur and individuals experience a feeling of self rejection and negative self attitudes, and if the normative structure of their membership group fails to provide them with self-enhancing experiences, they will lose the motivation to conform to normative behavioral patterns endorsed by the group. Alternate behavioral patterns which serve a self-enhancing function will develop. Because these behaviors do not conform to normative standards, they are labeled as "deviant" or "delinquent" by the normative group. In short, Kaplan's theory suggests that low self-esteem predisposes a person to delinquent behavior. For an elaboration of the theory and the evidence in support of the theory obtained in the West, see Kaplan (1975; 1980; 1982), Kaplan and Robbins (1983), Kaplan, Johnson, and Bailey (1986), and Leung and Drasgow (1986). A study conducted in Taiwan has provided data in support of Kaplan's formulation (Su and Yang, 1964). In the study, 36 delinquent and

36 normal youths were asked to describe themselves (the actual self), the person they would like to be (the ideal self), and the person their family would like them to be (the family self) by sorting 70 self-referent statements according to the Q-sort method. Three types of discrepancy scores were calculated, namely, actual-ideal, actual-family, and ideal-family. Results indicated that the delinquent subjects showed a higher level of discrepancy in all three areas than did the control subjects. In other words, juvenile delinquents were less satisfied with themselves and experienced more conflict between their personal ideals and family expectations.

Another study conducted in Taiwan also provided data in support of Kaplan's formulation. Lin (1984b) compared a group of 773 male juvenile delinquents with a control group of 731 male school youths. Both groups completed, among other things, a modified version of the Self-Criticism Scale from the Tennessee Self-concept Scale, which measures the extent to which social approval is desired, and a set of items taken from the MMPI that were found to be able to distinguish juvenile delinquents from non-delinquents. His results indicated that the delinquent group showed more desire for social approval. Based on Kaplan's framework, it may be argued that delinquent youths suffer from lower self-esteem and hence are more in need of social approval to bolster their self-worth.

Kaplan's theory was also tested and expanded in Hong Kong. Leung and Lau (1988) proposed that self-concept can be conceptualized as multi-dimensional, and that different components of self-concept may be related to delinquent behavior differently. Their hypothesis was tested with 1668 high school children (grades 7 to 9) from three secondary schools in Hong Kong. All the variables tested were based on self-report measures, including delinquent behavior which was measured by a 15 item scale. With the use of path analytic techniques, Leung and Lau (1988) showed that delinquent behavior was related to poor academic self-concept, poor relationships with family and school, but favorable social and physical self-concepts. Thus, their results have provided a more intricate relationship between self-concept and delinquent behavior, and have extended the scope of Kaplan's theory. Consistent with the results of the studies reviewed earlier, Leung and Lau (1988) also found that the influence of peer approval on delinquent behavior is stronger than that of family and school approval.

Hwang and Hwang (1982) studied 313 juvenile inmates in Taiwan with a modified version of the Tennessee Self-concept Scale and obtained results that are somewhat consistent with the conclusions of Leung and Lau (1988). Hwang and Hwang (1982) found that the inmates reported a more negative self-concept and lower self-satisfaction than normal students. But there was no significant difference in social self between these two groups. However, in contrast to the results of Leung and Lau (1988), Hwang and Hwang found that the inmates reported a more negative level of physical self.

Finally, a recent study comparing the relationship between misconduct and family environments and values across three cultures provides an opportunity to examine the universality of the processes underlying misconduct (Feldman et al., 1991). The study involved 10th and 11th grade adolescents from Hong Kong (N=141), Australia (N=155), and the U.S. (N=155). Misconduct was measured by a 17-item self-report scale. Values were measured by 16 items from the Chinese Value Survey (Chinese Culture Connection, 1987) and 24 items from the Rokeach Value Survey (Rokeach, 1973). Five factors were identified with this value instrument through factor analysis, namely, well-socialized behavior (e.g., polite, responsible), universal pro-social (e.g., equality, peace), outward success (e.g., wealth, power), competence (e.g., independent, imaginative), and traditional values (e.g., rites and rituals, noncompetitiveness). In addition, individualism-collectivism was measured by a 16 item scale (Triandis, Kashima, Shimada, and Villareal, 1986), and factor analysis revealed three factors, namely, general individualism (e.g., what happens to me is my own doing), honors to individuals (e.g., if a child wins the Nobel prize parents should not feel honored), and family as living unit (e.g., aging parents should live at home with their adult children). Family practices and functioning were measured by the Family Environment Scale (Moos and Moos, 1974), which includes scales on cohesion, expressiveness, conflict, independence, achievement orientation, intellectual-cultural orientation, active recreational orientation, moral-religious emphasis, organization, and control. Eight measures of parenting developed by Dornbush, Ritter, Leiderman, Roberts, and Fraleigh (1987) were also used, which include monitoring of the adolescent, mother and father authoritativeness, mother and father authoritarianism, parental involvement in adolescent decision-making, acceptance of diversity, and emphasis on conformity. Factor analysis of these scales suggests that three general factors can be extracted: the accepting-engaged family factor includes acceptance of diversity, intellectual-cultural orientation, and cohesion. The demanding family factor includes control, achievement orientation, and conformity. The autocratic family factor includes conflict, the authoritarian father and the authoritarian mother. Finally, monitoring from the Dornbush et al. (1987) measures was maintained as a separate family factor.

Using a series of regression analyses, Feldman et al. (1991) were able to show that across the three cultures, misconduct was negatively related to parental monitoring and the family as a unit, but positively related to outward success. In other words, adolescents reported a lower level of misconduct if they perceived a higher level of monitoring from their parents, they believed that parents should live with their adult children, and they regarded such values as power and wealth as less important.

Applicability of Western Theories in Chinese Societies

Based on the above review, it is tempting to conclude that the processes underlying delinquent behavior are similar in both Chinese and Westerners, and that major theoretical models developed in the West are able to explain delinquent behavior equally well in Chinese societies. One may argue, however, that there are at least three more explanations for this convergence. First, except for Feldman et al. (1991), all the studies reviewed are mono-cultural and are therefore less sensitive in detecting cultural differences. Second, most of the studies are guided by western theories, and there is rarely any attempt to develop indigenous concepts to compete with the western concepts. Thus, it is not certain whether the western theories can provide a comprehensive explanation for delinquent behavior or whether some indigenous concepts may go even further in explaining delinquent behavior in Chinese societies. Third, previous studies tend to examine fairly general hypotheses, such as the hypothesis that a poor relationship with family is related to delinquent behavior, and it is not surprising that cross-cultural generality is often confirmed. It is still possible that, with more complicated research designs, the processes underlying delinquent processes may be found to show some cultural variation. A few directions for this line of inquiry are reviewed below.

Cultural Variations in the Processes Underlying Delinquent Behavior

Parental Style

Considerable research has shown that parental warmth and parental control are two major, independent parental styles in the West (Rohner and Rohner, 1981). However, Rohner and Pettengill (1985) argued and confirmed that these two dimensions are related in South Korea. Consistent with the Confucian ideology, parents often exert strong influence over their children and children are expected to respect the wisdom of their parents and show deference to them in the Korean culture. It follows that the perception of parental control may actually be related to a feeling of parental warmth and acceptance, which was exactly what Rohner and Pettengill (1985) found.

Lau and Cheung (1987) argued that the results of Rohner and Pettengill (1985) need to be qualified because parental control can be conceptualized as functional and dysfunctional. They reported that dysfunctional control, which refers to a style that is dominating and authoritarian, was related to poor self-esteem, lower perceived parental warmth, and lower perceived family harmony. On the other hand, functional control, which refers to a style that helps children to organize their activities, was related to positive self-esteem, higher perceived parental warmth, and higher perceived family harmony.

Given that Koreans and Chinese both share the Confucian heritage and that major value surveys confirm that Koreans and Chinese show similar value profiles (e.g., Hofstede, 1983), the results of Lau and Cheung (1987) and of Rohner and Pettengill (1985), may provide a basis for speculating about how the autocratic parental style may be related to delinquent behavior in Chinese societies. It is possible that because of the higher acceptance of parental control in Chinese societies, functional control may bear little relationship with delinquent behavior, and may even reduce delinquency. On the other hand, because of the lower acceptance of parental control in Western societies, it is possible that functional control may be related to a higher level of delinquent behavior. Some initial evidence has been provided by Feldman et al. (1991) to support this speculation. Specifically, an autocratic family style was correlated positively with misconduct for American and Australian subjects, but this correlation was non-significant for Chinese subjects. Unfortunately, this cultural difference disappeared when a finer analysis with multiple regression was applied. In any event, this line of reasoning deserves some attention in future research.

Group Orientation

Most juvenile delinquency is committed by groups, and social influence obviously plays a significant role in the enactment of delinquent behavior. In fact, a previous section concludes that peer influence has the largest impact on the occurrence of delinquent behavior. Research has shown that groups exert a stronger influence on members in Chinese societies. For instance, in a large-scale value survey, Hofstede (1980) characterized Hong Kong and Taiwan as collectivistic. In general, Chinese tend to make a stronger distinction between ingroups and outgroups, and are more likely to make an effort to remain in a group and sacrifice their self-interest for the group (e.g., Hsu, 1970; Leung and Bond, 1984). In addition, this collectivistic orientation also tends to lead to a closer adherence to group norms.

How is group orientation related to delinquent behavior in Chinese societies? In the absence of relevant data, only some general hypotheses can be developed. In line with the arguments proposed by Hirschi (1969) and Naroll (1983), the stronger social ties between adolescents with family, relatives, and school in Chinese societies may provide a partial explanation for the lower crime rate in these societies as compared to the West. In fact, in an extensive review of the literature, Triandis (1990) has also concluded that crime should be and has been lower in collectivist than in individualist societies for a similar reason. It should be noted that this argument is consistent with some of the explanations for the lower level of juvenile delinquency in Chinese societies given in a previous section.

The strong group orientation in Chinese societies, however, may be a two-edged sword with regard to its effect on delinquent behavior. In delinquent groups, such as street gangs, the dominant values and norms are obviously consistent with the enactment of delinquent behavior. It follows that a stronger group orientation and a closer adherence to group norms may breed more delinquent behavior. In addition, members may even construe the enactment of delinquent behavior as a means to promote the well-being of the group and thus are more committed to such behavior. For instance, a street gang may decide to beat up people to establish the name of the gang. Individual members may be over-zealous about establishing the name of the group and beat up more people than was required by the original plan. Some indirect evidence is available to support this reasoning. Bond and Wang (1983) have reviewed quite a few cases in which Chinese were extremely brutal in their treatment of outgroup members. For instance, during the Cultural Revolution in Mainland China, landlords were often beaten to death by otherwise law-abiding, timid villagers. Bond and Wang (1983) argue that one interpretation of this unjustified brutality is that the wrongdoers see the brutal acts not as aggression, but as a just defense of the well-being of the group. An interesting corollary of this argument is that juvenile crime may be more frequently committed by groups in Chinese societies than in the West. Needless to say, all these hypotheses should be examined in future research.

Indigenous Phenomena

Chinese societies are different from Western societies in many ways, and a number of phenomena are prevalent in Chinese societies which are rare in the West. The investigation of these indigenous phenomena is likely to throw new light on our understanding of delinquent behavior and extend our theories. A good example is given by the recent effort to control population growth in Mainland China (such as by raising the legal marriage age and by the one-child policy), which inevitably alters the traditional family pattern and may result in more juvenile delinquency (Wei, 1983). In particular, the one-child policy has generated quite a lot of social concern and research activities. In 1980, the government in Mainland China began to advocate the one child per family policy to alleviate the population expansion problem. Thus, in the past 10 years, one-child families have come to abound in urban areas in China. In the West, there has been debate as to whether children from one-child families are more likely to show psychological maladjustment. The exploration of the behavior of single children in China may shed new light on this debate. Some initial work has shown that only children have more behavior problems than children with siblings (Tao and Chiu, 1985). In a large scale survey conducted in Nanjing, Tseng, Tao, Jing, Chiu, Yu, and Kameoka (1988) found a more complex pattern. Chinese boys who were only children and were cared for by grandparents tended to become more anxious and aggressive.

It is also worth noting that grandparents as "caretakers" of children are relatively more common in Chinese societies than in the West. The influence of grandparents on delinquent behavior in adolescents is definitely a relevant and important topic for research in Chinese societies, but it is almost meaningless in the West.

Another example of indigenous phenomena is that cities in Mainland China are undergoing rapid urbanization, and it is interesting to explore how this change may be related to the occurrence of juvenile delinquency. For instance, many people have moved from traditional courtyard houses to modern flats in Beijing, and this environmental change has been found to be related to the occurrence of delinquent behavior in adolescents (Ekblad and Werne, 1990).

Finally, Shaw (1985) identified three types of youths in Taiwan in an anthropological study. "Hao-hsüeh-sheng" (good students) follow social conventions and norms, respect parents and teachers, study hard, avoid indecent places and bad habits, and speak Mandarin instead of Taiwanese with teachers. "Kha-a" refers to youths who wear trendy clothes, enjoy mixing with the opposite sex and westernized entertainments such as discos and MacDonalds, smoke cigarettes and use drugs of a western origin, and disregard rules set by adults. "Liu-mang" refers to youths who are often involved in fights and gambling, but who tend to stay away from the opposite sex. They go to restaurants to drink rather than discos and bars, and use drugs of a Chinese origin. They emphasize loyalty and devotion to the ingroup and are likely to be members of delinquent gangs. Because Taiwan is subject to a high level of western influence, kha-a probably represent a pattern of deviance under the influence of westernization, whereas liu-mang represent an indigenous pattern of deviance. In a large-scale study, Yang, Yue, and Wu (1991) developed measures to identify these types of youths. They further showed that compared with liu-mang, kha-a showed a poorer relationship with parents, were more concerned with social status as a life goal, showed a higher level of sensation-seeking, impulsiveness and aggressiveness, a lower level of self-discipline, and displayed more delinquent behavior and more disrespect for the police. Our understanding of the processes underlying kha-a and liu-mang behaviors is obviously rudimentary, and this topic awaits in-depth exploration in Taiwan as well as in other Chinese societies. The concept of loyalty among liu-mang and the dynamics in liu-mang groups also deserves special attention as such work may lead to the development of important indigenous concepts and theories.

Conclusions and Suggestions for Future Research

Inadequate Research

A number of conclusions can be drawn from the above review. The most obvious one is probably the dearth of theory-guided research that has been conducted in Chinese societies. The lack of empirical data on the subject should not be taken to mean that there is little concern for juvenile delinquency in Chinese societies. Quite the reverse, juvenile crime has generated a high level of social concern and extensive speculation about its causes and prevention in China (e.g., Wang, 1985), Taiwan (e.g., Chang, 1991), and Hong Kong (e.g., Y. W. Cheung, 1985). It is unclear why the attention that juvenile crime receives does not translate into more rigorous research activities. In any event, more theory-guided empirical work is needed for a better understanding of the dynamics behind juvenile delinquency in Chinese societies.

Indigenous Concepts and Theories

Many observers have noted that the West has dominated the non-western world by a form of intellectual colonialism. Theories developed in the West are often imported into and applied in non-western countries, whereas indigenous concepts and theories usually receive minimal attention. Psychological research in Chinese societies unfortunately fits this description (e.g., Bond, 1986; Yang, 1986), and research on juvenile delinquency in Chinese societies is also no exception to this pattern. Virtually all empirical studies conducted are guided by western theories, and results are generally supportive of these imported theories. It has been pointed out in a previous section that, thus far, only very general hypotheses derived from western theories have been tested. It is entirely possible that when indigenous concepts and theories are taken into account and more intricate hypotheses are being put to test, cultural differences will begin to emerge. Some general areas for uncovering the uniqueness of delinquent behavior in Chinese societies have already been discussed.

The development of more locally sensitive theories of delinquent behavior will also contribute to the development of truly universal theories. Only when the cultural limitations of western theories are identified can they be refined and improved for universal applications (see Leung, 1988; Pepitone and Triandis, 1988, for an elaboration of this argument). Thus, future research efforts in the area of delinquent behavior should intensify the search for cultural uniqueness while bearing in mind the broad goal of the eventual development of truly universal theories.

Cross-cultural Research

Most of the empirical work on juvenile delinquency in Chinese societies is mono-cultural. While mono-cultural work is essential for the development of indigenous theories, cross-cultural comparisons provide the basis for identifying what is culture-specific and what is culture-general

(Triandis, 1980). Obviously, we need a balance of both types of research for establishing a clear picture of the causes and patterns of juvenile delinquent behaviors in Chinese societies.

It is also worth noting that while Chinese living in China, Taiwan, and Hong Kong do share a common Chinese heritage (e.g., Bond, 1986; Hofstede, 1980), subtle differences may exist among these three groups of Chinese since they live in very different social, economic and political environments. For instance, Epstein (1986) has compared the reformatory education organizations for juvenile offenders in Taiwan, China, and Hong Kong and concluded that reformatory institutions in Taiwan and China are similar in their prison-like set-up and the political nature of the institutionalization, whereas such institutions in Hong Kong rely more on rewards and incentives to channel their inmates back to a normal pattern of life. Comparative studies involving these three societies may uncover systematic similarities and differences that are important for theory development.

References

Akers, R. L., and Cochran, J. K. (1985). Adolescent marijuana use: A test of three theories of deviant behavior. *Deviant Behaviour*, 6: 323–346.

Bloom, A. H. (1977). A cognitive dimension of social control: The Hong Kong Chinese in cross-cultural perspective. In A. A. Wilson, S. L. Greenblatt, and R. W. Wilson (Eds.), *Deviance and social control in Chinese society* (pp. 67–81). New York: Praeger.

Bond, M. H. (1986). *The psychology of the Chinese people*. Hong Kong: Oxford University Press.

Bond, M. H., and Hwang, K. K. (1986). *The social psychology of Chinese people*. In M. H. Bond (Ed.), *The psychology of the Chinese people* (pp. 213–266). Hong Kong: Oxford University Press.

Bond, M. H., and Wang, S. H. (1983). Aggressive behavior in Chinese society: The problem of maintaining order and harmony. In A. P. Goldstein and M. Segall (Eds.), *Global perspectives on aggression* (pp. 58–74). New York: Pergamon Press.

Chang, C. H. (1991, October). *Social change and youth problems* (In Chinese). Paper presented at the Annual Conference on Educational Psychology of the Chinese Psychological Association, Nanjing, PRC.

Chang, T. H., and Yang, K. S. (1975). *Psychology* (In Chinese). Taiwan: San Ming Publishing Company.

Chen, K. H. (1966). *A study of the family environment and social background of juvenile delinquents in Taipei* (In Chinese). Taipei: Literature Committee of Taipei.

Cheung, F.M.C. (1986). *An overview of Chinese MMPI research in Hong Kong* (Occasional paper). Hong Kong: The Chinese University of Hong Kong, Centre for Hong Kong Studies.

Cheung, M. K. (1985). *Some social correlates of juvenile misbehaviour in Hong Kong*. Senior thesis, The Chinese University of Hong Kong, Department of Sociology.

Cheung, Y. W. (1985). Family and beyond: The past and future of adolescent delinquency research in Hong Kong (In Chinese). Paper presented at the Second Conference on Modernization and Chinese culture, The Chinese University of Hong Kong, Hong Kong.

Cheung, Y. W., and Ng, M. C. (1988). Social factors in adolescent deviant behavior in Hong Kong: An integrated theoretical approach. *International Journal of Comparative and Applied Criminal Justice*, 12: 27–45.

The Chinese Culture Connection. (1987). Chinese values and the search for culture-free dimensions of culture. *Journal of Cross-Cultural Psychology*, 18: 143–164.

Chu, R. L, and Yang, K. S. (1978, June). *The influence of family and community environment on problem behaviors of secondary school students* (In Chinese). Paper presented at the Symposium on Youth Problems in a Society in Transition, Taipei.

Chuang, Y. J. (1986). *Psychopathic personality and criminal behavior* (In Chinese). Taipei: Legal Department.

Cloward, R., and Ohlin, L. (1960). *Delinquency and opportunity: A theory of delinquent gangs*. New York: Free Press.

DeFleur, L. (1969). Alternate strategies for the development of delinquency theories applicable to other cultures. *Social Problems*, 17: 30.

Domino, G., and Hannah, M. T. (1987). A comparative analysis of social values of Chinese and American children. *Journal of Cross-Cultural Psychology*, 18: 58–77.

Dornbush, S. M., Ritter, P. L., Leiderman, P. H., Roberts, D. F., and Fraleigh, M. J. (1987). The relation of parenting style to adolescent school performance. *Child Development*, 58: 1244–1257.

Duke, D. L. (1977). Why don't girls misbehavior more than boys in school? *Journal of Youth and Adolescence*, 7: 515–523.

Ekblad, S. (1986). Social determinants of aggression in a sample of Chinese primary school children. *Acta Psychiatrica Scandinavica*, 73: 515–523.

———. (1988). Influence of child-rearing on aggressive behavior in a trans-cultural perspective. *Acta Psychiatrica Scandinavica*, 78: 133–139.

Ekblad, S, and Olweus, D. (1986). Applicability of Olweus' aggression inventory in a sample of Chinese primary school children. *Aggressive Behavior*, 12: 315–325.

Ekblad, S., and Werne, F. (1990). Housing and health in Beijing: Implications of high-rise housing on children and the aged. *Journal of Sociology and Social Welfare*, 1: 51–77.

Epstein, I. I. (1986). Reformatory education in Chinese society. *International Journal of Offender Therapy and Comparative Criminology*, 30: 87–100.

Feldman, S. S., Rosenthal, D. A., Mont-Reynaud, R., Leung, K., and Lau, S. (1991). Ain't misbehavin': Adolescent values and family environments as correlates of misconduct in Australia, Hong Kong, and the United States. *Journal of Research on Adolescence*, 1: 109–134.

Freedman, D. G. (1971). An evolutionary approach to research in the life cycle. *Human Development*, 67: 87–99.

———. (1974). *Human infancy: An evolutionary perspective*. Hillsdale, NJ: Lawrance Earlbum.

Hagan, J. (1977). *The disreputable pleasures: Crime and deviance in Canada*. Toronto: McGraw-Hill Ryerson.

Hagan, J., Gillis, A. R., and Simpson, J. (1985). The class structure of gender and delinquency: Toward a power-control theory of common delinquent behavior. *American Journal of Sociology*, 90: 1151–1326.

Hagan, J., Simpson, J., and Gillis, A. R. (1987). Class in the household: A power-control theory of gender and delinquency. *American Journal of Sociology*, 92: 788–816.

Hinde, R. A. (1974). *Biological bases of human social behavior*. New York: McGraw-Hill.

Hindelang, M. J., Hirschi, T., and Weis, J. G. (1981). *Measuring delinquency*. Beverly Hills, CA: Sage.

Hirschi, T. (1969). *Causes of delinquency*. Berkeley: University of California Press.

Ho, D.Y.F. (1986). Chinese patterns of socialization: A critical review. In M. H. Bond (Ed.), *The psychology of the Chinese people* (pp. 1–37). Hong Kong: Oxford University Press.

Hofstede, G. (1980). *Culture's consequences: International differences in work-related values*. Beverly Hills, CA: Sage.

———. (1983). Dimensions of national cultures in fifty countries and three regions. In J. B. Deregowski, S. Dziurawiec, and R. C. Annis (Eds.), *Expiscations in cross-cultural psychology* (pp. 335–355). Lisse: Swets and Zeitlinger.

Hsi, R. C. (1982, December). Further analysis of causes of juvenile delinquency (In Chinese). In C. I. Wen, K. S. Yang, and Y. Y. Li (Eds.), *Proceedings of the Conference on Problems of Crime in a Society in Transition and Its Prevention*. Taipei, Taiwan.

Hsu, F.L.K. (1970). *Americans and Chinese*. New York: Natural History Press.

Hwang, K. K., and Hwang, S. L. (1982). Self-concept, values, and attitude toward crime among criminals from low social class (In Chinese). In C. I. Wen, K. S.

Yang, and Y. Y. Li (Eds.), *Proceedings of the Conference on Problems of Crime in a Society in Transition and Its Prevention*. Taipei, Taiwan.

Johnson, R. E. (1979). *Juvenile delinquency and its origins*. Cambridge: Cambridge University Press.

Kagan, J., Kearsley, R. B., and Zelazo, P. R. (1978). *Infancy: Its place in human development*. Cambridge, MA: Harvard University Press.

Kaplan, H. B. (1972). Toward a general theory of psychosocial deviance: The case of aggressive behavior. *Social Science and Medicine*, 6: 593–617.

———. (1975). *Self-attitudes and deviant behavior*. Santa Monica, CA: Goodyear.

———. (1980). *Deviant behavior in defense of self*. New York: Academic Press.

———. (1982). Self-attitudes and deviant behavior: New directions for theory and research. *Youth and Society*, 14: 185–211.

Kaplan, H. B., Johnson, R. J., and Bailey, C. A. (1986). Self-rejection and the explanation of deviance: Refinement and elaboration of a latent structure. *Social Psychology Quarterly*, 49: 110–128.

Kaplan, H. B., and Robbins, C. (1983). Testing a general theory of deviant behavior in longitudinal perspective. In K. T. van Dusen and S. A. Mednick (Eds.), *Prospective studies of crime and delinquency* (pp. 117–146). Boston: Kluwer-Nijhoff.

Lai, B. J. (1988). *A study of the causes of delinquent behavior in students and the prevention of delinquent behavior in Taiwan* (In Chinese). Report of the Prevention of Juvenile Delinquency Research Programme of the Taiwan Government.

Lau, S., and Cheung, P. C. (1987). Relations between Chinese adolescent's perception of parental control and organization and their perception of parental warmth. *Developmental Psychology*, 23: 726–729.

Lau, S., and Leung, K. (1992). Self-concept, delinquency, relations with parents and school, and Chinese adolescents' perception of personal control. *Personality and Individual Differences*, 13: 615–622.

Lemert, E. M. (1967). *Human deviance, social problems, and social control*. Englewood Cliffs, NJ: Prentice-Hall.

Leung, F.K.W. (1992). *Clinical utility of the MMPI in the evaluation of delinquent boys with mid to severe behavioral problems*. Unpublished master's thesis, The Chinese University of Hong Kong, Department of Psychology.

Leung, K. (1988). Theoretical advances in justice behavior: Some cross-cultural inputs. In M. H. Bond (Ed.), *The cross-cultural challenge to social psychology* (pp. 218–229). Newbury Park, CA: Sage.

Leung, K., and Bond, M. H. (1984). The impact of cultural collectivism on reward allocation. *Journal of Personality and Social Psychology*, 47: 793–804.

Leung, K., and Drasgow, F. (1986). Relation between self-esteem and delinquent behavior in three ethnic groups: An application of item response theory. *Journal of Cross-Cultural Psychology*, 17: 151–167.

Leung, K., and Lau, S. (1988). Effects of self-concept and perceived disapproval of delinquent behavior in school children. *Journal of Youth and Adolescent*, 18: 345–359.

Lin, P. C. (1984a). Social desirability, personality traits and juvenile delinquency (In Chinese). *Journal of Education and Psychology*, 7: 1–17.

Lin, Y. Y. (1984b). *A study on juvenile violent crime* (In Chinese) (Research Report). Taiwan: Minister of Law, Criminal Research Center.

Liu, S. S. (1990). The importance of family education in light of the recidivism of Juvenile criminals (In Chinese). *Qingshaonian tantao*, 1: 28–30.

Lo, M. Y. (1966). Assessment and investigation of juvenile delinquents in Northern Taiwan (In Chinese). *Assessment Annual*, 13: 30–39.

Lu, M. C., and Chuang, Y. C. (1992). An empirical study on the single-parent families and factors related to adolescent delinquency (In Chinese). *Tunghai Journal*, 33: 247–284.

Ma, C. C. (1978). A comparative study of the personality profile of normal and delinquent youths in Taiwan (In Chinese). *Police Academy Journal*, 9: 43–53.

Matza, D. (1964). *Delinquency and drift*. New York: Wiley.

Merton, R. K. (1938). Social structure and anomie. *American Sociological Review*, 3: 672–682.

Mok, B. H. (1985). *Problem behaviour of adolescents in Hong Kong: A socio-cultural perspective* (Occasional paper No. 7). Hong Kong: The Chinese University of Hong Kong, Centre for Hong Kong Studies.

Moos, R. H., and Moos, B. S. (1974). *Family environment scale*. Palo Alto, CA: Consulting Psychology Press.

Naroll, R. (1983). *The Moral Order*. Beverly Hills, CA: Sage.

Ng, A. (1975). *Social causes of violent crime among young offenders in Hong Kong*. Hong Kong: The Chinese University of Hong Kong, Social Research Centre.

———. (1980). *Family relationship and delinquent behaviour*. Unpublished doctoral dissertation, Columbia University, School of Social Work.

Pepitone, A., and Triandis, H. C. (1988). On the universality of social psychological theories. *Journal of Cross-Cultural Psychology*, 18: 471–498.

Quay, H. C., and Werry, J. S. (1972). *Psychopathological disorders of childhood*. New York: Wiley.

Quinney, R. (1977). *Class, state, and crime*. New York: McKay David.

Rohner, R. P., and Rohner, E. C. (1981). Parental acceptance-rejection and parental control: Cross-cultural codes. *Ethnology*, 20: 245–260.

Rohner, R. P., and Pettengill, S. M. (1985). Perceived parental acceptance–rejection and parental control among Korean Adolescents. *Child Development*, 56: 524–527.

Rokeach, M. (1973). *The nature of human values*. New York: The Free Press.

Rutter, M., and Giller, H. (1983). *Juvenile delinquency: Trends and perspectives.* Suffolk: Penguin Books.

Ryback, D., Sanders, A. L., Lorentz, J., and Koestanblatt, M. (1980). Child-rearing practices reported by students in six cultures. *Journal of Social Psychology,* 110: 153–162.

Segall, M. H. (1988). Cultural roots of aggressive behavior. In M. H. Bond (Ed.), *The cross-cultural challenge to social psychology* (pp. 208–217). Newbury Park, CA: Sage.

The Seville Statement on violence. (1990). *American Psychologist,* 45: 1167–1168.

Shaw, T. A. (1985). *Youth culture in the Chinese setting: An outline of conclusions tentatively drawn in the final stage of anthropological fieldwork.* Unpublished manuscript, Columbia University, Department of Anthropology.

Sollenberger, R. T. (1968). Chinese–American child-rearing practices and juvenile delinquency. *Journal of Social Psychology,* 74: 13–23.

Su, H. Y., and Yang, K. S. (1964). Self-concept congruence in relation to juvenile delinquency. *Acta Psychologica Taiwanica,* 6: 1–9.

Sutherland, E. H., and Cressey, R. R. (1978). *Criminology* (10th ed.). Philadelphia: J. B. Lippincott.

Tao, K., and Chiu, J. H. (1985). The one-child policy per-family policy: A psychological perspective. In W. S. Tseng and D.Y.H. Wu (Eds.), *Chinese culture and mental health* (pp. 153–165). London: Academic press.

Triandis, H. C. (1980). Introduction to *Handbook of cross-cultural psychology.* In H. C. Triandis and W. W. Lambert (Eds.), *Handbook of cross-cultural psychology* (pp. 1–14). Boston, MA: Allyn and Bacon.

———. (1990). Cross-cultural studies of individualism and collectivism. In J. Berman (Ed.), *Nebraska symposium on motivation 1989* (pp. 41–133). Lincoln, NB: University of Nebraska Press.

Triandis, H. C., Kashima, Y., Shimada, E., and Villareal, M. (1986). Acculturation indices as a means of confirming cultural differences. *International Journal of Psychology,* 21: 43–70.

Tsai, H. H. (1990). *A study on the relationship between family and juvenile delinquency* (In Chinese). Unpublished master's thesis, National Taiwan University, Department of Sociology.

Tseng, W. S., Tao, K., Jing, H., Chiu, J., Yu, L., and Kameoka, V. (1988). Family planning and child mental health in China: The Nanjing survey. *American Journal of Psychiatry,* 145: 1396–1403.

Turk, A. T. (1971). *Criminality and legal order.* Chicago, IL: Rand McNally.

Wang, C. C. (1985). Some statistics about juvenile delinquents in our country (In Chinese). *Nanfang qingshaonian yanjiu,* 3: 32–35.

Wang, S. N. (1987). *Testing criminological theories in an oriental society.* Unpublished doctoral dissertation, University of Arizona, Department of Sociology.

Wei, Z. L. (1983). Chinese family problems: Research and trends. *Journal of Marriage and the Family*, 45: 943–948.

Wilkins, L. T. (1980). World crime: To measure or not to measure? In G. R. Newman (Ed.), *Crime and deviance: A comparative perspective* (pp. 17–41). Beverly Hills, CA: Sage.

Wilson, R. W. (1974). *The moral state: A study of the political socialization of Chinese and American children*. New York: The Free Press.

Yang, K. S. (1981). Problem behavior in Chinese adolescents in Taiwan: A classificatory-factorial study. *Journal of Cross-Cultural Psychology*, 12: 179–193.

——— . (1986). Effects of family factors on child behavior: A review of empirical studies in Taiwan (In Chinese). *Acta Psychologica Taiwanica*, 15: 7–28.

Yang, K. S., Wu, E. C., and Yue, D. H. (1986). *The psychological orientation of juvenile delinquents in Taipei and the prevention of juvenile delinquency* (In Chinese). Report submitted to the Taipei Police Bureau.

Yang, K. S., Yue, D. H., and Wu, E. C. (1991). Normal and delinquent syndromes of Chinese youth in Taiwan: Quantitative differentiation and psychological profiles. *Proceedings of the National Science Council, Part C: Humanities and Social Sciences*, 1: 260–279.

Yu, H. Y., Wei, C. H., and Hsu, K. H. (1987). A preliminary exploration of the family factors related to criminal behavior of adolescents (In Chinese). *Xuchang shizhuan xuebao*, 3: 98–103.

The Academic, Personality, and Physical Outcomes of Chinese Only Children: A Review[*]

Toni Falbo, Dudley L. Poston, Jr., and Xiao-tian Feng

Introduction

This chapter reviews much of the scientific research conducted about only children in China and in the West. The conclusions are remarkably consistent with those of David Wu in Chapter 1. We describe the research we have conducted in China not only in terms of our findings about only children but also in terms of our own increasingly sophisticated methodology. We attempt to explain why concern about only children in China persists despite the accumulation of evidence which indicates that only children on the average are not "little emperors."

The One-Child Policy

In 1979, People's Republic of China stunned the world by announcing the most ambitious family planning policy ever undertaken in human history. Based on the population projections of high-ranking Communist Party officials, the Central Government determined that unless new families were limited to one child per family, the rate of economic development in China would be substantially reduced. Furthermore, allowing new families to have more than two children would exacerbate the already severe degradation of the environment, with famine a real possibility. To avoid these problems and accelerate economic development, a family planning policy, later known as the One-Child Policy, was initiated which stated that

[*] Some paragraphs in this chapter are excerpts from the Method and Discussion sections in an article published in Child Development (1993) by the present authors with the permission of the Society for Research in Child Development.

each new family should contain only one child. This policy was given a high, national priority and much of the nation's resources and attention were devoted to increasing the number of one-child families. The goal was to reduce the rate of population growth so that China's population would be about 1.2 billion at the beginning of the 21st Century (Banister, 1987; Greenhalgh and Bongaarts, 1987; Hardee-Cleaveland and Banister, 1988).

In major urban areas and agricultural communes, the Party had succeeded in 1971 in implementing a two-child policy by establishing a nationwide family planning system, including the mass distribution of contraceptives to married couples, saturation propaganda about the importance of family planning, and workplace enforcement of the policy (Croll, Davin, and Kane, 1985).

In early 1979, they decided to use this system and infrastructure to attain a new goal, allowing newly formed families to have only one child. At first, the one-child policy was vigorously implemented in both urban and rural areas. But then, in the face of mounting pressure from local officials who complained of local opposition, many waivers were established, including allowing rural parents with an only child girl to try again to have a son (Greenhalgh, 1986; Tien, 1992). Complicating matters further, the Central Committee decided also to decollectivize farming, inadvertently disabling the system that was necessary to enforce the one-child policy (Hardee-Cleaveland and Banister, 1988). Consequently, many rural families formed since 1979, have second children, especially if the firstborn was a girl. Nonetheless, their final family size is substantially smaller than what was common during the 60s (Coale, Wang, Riley, and Lin, 1991).

In urban China, the family planning system was not as much affected by the changes in agricultural policy, and most families formed in the 80s are one child families. For example, in Beijing and Shanghai 86 percent and 91 percent, respectively, of all babies born in 1985 had no siblings (Gu, Poston, and Shu, 1987). Given the fact that about one-fifth of the world's current population lives in China, it is surely true that there are more only children living in China today than in any other country.

Little Emperors

Soon after the implementation of the one-child policy, critics in the West and in China wondered whether this policy would ruin the character of the Chinese people. They argued that only children in their families were like the sun around which rotated their parents and grandparents (the first chapter of this book describes and documents this belief). Such a configuration was thought to spoil the child, producing what is popularly called, a "little emperor." In response, many Chinese social scientists conducted studies to determine if this concern was justified and if so, what could be done to improve the children's character.

However, the quality of these studies varies substantially as does the conclusions reached about only children. Most of the studies published in scholarly journals in China were by scholars in psychology and education. This accumulation of scholarly publications about only children tells us as much about the status of such research in China as it does about the status of only children in China. Compared to Western-style research, many of these Chinese studies are lacking not only in their theoretical, but also in their methodological aspects. Most of the studies were driven mainly by the practical need to know if only children were different from others. Therefore, these studies tend to compare the characteristics of only children with those of non-only children, without considering the layers of social context in which the children live. Furthermore, these studies are often conducted in isolation, without reviewing the results of previous studies. For example, during the 80s, more than sixty articles comparing only children to others were published in scholarly journals in China. Unfortunately, few showed any awareness of the others, and therefore, most used unique indices and drew conclusions without any effort to reconcile these results with those of previous investigators. Consequently, no body of knowledge had accumulated in China about only children. Each scholar tended to rely on his or her own study when drawing conclusions about only children.

Given this, it should not be surprising that one of the methodological flaws of this literature is that since each study uses its own indices of academic, personality, and physical outcomes, it is difficult to make comparisons of the results. Further, many studies have not revealed how the characteristics studied were measured, making evaluation and replication of these studies impossible.

Putting aside these limitations, some studies concluded that only children possess different characteristics than non-only children. These differences were noted as manifesting themselves in academic and physical characteristics, as well as in the character of these children.

For example, in an article on the character and virtues of only children, Yang (1983) draws a clear conclusion: "only and non-only children tend to show developmental differences in two aspects, only children were better in physical condition and intelligence.... Only children were worse in virtues and behavioral habits than non-only children." This finding is common among those studies reporting differences between only children and others.

In contrast, other studies have concluded that only children do not differ from others in their psychological characteristics and behavior. For example, Chen (1985) considered the "collective orientations" of 964 children from urban and rural primary schools and kindergartens in the Beijing Municipality. He obtained personality data from three sources: the children's teachers, parents, and peers. Irrespective of age, gender, or residence, only children were found to be as likely as their peers with siblings to show socially desirable levels of collective orientation.

Studies of Chinese Children Published in English

Although at least sixty Chinese studies have been published in Chinese journals, a few studies of Chinese only children have been published in Western journals. The ones which have received the most attention will be described here.

Chinese Researchers

Jiao, Ji, and Jing (1986) evaluated the peer prestige of children ranging in age from 4 to 10 years from the urban and rural areas of the Beijing Municipality. Originally, they tested 975 children by asking them a series of questions about the classroom behavior of their classmates. For example, each child was asked to indicate which classmate "... is the one who usually is the leader and offers new ideas?" Instead of doing a within classroom analysis or covarying background factors during data analysis, the investigators chose to match the only children with non-only children in their sample. In this way, they reduced the number of children in their sample to 360 (180 matched pairs). The matching procedure was not described in any detail, but the point of it was to select from the non-only child pool, children who were comparable to the onlies in terms of the occupational and educational status of their parents, whether the family was nuclear or three generational in structure, and the gender of the child.

The results of this study indicated that only children were at a severe disadvantage in terms of the peer evaluations of their social behavior. Without exception, the comparisons between onlies and others indicated that onlies were problematic: specifically, they were found to be low in cooperation with peers and peer prestige and high in egocentricism, as seen by their peers. The authors attributed the poor performance of only children to the excessive indulgence of their parents. Children who had the worst peer evaluations tended to come from nuclear one-child families; while those with the best evaluations tended to come from three-generational multi-child families.

Another, more sociological study, involved a survey of 800 households in and near Tianjin, a port city near Beijing (Bian, 1987). The author did not measure the children's outcomes, but instead, examined such factors as family income and time spent with children and compared one-child to multiple-child families. His results indicated that the per capita incomes of one-child families were not only higher, but also more stable than those of multiple child families throughout the childrearing period of the family. On the average, families with only one child spent more on their children than larger families spent on each child. Furthermore, these families spent more money on the child than they spent on any other family member. This high level of expenditure was found regardless of the family income. In terms of the amount of time parents spent with children, Bian's survey indicated that "… single children's parents spend approximately double the time that those of the non-single child do on the rearing of their children" (Bian, 1987). This survey also reported that the Chinese families were changing from an extended one to a nuclear one. His study suggested that a preferred family pattern among upwardly mobile, young Chinese families was a one-child, nuclear family. Most of the reasons for this shift, Bian noted, may be seen as part of a modernization shift in which young Chinese people were aiming towards a modern, technological life, in which one's traditional obligations to family members had changed. In the midst of this change, young parents were often confused about how to rear their children, and this confusion was resulting in a pattern of material overindulgence and parental high expectations for the child. Although no direct observations of the children were made in Bian's survey, he blamed faulty childrearing as the main reason for their reputedly undesirable characteristics of some children, e.g., greediness, willfulness, selfishness, fussy eating habits, and so forth.

Our Early Research

We have published several articles about Chinese children, comparing the outcomes of only children to those of non-only children. The first survey conducted in this series was that of Mei-Yu Yu and her medical colleagues, who in 1980 collected information about 1,069 kindergarten and primary school children ranging in age from 3 to 9 years and living in Changsha, the capital of Hunan. The children were evaluated by their teachers in terms of academic performance in school and according to a list of nine personal attributes. These data were analyzed and the results published by Poston and Yu (1985). The results indicated that only children scored higher than others in both mathematics and verbal achievement. In terms of the nine personal attributes, only children were rated as more cooperative and less hostile than children with siblings. In only two attributes did onlies clearly perform worse than their peers and these attributes were their fussy eating habits and their fascination with fancy dress. The remaining attributes produced no differences between only children and others: lacking in self-care, careless about property, timid, disrespectful for elders, and unenthused about manual labor.

In 1985, Falbo had the opportunity to work with Chinese colleagues at the Institute of Psychology, a unit of the Chinese Academy of Sciences in Beijing, to evaluate only children in urban schools. These children were evaluated in terms of their academic, personality, and physical outcomes, since most Chinese adults think of these three dimensions when talking about the quality of children. What was special about these data is that the first, second, and third graders of this sample had all been born just before the beginning of the one-child policy and therefore, were largely from one and two child families. Currently, the early grades in Beijing City are almost completely filled with only children and direct comparisons between only children and others within classrooms or schools is not possible. We asked the teachers in 1985 to complete a form which asked for the child's most recent mathematics and verbal scores and for the teacher to rate each child on a list of 31 attributes. This list consisted of the nine originally used by the Shanghai group and 22 additional ones. These additional ones, our Chinese colleagues had indicated, were part of the Little Emperor stereotype or were considered important attributes by Chinese adults for schoolchildren to possess.

We could have selected a personality instrument developed in the U.S. and translated it into Chinese for use in our surveys of Chinese schoolchildren. However, our goal was not to evaluate the adjustment of Chinese children using Western standards, but to evaluate the adjustment of Chinese children using Chinese standards. The 31 attributes were originally presented to teachers in terms of a checklist, with the teacher asked to choose between two polar opposites, such as "selfish — selfless."

In addition, parents were asked to complete a questionnaire, indicating their occupations and educational attainment, the number and types of people in their household, and the height and weight of their children.

The results of this study were published in 1989 (Falbo et al., 1989) and indicated that the only children in this sample of 775 schoolchildren scored higher in verbal scores, and were both taller and heavier than the children from two-child families. The only significant statistical interaction indicated that the only child advantage in achievement was most pronounced among first graders.

In this survey, the personality attributes were scored in terms of two scales which we created as a result of factor analyses. Most of the attributes were combined to be part of a Virtue or Competence scale. The factor analysis of the 31 attributes had indicated that most of the attributes loaded on two factors, the first reflecting moral virtues, such as selflessness and respect for elders, and the second reflecting basic competence, such as confidence and ability. At any rate, only children did not score significantly different from others on either the virtue or competence scores.

While these results were consistent with the pattern reported by many other Chinese studies, we were concerned that they may not be generally applicable to other Chinese areas. In particular, many of the parents in the Beijing sample were professionals, for whom a small family size was more normative even before the initiation of the one-child policy. We reasoned that it could well be the case that these sophisticated urbanites are more adept at rearing only children than their less sophisticated countrymen. Furthermore, the Beijing sample consisted entirely of only children and second borns of two-child families.

Therefore, we took an opportunity in 1987 to work with colleagues at Jilin University and dedicated it to the replication and extention of our Beijing survey. Jilin Province is in northeastern China, sharing a border with North Korea. Our sample consisted of schoolchildren living in and around Changchun, the provincial capital. Changchun has two major industries, automotive assembly and motion picture making. Our sample contained the children of professionals, industrial workers, and peasants. Because there was a wider range of family sizes available, we felt that the results from this sample would be more representative of Chinese children overall. We selected first and fifth graders for this sample, in order to determine if being born before or after the initiation of the 1979 policy had an influence on whether the only children were significantly different from others. In all, there were 1,460 schoolchildren, half born before 1979, and the other half after 1979.

Not only did we improve our methodology by increasing the hetero-geneity of the sample, we also improved the quality of the information we obtained about each child by asking both parents and teachers to evaluate the children's personality attributes and by directly measuring the children's height and weight.

We found that regardless of whether only children were born before 1979 or after 1979, lived in urban or rural areas, or were male or female, there were no significant differences between them and their counterparts with siblings in their academic achievements or in the personality evalua-tions given them by either their teachers or parents (Poston and Falbo, 1990a, 1990b). Curiously enough, only children were significantly smaller in both height and weight than others. We suspected this was due to their average younger age for this sample.

We also combined the Beijing and Jilin samples (Falbo et al., 1989) and divided the children in terms of three major categories of fathers' occupation: professionals, industrial workers, and farmers. We wondered if only children brought up by professionals would have better outcomes than only children brought up by less educated peers. We analyzed the physical, personality, and academic achievement data and found that the only child advantage in academics was found for urban children, that is, children of industrial and professional fathers. Rural only children had lower scores than non-only children on verbal achievement, but they scored similarly on mathematics scores. We explained this in terms of the preschool ex-periences of urban versus rural children. Almost all urban children come from two-parent families where both parents are fully employed and the parents place their young children in preschools, often associated with their place of employment. In contrast, rural children rarely attend preschools and are frequently cared for by grandparents, many of whom are illiterate.

We also used the Jilin Province data to evaluate the incidence of obesity among Chinese children; press reports in China had suggested that the number of obese children in China had increased because the parents of only children tended to overindulge their children with food. We calculated the body mass indices (Weight/Stature^2) of the Jilin children and compared these scores against U.S. standards (the only available ones, using this index); we found that about 4% of the sample was obese, meaning that they scored at or above the 90% level. Although these children were more likely to be male and urban, they were no more likely to be only children than were the nonobese children (Falbo, 1990).

Thus, our studies of Chinese children have indicated that only children, especially those living in urban areas, tend to do better in school tests, notably those assessing verbal and mathematics skills. Our Jilin Province results indicated that this only child advantage did not hold for rural onlies.

Taken together, the studies published in the West, combined to provide a complex picture of the adjustment of only children, with the Jiao et al. study providing the most negative view, while the results from both our Beijing and Jilin surveys providing the most positive view of the differences between onlies and others.

In terms of physical outcomes, the results were also complex, with the Beijing only children being larger and the Jilin only children being smaller than their counterparts. Analyses of the body mass indices of the Jilin sample indicated that the incidence of obesity overall was lower there than in the U.S., and that only children were no more likely to be obese.

Studies of Western Only Children

These limitations in the Chinese knowledge base about only children are reminiscent of the early years of research on only children in the West. Since the founding of modern psychology, there has been a constant interest in the importance of birth order and family size as determinants of an individual's outcomes. The presence of siblings was assumed to be essential for a child to develop normally, and one's position among one's siblings was thought to have profound effects on an individual's developmental outcomes. These assumptions permeated the research of E.W. Bohannon (1898), a student of G. Stanley Hall. Bohannon and others had amassed a data archive about of 1001 "peculiar and exceptional children," of which 46 were only children. Two-thirds of these only children exhibited what Bohannon described as "disadvantageous peculiarities," especially an inability to interact with peers. On the basis of Bohannon's findings, G. Stanley Hall is said to have concluded, "Being an only child is a disease in itself" (Neal, 1927).

It is possible that this position was more correct for Hall's times, the end of the nineteenth century, than for now, the end of the twentieth century in the U.S. In the late 19th Century, most American families lived in rural settings and had large families. Rural homes were scattered across vast distances limiting the opportunities that children of different families had to interact with each other. Large families ensured that children had other children to play with. If a child did not have siblings, it was likely that he or she had few opportunities to play with other children. This changed as the population of the U.S. began clustering into newly created urban and suburban areas. Today, more than 75 percent of Americans live in urban centers.

It took 30 years before Hall's conclusion was challenged by the results of studies of normal populations. Since the turn of the century, there have been many empirical studies comparing only children to others. Norman Fenton (1928), for example, published an article which focused on the personality and social adjustment of a sample of Californians, who ranged in age from kindergarteners to college students. He found that the scores of only children generally overlapped those of their peers.

Recently, Falbo and Polit (1986) conducted a quantitative review of the hundreds of studies conducted in the West since then and found that the outcomes of only children were similar to the outcomes of others in adjustment and sociability. Small, but significant differences were found between only children and later borns, particularly those from larger families, in the areas of achievement and intelligence. Here, the outcomes of only children were better than those of non-onlies.

Subsequently, Polit and Falbo (1987) expanded their quantitative review in the personality area by increasing the number of studies included. Sixteen dimensions of personality were considered and the results indicated that the personality outcomes of only children were indistinguishable from the outcomes of others in 14 of these dimensions. It was only in achievement motivation and self-esteem that significant differences were found, and here, the advantage was with only children.

In their third and last quantitative review of the Western literature, Polit and Falbo (1988) expanded their quantitative review of intellectual abilities, and found that while the intellectual advantage of only children was found across most traditionally measured forms of intellectual abilities, it was greatest in the verbal areas.

More recent publications (Blake, 1989; Dawson, 1991) describing the results of national surveys of Americans have supported the conclusions of the three Falbo and Polit quantitative reviews.

It is important to note that not every study in this body of Western literature has yielded the same results. In the birth order and family size area, the overall picture must be drawn from a mixture of the results of individual studies. The results of some studies have indicated that only children had advantaged outcomes; other studies have indicated that only children had disadvantaged outcomes; still other studies found no significant differences between only children and others. In this regard, the Chinese and Western results are similar.

The Western mixture is brought about by a variety of factors, particularly the fact that most studies in this literature were based on selected samples, such as clinic populations or college undergraduates. In addition, the one-child family has not been a common family size in the West and social and economic events have frequently affected the reasons why the proportion of only children within a birth cohort varies. For example, some selected samples contain groups of only children who are advantaged (i.e., the children of dual career couples), while other selected samples contain groups of only children who are disadvantaged (i.e., the children of unemployed fathers). To the extent that individual studies do not account for these background factors, the results for only children are likely to vary from study to study.

It became clear to us that if anyone was to be able to draw conclusions about only children in general, random samples, selected to be representative of a given geographic area at one point in time, were needed.

Our 1990 Survey of Chinese Children

Based on this argument, we obtained funding in 1989 from the National Institutes of Health to conduct a survey of a representative sample of 4,000 schoolchildren in China. Because this project used many state-of-the-art methodologies to evaluate Chinese only children, these methodologies will be described here. There are two aspects of the methodologies used in this project which are critical. One of the methodological innovations consists of the sampling technique we used to generate four representative samples of Chinese schoolchildren. The second consists of the variety and nature of the instruments we developed for assessing the children's personalities and academic achievements.

Sampling Technique

We employed a multi-stage cluster sampling approach to select a total sample of 4,000 schoolchildren, or 1,000 from each of the three provinces of Anhui, Gansu, and Hunan Provinces, and from the Beijing Municipality (the capital city and its surrounding eight rural counties). We chose Beijing as one of our four provinces because much of the previous research on Chinese only children has been done in Beijing, although none of this earlier research was based on a representative sample of the entire Municipality. We decided to collect data on schoolchildren in Anhui, Gansu, and Hunan provinces because these provinces have also been the sites of some of the previous research on only children, and of equal importance, these three provinces, along with Beijing, represent a wide range of demographic, economic, social, and geographic characteristics (China Population Information and Research Center, 1990). Beijing is the capital city of China, and thus, its political and economic nerve-center; by far it is the most socioeconomically developed of the four sites included in the study. On the other hand, the three provincial sites have economic and social levels of development more in line with those of China as a whole. The four sites are also distributed fairly well geographically, with Anhui in the east, Hunan in the southwest, Gansu in the northwest, and Beijing in the north. Hunan and Gansu also include many of the country's ethnic minorities (Poston and Shu, 1987); Anhui is one of the least urbanized provinces in China.

The 4,000 schoolchildren were drawn from primary schools in each of the four provinces. Schools were selected for inclusion following a multi-stage cluster random sampling strategy. Our goal in each province was to choose a sample of 1,000 schoolchildren, 500 from the third grade and 500 from the sixth grade. We desired this distribution by grade because of the tremendous increase after 1979 in the numbers of only children in China. We wanted children in the sample, some of whom were born before 1979 (these would be sixth graders around 12 years of age in 1990), and others of whom were born after 1979 (third graders around nine years of age in 1990). We wanted to be able to draw a sample from which we could generalize fairly well to the third and sixth graders in the province. Unfortunately, lists of all the third and sixth graders in each province from which we could draw a random sample did not exist. But we did have a list of the urban and rural counties of each province.

We first ascertained the percentage of the province that was classified as urban in 1985, the most recent year for which we had urban distribution data available at the time we were preparing to conduct this survey (January, 1990). We selected the capital city of each province, plus an additional two to five randomly selected urban districts (depending upon the province's urban distribution) from which to draw our samples of urban schools. If the province was about 20 percent urban (as was the case with Anhui), 10 schools were selected from the capital city and the other randomly selected urban districts. We then randomly selected seven or eight rural counties so that the remaining schools would be drawn from these counties. The schools were selected randomly from a list of all elementary schools in each of the sampled urban districts and rural counties. For each rural county in our sample, we took a random sample of about five to eight schools, and we did the same for each of the sampled urban districts and the capital cities of Anhui and Hunan. For Beijing City and Lanzhou City (Gansu province) we randomly chose a larger number of schools, owing to their much larger populations in relation to the other sampled urban districts; thus we randomly selected 32 schools from Beijing City, and eight from Lanzhou City.

From each of the sampled schools, we then randomly selected one third grade and one sixth grade classroom. Within each sampled third and sixth grade classroom five girls and five boys were selected randomly to participate in the survey. In this way, each of the 50 schools sampled in each province contributed 20 students. Thus, our sample consisted of 4,000 schoolchildren from 200 schools in all.

Instrumentation

This study expanded and refined the kind of information we obtained in terms of the personality and academic achievement outcomes of Chinese schoolchildren. In terms of *personality*, the major improvement involved the inclusion of children as evaluators of personality attributes. Our results from the use of the attributes checklist suggested that parents and teachers did not rate only children as better or worse than their peers. Perhaps, we reasoned, the children themselves or their peers would regard only children as different from children with siblings. To test this possibility, we had to alter our checklist so that children who had no more than a third grade reading level could use it to evaluate themselves and other children. From the outset it was clear that the characters for some of the items would have to be simplified so that third graders could read them. These revisions were made on all forms of the checklist so that all checklists, even those used by adults, would be identical. During a December, 1989, pilot test, the parents, teachers, and children were asked to complete the checklist. The Chinese administrators took notes of any problems that the 160 children in the pilot had while completing the checklists and shared them with us during a Beijing meeting in January, 1990. To solve these problems we made one more revision, involving the simplification of one item and the addition of one item, resulting in the final instrument "The 32 Attributes Checklist."

The English translation of the desirable pole for the 32 attributes follows: good manners, doesn't like to cry, keeps trying until finishes task, not squeamish, likes to tell others his/her own ideas, likes to do things better than others, cares about what other people think about him/her, does things resolutely, not selfish, always feels sympathy for others, has his/her own ideas and is determined, capable, kind and docile, likes to solve problems on own, confident, likes to help others, likes to be a leader, cooperative, brave, handles objects with care, likes to share, doesn't like to show off, doesn't start fights, respects elders, doesn't like to dress up, likes to do manual labor, modest, never lies, likes to participate in group activity, pays attention to lecturing teacher, does homework by him/herself, likes to volunteer to answer teacher's questions. A copy of the checklist in Chinese follows this chapter in an appendix.

Refinements in the academic *achievement instruments* involved adding to the school-based assessments of the child's mathematics and verbal skills made by the child's classroom teacher. These school-based assessments were made at the end of each of the two semesters for the 1989-90 school year and we considered them useful because they reflected how well the student was perceived to be performing according to the standards of his or her own classroom.

We averaged the scores from the fall and spring semester's school-based tests separately for their mathematics and verbal tests, resulting in two, school-based mean scores per student. These scores varied depending on the content of the tests and the standards used by each classroom teacher to evaluate the students' performance.

We also created a second type of assessment for the purpose of assessing all students with the same instruments in mathematics and Chinese in order to have common academic achievement measures to assess all the students in our sample. We called these the standard achievement tests and we devised third and sixth grade verbal tests and a sixth grade mathematics test, based on contemporary exams used by Chinese educators . We either obtained the sample exams directly from teacher organizations or we invented items similar to those presented in third or sixth grade Chinese textbooks.

We used a third grade mathematics exam created by Stevenson and his colleagues (Stevenson, 1989) in order to be able to determine the extent to which our scores resembled his Chinese scores.

The original versions of these four exams (two grades by two content areas) underwent two pilot tests. In the fall of 1989, we administered the tests to 30 third and sixth graders from a working class school in Beijing. A working class school in Beijing was selected because it was thought to be more typical of the schools in China. While the Stevenson exam appeared to be of an appropriate length and difficulty, the other exams contained several items that were either too easy or too difficult. These problematic items were replaced with items of more moderate difficulty.

The revised exams were then used in a second pilot test, in December, 1989 and involved 160 schoolchildren, 40 from each of the four participating provinces. In each province, the pilot sample was equally divided by region (urban/rural), grade (third/sixth), and gender (girls/boys). We correlated the student's performance on each item of these second pilot tests with their school-based math and verbal scores. These correlations ranged from .45 to .58. In addition, in Hunan province, the students were administered the achievement tests twice (with two weeks intervening), and the test-retest correlations were all in the .80s, with the exception of the Stevenson test, with a test-retest correlation of .59.

Because the provinces varied substantially in many ways, notably in terms of their degree of economic development and their implementation of the one-child policy, we chose to analyze our data separately by province. In all analyses, the independent variables were: Birth Category (only, first, and later born), Gender (boys and girls), and Region (urban and rural). Although there was a strong central tendency for third graders to be roughly 10 years old and sixth graders to be roughly 13 years old, the range of ages within each grade was fairly wide, spanning six years in all four provinces. Because of the broad range of ages present in each grade, the child's age was covaried.

Our Results

We will now briefly describe the results of our study; a more complete description can be found in Falbo and Poston (1993). One of the most important findings was that most children in our sample are growing up with siblings. Beijing had the largest percentage (56%) of only children, and the other provinces had much lower percentages: 21% (Anhui), 24% (Gansu), and 23% (Hunan). Most Chinese (about 80 percent) live in rural areas and most rural families formed since the one-child policy contain two or three children.

The outcome area providing the most consistent results was achievement, where there were fairly consistent only child effects in verbal achievement in three of the four provinces. Here, only children outscored others. In mathematics, there was some variation by region and province, but where differences were found between only children and others, only children were never found to score significantly lower than both first and last borns, and they usually scored higher than at least one nononly child group. Perhaps, the parental pressure which Wu described in the first chapter of this book has had the effect of enhancing the verbal skills of Chinese only children.

It is in the area of personality attributes that few results about only children were found. Few significant multivariate and univariate effects were found here and the direction of these differences was generally not consistent. We scored the checklist in terms of a summation of the number of positive attributes the target child was given by his or her teacher, parent, classmate, and self. These results indicate that in the area of personality, there is no single only child effect. It was only in Beijing that only children distinguished themselves by receiving significantly less favorable personality evaluations than either first or last borns. This finding applied solely to male only children and to peer and self evaluations, however. In another province, there were birth order effects, in both peer and teacher ratings, but here the scores of only children were always similar to one other group; they failed to stand out. Furthermore, in a third province, only children received a lower personality evaluation from their parents than did children with siblings. This finding was particularly curious since teachers, peers, and the children themselves did not regard these same children as especially lacking in positive attributes.

We found that only children were physically larger than their classmates in two provinces. This finding suggests that the benefits derived from possessing the one-child certificate may well be providing better nutrition and overall health care for only children in these two provinces. It is unclear why this effect is not found in all of the provinces, since possessing this certificate is associated with benefits in all four. We plan to investigate this finding in future analyses of our 1990 survey data. Perhaps in Hunan and Beijing, the benefits associated with the one-child certificate are greater than in Anhui or Gansu. Or, perhaps the difference in the educational levels of parents with and without only children is more extreme in Hunan and Beijing than in the other two provinces. The educational level of mothers has been found to be strongly related to their children's height and weight in many developing countries (Tucker and Young, 1989). In any case, where significant, the physical size difference was found in only one of the two dimensions, either height or weight. Thus, in Hunan, onlies weighed significantly more than others, but there were no differences in height. In Beijing, only children were taller than their classmates, but there were no differences in their weights.

The fact that the same results were not found in each provincial sample points to the fact that the factors determining the outcomes of children are not constant across the four provinces. Instead there has been substantial variation, probably caused by variation among the provinces in such factors as the quality of the schools, the level of modernization, the dynamics of family processes, and the implementation of the one-child policy. Our future research will focus on trying to explain this variation by considering these possible sources.

The acknowledgement of this variation, however, represents an important advance in our thinking about only children. The literature about only children, starting with Bohannon's (1898) work, has followed the style of discussing the results of a given study in the present verb tense, and suggesting that the results of that study are universally true about only children. It should be clear from the present review that the social and economic factors that cause a child to be an only child vary substantially from time to time, place to place, and even family to family. These same factors have at least as strong an influence on children's outcomes as does their sibling condition.

The Persistence of Beliefs

In view of the fact that the research about only children in China as well as in the West does not indicate that only children are reliably different from others in undesirable ways, why do so many Chinese and Westerners prefer to believe that only children are prone to such problems as selfishness and bad manners? Falbo (1991) has written about the psychological origins of this persistence in a recent chapter; the story line goes as follows.

In China, the perception that these "little emperors" are a problem may well derive from the fact that the Chinese place much more emphasis on the position of a child among his or her siblings than do Westerners. Within the Chinese family, siblings refer to each other in terms of their relative age and gender. For example, younger sisters are called mei mei by their older siblings. To outsiders, children identify themselves in terms of their position among their siblings. If you ask a rural boy to identify himself, for example, the boy will typically not give his name, as is common in the

West, but will describe himself as the second son of Li (his father's family name). Consequently, it is likely that the identities of most Chinese people are much more firmly attached to their sibling position than are the identities of Western people. Furthermore, kinship relationships tend to form the basis of the daily lives of most Chinese, determining where they live, what work they do, and how they are regarded in their communities. Thus, the elimination of sibling relationships would seem to most Chinese as a threat to the social reality for most contemporary Chinese people.

In addition, many Chinese continue to believe that only children are "little emperors," despite the research results presented in the first chapter of this book and in our own results (Falbo and Poston, 1993) because most Chinese do not consider the fact that rural children are different from urban children, and only children in China are predominately urban. In Western research conducted in the early part of this century, it was typical for investigators to examine the incidence of specific birth orders within problem or success groups and to conclude that there was something about birth order that caused the outcome. This approach was often criticized (Price and Hare, 1969) because investigators failed to consider the incidence of specific birth order or family size categories within the relevant birth cohort. For example, in the U.S., a high proportion of families was formed after World War II, resulting in a surge of first births between 1947 and 1950. Between 39 and 43 percent of all Americans of this birth cohort are firstborns. Thus it is not surprising that firstborns predominated in samples drawn from this birth cohort, be they National Merit Scholarship finalists (Altus, 1967) or stripteasers (Skipper and McCaghy, 1970). Unfortunately, because most Chinese are unaware of the Price and Hare critique, they are still making this mistake. They presume that because only children are currently found to predominate in certain success or failure groups such as overweight children in Beijing (WuDunn, 1991), it is their lack of siblings, and not their sheer predominance within the urban birth cohort, that is the cause.

Related to this we found very profound regional differences in our results (Falbo and Poston, 1993). Children living in urban areas have more academic skills, less desirable personalities, and greater size, both in height and weight than do rural children. The fact that only children disproportionately reside in urban areas means that only children as a group have higher academic skills, less desirable personalities, and greater size than other children. Our statistical analyses control for region of residence when comparing the outcomes of children. But most lay observers do not control for regional differences when evaluating only children. They see big, smart children lacking in such traditional virtues as selflessness and enthusiasm for manual labor. This tends to confirm the "little emperor" stereotype.

Throughout the world, most adults alive today grew up with siblings. This simple fact has two psychological implications. First, it helps to determine what we define as normal. In general, what we think of as normal is largely determined by what we think is common. But there is more to it than that. What is normal is also largely determined by traditional views about what is right.

Being an only child is still associated with loss in the U.S. That is, American only children are disproportionately likely to grow up in single parent homes; that is, they are more likely to have divorced parents, to have lost one parent by death, or to have no contact with their fathers (Blake, 1989; Dawson, 1991). A similar finding about Swedish only children was reported by Wallden (1990). A child from such a background may idealize the two-parent, multiple-child family, particularly if their single parent repeatedly expresses regret about not having more children and a "more normal family life."

Polit (1982) found that children expressed regret about not having more siblings or having too many siblings depending on their mothers' expressed desires. Single or married mothers reported that their only children strongly wanted a brother or sister if the mother had also expressed to the interviewer a strong desire for more children. Conversely, mothers of three children (the largest family size in Polit's sample) would report that their first-born children frequently expressed a desire to have no siblings if the mother had independently expressed the belief that she had had too many children. The apparent correlation between mothers' and children's desire for siblings could reflect the mother's transmission of her own wishes onto her child. This correlation could also reflect the child's identification with his or her mother and their shared values and feelings.

A second psychological implication of the fact that most of us grew up with siblings is that our relationships with our siblings has become part of our self-concepts. As Tesser (1980) theorized, many of our evaluative notions about ourselves are based on our early experiences of comparing ourselves to our siblings. To illustrate, siblings judge themselves as taller, smarter, or clumsier than their siblings.

Given these patterns, how do people without siblings develop evaluative notions about themselves? Although no systematic study of this process exists, it seems likely that only children acquire evaluative notions from other children, such as cousins, classmates, and neighbors, as well as from their parents and other adult caretakers. The evidence from our 1990 survey suggests that only children in China acquire notions of their own attributes in about equal measure to those of other children.

Summary

Since the early 1970s, the People's Republic of China has been engaged in one of the most far-reaching family planning programs in history. In 1979, they began the one-child policy, which was intended to improve their quality of life by encouraging economic development and reducing environmental degradation. However, some Chinese psychologists and Western journalists responded negatively to the policy because it strongly encouraged new families to have just one child. These critics argued that the policy would create a generation of "little emperors," or spoiled brats. Research conducted early in the 1980s tended to confirm that Chinese only children had undesirable qualities. However, more mixed results about only children were revealed by research conducted later in the 1980s. Finally, the results of our survey of 4,000 Chinese schoolchildren were presented in terms of evaluating the academic, personality, and physical outcomes of only children. These results in general do not support the view that Chinese only children are "little emperors."

References

Altus, W. D. (1967). Birth order and its sequelae. _International Journal of Psychiatry_, 3(1): 23–39.

Banister, J. 1987. _China's changing population_. Stanford: Stanford University Press.

Bian, Y. (1987). A preliminary analysis of the basic features of the lifestyles of China's single child families. _Social Sciences in China_, 8(3): 189–209.

Blake, J. (1966). Ideal family size among white Americans: A quarter of a century's evidence. _Demography_, 3(1): 154–173.

———. (1989). _Family size and achievement_. Berkeley: University of California Press.

Bohannon, E. W. (1898). The only child in a family. _The Pedagogical Seminary_, 4: 475–496.

Chen, K. (1985). A preliminary study of the collective orientation of the only child. _Acta Psychologica Sinica_, 3: 264–269.

China Population Information and Research Center. (1990). _China's Fourth_

National Population Census data sheet. Beijing: China Population Information and Research Center.

Coale, A. J., Wang, F., Riley, N. E., Lin, F. (1991). Recent trends in fertility and nuptiality in China, *Science*, 251: 389–393.

Croll, E., Davin, D., Kane, P. (1985). *China's one-child policy*. New York: St Martin's Press.

Dawson, D. A. (1991). Family structure and children's health and well-being. *Journal of Marriage and the Family*, 53: 573–584.

Falbo, T. (1990). Politicas y logros de los hijos Unicos en China. *Revista de psicologia social y personalidad*, 6(1–2): 39–56.

———. (1991). Social norms and the one-child family: Clinical and policy implications. In J. Dunn and F. Boer (Eds.), *Children's sibling relationships: Developmental and clinical issues* (pp. 71–82). Hillsdale, NJ: Erlbaum.

Falbo, T., and Polit, D. F. (1986). A quantitative review of the only child literature: Research evidence and theory development. *Psychological Bulletin*, 100: 176–189.

Falbo, T., and Poston, D. L., Jr. (1993). The academic, personality, and physical outcomes of only children in China. *Child Development*, 64: 18–35.

Falbo, T., Poston, D. L., Jr., Jing, Q., Wang, S., Gu, Q., Yin, H., and Liu, Y. (1989). Physical, achievement, and personality characteristics of Chinese children. *Journal of Biosocial Science*, 21: 483–495.

Feng, X. T. (1990). Wuo guo du sheng zi nu yan jiu de xian zhuang fen xi [The present status and critique of only child studies in China]. *Jiang-Hai Xue-Kan [Middle China Journal]*, no. 1.

Fenton, N. (1928). The only child. *Journal of Genetic Psychology*, 35: 546–556.

Greenhalgh, S. (1986). Shifts in China's population policy, 1984–1986: Views from the central, provincial and local levels. *Population and Development Review*, 12: 491–515.

Greenhalgh, S., and Bongaarts, J. (1987). Fertility policy in China: Future options. *Science*, 235: 1167–1172.

Gu, B. C., Poston, D. L., and Shu, J. (1987). *The People's Republic of China population data sheet*. Austin: The University of Texas Printing Division.

Hardee-Cleaveland, K., and Banister, J. (1988). Fertility policy and implementation in China, 1986–88. *Population and Development Review*, 14: 245–286.

Jiao, S. L., Ji, Q. P., and Jing, Q. C. (1986). Comparative study of behavioral qualities of only children and sibling children, *Child Development*, 57: 357–361.

Neal, E. (1927). The only child. *Mental Health Bulletin*, 5(9): 1–3.

Polit, D. F. (1982). *Effects of family size: A critical review of literature since 1973* (Contract No. N01-HD-12816). Bethesda, Maryland: National Institutes of Health.

Polit, D. F., and Falbo, T. (1987). Only children and personality development: A quantitative review. *Journal of Marriage and the Family*, 49: 309–325.

————. (1988). The intellectual outcomes of only children. *Journal of Biosocial Science*, 20: 275–285.

Poston, D. L., and Falbo, T. (1990a). Academic performance and personality traits of Chinese children: "Onlies" versus others. *American Journal of Sociology*, 96: 433–451.

————. (1990b). Scholastic and personality characteristics of only children and children with siblings in China. *International Family Planning Perspectives*, 16: 45–48.

Poston, D. L., and Shu, J. (1987). The demographic and socioeconomic composition of the major minority groups in China. *Population and Development Review*, 13: 703–722.

Poston, D. L., and Yu, M. Y. (1985). Quality of life, intellectual development and behavioural characteristics of single children in China: Evidence from a 1980 survey in Changsha, Hunan province. *Journal of Biosocial Science*, 17: 127–136.

Price, J. S., and Hare, E. H. (1969). Birth order studies: Some sources of bias. *British Journal of Psychiatry*, 115: 633–646.

Shanghai Preschool Education Study Group. (1980). Family education of only children. *Zhongquo funü*, 5: 16.

Skipper, J. K., Jr., and McCaghy, C. H. (1970). Strip-teasers: The anatomy and career contingencies of a deviant occupation. *Social Problems*, 17: 391–405.

Stevenson, H. (Personal Communication, 1989).

Tesser, A. (1980). Self-esteem maintenance in family dynamics. *Journal of Personality and Social Psychology*, 39: 77–91.

Tien, H. Y. (1992). Second thoughts on the second child: A talk with Peng Peiyun. In D. L. Poston, Jr. and D. Yaukey (Eds.), *The Population of Modern China* (pp. 421–26). New York: Plenum.

Tucker, K., and Young, F. W. (1989). Household structure and child nutrition: A reinterpretation of income and mother's education. *Social Indicators Research*, 21: 201–221.

Wallden, M. (1990). *Sibling position and mental capacity — Reconsidered* (Research Report No. 31). University of Stockholm, Department of Sociology.

WuDunn, S. (1991, August 26). China's young are finding that fat no longer means fortune. *New York Times*.

Yang, Z. (1983, February 25). The existing problems in character and virtues and reasons why of the only children. *Guangming ribao*.

12

Crossing the Border:
Chinese Adolescents in the West

Doreen A. Rosenthal and S. Shirley Feldman

When you cross the border, obey the local custom.
— A Chinese saying

Today's world, more so than ever before, is characterised by the mobility of its people. Changing one's original geographic and cultural location for that of another — either long-term as immigrants or refugees, or short-term as temporary sojourners or tourists — has become a relatively commonplace phenomenon. For those Chinese who now find themselves as long-term settlers in locations other than their country of birth the reasons for moving may have been social, economic, or political. Whatever the reason, there is now a substantial Chinese Diaspora, with Chinese immigrants or refugees settled in many countries of the world, both in other parts of Asia and in the West. It is the ways in which the adolescent children of these settlers cope with and adapt to a new environment — the bridging of two cultures — that are the focus of this chapter.

The concept of acculturation is used to refer to those changes that groups and individuals undergo when they come in contact with another culture. Berry, Kim, Minde, and Mok (1987) suggest that the changes which occur as a result of acculturation may be grouped in five categories. These relate to the physical environment (such as the change from a rural to an urban environment — a common occurrence for immigrants), to biological factors (such as changes in nutritional status and the conse-quences of this), to culture (where original cultural institutions such as the religious, linguistic, and political become altered), to new social relation-ships (where new ingroup allegiances may arise), and changes within the individual as she or he attempts to adapt to a new cultural milieu (such as changes in behaviour or mental health). Our concern is with the last of these categories.

At the individual level, acculturation "entails changes in behavior, values and attitudes, and identity" (Williams and Berry, 1991, p. 633). Acculturation has also been conceptualised as a resocialisation process (Taft, 1985, 1986) with the assumption that increased contact with the host culture will lead to a shift away from the traditional values, attitudes, and behaviour of the culture of origin, especially over several immigrant generations. Current models of acculturation, however, emphasize the selective, multidimensional nature of that process. The neglect of old, and adoption of new, norms may vary from one behavioural or attitudinal domain to another, and may be affected in diverse ways, at different rates, and at various times. Thus, acculturation is considered an uneven process; "core" elements of a culture may be resistant to change, whereas peripheral features may change more rapidly (Berry, 1980; Bond and Yang, 1982; Rokeach, 1979; Triandis, Kashima, Shimada, and Villareal, 1986. For a fuller discussion of the acculturation process see the work of Berry and his colleagues, for example, Berry, 1990).

The ease or difficulty of the task of coping with an unfamiliar culture depends on factors such as the degree of similarity or difference between the old and the new cultures, the reason for change and the abruptness of that change, the extent to which the new culture is all-encompassing in the life of the new settler, as well as demographic, social and psychological characteristics of the individual (Zheng and Berry, 1991). Most writers assume that the process of acculturation involves conflict and stress for the individual — conceptualised as "acculturative stress" (Berry et al., 1987; Chataway and Berry, 1989), "culture shock" (Furnham and Bochner, 1986; Oberg, 1960), or "bicultural conflict" (Sue and Sue, 1971; Taft, 1985) — and results in psychological turmoil, identity problems, and maladaptive behaviour. Such a view neglects the possibility that individuals may successfully integrate the two cultures to which they are exposed (Burns and Goodnow, 1985; Rosenthal, Bell, Demetriou, and Efklides, 1989; Taft, 1977).

In this chapter, we examine the process of acculturation for Chinese immigrant youths who now live in a western culture. Our focus on adolescents enables us to study acculturation at a particularly crucial developmental stage. In western cultures at least, adolescence is a time when youth commonly struggle with issues of autonomy and separation from parents, and with concerns about establishing a sense of identity. It is also a time of increased peer influence. In addition to resolving the normative developmental concerns of this life stage, immigrant adolescents often have the added difficulties of coping with conflicting cultural values (most commonly represented by peers and the broader social context) and parents who disapprove of their chosen modes of acculturation (Lee, 1988; Naditch and Morrissey, 1976). As a result, many writers have argued that during this developmental period immigrant children are in greatest conflict with their parents and at highest risk for experiencing varied problems of adjustment (Banchevska, 1981; Rosenthal, 1984; Sluzki, 1979; Stoller, 1981). Because of their immersion in the world of school and peers, adolescents of immigrant status, or those whose parents were immigrants, are regularly confronted with the task of dealing with two cultures simultaneously — an especially hard task when there are substantial differences between the cultures. For these adolescents, then, to the developmental tasks common to their non-immigrant peers, several others must be added. In making choices between traditional behaviours and attitudes of their culture of origin and those of their host culture, these youths must balance loyalty to their parents and their ethnic group with their need for acceptance in the host culture. The process of taking on new behaviours and values sanctioned by the host culture must be tempered by their allegiance to parents and traditional ways, and by the effects on their own socioemotional development of the choices they make. A crucial feature of the development of minority youth is the extent to which they can integrate a satisfying and satisfactory sense of their ethnicity — an ethnic identity — within a broader and more complete sense of self-identity. It is these aspects of the experience of adolescence for Chinese youth residing in the West that are the focus of this chapter.

What happens to the lives of Chinese immigrants who make the leap from the East to the West? There is ample evidence to suggest that acculturative stress will be high for these people. Chinese and Anglo–Western cultures are profoundly and fundamentally different in their values. On the important dimension of individualism-collectivism, Chinese and western cultures vary dramatically (The Chinese Culture Connection, 1987; Hofstede, 1980, 1983; Leung and Bond, 1984), with considerable divergence between these two cultures on issues of personal freedom, conformity, and collective welfare (Bond, 1986; Hsu, 1981; Triandis et al., 1986). The Chinese are described as being situation-centered, valuing family and tradition, harmony, emotional restraint, conformity, and obedience to authority (Ho, 1986; Sung, 1985; Yang, 1970) while the West prizes individualism, autonomy, and original thinking (Feather, 1986; Gardner, 1989; Hsu, 1972). Chinese traditionally place greater significance upon social and moral values than upon personal values and competence in the service of individualistic goals or self-fulfilment.

The contrast between the Chinese emphasis on collectivism and the well-being of the group and the western emphasis on individualism is seen particularly clearly in their contrasting family environments and socialisation practices. The family has been described as the pivot of Chinese culture. Cohesion among family members, dependence on the family, unquestioning acceptance of parental authority, preservation of the status quo, and profound loyalty are encouraged as a means of preserving the family system (Bond and Hwang, 1986; Harrison, Serafica, and McAdoo, 1984). With its emphasis on conformity, obedience, and respect for tradition, the Chinese family has been described as demanding, structured, and authoritarian (Fong, 1973; Ho, 1986; Kriger and Kroes, 1972; Vernon, 1982; Wolf, 1970; Yang, 1986). Proverbial expressions of Chinese parenting styles note that: "The stick produces a dutiful son" (Wu, 1966) and "A dull metal can be sharpened by constant grinding" (Cheng, 1946). In contrast, the western family, with its emphasis on autonomy, individualism, and creativity, is described as accepting, moderately structured, child-centered, and democratic (Baumrind, 1971; Maccoby and Martin, 1983). Unlike the Chinese family, the western family places marked stress on assisting children to become physically and psychologically separated from their parents, and children are strongly encouraged to be self-reliant and independent (Alwin, 1988; Rosenthal and Bornholt, 1988; Steinberg and Silverberg, 1986).

It is worth noting, however, that values and childrearing practices of the Chinese are changing in their homelands. Children and their families in Hong Kong and Taiwan are moving away from traditional Chinese practices and attitudes (Dawson and Ng, 1972; Ho and Kang, 1984; Lin and Fu, 1990). This development has been associated with industrialisation, economic advancement, and higher levels of education (Martin, 1975; Mitchell and Lo, 1968). Indeed, it has been suggested that in these countries, such typically western values as personal competence and autonomy are increasingly more important (Lau, 1988; Lin and Fu, 1990), implying a gradual shift towards individualism and self-orientation (Yang, 1986). Notwithstanding these changes, the significant contrasts between the Chinese and the western cultural contexts provide us with an opportunity to study the acculturation process in a group which is assumed to be subjected to considerable pressures in coping with two divergent cultures.

A further source of pressure for Chinese people in the West, rests in depictions of them, along with other Asians, as a "model minority". This stereotype is presented in widely read newspapers and magazines and perpetuates the image of Asian immigrants and, in particular, their children as high achievers who have successfully adapted to the western way of life. The academic success of Asians in the West has been a consistent theme in the popular press (Australian, 1992; Brand, 1987; *New York Times*, 1986) and the superior performance of these students has been demonstrated in a number of studies in several western countries: in the United States by Ahn Toupin and Son (1991), Dornbusch, Ritter, Leiderman, Roberts, and Fraleigh (1987), Hirschman and Wong (1986), Stevenson, Lee, and Stigler (1986), Sue and Zane (1985), and Vernon (1982) and in Australia by Anderson and Vervoorn (1983), Chan (1987), Chiu and Tan (1986), and McAdam (1972). This academic excellence has been achieved at some cost according to the work of Dion and Toner (1988), who found that Chinese students in Canada had higher levels of anxiety associated with taking tests than did their Anglo– or European–Canadian peers. Other researchers suggest that the model minority stereotype raises the question of discrimination, for it perpetuates social distancing and competition and is maintained at some personal cost to Asian minorities in a western Country. It has been argued that the stresses associated with living up to the achieving Asian stereotype have negative consequences for the psychological well-being of some Asians (Ahn Toupin and Son, 1991; Chen and Yang, 1986; Sue and Zane, 1985).

In spite of their obvious importance, not only as an object of study in their own right, but also as a group whose very differences from western culture provide clear markers of the acculturation process, the acculturation of Chinese residing in the West has been rarely been the focus of re-searchers' concerns. Most research in the United States has focussed on the adaptation of Blacks and Hispanics (Spencer and Dornbusch, 1990) and in Australia on ethnically, but not racially, distinct minority groups such as Greeks and Italians (Rosenthal et al., 1989; Rosenthal and Cichello, 1986; Rosenthal and Hrynevich, 1985). The sparse research on adolescents of Asian descent has tended not to differentiate between Asian cultures (but see the work of Berry and his colleagues). While there are undoubted similarities in these cultures, there are subtle differences between them, and in the ways in which members of different Asian cultures have been received and perceived by the host society. For example, in the United States, there was considerable hostility towards Japanese-Americans at the time of World War II — hostility not experienced by Americans of Chinese descent. Currently, in Australia, while there is evidence of some hostility to Asian immigrants, this is directed more at the recently arrived Vietnamese refugees than towards the more settled Chinese community.

Apart from some exploration of the factors associated with Asian ethnic identity (to be discussed in a later section of this chapter), most of the few published studies of Chinese or Asian adolescents living in the West have focussed on their mental health — their use of mental health services (Atkinson and Gim, 1989) or the incidence of psychological dysfunction (Chataway and Berry, 1989; Mumford, Whitehouse, and Platts, 1991; Zheng and Berry, 1991) — or their academic achievements (see above). One exception to this is the study of personality characteristics of Asian–Canadian university students reported by Dion and Yee (1987). Unlike their Anglo– or European–Canadian counterparts, these Asian students reported personality characteristics that were consistent with aspects of the Confucian ethic. They scored higher on qualities that reflected the importance of harmony, a de-emphasis of individuality, and a desire to avoid conflict.

In terms of mental health, Berry and his colleagues have found that Chinese university students in Canada exhibit higher levels of dysfunction than their French– and English–Canadian counterparts (Chataway and Berry, 1989), a finding confirmed in a study of somewhat older students, with evidence for lower psychological health among Chinese sojourners than among non-Chinese Canadians and longer-settled Chinese–Canadians (Zheng and Berry, 1991). A search of the literature since 1980 revealed only one study which explored the acculturation of school-aged Chinese in the West. Leong and Tata (1990) found that work-related values were related to these elementary school children's level of acculturation (measured here by traditional behaviours and self identification as an Asian), with children who were more western-identified expressing higher levels of occupational values relating to self-realisation, prestige, and money than their more Chinese-identified peers.

It is against this background of meagre research that we report our studies of Chinese high schoolers living in two western cultures. For this task, we draw upon our published papers on the acculturation of first- and second-generation Chinese immigrants living in Australia and the United States (Chui, Feldman, and Rosenthal, 1992; Feldman, Mont-Reynaud, and Rosenthal, 1992; Feldman and Rosenthal, 1990; Rosenthal and Feldman, 1991a, 1991b). Our research confronts several problems familiar to cross-cultural researchers. First, we are sensitive to the need to modulate western ethnocentric bias which inevitably creeps into the design of research and which, in particular, guides the choice of items to be included in research instruments. Following the example of The Chinese Culture Connection (1987) our research incorporates measures derived from both Chinese and western instruments. Secondly, our research responds to the call to study acculturation in more than one immigration context (Yang, 1986). In contrast to other work which has focussed on immigrant groups in a single host culture, we study acculturation of Chinese behaviours and values among immigrant adolescents in two Western contexts — the United States and Australia. These host cultures were selected because they share a number of common features. Both are English-speaking, industrialised, capitalistic western nations, with a common English heritage and shared historical roots. Although there are some distinctions between the two cultures based on size, political power, and economic factors, similarities in values between the cultures are impressive. For example, studies of American and Australian adolescents reveal the importance in both cultures of autonomy, responsibility, and honesty, and the relative unimportance of conformity to authority and social convention (Feather, 1980). In terms of family environments and practices, those of the United States and Australia seem very similar (Funder, 1991; Noller and Callan, 1991).

We studied first- and second-generation Chinese youth residing in the West to test the assumption that acculturation proceeds slowly, over several generations. First-generation youth are those born in Hong Kong and who migrated to the West with their families. We studied 82 such youth from the USA and 62 from Australia. Second-generation youth are those who were born in the West, but those parents and grandparents were born in Hong Kong. In the USA we had 68 second-generation Chinese youths and 34 in Australia. Both first- and second-generation youths, while differing in the length of time that their families have lived in the West, have parents who were born and raised in Hong Kong, and thus likely to bring Chinese values to the task of socializing their children. Nevertheless, the changing values of Chinese in their homelands, noted earlier, might hasten acculturation since recent immigrants (parents of our first-generation youths) may be more like their western counterparts in values than immigrants of longer standing (parents of second-generation youths). We also used samples of respondents from Hong Kong. Anglo–Australians. and Euro–Americans, so that we were able to assess any shift either towards the norms of the host country or away from the norms of the culture of origin. These comparison groups, each of approximately 100 respondents, were selected to maximize comparability between the acculturation and comparison sample.

Respondents were drawn from high schools in the three countries. In order to establish some comparability, we restricted the sample to students in 10th or 11th grade, aged between 15 and 18 years, whose parents had received some formal education. Demographic data showed that the groups (three in Australia, three in the United States, and one in Hong Kong) did not differ in age, ratio of males to females, or in percentage of fathers employed full-time. Although there were differences in birth order and mother work status, these variables were not, in general, expected to influence our results in important ways, since most students were first- or second-born and had mothers who were in the paid labour force. Somewhat more problematic was the finding that the educational level of Hong Kong parents was notably lower than that of other groups, a not surprising finding given the different educational systems and different expectations for high school completion in Hong Kong, Australia, and the United States. Comparison of the educational attainment of fathers in each country to census data for that country showed that fathers in all groups, including those in Hong Kong, were more educated than their census counterparts. Fathers of the immigrant Chinese samples in the United States and Australia were significantly more educated than their Hong Kong counterparts.

An issue of importance is the extent to which the cultural context influences the process of acculturation. Despite the similarities between the American and Australian cultures, the place of the Chinese minority in each country is somewhat different. In the United States, especially in San Francisco where this research was carried out, the Chinese community is substantial and congregated in select areas. In many instances they actually form a majority, or near majority, in a given neighbourhood, and virtually all daily transactions can be conducted in Chinese with fellow compatriots. In contrast, in Australia (including Melbourne, the site of this research), the Chinese community is small, fragmented, geographically dispersed, and relatively powerless. Moreover, until recently, Australia had an immigration policy which severely restricted the inflow of Asian immigrants, with resultant stigmatisation of that group in society. Indeed, in both societies the Chinese face both subtle and sometimes overt racism (Kitano and Sue, 1973).

Research evidence suggests that the extent of acculturation is influenced by features of the ethnic community such as its status (Driedger, 1975; Tajfel, 1981), density of the neighbourhood (Garcia and Lega, 1979), and institutional completeness (Rosenthal and Hrynevich, 1985). For example, Triandis et al. (1986) argue that the more power the immigrant group has in its new setting, the less likely they are to accommodate to new cultural norms. Similarly, the denser the population of immigrants, the slower acculturation is likely to be. Thus we expected that the different environments experienced by Chinese immigrants in the two cultures may lead to more rapid acculturation in Australian– than American–Chinese.

Two related types of acculturation studies were carried out. These studies overlapped considerably in the questions addressed, but varied in some important details. In all the studies, we relied on our adolescent informants' self-reports and their perceptions of family environments. In the first studies, we examined the extent to which perceived family environments and adolescent values became acculturated over time. Our central focus was on whether there was a shift away from the patterns of the culture of origin towards those of the host culture. In the second series of studies, we examined three adolescent socioemotional outcomes — namely autonomy, misconduct, and distress. For these outcomes we addressed the question of mean differences among the four groups — the Hong Kong, first- and second-generation Chinese adolescents living in the West, and Australian or American youths. Another issue of concern was the need to go beyond simple descriptions of group differences in level of some outcome or some mechanism as indices of acculturation. It is possible that the process of acculturation, as measured by a particular outcome, is subject to different influences over time, or in different cultural contexts. Thus, another important aspect of the acculturation process is in terms of the organisation (or nomological net) of a given construct. A further focus of the research, therefore, was whether the patterns of relations between adolescent outcomes and possible mechanisms of change were similar or different across generations and in different Western contexts.

Family Environments and Adolescent Values

Acculturation can only be assessed when the culture of origin (in this case Hong Kong) differs from the host culture (Australia or the USA) in the attributes of interest. In seeking to locate some mechanisms (or proximal influences) by which culture, a distal variable, would impact on adolescent outcomes we had, in our cross-cultural studies (Feldman and Rosenthal, 1991; Feldman and Rosenthal, 1993; Feldman, Rosenthal, Mont-Reynaud, Lau, and Leung, 1991), chosen two domains of variables — family environments and adolescent values. We had two reasons for doing so. First, in the extant literature, these domains have been used to describe differences between cultures, especially Chinese and western cultures. Thus these constructs are ones which are likely to reveal changes over time as acculturation occurs. Moreover, they present as excellent candidates for serving as vehicles to translate distal cultural influences into more proximal influences on adolescents.

In our cross-cultural research we assessed four dimensions of family environments based on our reading of both western and Chinese family functioning and parental styles — accepting/engaged parenting, demanding parenting, autocratic parenting, and monitoring. These were derived from a factor analysis of a battery of paper-and-pencil tests (Feldman and Rosenthal, 1991). We found western family environments were more likely than those of Hong Kong adolescents to be regarded as accepting/engaged — characterised by family members spending time together, accepting different viewpoints of family members, cohesion, and authoritative parenting — and less likely to be demanding[1], a family style characterised by parental control, involvement in adolescents' decisions, limit setting, and family organisation.

Values — generalised and relatively enduring beliefs concerning what is desirable or undesirable — also differ across cultures. As noted earlier, Chinese, Australian, and American cultures differ in the value ascribed to personal freedom, conformity, collective welfare, obedience and respect for parents, and maintaining harmony (Bond, 1988; Feather, 1980, 1986; Poole, 1986; Rokeach, 1973; The Chinese Culture Connection, 1987; Yang, 1986). We derived eight different value scores in from a factor analysis of both Chinese and Western value scales in our cross-cultural research (Feldman et al., 1991). Of these, four — namely the valuing of universal prosocial behaviours (such as equality, peace, justice), tradition, outward success (wealth, power, status), and the family as a residential unit (elderly parents should live with adult children, unmarried adult children should live with parents) — revealed differences between western and Chinese adolescents. Specifically, Hong Kong youths placed more value on prosocial outcomes, tradition, and the family as a residential unit, and less value on outward success than did western youths.

In our acculturation studies, then, we searched for evidence of a shift

---

[1] For the demanding family environment this occurred for the United States sample only, although there was a similar non-significant trend for the Australian sample.

from Chinese to western norms in these two family environment dimensions and four adolescent values. As shown in Table 1 there was evidence of acculturation in the accepting/engaged dimension for both the American and Australian samples[2]. Acculturation occurred more rapidly for the Chinese–Australians than for the Chinese–Americans, but in both cases it remained incomplete, with the Chinese adolescents still differing from their western counterparts in perceptions of this aspect of family environment. The pattern for the demanding dimension was different and highlights the need to sample groups representing both the old and the new cultures. Our results suggest that immigrant adolescents perceive heightened expectations and greater control by their parents than their non-immigrant peers. This could be a function of an understandable response by parents to the anxieties and stresses associated with immigration and with being members of a minority group. Alternatively, these Chinese adolescents may be using the behaviour of western parents as a yardstick against which they measure their own parents' behaviour. Hong Kong adolescents, on the other hand, may be more accepting of parental restrictiveness and control.

As Table 1 shows, in both the American and Australian studies, acculturation of values began early and was already evident among the first-generation. First-generation Chinese youth living in the West differed from their Hong Kong counterparts in that they placed less value on tradition, prosocial behaviour, and the family as a residential unit, and more value on success. Subsequent acculturation was modest, occurring only for the value of the family as a residential unit. However, acculturation of this value was not complete — second-generation Chinese continued to place greater value on family members living together than did western students. In Australia, on all other values, second-generation Chinese youth were indistinguishable from the Anglo–Australian counterparts. In contrast, in the United States, where the Chinese are congregated in ethnic enclaves, second-generation Chinese–American teenagers continued to differ from

---

[2] For the values and family environment scores, we took account of possible cultural biases in responding to general evaluative scales (Triandis et al., 1986); each individual's score was first standardised across the items before being averaged to form the composites. In this way the subject's score reflected the salience of that composite relative to other composites for that individual. For the adolescent outcomes scores were standardised separately in the United States and Australian studies, with the mean set at 50 and the standard deviation at 10.

Table 12.1 Acculturation of Family Environments, Adolescent Values, and Adolescent Outcomes in Chinese Adolescents in USA and Australia: Mean Scores

Score	EAm	CAm2	CAm1	HK
Family Environment				
Accepting/engaged	53.8**	51.3*	49.2	48.7
Demanding	49.9**	52.5	53.0***	47.9
Adolescent Values				
Prosocial	52.2	53.8	52.6*	54.6
Tradition	41.7	42.0	42.3**	44.3
Family as residential unit	2.4***	3.3*	3.7**	4.4
Outward success	49.4*	47.3*	49.7***	44.6
Adolescent Outcomes				
Autonomy expectations[1]	44.7***	50.6*	54.0	54.3
Misconduct	55.0**	48.2	46.7	46.4
Distress	42.6***	50.6	52.7	53.1
	AAust	CAust2	CAust1	HK
Family Environment				
Accepting/engaged	55.0*	52.3	52.1***	48.7
Demanding	48.2***	54.1	52.9***	47.9
Adolescent Values				
Prosocial	52.7	52.1	52.2*	54.6
Tradition	41.8	42.3	42.7*	44.3
Family as residential unit	2.5***	3.1***	3.9*	4.4
Outward success	48.7	50.3	49.4***	44.6
Adolescent Outcomes				
Autonomy expectations[1]	44.3**	49.3	52.5	54.3
Misconduct	53.7+	50.4**	44.5***	46.4
Distress	46.4	46.4+	50.2**	53.1

Note: [1] High score = Low autonomy expectations
Significant differences between adjacent groups: $+P < .10$; $*P < .05$; $**P < .01$; $***p < .001$
EAm = Euro–Americans; CAm = Chinese–Americans; CAust = Chinese–Australians; HK= Hong Kong; AAust= Anglo–Australians

Euro–American youth in that they still placed more value on prosocial behaviour and less on outward success.

In sum, the experience of living in a western country had an impact on Chinese adolescents from Hong Kong. Their perceptions of some aspects of their family environment and their values shifted towards those of the host country. In general, these changes were already apparent in first-generation youth. It is notable that somewhat more rapid change in the second-generation occurred for adolescents' values than for perceptions of family environments. This is not surprising, given that the former represent beliefs that these youths themselves hold dear while that latter essentially reflect the behaviour of their Hong Kong-born and bred parents. It is interesting, in the light of purported recent changes in Hong Kong, that adolescents' perceptions of family environments (and thus their parents' values) were similar across generations. Thus, the expectation that recent immigrants — through the impact of modernisation — may hold less traditional values (albeit through the eyes of their adolescent children) than immigrants of longer standing was not borne out by our findings.

Adolescent Outcomes

We were interested in the extent to which the acculturation process impacted on the development of Chinese youths in the West. Socioemotional outcomes were selected for study if previous empirical research had shown that there were significant differences between Chinese and western respondents on the outcome in question and, additionally, if that outcome met at least one of the following criteria: (1) it reflected behaviours or attitudes that are an important aspect of adolescence in at least one of the cultures studied; or (2) the outcome was valued differently in the Chinese culture and in the West. We settled on three outcomes, one positive — expectations of autonomy — and two negative or undesirable outcomes — misconduct and distress.

Behavioural autonomy is, to some extent, positively valued in both cultures. However, consistent with the western emphasis on individualism, achieving autonomy has been defined as one of the central tasks of adolescence in western cultures. As a result, early behavioural autonomy is more highly valued and a more salient issue in western than in Chinese cultures and is, as we have seen, more strongly promoted by western than by Chinese parents. The two negative outcomes — misconduct and distress — have been reported to occur with differential frequency in western and Chinese cultures. Western children from an early age are characterised as being more aggressive and lower in restraint than Chinese children. Thus it is not surprising that, at adolescence when the level of misconduct increases in most cultures, misconduct and delinquency occur more often among western than Chinese youths (Cameron, 1985; Cheng, 1946; Hong Kong Census and Statistics Department, 1988; US Federal Bureau of Investigation, 1987. See also Leung and Fan, this volume). In contrast, it has been conjectured that since Chinese youths are less likely to "act out" their distress, they are likely to turn inward and to feel subjectively more distressed than western youths.

In contrast to the pattern found for family environments and adolescent values, the adolescent outcomes showed gradual rather than rapid acculturation (see Table 1).[3] For example, in both the American and Australian studies, second-generation youth, despite being born and raised in the West, nonetheless had significantly later expectations for autonomy, showed markedly less misconduct, and, in the American study, reported more distress than their western classmates. There is evidence that acculturation may be proceeding at a slower pace in the United States than in Australia. First-generation Chinese youths in America and their Hong Kong counterparts were alike on all of the adolescent outcomes, whereas first-generation Chinese youths resident in Australia reported less distress *but* higher levels of misconduct than youths in Hong Kong. Levels of misconduct rose substantially among second-generation Chinese-Australians.

As we argued previously, it is important in studies of acculturation to investigate whether the organisation of constructs — patterns of correlations — among the populations of interest differs from those prevailing in their country of origin or the host country. This question of similarities or differences in organisation of an adolescent outcome is quite different from the usual question investigated in acculturation studies and, to the best of our knowledge has not been addressed before. It is, however, a powerful way to consider the influence of a shift from one culture to another. We thus examined whether the organisation of the constructs differed across the samples.

To address this question, we used stepwise regression analyses. In separate analyses, each adolescent outcome was regressed on all eight adolescent values and four family environments for each group. We then compared the slopes of the regression places (by means of an ANCOVA), first for the four groups in the United States study (Hong Kong, first- and second-generation Chinese–American, and American adolescents) and, second, for those groups in the Australian study (Hong Kong, first- and second-generation Chinese–Australian, and Australian adolescents). The results were clear-cut. For all except one adolescent outcome (misconduct for the Australian study), the first- and second- generation Chinese living in the West did not differ from either anchor group (Hong Kong and American

---

[3] See Note 2.

or Australian youths) in the way adolescent outcomes were related to the family environments and values of youths. Thus, despite mean differences in autonomy expectations, misconduct, and distress, and despite differences among the groups in terms of important aspects of family environment and adolescent values, the patterning of associations with adolescent outcomes, with one exception, was similar across the acculturation groups and Chinese adolescents in their culture of origin as well as adolescents from the western host cultures, with modest to moderate significant correlations of the order of 0.20 to 0.45. This finding is consistent with those described in our other cross-cultural studies (Feldman and Rosenthal, 1990, 1991; Feldman et al., 1991).

Many of the results about the relationship between adolescent outcomes, family environments, and adolescent values are consistent with other reports in the literature. What is important here is the finding that adolescents' expectations of behavioural autonomy, their level of distress, and — in the United States study — their misconduct are influenced similarly by their values and their perceptions of family environment, irrespective of cultural background and/or experience of immigration. Despite differences in these last factors among our Chinese and western adolescents, parental acceptance and control have essentially the same effect on Hong Kong, western, and first- and second-generation Chinese immigrant youths. Similarly, the values that these youths hold have similar associations with adolescent outcomes in the individualistic West, the collectivist Chinese in Hong Kong, and among Chinese immigrants. Without addressing the question of the relationships between adolescent outcomes, family environments, and adolescent values we would have had only a restricted picture of the nature of the acculturation process and would have overlooked the robustness of these relationships across a variety of cultural influences and experiences.

These studies of adolescent outcomes, values, and family environments have added to our understanding of the lives of Chinese youths in the West. However, they have so far ignored a crucial element in the psychological functioning of these and other minority adolescents. We turn now to consider the nature and role of ethnic identity.

Ethnic Identity

The major developmental task for adolescents in western cultures, and one which subsumes all others, has been defined as the establishment of a stable, coherent sense of identity. Westerners' concern with identity achievement, expressed in both popular culture and in academic writings and research, has its genesis in those cultures' stress on the individual and his or her fundamental need for individual autonomy. Adolescents construct a sense of who they are and what they may become, achieving in that process a sense of self-worth and psychological cohesiveness, by integrating childhood identifications, personal inclinations and competencies, and the opportunities afforded by society. This ability to know and understand oneself as a unique individual with a particular place in the world is influenced strongly by the many social contexts in which each adolescent lives and functions.

For youths from ethnic minority groups, the process of identity formation is more complex because of their exposure to alternative sources of identification — their own ethnic group and the mainstream culture. Erikson (1968) has argued that achieving a sense of identity involves not just the "core of the individual" but also "the core of the communal culture" (Erikson, 1968, p. 2). Ethnic group membership provides for individuals not only a cultural identity and a set of prescribed norms, values, and social behaviours, but also, ideally, gives them a sense of belonging and group pride. The extent to which individuals adopt an identity based on their subjective identification with an ethnic group is a critical element in determining their response to the world in which they live. It has been suggested that ethnic identity provides the individual with a means of interpreting the world and future opportunities and thus is a potent conceptual framework for interpreting his or her ongoing experience or "fit" between the self and the environment (Gibbs and Huang, 1989).

The close links between a positive ethnic identity and the achievement of a sense of personal identity, as well as the importance of ethnicity as an identity issue, have been demonstrated by Phinney and Alipuria (1990). The task of integrating one's ethnic identity into a personal sense of self may be especially complex for adolescents growing up in a mainstream culture which differs significantly from their culture of origin in its values and behavioural norms since ethnic identity is a product not only of the individual and his or her relation to the ethnic group but of the relation between that group and the wider social setting. In particular, minority adolescents may face issues of prejudice and discrimination as well as structural barriers which limit their aspirations and achievements. If ethnic minority youth are to be well-functioning members of the mainstream society, their sense of ethnic identity, of belonging to a personally valued community, must be integrated with their subjective experiences in the world at large.

In conceptualising ethnic identity, researchers have focussed on the multifaceted rather than unitary nature of the construct. Subjective self-identification as a member of an ethnic group is a key component since this locates the individual within a particular cultural framework. A second critical component is the extent to which individuals take on the culture's "baggage", that is, their participation in activities consistent with those of the group and their knowledge of cultural norms. A third important component of ethnic identity is the evaluation of their culture of origin — their ethnic pride. While individuals may identify themselves as members of an ethnic group, they need not necessarily have positive feelings about that group.

Another focus of concern has been with the shift in commitment to one's ethnic group over time, with several studies showing ethnic identity to be weaker among those who have lived longer in the new country (Chan, 1987; Rogler, Cooney, and Ortiz, 1980). There is some evidence for erosion of ethnic identity in later generations of immigrants (Connor, 1977; Constantinou and Harvey, 1985; Fathi, 1972) although several studies have suggested that this erosion plateaus after the second generation (e.g., Wooden, Leon, and Tashima, 1988) or that a resurgence occurs, with stronger identification in third and subsequent generations (Scourby, 1980; Ting-Toomey, 1981).

Little attention has been paid to the interrelationships between the different components of ethnic identity and even less to the question of whether some aspects of ethnic identity are more open to change than others. We can draw on acculturation research to make some predictions about the process of change over time. Some researchers (e.g., Bond and Yang, 1982; Keefe and Padilla, 1987; Triandis et al., 1986) have argued that elements of the culture that are central and invisible, such as values, may be more resistant to change than those, such as behaviours, which are peripheral and visible. Thus it is possible that ethnic pride or loyalty remains constant over generations of immigrants although cultural awareness may decline and, over time, the individual may engage in fewer culturally approved behaviours.

What factors influence the salience and strength of ethnic identity? Support for the maintenance of a positive ethnic identity comes from the nature of the ethnic community — the extent to which the community provides for the needs of its members, its size and geographical dispersion, its cohesiveness — and its position in the wider society. Taifel (1978) points out that members of disparaged minority groups face the problem of having to live with negative images of their group. He describes a number of strategies open to these individuals to preserve their self-image, including identifying with the majority culture, or re-evaluating and enhancing their group's image ("Black is beautiful"). While both strategies have been identified in minority youth (Giles, Rosenthal, and Young, 1985; Hogg, Abrams, and Patel, 1987; Milner, 1984; Ullah, 1985, 1987), many studies have affirmed the notion of biculturality or dual identity, suggesting that individuals do not have to choose between two conflicting or competing identities (e.g., Hutnick, 1986; Rosenthal and Hrynevich, 1985; Ting-Toomey, 1981). Rather than considering maintenance of an ethnic identity to be incompatible with identification with the dominant culture, Berry (1980) argues that it is possible to maintain or enhance one's ties with both groups.

The study of ethnic identity has largely been confined to studying racially distinct groups such as minorities of colour. For these groups, the option of complete assimilation into the mainstream culture is not available and, unlike racially similar minority groups, such as European immigrants in the United States, issues of prejudice and discrimination have been more virulent and widespread. Sue (1973) documents the long-term experience of cultural racism by Asians in the United States and others have drawn attention to the potential conflict inherent in the identification of Chinese–Americans, born and acculturated in the United States, as "American" and their appearance to others as primarily "Chinese" (Chen and Yang, 1986). For these youths, issues of ethnic identity are likely to be highly salient.

While there has been some research into the development, nature, and maintenance of ethnic identity among Black adolescents, and the consequences for this on their psychological well-being (Cross, 1987; Ogbu, 1985; Spencer, 1982; Spencer and Dornbusch, 1990), there has been surprisingly little study of adolescents of Asian — and specifically Chinese — descent, a significant racially distinct and numerically large group in the United States (Kim, 1981). To some extent, this may be explained by the belief that Asians are a model minority. Thus, the problems of identity conflicts and poor self-image associated with being a member of a denigrated minority group may be lessened for Asian–Americans. Nevertheless, Sue (1973) suggests that there is considerable evidence of social and economic discrimination against Asian-Americans.

Phinney and her colleagues (Phinney, 1989; Phinney and Alipuria, 1990) have highlighted some of the complexities of this issue in their work on ethnic identity formation and the importance of ethnic identity as one component of self-identity. Phinney adopts Erikson's model and examines two independent facets of ethnic identity, exploration of, and commitment to, that identity. In a study of tenth-graders of Asian, Black, and Hispanic backgrounds, Phinney (1989) found that higher levels of self-esteem were associated with a committed ethnic identity. In a study of older adolescents, the self-esteem of Asian–Americans, unlike that of Blacks and Hispanics, was not related to exploration, that is, their need to find out about their ethnic background and its role in their lives. For all three groups — Asians, Blacks and Hispanics — self-esteem was positively related to a commitment to an ethnic identity. Taken together, these results suggest that much of the early research which focussed on the potentially damaging effect of minority status on self-esteem (Clark and Clark, 1947; Cross, 1987) failed to take account on the subtleties of ethnicity. Rather than relating self-esteem to subjective or objective measures of ethnic group membership, Phinney's research suggests that self-esteem of minorities is influenced by the extent to which one has thought about issues regarding ethnicity (exploration) and resolved these issues (commitment).

In our studies of ethnic identity we focussed on adolescents of Chinese descent, using the same sample as described earlier (Rosenthal and Feldman, 1992a, 1992b). This enabled us to study an ethnic minority group which has had a long history of immigration to these two western cultures, Australia and the United States, but for whom issues of ethnic identity are still salient. In designing our research we were guided by questions relating to the multiple aspects of ethnic identity, the ways in which these may change over time, and factors which may influence both change and stability.

Our interest in the study of ethnic identity was threefold and partly parallels that of our other studies. First we addressed the question of the importance of various components of ethnic identity and the relationships between them. We did this by assessing the following three areas. Subjective self-identification as a member of the ethnic group was asking adolescents how Chinese they felt themselves to be. Behaviour/knowledge was assessed by their participation in activities consistent with those of their cultural group such as language, religious affiliation, participation in clubs and organisations, food preferences, and traditional celebrations. Third, we assessed cultural pride or the evaluation given to their culture of origin. In addition we asked about the cultural composition of their social networks, and their willingness to consider exogamy. As a second focus, we examined changes over time by comparing first- and second-generation Chinese students residing in the West. Finally, we explored the effect of cultural

context on strength and maintenance of ethnic identity by comparing
Chinese youths in Australia to those in the United States. The results are
summarised in Table 12.2.

As in our earlier studies, there were a number of replicated findings in
the Australian and American contexts. In particular, second-generation
Chinese youth, compared to first-generation, less often reported feeling
totally or mostly Chinese, scored lower on the Chinese behavior/knowledge
index, and were more open to exogamy. Notably, however, first- and second-
generation youth did not differ on ethnic pride, that is, they were alike in
the extent to which they felt positive about being Chinese. In Australia, but
not in the United States, first-generation Chinese were much more likely to
have totally or mostly Chinese friends than were second-generation youths,
although even the first-generation Chinese–Australians had significantly
fewer Chinese friends than their American peers.

The cultural context also influenced the results although only in terms
of social relations. Specifically, in Australia with its dispersed Chinese
population, Chinese adolescents were less likely to interact primarily with
Chinese friends either at school or during the weekend, and they were more
likely to consider exogamy, than were Chinese youths in the United States.

Correlations between the components of ethnic identity were moderately high for both Chinese–Australian and Chinese–American youths,

**Table 12.2 Ethnic Identity in First- and Second-generation Chinese Youth
Residing in USA or Australia**

	USA		Australia	
Score	CAm1	CAm2	CAust1	CAust2
Ethnic Identification				
"Feel totally or mostly Chinese"	58%	18%	66%	17%
Ethnic Social Relations				
Mostly Chinese school friends	59%	62%	30%	6%
Mostly Chinese weekend friends	74%	78%	51%	21%
Marriage partner only or preferably Chinese	62%	49%	51%	37%
Ethnic behavior and knowledge[1]	2.8	2.4	2.7	2.3
Ethnic pride[1]	3.1	3.0	3.0	3.0

Note: [1] 4-point scale: 4 = high
CAm1 and 2 = First- and second-generation Chinese-Americans
CAust1 and 2 = First- and second-generation Chinese-Australians

suggesting that these facets of ethnic identity overlap to some extent but are not identical. This finding, together with the stability over time of one aspect of ethnic identity, namely cultural pride, but not others, demonstrates the importance of analysing separately the distinctive components of ethnic identity.

In our findings on ethnic identity, there was significant variability in the responses of adolescents. Some were knowledgeable about their culture of origin, others knew relatively little; some were proud of their ethnic heritage, others were not. Furthermore, there was variability in both the first- and second-generations. This led us to wonder about the process by which Chinese youths in the West establish their ethnic identity. The process seemed to us especially interesting among Chinese youths who are less able to deny their heritage than other ethnic groups, given that they are a "visible minority", readily labelled as Chinese by others as well as by themselves.

The family has been implicated as a significant force in the process of forging an identity, for it provides the child with his or her first experiences as a member of a particular ethnic group. Family members are powerful sources of information which gives the child a cultural context, a lens through which the world is viewed. In particular, at least four aspects of parenting have been associated with adolescents' developmental outcomes. At all ages, adaptive outcomes have been related to parental warmth and acceptance and a regulated environment where rules are provided and enforced (Maccoby and Martin, 1983, Rohner, 1986). Parental monitoring, in which parents keep tabs on their adolescents (Dornbusch et al., 1987; Patterson, Bank, and Stoolmiller, 1990) is also associated with positive (adult sanctioned) outcomes. In addition, identity exploration and ego development have been facilitated by a parenting style which promotes autonomy, in which family members are free to express dissent and tolerate disagreement with each other (Grotevant and Cooper, 1986; Hauser, Powers, Noam, Jacobson, Weiss, and Follansbee, 1984).

We speculated that each of these parental behaviours provides adolescents with positive role models, leading adolescents to internalise not only behaviour related to specific parenting practices, but also other characteristics of their parents, including the parents' ethnic culture. Thus we predicted that the pride adolescents feel in their ethnicity, the positive or negative evaluation of their cultural heritage, is likely to be influenced by good parenting practices. In contrast, knowledge and behavioral expressions of ethnicity (such as speaking Chinese, eating Chinese food, going to Chinese places of worship) are less likely to be influenced by psychological aspects of parenting and more likely to be influenced by parental example of engaging in these ethnic behaviours, direct instruction, and enforcement of these behaviors.

To evaluate these hypotheses we used the same sample of respondents as in the other studies. Given that the two generations of Chinese students did not differ in ethnic pride, we combined them into one undifferentiated sample and replicated the study in two cultural contexts — in Australia and the United States.

Our hypothesis, that perceived parenting behaviour would be associated with ethnic pride but not the behavioural or knowledge components of ethnic identity, was supported in both cultural contexts. Multiple regression analyses indicated that three of the four parenting behaviours — warmth, control, autonomy-promotion — made independent and unique (albeit modest) contributions to youths' positive evaluation of their ethnicity. In contrast, the extent to which adolescents engaged in behaviours which denote their ethnic culture was not influenced by perceived styles of parenting. In sum, disengaging the affective component of ethnic identity from behaviours has enabled us to demonstrate a subtle and complex relationship between perceived parenting behaviour and Chinese youths' ethnic identity. If parents provide a warm family environment where rules are explicit and some control is exercised over adolescent behaviour, but where adolescents are allowed flexibility and given the opportunity to develop a sense of autonomy, then adolescents will feel good about their (and their parents') cultural heritage.

We can draw the following conclusions from our study of ethnic identity among Chinese youths from immigrant families residing in the West. Diverse aspects of ethnic identity show different patterns of development. Whereas behaviour, knowledge, and social networks change across generations, ethnic pride — identified as a core aspect of ethnic identity — does not. It appears that, although some acculturation to western norms occurs with increasing periods of residence in the West, vital psychological ties with the ethnic community, essential for the maintenance of a cultural consciousness, are resistant to change.

Our findings also shed some light on the question of what factors produce "well-functioning" minority youth (Spencer and Dornbusch, 1990). In particular, there is a concern with youths' readiness to take on a positive, satisfying ethnic identity as part of their construction of a sense of self, so that they can fit harmoniously both within their ethnic culture and within the host culture of which they are also a part. We have shown that the

perceived quality of family relationships influences adolescents' evaluations of their ethnic group membership. What parents are perceived to do in
the family, the environment they create in which family life is played out,
has an impact on the pride and positive feelings that youth have about their
ethnic heritage.

Summary and Conclusions

In sum, many of the results that emerged from our studies affirm that
adolescents who are part of two cultures are psychologically distinct from
youths who do not have this experience. We have studied only a few of the
possible domains of behaviour and psychological functioning which are
significant for adolescents. However, one noteworthy feature of the findings is that we have confirmed that the process of acculturation does not
necessarily proceed in a linear fashion, nor does it proceed at the same rate
for all the domains we studied. For example, we may question why the pace
of acculturation for adolescent outcomes such as behavioural autonomy
was relatively slow, certainly for Chinese youths in the United States, while
acculturation of values occurred more rapidly, being already evident among
our first-generation Chinese. There may be several explanations for this. It
is possible that families who emigrated from Hong Kong are self-selected
and differ from those that remained in important ways and, in particular, in
being entrepreneurial and valuing western notions of outward success and
achievement. Alternatively, it may be that the persuasive cultural messages
of the western mass media, combined with the pervasive material comforts
in western nations, enhances the appeal of western values, especially to
adolescents. At the same time, these adolescents are part of a family
environment which they regard as retaining many of the features of traditional Chinese families. Given the significance of the family unit in the
Chinese culture and its effectiveness in transmitting standards of conduct, it
is not surprising that adolescents are also to shed behaviours that conform
to cultural norms.

Insofar as values are internal and not directly observable and thus not
open to parental criticism in the way that overt behaviours are, the apparent
faster rate of change for values than for behaviours should not surprise us.
Moreover, these Chinese youths, like their western peers, are at a time in
their lives when values are particularly salient as they work towards adopting a coherent value stance on a number of issues. In their search, they are
free to experiment with different values in a way not open to their parents,

who already have the responsibility of passing on to their children a prescribed set of cultural values. Thus, these Chinese adolescents in the West may be exploring new western values now, but may not hold these values when, as parents, they wish to connect their children to their Chinese heritage.

Our findings also highlight the need to consider the process of acculturation within a particular social context. There were remarkable consistencies between the Chinese youths in the United States and Australia, attesting to a certain robustness of the findings. Whether Chinese youths live in predominantly Chinese neighbourhoods, interacting with fellow nationals at school and elsewhere (as in San Francisco), or whether they live dispersed among the local population with only a handful of other Asian students in the school (as in Melbourne), changes in values and family environments towards those of the host culture begin during the first generation. Nevertheless, when we turned to adolescent outcomes, the picture was different. The faster pace of acculturation that occurred for the Chinese–Australians warrants attention. It is likely that these youths, in the absence of large numbers of Chinese peers, very quickly learn to model their behaviour on that of their Australian schoolmates.

In drawing conclusions from our research about the process of acculturation, we should note the limitations of that research. We have studied only a small set of adolescent outcomes and possible influences on these. Furthermore, we have restricted our samples of Chinese immigrant samples to a particular group — adolescents from intact families who have left Hong Kong to live in western countries. The findings of relatively rapid onset and extensive acculturation of some outcomes, values, and family environments may well be influenced by the developmental stage of our respondents. It should not be assumed that similar findings will be found among younger subjects who may be more influenced by parents than by peers and the wider culture, or among adults who, in their parenting roles, may consciously and deliberately attempt to preserve and transmit their Chinese heritage to the next generation.

What would we find if, for example, we had included Chinese immigrant adolescents with divorced parents in our sample? It is likely that there would have been differences between these youths and their counterparts from intact families on all our adolescent outcomes as well as in the associations between these outcomes and other factors. Again, we studied Chinese immigrants from Hong Kong whose experience of immigrating to the West is probably less traumatic than the experience of, say, people from small rural Chinese communities. The example serves to remind us of the need, in assessing the impact of settlement in the West, to be aware of the current nature of the culture of origin. To what extent, for example, has modernization caused a shift within that culture which narrows the gap between the old and the new? In our cross-cultural research, the findings that Hong Kong Chinese and western family environments were perceived to be similar on a number of dimensions, as were adolescent values, suggest two possibilities: either Chinese–Western differences are no longer as pervasive as in the past or Hong Kong is not typical of other, less western-ised Chinese communities. In order to determine which alternative is correct, we need research using respondents from other Chinese countries to provide baseline data.

Bond's study of values in 21 cultures (Bond, 1988) sheds some light on this issue, while at the same time pointing to its complexity. Using Rokeach's Values Survey, Bond found both similarities and differences among the values of Hong Kong and Australian university students and other Chinese groups. For example, Hong Kong Chinese and Australians were similar in their valuing of personal morality and different from Chinese in Taiwan and Malaysia. On the other hand, Hong Kong and Malaysian Chinese tended to value politeness and responsibility to a greater extent than did the Australian students. Similar complex patterns were obtained for the clusters of values measured by the Chinese Value Survey. These findings suggest that shifts in cultural values may be specific either to the value or the culture, or to both of these.

As a final example, we would expect to find the process of accultura-tion among Chinese youths to be different if we were to select, as our target groups, Chinese who had immigrated to countries such as Singapore or Malaysia where they are not a "visible" minority as in the West by virtue of their physical characteristics, are present in large numbers, and are living in an Asian country with similar values and norms of behaviour.

These and other gaps in the study of the coping and adaptation of Chinese immigrants remain to be filled. What is needed are studies that are methodologically rigorous and that ask sophisticated questions as to how the transition from one culture to another may influence the lives of children, adolescents, and their families. Our research has shown the need to distinguish between the stress of immigration and the process of learning to live adaptively in a new society. Whether this process results in a cultural synthesis, whereby a new cultural identity evolves — an amalgam of East and West, based on elements of both the old and the new cultures, or whether these Chinese settlers eventually abandon the values and norms of their culture of origin, remains to be investigated.

References

Ahn Toupin, E.S.W., and Son, L. (1991). Preliminary finding on Asian–Americans: "The model minority" in a small private East Coast college. *Journal of Cross-cultural Psychology*, 22: 404–417.

Alwin, D. F. (1988). From obedience to autonomy: Changes in traits desired in children, 1924–1978. *Public Opinion Quarterly*, 52: 33–52.

Anderson, D. S., and Vervoorn, A. E. (1983). *Access to privilege: Patterns of participation in Australian post-secondary education*. Canberra: Australian National University Press.

Asians take top honours in HSC results. (1992, January 14). *Australian*, p. 3.

Atkinson, D. R., and Gim, R. H. (1989). Asian–American cultural identity and attitudes toward mental health services. *Journal of Counseling Psychology*, 36: 209–212.

Banchevska, R. (1981). Uprooting and settling: The transplanted family. In L. Eitinger and D. Schwartz (Eds.), *Strangers in the world* (pp. 107–132). Vienna: Hans Huber.

Baumrind, D. (1971). Current patterns of parental authority. *Developmental Psychology Monograph*, 4: 1.

Berry, J. W. (1980). Acculturation as varieties of adaptation. In A. M. Padilla (Ed.), *Acculturation: Theory, models and some new findings* (pp. 9–25). Boulder, CO: Westview Press.

————. (1990). Psychology of acculturation: Understanding individuals moving between cultures. In R. W. Brislin (Ed.), *Applied cross-cultural psychology* (pp. 232–253). Newbury Park, CA: Sage.

Berry, J. W., Kim, V., Minde, T., and Mok, D. (1987). Comparative studies of acculturative stress. *International Migration Review*, 21: 491–511.

Bond, M. H. (Ed.) (1986). *The psychology of the Chinese people*. Hong Kong: Oxford University Press.

————. (1988). Finding universal dimensions of individual variation in multicultural studies of values: The Rokeach and Chinese value systems. *Journal of Personality and Social Psychology*, 55: 1009–1015.

Bond, M. H., and Hwang, K. (1986). The social psychology of Chinese people. In M. H. Bond (Ed.), *The psychology of the Chinese people* (pp. 213–266). Hong Kong: Oxford University Press.

Bond, M. H., and Yang, K. S. (1982). Ethnic affirmation versus cross-cultural accommodation: The variable impact of questionnaire language on Chinese-bilinguals in Hong Kong. *Journal of Cross-cultural Psychology*, 13: 169–185.

Brand, D. (1987, August). The new whiz kids: Why Asian–Americans are doing so well and what it costs them. *Time Magazine*, 42–51.

Burns, A., and Goodnow, J. J. (1985). *Children and families in Australia* (2nd ed.). Sydney: Allen and Unwin.

Cameron, R. J. (1985). *Australia's youth population, 1984: A statistical profile*. Canberra: Australian Bureau of Statistics.

Chan, H.K.Y. (1987). *The adaptation, life satisfaction and academic achievement of Chinese senior school students in Melbourne*. Unpublished doctoral dissertation, Monash University, Melbourne, Australia.

Chataway, C. J., and Berry, J. W. (1989). Acculturation experiences, appraisal, coping, and adaptation: A comparison of Hong Kong Chinese, French, and English students in Canada. *Canadian Journal of Behavioural Science*, 21: 295–309.

Chen, C. L., and Yang, D.C.Y. (1986). The self-image of Chinese–American adolescents: A cross-cultural comparison. *International Journal of Social Psychiatry*, 32: 19–26.

Cheng, C. K. (1946). Characteristic traits of the Chinese people. *Social Forces*, 25: 146–155.

Chinese Culture Connection (1987). Chinese values and the search for culture-free dimensions of culture. *Journal of Cross-cultural Psychology*, 8: 143–164.

Chui, E., and Tan, E. S. (1986). *Socialization of Australian-born Chinese*. Paper presented at the Ethnicity and Multiculturalism National Research Conference. A.I.M.A., Melbourne, May.

Chui, M. L., Feldman, S. S., and Rosenthal, D. A. (1992). The influence of immigration on parental behavior and adolescent distress in Chinese families residing in two western nations. *Journal of Research on Adolescence*, 2: 205–240.

Clark, K. B., and Clark, M. P. (1947). Racial identification and preference in Negro children. In T. M. Newcomb and E. L. Hartley (Eds.), *Readings in social psychology* (pp. 169–178). New York: Holt, Rinehart and Winston.

Connor, J. W. (1977). *Tradition and change in three generation of Japanese–Americans*. Chicago: Nelson-Hall.

Constantinou, S., and Harvey, M. (1985). Dimensional structure and intergenerational differences in ethnicity: The Greek Americans. *Sociology and Social Research*, 69: 234–254.

Cross, W. E. (1987). A two-factor theory of black identity: Implications for the study of identity development in minority children. In J. S. Phinney and M. J. Rotheram (Eds.), *Children's ethnic socialization: Pluralism and development* (pp. 117–133). Newbury Park, CA: Sage.

Dawson, J.L.M.B., and Ng, W. (1972). Effects of parental attitudes and modern exposure on Chinese traditional–modern attitude formation. *Journal of Cross-cultural Psychology*, 3: 210–217.

Dion, K. L., and Toner, B. B. (1988). Ethnic differences in test anxiety. *Journal of Social Psychology*, 128: 165–172.

Dion, K. L., and Yee, P.H.N. (1987). Ethnicity and personality in a Canadian context. *Journal of Social Psychology*, 127: 175–182.

Dornbusch, S. M., Ritter, P. L., Leiderman, P. H., Roberts, D. F., and Fraleigh, M. J. (1987). The relation of parenting style to adolescent school performance. *Child Development*, 58: 1244–1257.

Dreidger, L. (1975). In search of cultural identity factors: A comparison of ethnic students. *Canadian Review of Sociology and Anthropology*, 12: 150–162.

Erikson, E. H. (1968). *Identity: Youth and crisis*. New York: Norton.

Fathi, A. (1972). Some aspects of changing identity of Canadian Jewish youth. *Jewish Social Studies*, 34: 23–30.

Feather, N. T. (1980). Values in adolescence. In J. Adelson (Ed.), *Handbook of adolescent psychology* (pp. 247–294), New York: Wiley.

———. (1986). Value systems across cultures: Australia and China. *International Journal of Psychology*, 21: 697–715.

Feldman, S. S., Mont-Reynaud, R., and Rosenthal, D. A. (1992). When East moves West: The acculturation of values of Chinese adolescents in the United States and Australia. *Journal of Research on Adolescence*, 2: 147–174.

Feldman, S. S., and Rosenthal, D. A. (1990). The acculturation of autonomy expectations in Chinese high schoolers residing in two western nations. *International Journal of Psychology*, 25: 259–281.

———. (1991). Age expectations of behavioral autonomy in Hong Kong, Australian, and American youths: The influence of family variables and adolescent values. *International Journal of Psychology*, 26: 1–23.

———. (1993). Culture makes a difference ... or does it? A comparison of adolescents in Hong Kong, Australia, and the U.S.A. In R. Silbereisen and E. Todt (Eds.), *Adolescence in context: The Interplay of family, school, peers, and work in adjustment*. New York: Springer.

Feldman, S. S., Rosenthal, D., Mont-Reynaud, R., Lau, S., and Leung, K. (1991). Ain't misbehavin': Adolescent values and family environments as correlates of misconduct in Australia, Hong Kong, and the United States. *Journal of Research in Adolescence*, 1: 109–134.

Fong, S.L.M. (1973). Assimilation and changing social roles of Chinese Americans. *Journal of Social Issues*, 29: 115–128.

Funder, K. (Ed.). (1991). *Images of Australian families*. Sydney: Longman Cheshire.

Furnham, A., and Bochner, S. (1986). *Culture shock: Psychological reactions to unfamiliar environments*. London: Methuen.

Garcia, M., and Lega, L. (1979). Development of a Cuban ethnic identity questionnaire. *Hispanic Journal of Behavioral Sciences*, 1: 247–261.

Gibbs, J. T., and Huang, L. N. (1989). A conceptual framework for assessing and treating minority youth. In J. T. Gibbs and L. N. Huang (Eds.), *Children of color* (pp. 1–29). San Francisco: Jossey-Bass.

Giles, H., Rosenthal, D. A., and Young, L. (1985). Perceived ethnolinguistic vitality: The Anglo– and Greek–Australian setting. *Journal of Multilingual and Multicultural Development*, 6: 253–269.

Gradner, H. (1989). *To open minds: Chinese clues to the dilemma of contemporary education*. New York: Basic Books.

Grotevant, H., and Cooper, C. (1986). Individuation in family relationships: A perspective on individual differences in the development of identity and role-taking skills in adolescence. *Human Development*, 29: 82–100.

Harrison, A., Serafica, F., and McAdoo, H. (1984). Ethnic families of color. In R. D. Parke (Ed.), *Review of child development research 7: The family* (pp. 329–365). Chicago: University of Chicago Press.

Hauser, S., Powers, S., Noam, G., Jacobson, A., Weiss, B., and Follansbee, D. (1984). Familial contexts of adolescent ego development. *Child Development*, 55: 195–213.

Hirschman, C., and Wong, M. G. (1986). The extraordinary attainments of Asian-Americans: A search for historical evidence and explanations. *Social Forces*, 65: 1–27.

Ho, D.Y.F. (1986). Chinese patterns of socialization: A critical review. In M. H. Bond (Ed.), *The psychology of the Chinese people* (pp. 1–37). Hong Kong: Oxford University Press.

Ho, D.Y.F., and Kang, T. K. (1984). Intergenerational comparisons of child-rearing attitudes and practices in Hong Kong. *Developmental Psychology*, 20: 1004–1006.

Hofstede, G. (1980). *Culture's consequences: International differences in work-related values*. Newbury Park, CA: Sage.

———. (1983). National cultures revisited. *Behaviour Science Research*, 18: 285–305.

Hogg, A., Abrams, D., and Patel, Y. (1987). Ethnic identity, self-esteem and occupational aspirations of Indian and Anglo–Saxon British adolescents. *Genetic, Social and General Psychology Monographs*, 113: 487–508.

Hong Kong Census and Statistics Department. (1988). *Crime and its victims in Hong Kong 1986* (A report on the crime victimization survey conducted in January 1987 by the Census and Statistics Department, Hong Kong Government).

Hsu, F.L.K. (1972). American core value and national character. In F.L.K. Hsu (Ed.), *Psychological Anthropology* (pp. 241–261). Cambridge, MA: Schenkman.

———. (1981). *Americans and Chinese: Passage to differences* (3rd ed.). Honolulu: University of Hawaii Press.

Hutnik, N. (1986). Patterns of ethnic minority identification and modes of social adaptation. *Ethnic and Racial Studies*, 9: 150–167.

Keefe, S. E., and Padilla, A. M. (1987). *Chicano ethnicity*. Albuquerque: University of New Mexico Press.

Kim, J. (1981). *The process of Asian–American identity development: A study of Japanese American women's perceptions of their struggle to achieve positive identification*. Unpublished doctoral dissertation, University of Massachusetts.

Kitano, H. L., and Sue, S. (1973). The model minorities. *Journal of Social Issues*, 29: 1–9.

Kriger, S. F., and Kroes, W. H. (1972). Child-rearing attitudes of Chinese, Jewish, and Protestant mothers. *Journal of Social Psychology*, 86: 205–210.

Lau, S. (1988). The value orientations of Chinese University students in Hong Kong. *International Journal of Psychology*, 23: 583–596.

Lee, E. (1988). Cultural factors in working with Southeast Asian refugee adolescents. *Journal of Adolescence*, 11: 167–179.

Leong, F.T.K., and Tata, S. P. (1990). Sex and acculturation differences in occupational values among Chinese–American children. *Journal of Counseling Psychology*, 37: 208–212.

Leung, K., and Bond, M. (1984). The impact of cultural collectivism on reward allocation. *Journal of Personality and Social Psychology*, 47: 793–804.

Lin, C. C., and Fu, V. R. (1990). A comparison of child-rearing practices among Chinese, immigrant Chinese, and Caucasian–American parents. *Child Development*, 61: 429–433.

Maccoby, E. E., and Martin, J. (1983). Socialization in the context of the family: Parent-child interaction. In E. M. Hetherington (Ed.), *Handbook of child psychology, Vol. 4: Socialization, personality, and social development* (pp. 1–102). New York: Wiley.

Martin, R. (1975). The socialization of children in China and Taiwan: An analysis of elementary school textbooks. *China Quarterly*, 62: 242–262.

Masuda, M., Matsumoto, G. H., and Meredith, G. M. (1970). Ethnic identity in three generations of Japanese Americans. *Journal of Social Psychology*, 81: 199–207.

McAdam, K. (1972). The study methods and academic results of overseas students. In S. Bochner and P. Wicks (Eds.), *Overseas students in Australia*. Sydney: University of New South Wales Press.

Milner, D. (1984). The development of ethnic attitudes. In H. Tajfel (Ed.), *The social dimension: European developments in social psychology* (Vol. 1, pp. 89–110). Cambridge: Cambridge University Press.

Mitchell, R. E., and Lo, I. (1968). Implications of changes in family authority relations for the development of independence and assertiveness in Hong Kong. *Asian Survey*, 8: 309–322.

Mumford, D. B., Whitehouse, A. M., and Platts, M. (1991). Sociocultural correlates of eating disorders among Asian schoolgirls in Bradford. *British Journal of Psychiatry*, 158: 222–228.

Naditch, M. P., and Morrissey, R. F. (1976). Role stress, personality, and psychopathology in a group of immigrant adolescents. *Journal of Abnormal Psychology*, 85: 113–118.

Noller, P. and Callan, V. (1991). *The adolescent in the family*. London: Routledge.

Oberg, K. (1960). Culture shock: Adjustment to new cultural environments. *Practical Anthropology*, 7: 177–182.

Ogbu, J. (1985). A cultural ecology of competence among inner-city Blacks. In M. Spencer, G. Brooks, and W. Allen (Eds.), *Beginnings: The social and affective development of black children* (pp. 45–66). Hillsdale, NJ: Lawrence Erlbaum.

Patterson, G. R., Bank, L., and Stoolmiller, M. (1990). The preadolescent's contributions to disrupted family process. In R. Montemayor, G. R. Adams, and T. P. Gullotta (Eds.), *From childhood to adolescence: A transitional period?* (Vol. 2, pp. 107–133). Newbury Park, CA: Sage.

Phinney, J. S. (1989). Stages of ethnic identity development in minority group adolescents. *Journal of Early Adolescence*, 9: 34–49.

Phinney, J. S., and Alipuria, L. (1990). Ethnic identity in college students from four ethnic groups. *Journal of Adolescence*, 13: 171–183.

Poole, M. (1986). Perspective on the aspiration, values, and achievements of Australian adolescents. In C. Bagley and G. Verma (Eds.), *Personality, cognition and values* (pp. 24–76). London: Macmillan.

Rogler, L., Cooney, R., and Ortiz, V. (1980). Intergenerational change in ethnic identity in the Puerto Rican family. *International Migration Review*, 14: 193–214.

Rohner, R. P. (1986). *The warmth dimension: Foundations of parental acceptance-rejection theory*. Newbury Park, CA: Sage.

Rokeach, M. (1973). *The nature of human values*. New York: The Free Press.

———. (1979). From individual to institutional values: With special reference to the values of science. In M. Rokeach (Ed.), *Understanding human values* (pp. 47–70). New York: The Free Press.

Rosenthal, D. A. (1984). Intergenerational conflict and culture: A study of immigrant and nonimmigrant adolescents and their parents. *Genetic Psychology Monographs*, 109: 53–75.

Rosenthal, D. A., Bell, R., Demetriou, A., and Efklides, A. (1989). From collectivism to individualism? The acculturation of Greek immigrants in Australia. *International Journal of Psychology*, 24: 57–71.

Rosenthal, D. A., and Bornholt, L. (1988). Expectations about development in Greek and Anglo-Australian families. *Journal of Cross-cultural Psychology*, 19: 19–34.

Rosenthal, D. A., and Cichello, A. (1986). The meeting of two cultures: Ethnic identity and psychosocial adjustment of Italian–Australian adolescents. *International Journal of Psychology*, 21: 487–501.

Rosenthal, D. A., and Feldman, S. S. (1991a). The influence of perceived family and personal factors on self-reported school performance of Chinese and western high school students. *Journal of Research in Adolescence*, 1: 135–154.

——— . (1991b). The acculturation of Chinese immigrants: Perceived effects on family functioning of length of residence in two cultural contexts. *Journal of Genetic Psychology*, 151: 493–514.

——— . (1992a). The relationship between parenting behaviour and ethnic identity in Chinese–American and Chinese–Australian adolescents. *International Journal of Psychology*, 27: 19–31.

——— . (1992b). The nature and stability of ethnic identity in Chinese youth: Effects of length of residence in two cultural contexts. *Journal of Cross-cultural Psychology*, 23: 214–227

Rosenthal, D. A., and Hrynevich, C. (1985). Ethnicity and ethnic identity: A comparative study of Greek–, Italian– and Anglo–Australian adolescents. *International Journal of Psychology*, 20: 723–742.

Scourby, A. (1980). Three generations of Greek Americans: A study in ethnicity. *International Migration Review*, 14: 43–52.

Sluzki, C. E. (1979). Migration and family conflict. *Family Process*, 18: 379–390.

Spencer, M. (1982). Personal and group identity of Black children: An alternative synthesis. *Genetic Psychology Monographs*, 106: 59–84.

Spencer, M. B., and Dornbusch, S. M. (1990). Minority youth in America. In S. S. Feldman and G. R. Elliott (Eds.), *At the threshold: The developing adolescent* (pp. 123–146). Cambridge, MA: Harvard University Press.

Steinberg, L., Mounts, N. S., Lamborn, S. D., and Dornbusch, S. M. (1991). Authoritative parenting and adolescent adjustment across varied ecological niches. *Journal of Research on Adolescence*, 1: 19–36.

Steinberg, L., and Silverberg, S. (1986). The vicissitudes of autonomy in early adolescence. *Child Development*, 57: 841–885.

Stevenson, H. W., Lee, S. Y., and Stigler, J. (1986). Mathematics achievement of Chinese, Japanese and American children. *Science*, 231: 693–699.

Stoller, A. (1981). Foreigners in our time: The present situation. In L. Eitinger and D. Schwarz (Eds.), *Strangers in the world* (pp. 27–41). Vienna: Hans Huber.

Sue, D. W. (1973). Ethnic identity: The impact of two cultures on the psychological of development of Asians in America. In S. Sue and N. N. Wagner (Eds.), *Asian Americans: Psychological perspectives* (pp. 140–149). Ben Lomond, CA: Science and Behavior Books.

Sue, S., and Sue, D. W. (1971). Chinese–American personality and mental health. *Amerasia Journal*, 1: 36–49.

Sue, S., and Zane, N.S.W. (1985). Academic achievement and socioemotional adjustment among Chinese university students. *Journal of Counselling Psychology*, 32: 570–579.

Sung, B. L. (1985). Bicultural conflicts in Chinese immigrant children. *Journal of Comparative Family Studies*, 16: 255–269.

Taft, R. (1977). Coping with unfamiliar cultures. In N. Warren (Ed.), *Studies in cross-cultural psychology*, (Vol. 1, pp. 121–151). London: Academic Press.

———. (1985). The psychological study of the adjustment and adaptation of immigrants in Australia. In N. T. Feather (Ed.), *Australian psychology: Review of research* (pp. 364–386). Sydney: Allen and Unwin.

———. (1986). Methodological considerations in the study of immigrant adaptation in Australia. *Australian Journal of Psychology*, 38: 339–346.

Tajfel, H. (1978). *The Social psychology of minorities*. New York: Minority Rights Group.

———. (1981). *Human groups and social categories: Studies in social psychology*. New York: Cambridge University Press.

Ting-Toomey, S. (1981). Ethnic identity and close friendship in Chinese–American college students. *International Journal of Intercultural Relations*, 5: 383–406.

Triandis, H. C., Kashima, Y., Shimada, E., and Villareal, M. (1986). Acculturation indices as a means of confirming cultural differences. *International Journal of Psychology*, 21: 43–70.

Ullah, P. (1985). Second generation Irish youth: Identity and ethnicity. *New Community*, 12: 310–320.

———. (1987). Self-definition and psychological group formation in an ethnic minority. *British Journal of Social Psychology*, 26: 17–23.

U.S. Federal Bureau of Investigation. (1987). *Uniform crime reports for the United States 1986*. Washington, DC: U.S. Department of Justice, Uniform Crime Report Program.

Vernon, P. E. (1982). *The abilities and achievements of orientals in North America*. New York: Academic Press.

Why Asians are going to the head of the class. (1986, August 3). *New York Times*.

Williams, C. L., and Berry, J. W. (1991). Primary prevention of acculturative stress among refugees: Application of psychological theory and practice. *American Psychologist*, 46: 632–641.

Wolf, M. (1970). Child training and the family. In M. Freedman (Ed.), *Family and kinship in Chinese society* (pp. 37–62). Stanford, CA: Stanford University Press.

Wooden, W., Leon, J., and Tashima, E. (1988). Ethnic identity among sansei and yonsei church-affiliated youth in Los Angeles and Honolulu. *Psychological Reports*, 62: 268–270.

Wu, Y. H. (1966). Cong renleixue guandian kan muqian Zhongguo ertong de yangyu wenti [An anthropologist looks at Chinese child method]. *Si yu yan*, 3: 3–7.

Yang, K. S. (1970). Authoritarianism and evaluation of appropriateness of role behavior. *The Journal of Social Psychology*, 80: 171–181.

———. (1986). Chinese personality and its change. In M. H. Bond (Ed.),

The psychology of the Chinese people (pp. 106–170). Hong Kong: Oxford University Press.

Zheng, X., and Berry, J. W. (1991). Psychological adaptation of Chinese sojourners in Canada. *International Journal of Psychology*, 26: 451–470.

13

Cultural Adjustment and Differential Acculturation among Chinese New Immigrant Families in the United States

Kam-fong Monit Cheung

Since the 1950s, the Chinese population in the United States has been increasing significantly: 117,140 in 1950; 237,292 in 1960; 435,062 in 1970; 812,178 in 1980; and 1,645,472 in 1990 (U.S. Census, 1950; 1960; 1970; 1980; 1990). This trend projects that the Chinese population will have escalated to over 2.5 million by the year 2000. The increase can be attributed to several factors. One factor is the increasing immigration quota authorized by U.S. immigration acts, such as the Immigration and Nationality Act, the Immigration Reform and Control Act, and the 1990 Immigration Act (See Table 13.1 for statistics on Chinese immigrants). A second factor stems from various political and economic situations, such as Hong Kong's 1997 issue, China's Tiananmen Square massacre in 1989, and Taiwan's economic growth and outward expansion, all of which pull new immigrants into a country with opportunities. A third factor, as expressed by many new immigrants, is the strong desire for family reunification. According to the U.S. 1990 Census, there are 543,208 foreign-born Chinese, which constitutes one third of the total Chinese population in the United States. Among these immigrant families, many have experienced adjustment difficulties. Even in a shared household, each family member may adjust to the new culture at a different rate and with a different attitude. Different expectations of the new culture can create family tension and conflict. This chapter will illustrate how the changing environmental factors, combined with traditional Chinese culture, affect the lives of Chinese people in a "foreign" land.

Focusing on adjustment difficulties of adult children and their elderly parents, this chapter will first review the literature and discuss some of the major adjustment problems facing Chinese new immigrant families. Then, it will use a conceptual framework to analyse how an individual's cultural

Table 13.1: **Asian and Chinese Immigrants in the United States**

Year	U.S. population at decade's end	Total immigrants in the decade	Asian immigrants in the decade	Chinese immigrants Total in the decade	Chinese immigrants % of total immigrants	Chinese immigrants % of Asian immigrants
1821–1830	12,866,000	143,439	33	NA	NA	NA
1831–1840	17,069,000	599,125	55	NA	NA	NA
1841–1850	23,192,000	1,713,251	141	NA	NA	NA
1851–1860	31,443,000	2,598,214	41,538	41,397	1.6%	99.9%
1861–1870	39,818,000	2,314,824	64,759	64,301	2.8	99.3
1871–1880	50,156,000	2,812,191	124,160	123,201	4.4	99.2
1881–1890	62,948,000	5,246,613	69,942	61,711	1.2	88.2
1891–1900	75,995,000	3,687,564	74,862	14,799	.4	19.8
1901–1910	91,972,000	8,795,386	323,543	20,605	.2	6.4
1911–1920	105,711,000	5,735,811	247,236	21,278	.4	8.6
1921–1930	122,775,000	4,107,209	112,053	29,907	.7	26.7
1931–1940	131,669,000	528,431	16,081	4,928	.9	30.6
1941–1950	151,326,000	1,035,033	32,360	16,709	1.6	51.6
1951–1960	179,323,000	2,514,479	125,249	9,657	.4	7.7
1961–1970	203,302,000	3,321,677	427,642	34,764	1.0	8.1
1971–1980	226,546,000	4,493,314	1,588,178	124,326	2.8	7.8
1981–1990	248,709,873	7,338,000	2,817,400	451,800	6.2	16.0

Sources: Mangiafico, 1988; *Statistical abstract of the United States*, 1993.

Table 13.2: Asian Population in the United States: 1990 Census

State	State total population	Asian & Pacific islanders (A.P.I.) population		
		State total A.P.I. population	% of state total population	% of U.S. total A.P.I. population
Alabama	4,040,587	21,797	0.54	0.30
Alaska	550,043	19,728	3.59	0.27
Arizona	3,665,228	55,206	1.51	0.76
Arkansas	2,350,725	12,530	0.53	0.17
California	29,760,021	2,845,659	9.56	39.12
Colorado	3,294,394	59,862	1.82	0.82
Connecticut	3,287,116	50,698	1.54	0.70
Delaware	666,168	9,057	1.36	0.12
Florida	12,937,926	154,302	1.19	2.12
Georgia	6,478,216	75,781	1.17	1.04
Hawaii	1,108,229	685,236	61.83	9.42
Idaho	1,006,749	9,365	0.93	0.13
Illinois	11,430,602	285,311	2.50	3.92
Indiana	5,544,159	37,617	0.68	0.52
Iowa	2,776,755	25,476	0.92	0.35
Kansas	2,477,574	31,750	1.28	0.44
Kentucky	3,685,296	17,812	0.48	0.24
Louisiana	4,219,973	41,099	0.97	0.57
Maine	1,227,928	6,683	0.54	0.09
Maryland	4,781,468	139,719	2.92	1.92
Massachusetts	6,016,425	143,392	2.38	1.97
Michigan	9,295,297	104,983	1.13	1.44
Minnesota	4,375,099	77,886	1.78	1.07
Mississippi	2,573,216	13,016	0.51	0.18
Missouri	5,117,073	41,277	0.81	0.57
Montana	799,065	4,259	0.53	0.06
Nebraska	1,578,385	12,422	0.79	0.17
Nevada	1,201,833	38,127	3.17	0.52
New Hamphire	1,109,252	9,343	0.84	0.13
New Jersey	7,730,188	272,521	3.53	3.75
New Mexico	1,515,069	14,124	0.93	0.19
New York	17,990,455	693,760	3.86	9.54
North Carolina	6,628,637	52,166	0.79	0.72
North Dakota	638,800	3,462	0.54	0.05
Ohio	10,847,115	91,179	0.84	1.25
Oklahoma	3,145,585	33,563	1.07	0.46
Oregon	2,842,321	66,269	2.44	0.95
Pennsylvania	11,881,643	137,438	1.16	1.89
Rhode Island	1,003,464	18,325	1.83	0.25
South Carolina	3,486,703	22,382	0.64	0.31
South Dakota	696,004	3,123	0.45	0.04
Tennensse	4,877,185	31,839	0.65	0.44
Texas	16,986,510	319,459	1.88	4.39
Utah	1,722,850	33,371	1.94	0.46
Vermont	562,758	3,215	0.57	0.04
Virginia	6,187,358	159,053	2.57	2.19
Washington	4,866,692	210,958	4.33	2.90
West Virginia	1,793,477	7,459	0.42	0.10
Wisconsin	4,891,769	53,583	1.10	0.74
Wyoming	453,588	2,806	0.62	0.04
Washington, D.C.	606,900	11,214	1.85	0.15
U.S. Total (50 states + D.C.)	248,709,873	7,273,662	2.92	100.00

Source: 1990 census of population and housing.

adjustment may create family conflict. This framework is based on the theory of differential acculturation, otherwise known as different rates of adjustment (see Atkinson, Morten, and Sue, 1989; Gibbs and Huang, 1989; Matsuoka, 1990). It postulates that the cultural identity of young immigrants varies according to their social attachment with their peers, but that most of them, at some point, consider American culture as an integral part of their development. On the other hand, older immigrants see the family as an important component of their life but identify the new and changing culture as a cause of their adjustment difficulties.

The conceptual framework leads to the discussion of how the new socialization process and the different levels of acculturation impact the parent-child relationship among newly immigrated Chinese families. Differential acculturation creates generation gaps in terms of values, expectations, and other cultural components among family members and thus causes family conflict. Through two case illustrations, the author offers a three-step analysis as a practical approach: the assessment of the cultural identity (or "cultural compartment") of each family member involved; a critical incident analysis to discover the source of conflict as related to cultural expectations; and a self-evaluation process for both children and parents to identify their adjustment difficulties. The analysis serves the function of assessing the family's capability to deal with external changes. The goals of such assessment are to unite the family, to help the family understand and appreciate cultural differences, and to facilitate an effective communication pattern within the family. This approach suggests that helping professionals empower family members to engage in the assessment process and handle family conflict in a culturally sensitive manner. A family-oriented approach is incorporated in this chapter because most Chinese people consider the family as an important entity for all significant events and occasions, including their adjustment process in a new country.

Cultural Adjustment and Problems among Immigrant Families

Aronowitz (1984) reviews the literature on the prevalence of adjustment problems among immigrant children. He focuses on the social and emotional aspects of adjustment and explains the causes of adjustment problems of children from both a psychodynamic perspective and a social-cultural orientation. The psychodynamic explanation treats migration as a form of traumatic separation, which creates attachment disorders, neurotic conflicts and behavioral disorders. This explanation, however, does not explain why many other immigrants do not suffer from these disorders even though they too have experienced the same traumatic separation from their country of origin. In terms of the social consequences of migration, Aronowitz (1984; 1992) explains that language difficulties, school-related and social stressors, and disturbance and disruption of family relationships are the major causes of adjustment problems.

Most of the literature referred to in Aronowitz's (1984; 1992) studies supports the fact that immigrant children and their families are under tremendous pressure because of relocation. It generalizes that most adjustment problems are related to social and cultural adjustment difficulties. With this socio-cultural perspective, it describes two school-based prevention programs designed for Chinese immigrant children and families in Canada. These programs provide a support group environment, direct and referral services, and a cultural liaison for school and community services. Although these programs are designed for children, it is important to encourage family members' involvement in order to minimize adjustment difficulties that affect family relationships.

This chapter focuses on socialization in a changing environment, different rates of cultural adjustment between children and parents, and cultural adjustment difficulties among Chinese immigrants in a new country, especially those that affect child-parent relationships. Cultural adjustment is an adaptation process to a new cultural environment and the term is used interchangeably in this chapter with acculturation; the latter is often used to address a need for cultural change, while the former is used here to illustrate a process of balancing change and conflict. Immigration is a cause of cultural adjustment because the change of cultural environment may create conflict within a person's own culture. To some new immigrants, cultural adjustment means adopting a new set of cultural values and being able to appear as a native person. This perception, however, may not represent all aspects of the reality because cultural adjustment may mean, at one extreme, accepting all aspects of a new culture, or at the other extreme, rejecting everything a new culture has offered. As a common expectation, acceptance has been described as a major result of acculturation (after a study by Herskovits in 1958). However, some immigrants who have a strong attachment to their original culture may find that adaptation to or acceptance of the new culture is difficult (Cheung, 1989). They may react to a new culture by avoiding or rejecting it. In other words, a person's adjustment to a culturally different environment is affected by his or her decision to make, or not to make, changes. Berry (1980) called this decision "varieties of adaptation": a person can move with or toward, against, or away from a new culture (p. 12).

Adjustment Problems among Chinese Families in the U.S.

There are many factors affecting how well Chinese families adjust themselves to a new country. Based on the literature on cultural adjustment (see Aronowitz, 1984), language, cultural acceptance, and family relationships are the most important determinants for "successful" cultural adjustment. Since language is often a major barrier to new immigrants, non-English speaking Chinese people prefer staying closer to a Chinatown. Therefore, Chinatown and adjustment will be a first factor to be discussed. A second factor is differential acculturation, or different rates of accepting a new culture, among family members. Younger immigrants are acculturated at a faster rate than older immigrants because of school and peer influences. A third factor is the perception of family tension that creates family conflict and problems.

Chinatown and Adjustment

The selection of a place of residence is one of the immediate concerns of new immigrants. According to the 1980 Census, the ten preferred states of residence for Chinese include California (325,882 Chinese residents), New York (147,250), Hawaii (55,916), Illinois (28,847), Texas (26,714), Massachusetts (24,882), New Jersey (23,432), Washington (17,984), Maryland (15,037), and Pennsylvania (13,769). The 1990 Census reports that 79 percent of the total Asian and Pacific Islander populations are residing in these ten states (see Table 13.2). Even today, most of the Chinese people in the U.S. live in cities of these states where a Chinatown is accessible to them. Especially for the newly migrated Chinese people, accessibility to a Chinatown is a necessity to ease cultural adjustment. Therefore, it is predicted that these ten states will still be the most preferable to Chinese families in the 1990s.

Historically, Chinatowns in San Francisco, Los Angeles, New York, Honolulu, Chicago, Houston, Boston, and Seattle were initially established for Chinese individuals to increase community cohesiveness and to achieve a sense of belonging. These needs were a response to the harsh exclusion laws and discriminatory practices against Chinese in the 1880s

(Mangiafico, 1988). Prior to 1965, for example, the population in New York's Chinatown consisted mainly of male sojourners who did not plan to stay in the U.S. permanently (Wong, 1982; 1987). Similarly, the early immigrants in Hawaii primarily lived in or close to the Honolulu Chinatown to help themselves acquire a cultural identity (Ip, 1972). These overseas labourers thought that their stay would only be temporary. A lack of commitment to settlement was a major explanation for why many Chinatown buildings were not constructed with a master plan in mind. However, in the last two decades, more Chinese people have looked for a "permanent stay" in the U.S. Since the 1965 Immigration Act, immigration preferences have been given to family members and to highly skilled technicians, scientists and other professionals. Because of residents' resistance to change, the condition of many Chinatowns has been deteriorating. "People oppose urban renewal because this program tends to disrupt their lifestyles and to cause [them] their [the] inconvenience of having to be relocated and to readjust in new localities" (Chow, 1984, p. 169). Many young immigrants who have recently migrated to the U.S. choose to stay away from the Chinatown area, while older immigrants prefer to be closer.

Another change related to Chinatowns is their expansion and shift of location. The increasing number of Chinese immigrants has brought to many major U.S. cities a greater demand for ethnic goods, as well as more capital and resources for new business and residential establishments. In Los Angeles (L.A.), California, for example, Chinese business has expanded to Monterey Park, a metropolitan area of L.A., with visible, huge Chinese grocery stores and gourmet chain-type restaurants which are operated with extended business hours. Another example is the Bellaire Chinatown in Houston, Texas — its size triples that of the downtown Chinatown and is still expanding. Although these new Chinatowns may not replace the cultural values of the old ones, they represent a rapid geographical expansion of the Chinese community. The changing face of Chinatown demonstrates the commitment of immigrants to stimulate the economic development of the U.S., for its own growth and for its immigrants' needs. These developmental trends, however, have also identified a clear picture of the social and cultural — sometimes conflicting — differences among immigrants.

From studies within the Chinatown territories, Ho (1992) reports that youth gang activities have become a threat throughout the country. The Chinese youth who engage in these violent acts tend to be (1) recent immigrants, (2) frustrated over racism and powerlessness within society,

(3) struggling with school work because of English language problems and/or cultural conflicts, and (4) associated with monetary gains through gang activities (see also Lyman, 1977). Violence in Chinatown has been causing many adjustment difficulties for Chinese families who choose to stay closer to this place for cultural preservation.

Differential Acculturation

Different rates of acculturation within a family can cause discomfort among family members because each person may hold a different set of values and attitudes based on the culture that is dominant within himself or herself. This "dominant culture" may be the culture of the individual's original country or of the new country. In order to understand the extreme adjustment difficulties facing Chinese families, major concepts from the theory of differential acculturation are discussed.

Theoretical Foundation

Acculturation is a process whereby immigrants and their descendants "adapt to their new cultural environment and thus learn to function comfortably in the context of norms that may differ greatly from those of their native country" (Rosenthal and Feldman, 1991, p. 495). Although U.S. culture is actually comprised of many diverse cultures, theories on acculturation often focus on two cultures — that of the immigrant's ethnic origin and that of the American "mainstream."

Richardson (1967), in a study on migration, theorizes three types of acculturation patterns: intra-ethnic, inter-ethnic, and extra-ethnic. Intra-ethnic acculturation is a complete identity with one's own culture. Inter-ethnic acculturation is a process of integrating one's ethnic culture with the dominant culture. Extra-ethnic acculturation is a complete integration of an individual into a community or culture other than his/her own ethnic community or culture. This theory, focused on integration patterns, is similar to Sue and Sue's (1973) conceptual scheme to classify Chinese Americans: the traditionalist who adopts Chinese values; the marginal person who adopts both Chinese and western values; and the Asian-American who develops Asian-American values.

Richardson's integration patterns identify the unique process of cultural assimilation but his model does not take into consideration the various cultures in the U.S. and the developmental perspective. Kearl and Hermes

(1984) suggest that the developmental cycles of different generations are important considerations in intergenerational analysis. In addition, a developmental perspective is necessary to allow for a better understanding of each generation's cultural values and expectations. Continuity of transmitting this developmental process from one generation to another is essential in order to minimize conflict (see Thompson, Clark, and Gunn, 1985). In other words, these theories imply that any interruption of this developmental process of cultural transmission, such as migration, would cause conflict.

Based on the unique developmental characteristics of minorities in the United States, Atkinson, Morten, and Sue (1989) have developed a five-stage Minority Identity Development (MID) model to link attitudes and behaviors with cultural identity. Stage one is the Conformity Stage, in which minority individuals prefer dominant cultural values to those of their own culture. Stage two is the Dissonance Stage, which indicates a conflict between depreciating and appreciating attitudes toward one's own culture. Stage three is the Resistance and Immersion Stage, in which the minority person completely endorses his/her own cultural view and rejects that of the dominant society. Stage four is the Introspection Stage, where "the minority individual experiences feelings of discontent and discomfort with group views rigidly held in the Resistance and Immersion Stage and diverts attention to notions of greater individual autonomy" (p. 42). Stage five is the Synergetic Articulation and Awareness Stage, in which the minority person experiences a sense of self-fulfillment with regard to cultural identity and adopts the best from different cultural views, his/her own or others.

The MID model describes the probability of immigrants undergoing different acculturation experiences even if they share a similar cultural background. A minority person or immigrant could start his/her cultural identity at any stage, become fixed at that stage, or move onto another stage when ready. The degree of closeness to one's ethnic culture depends on how strong the identity with that culture is and how much influence other cultures have had on that individual. These experiences may also be influenced by the social and cultural forces of the dominant culture, as well as the cultures of other ethnic groups.

The minority identity development process is similar to the integration patterns observed by Richardson, except that the MID model takes into consideration the multiple cultural characteristics of the U.S. In reality, these integration patterns or cultural identity development processes form a continuum of different adjustment levels. Each individual's adjustment level to a new culture depends on many factors, one of which is a need for assimilation. For example, Price's (1969) study on cultural assimilation discovered that an immigrant may need to be assimilated in terms of occupation, residence or language for immediate social and physical survival. However, this same individual can, at the same time, maintain his/her cultural identity with the ethnic community, prepare ethnic foods, and follow the traditional way of being oneself. Ip (1972) also agreed that the cultural adjustment process can operate at different rates — social adjustment comes first; cultural and psychological adjustment comes later. Price called this uneven assimilation. The author prefers to call it a compartmental adjustment process in which immigrants make gradual changes to various cultural components (inside their cultural compartment) based on a need for social adjustment and survival.

Cultural Compartment

A cultural compartment contains cultural elements (such as values, attitudes, language) that an individual has learned from his or her environment. This compartment may be locked (rejecting cultures different from those of the individual's ethnic origin), half-open (accepting new cultures while maintaining the learned ones), or wide-open (readily adopting new cultures). Each cultural compartment is uniquely defined based on individual experiences and characteristics. In the compartmental adjustment process, an immigrant may open or lock his or her cultural compartment in order to adjust to the pace of accepting or rejecting social or cultural changes. People with a half-open compartment (that is, either leaving their compartment doors flip-flapping or being indecisive about what components to change or maintain) may be in conflict within themselves and with those with open compartments or locked compartments. It is assumed that the definition of one's cultural compartment may change over time; a person's adjustment to any new culture is an ongoing process.

In the assessment of a person's cultural identity, three critical factors should be considered: (1) attitudes toward own culture and other cultures; (2) a felt need for cultural adjustment; and (3) age and sociohistorical background of the individual. It is important to assess which "cultural compartment" each individual identifies himself or herself with, especially in a multi-generational family, so that the source of conflict can be identified.

Differentiation Acculturation among Chinese People

Many studies on early Chinese immigrants (see, for example, Hsu, 1971; Lee, 1960; Sung, 1967) have portrayed the Chinese as a model minority who have been successfully assimilated into American culture. However, their study targets were mainly those early immigrants who came at least four to six decades ago and had finally settled in. Some of these early settlers had also established visible businesses in Chinatown with a profit-motive value comparable to that of an American capitalist. In addition, their adjustment difficulties were mostly hidden because they considered sharing problems with anyone outside their own family circle to be culturally inappropriate. Furthermore, the differences of age-related adjustment difficulties of these immigrants were not addressed.

Age is seen as a significant factor in a cultural assimilation process, as suggested in a study of Vietnamese refugees. Matsuoka (1990) suggests that young immigrants, especially adolescents, have adjustment difficulties because they "come to this country at a vulnerable period in their development" and try to "resolve issues associated not only with physical maturity but also with an acute sense of loss — the loss … of culture" (pp. 342–343). However, children and adolescents can easily learn new behaviors from school and the mass media for quick cultural adjustment. On the other hand, adults have a difficult time learning a new language, and re-learning values and attitudes — all are required for cultural assimilation.

In a study that addressed the social service needs of elderly Chinese immigrants, Cheung (1989) found that assimilation sounds too forceful to these immigrants and forceful assimilation is not harmonious with their cultural values. Unlike younger immigrants, the elderly have a strong cultural background that is difficult to discount. Thus, social services that focus mainly on assimilation are often considered unacceptable. Therefore, it is recommended that "services should focus on helping people adjust to, but not assimilate into, a new culture" (p. 459). This "assimilation vs. adjustment" perspective suggests that the dilemma of integrating a conflicting value and world view into an elderly person's rooted cultural system needs to be adequately addressed.

Recent literature has justified the importance of assessing differential acculturation among immigrants. The assessment of cultural identity (or cultural compartment) and age-related adjustment issues would assist the helping professional in identifying possible solutions to family conflict and in providing appropriate resources to Chinese immigrants.

Perception of Family Conflict

Theoretical Foundation

Family conflict can be explained by theories of intergenerational relationships. Theoretically, a generation can be defined as individuals who, together with others born during the same time period, have been predestined for "participation in certain historic events and existing orientations, norms, and values" which has shaped their specific consciousness (Garms-Homolova, Hoerning, and Schaeffer, 1984, p. 1). This definition, which is focused on the "sociohistorical and sociocultural space" that shapes an individual's behavioral characteristics and social expectations, explains the differences between and among generations. Family conflict occurs because each generation has had different experiences in the process of social transformation.

Garms-Homolova and associates (1984) use the generation model of German sociologist Karl Mannheim to explain family conflict. The model states that each generation — youth, adults, and older adults — has its potential to effect changes based on its sociocultural orientations. Youth, however, is the formative phase in which individuals have the maximum capability to "react to a changed situation by bringing forth new entelechies" (p. 3). When changes occur too rapidly, new experience patterns which differ from the traditional will be established. These new patterns of behavior may become a barrier to family relationships. Therefore, the researchers conclude that "the process of social and cultural change is also constitutive for the problem of intergenerational relationships" (p. 3).

Davis (1940), in a study of parent-child conflict, also states that such family conflict is inevitable but that its extent will depend on the rate of social change and the complexity and integration of the culture. It is not uncommon for children in the United States to have conflictive views with their parents because of their strong emphasis on self-determination, independence and individualism in a country where societal influences (such as mass media and peer groups) are often stronger than family ties (see discussions in Simic, 1990).

On the contrary, Bengtson, Mangen, and Landry (1984) studied family solidarity rather than conflict within U.S. families and found that "middle-aged children do constitute a potential resource for most aged family members, though increasingly fewer generations share the same household" (p. 63). Concerned with the issue of household sharing, Suitor and

Pillemer (1988) conducted an empirical study to examine family conflict when adult children and elderly parents live together. Surprisingly, they found relatively low parent-child conflict, especially when the adult child was older. Their finding could be explained by the fact that these adult children had a strong family value which was identified through their decision to co-reside with their elderly parents. Nevertheless, these people are seen to be the exception, rather than the norm, in today's capitalist-oriented societies.

Beyond building a theoretical foundation, most literature on family conflict focuses on the analytical aspect of the problem, such as explaining relationship difficulties (Martin, 1990; Suitor and Pillemer, 1988) and discussing the economic, psychological, or social implications that conflict may generate (Atkinson, Kivett, and Campbell, 1986; Hirshorn, 1991; Pett, Caserta and Hutton, 1988; Traub and Dodder, 1988; Walker, 1990). Very few studies focus on the practical aspect, such as suggesting ways to resolve conflict (Ikels, 1990) and measuring relationships for better understanding among people (Mantell, 1991). In addition, very few studies focus on conflict among members in Chinese families.

Traditional Chinese Families and Family Conflict

There are few studies on family conflict among Chinese Americans. However, this does not mean that conflict does not exist; conflict is often hidden. A Chinese adage, "Every family has a hard-to-read book," expresses that every family has its own hidden conflict or problem. Another adage, "Family repulses pass no doors," has been socializing Chinese people not to share family problems with outsiders. Direct referrals of problem sharing are not common. Therefore, the helping professionals have to focus their effort to identify those who may have experienced cultural adjustment problems in order to find ways to help resolve their dilemmas. Unfortunately, research in this area of outreach efforts to contact new immigrants is still lacking.

In order to understand how family conflicts are affecting Chinese families, Chinese traditional values should first be examined. However, Sue and Sue (1973) caution the use of the term "traditional" to generalize Chinese families: differences among them must also respected and accounted for. Nevertheless, they also suggest that studies of traditional Chinese values toward parent-child relationships would provide information for understanding the cultural expectations of Chinese immigrants. In the case of family conflict, this understanding can promote self-evaluation and family solidarity that stress a respect for differences.

In Chinese culture, the parent-child relationship is characterized as one of five essential relationships in the society and is ranked the second most important according to the philosophy of Confucius. It is expected that "elderly Chinese parents be supported by and live with their children" and elderly parents are "seen as playing a key role in the family and society so that caregiving for elderly persons can be maintained" (Cheung, 1989, pp. 457–458). The authority figure and disciplinary image of parents, as portrayed in folk tales, is an important social control mechanism. However, the values of this traditional relationship tend to be diminished when Chinese immigrants live away from their country. For example, many new immigrants in the U.S., men and women, perceive work as a social responsibility. Often not based on economic reasons, both parents of many Chinese families work. Mangiafico (1988) found that "the absence of parental control has somewhat weakened the traditional family ties — increasing cultural and intergenerational conflicts" (p. 119).

Second-generation Chinese have been a target of family conflict since Chen studied the cultural adjustment of the Chinese in New York in the 1930s. Chen (1941) found that parent-child conflict was caused mainly by different educational background and lack of mutual understanding. Recently, Takaki (1989) has also touched on the issue of cultural conflict experienced by second-generation Chinese Americans who search for the bridge to connect two cultures. Second-generation Chinese Americans have been given derisive appellations by Chinese immigrants born outside the United States: *zhu sheng* (*chok sing* in Cantonese) mainly given by Cantonese people, or *xiangjiao* (*Heungchiu* in Cantonese) commonly used among most Chinese cultures in the U.S. *Zhusheng* (bamboo pole) is a pipe wind instrument made of bamboo with a joint or knot inside that blocks the air passage from one end to the other; *xiangjiao* (banana) is apparently yellow outside but white inside. Both terms have been negatively used to indicate a lack of connection between two cultures. Takaki's research has found that many second-generation Chinese Americans are caught in between two cultures and feel "the pushes and pulls" of two worlds. The experience of many young Chinese has been perceived as a "dilemma of being caught in between ... being loyal to the parents and their ways and yet trying to assess the good from both (Chinese and American)" (Takaki, 1989, p. 260).

Only a few studies have focused on Chinese elderly immigrants' cultural adjustment and its impact on family relationships (for example, Chen, 1979; Cheung, 1989; Ikels, 1983). Cheung (1989) found that Chinese elderly persons living in the U.S. possess strong ethnic identity and a drive to maintain their dignity and to preserve their culture. However, they face not only individual adjustment difficulties and institutional discrimination, but also relational problems that result from "conflicting pushes to stay with one's own values, versus adopting the values of a new culture" (pp. 458–459). Like the American-born Chinese, many elderly Chinese who migrated to the U.S. also became caught between two worlds: the influence of a new American culture and the rooted value of a traditional Chinese culture. Cultural conflicts occurring between the younger generation and the elderly persons often create family tension.

Another study by Ikels (1983) found that many elderly immigrants have separate residences from their adult children as a solution to family tension. Sometimes adult children think that starting a new lifestyle is more adaptable than trying to deal with family conflict. Their adaptability, however, may widen the cultural gap between them and their elderly parents (Cheung, 1989). Since they are living in a different culture, some adult children may feel "less obligated to take care of their aged parents" (Cheung, Cho, Lum, Tang, and Yau, 1980, p. 492). Some people rationalize that "their parents may prefer living alone to avoid suffering from changes in lifestyle and to maintain their ethnic identity with their Chinatown peers" (Cheung, 1989, p. 459). Increasingly, many recent immigrants have moved to suburban areas where they can find a more spacious environment, while their elderly parents may maintain their residence in Chinatown (Chen, 1979; Cheung, 1989).

Intervention to Resolve Family Conflict

Aronowitz (1984) identifies three major types of intervention programs that have been designed to assist immigrant families. The first type is primary intervention programs which adopt "a model of education with curricular adaptation to specific immigrant problems such as identity conflicts, communication problems and unequal access to community resources" (p. 248). The second type is secondary intervention programs which establish support groups and community activities for immigrants. The third type is tertiary prevention programs which employ "a model for the delivery of social welfare services to immigrant families" (p. 250).

For Chinese immigrants, the primary and secondary intervention programs may work better. They provide opportunities for the immigrants to relate to others who have similar experiences in adjustment. Working with both parents and children is an important task because parents' positive attitudes to social change and new experiences are associated with children's perception of adequate adjustment (Aronowitz, 1992). In these programs, a self-help process matches the immigrant's expectation, along with Chinese philosophy, that "self governance is the best medicine to social illness." The evaluation model is also suggested by Gibbs and Huang (1989) to help minority youth assess their needs. These evaluative areas which can also be applied to Chinese children and their families include: (1) physical appearance; (2) affect; (3) self-concept and self esteem; (4) interpersonal competence; (5) attitudes toward autonomy; (6) attitudes toward achievement; (7) management of aggression and impulse control; and (8) coping and defense mechanisms. In addition to these eight areas, the author adds "attitudes towards differences" in the self-evaluation process. With an attitude of respect for differences, Chinese children learn to appreciate their family members' needs and differences in cultural adjustment.

Case Illustrations[1]

Differential Acculturation: An Analytical Approach

Based on the conceptual framework on cultural adjustment and differential acculturation, a practical approach is developed in order to analyze the adjustment difficulties facing Chinese immigrants in the U.S. This approach uses a cultural identity assessment model to examine various levels of individual adjustment to a new culture and uses a critical incident of family conflict to analyze whether differential acculturation plays an important role in explaining the conflict.

Two typical cases are presented to illustrate the use of this approach with immigrants to help them identify sources of conflict and possible solutions. This approach has three components:

1. A cultural identity assessment model — to assess the developmental process of the cultural identity of each individual within a family. Extended family members are usually included in the picture (directly or indirectly, depending on the extent of the

---

[1] All personal information has been changed to protect clients' confidentiality.

problem) to provide a broader view of various cultural expectations and possible age-related identity issues.

2. A critical incident analysis — to illustrate the importance of experience sharing between the young and the elderly. Each family
member involved in a conflict situation is invited to be present
when the conflict incident is revealed. Mutual understanding is the
goal for counseling so that the source of conflict can be identified.

3. A self-evaluation process — to promote each individual's self-
awareness of cultural differences within a family. The helping
professional would facilitate this self-awareness exercise with
each individual and then hold a combined meeting with all family
members involved. A cross-cultural perspective is used to guide
each individual to evaluate his or her cultural compartment and the
compartmental process from another cultural perspective so that
appreciation of other people's expectations can be acquired.

In the first case, "Three generations," a Chinese immigrant whose
wife and new-born son are American-born Chinese would like to resolve
conflict with his newly migrated father. The second case, "A family
scapegoat," was brought by a Chinese immigrant who felt depressed over
her life but found that her depression was actually caused by some covert
conflict of the cultural values between herself and her family.

Case 1: Three Generations[2]

Background

Tony (35) and Sue (28) married four years ago after Tony received his
doctoral degree from an Ivy-League university. Since graduation, he had
been working in a major industry company. Sue quit her work as a secretary
after their baby was born two years ago. Tony came to the United States to
pursue his college education ten years ago and met Sue at a Christmas party
organized by the Asian Americans Association in town. Sue was a second-
generation Chinese who did not speak or understand Chinese. Since their
wedding, Tony had asked his parents several times to join him in the U.S.
but they refused. Instead, they sent Tony's younger sister Yuen-yuen to

---

[2] This case combines the information from two cases, one of which is contributed
by Patrick Yip.

Tony so that she could pursue her studies in the U.S. After Tony's mother passed away two years ago, Tony asked his father again to come to the States and Mr. Chan said he would come to see his grandson. He came a year later, two days before his 61st birthday. Yuen-yuen (17) moved to share an apartment with two American friends before Mr. Chan's arrival.

Step 1: Assessing Cultural Identity and Differentiation Acculturation of Each Family Member

Father: Mr. Chan was a traditional Chinese fisherman who believed in ancestors and who treasured male children. He did not accept Tony's initial invitation to come to the U.S. because he had not reached elderly status; to depend on children when one is young is perceived as non-productive in Chinese culture. His 61st birthday, which marked the beginning of old age in his culture, would give him a respectful status. He believed that elderly parents should be supported by and live with their children, especially with the oldest son's family. Tony was the oldest and the only son and was Mr. Chan's favorite child. Therefore, his migration decision, made before his 61st birthday, was to provide an opportunity for Tony to honour his significant "age" milestone.

After coming to the U.S., Mr. Chan considered himself a "culturally handicapped" person. He pictured himself as "hearing impaired" because he did not understand English; "crippled" because he did not drive; "blind" because he found no T.V. programs to enjoy; "dumb" because no one understood him. Many times when he was alone at home, he called Tony at his office and said that he wanted to go back to Hong Kong (his original country), although he knew that he had no relatives to go back to. He did not find the new culture exciting and always said, "Coming to America wasn't my idea!" Tony had recently subscribed to a Chinese newspaper from Chinatown. After discovering that there was an Elderly Chinese Association, Mr. Chan rationalized his non-participation by saying that joining leisure clubs was a waste of his time and money. When asked about his cultural identity, Mr. Chan was proud to be Chinese and refused to become an American citizen.

Children: Tony was a marginal man caught between two cultures. He had acquired the Chinese value which dictated that the oldest son should take care of his elderly parents. At the same time, he also identified himself as a new immigrant who had been assimilated successfully into American life. Tony remembered quite well his decision to come to the U.S. Although he did not want to be a fisherman himself, he respected his father's occupation. However, he did not talk about his family with his classmates or friends in the U.S. He succeeded academically but not socially. Subsequently, he did not make friends with other students from Hong Kong. After college, he met Sue and took part in social activities with American-born Chinese, as well as other Americans. He found that his cultural assimilation was complete with his education and help from Sue.

Yuen-yuen experienced her adolescent development in the U.S. She felt that she could have more freedom and autonomy with her friends than with her brother. However, she found that peer pressure was much more difficult to handle than homework. She identified herself with a new generation (of Chinese immigrants) who could work well with local Americans. Independence was her first wish after graduating from high school. When she first came to the U.S., she felt that her adjustment was difficult only in the first few months because of the language barrier. Once she was used to the educational system and had got her driver's license, she found that she could be "perfectly" assimilated into American culture.

Daughter-in-law: A second generation Chinese born in the U.S., Sue would feel annoyed and uncomfortable if anyone called her "bamboo pole" or "banana." She explained that she was an American, just like any immigrant from Europe, who should melt into the American "mainstream culture." Not able to speak or understand Cantonese (the family's dialect) was not her fault because her parents had never given her the opportunity to practice. Sue considered herself an ABC (American-born Chinese) who did not and should not have any adjustment difficulties, except when trying to communicate with her father-in-law.

Grandson: Although Tony's son David was a baby, his cultural identity would be similar to Sue's. Having lost the opportunity to learn about Chinese culture, Sue said that she could not share any cultural heritage with her son. Tony found it easier for him to adopt the American way of life than trying to teach Sue Chinese. If both of them did not speak Chinese at home, they could not possibly expect their son to be bi-lingual. He hoped his father could teach his son Chinese.

Step 2: Describing a Critical Incident of Family Conflict

During the first family counseling session, Tony's father was very quiet. He politely said that he was not feeling well. Later when the entire family came to share and describe one of their conflict situations, he was much more alert and open. Tony's goal was to explain their misunderstanding to his father and try to reunite the family after his father had moved to China-town for two months. Tony's wife, Sue, smiled at the Chinese counselor when Tony started to tell his story in Chinese about a conflict situation with Mr. Chan.

> Tony was watching T.V. when dinner was ready. It was the first time Sue had prepared a whole fish for dinner.
> "You like it, Pa?" Tony asked his father as Mr. Chan used his chopsticks to pick up a small piece of fish.
> "It's all right, but I still prefer fresh fish in Hong Kong. They tasted better than this frozen thing," Mr. Chan said.
> "Tony, what did your dad say? He doesn't like my cooking?" Sue asked Tony.
> "No, honey. He just misses the fish he used to have back home," Tony replied.
> "Tell him that he is in America!" Sue said.

Tony's father was a fisherman in Hong Kong. Chinese fishermen are particular about the way they eat fish. A fish can never be chopped into pieces nor can it be turned to the other side after one side has been eaten. Chopping the fish or turning it over would mysteriously symbolize the exact things that would happen to their boat. For generations, Chan's family had believed in this folklore. The conflict began when Sue tried to turn the catfish and Mr. Chan yelled at her across the table to stop her from doing it.

> "Father, what do you want?" Tony asked.
> "Don't you remember that we never turned the fish whenever we had fish at home. It represents bad luck!" Mr. Chan was angry.
> "Yes, but we're in America," Tony replied.
> "I don't care where we are. And don't you forget that you didn't become who you are by chance." Mr. Chan meant he worked hard to send Tony to a famous university.
> "Tony, what's the matter with your dad? Is he losing his mind?" Sue complained.
> "Honey, he doesn't want you to turn the fish. He prefers just to take the entire bone out before we eat the other side." Tony tried to explain.

Sue was angry with her father-in-law's superstitious idea. Besides, she would have preferred not to cook a whole fish in the first place. When Mr. Chan tried to take the bone out with his fingers, she grabbed the fish away and threw it on the carpeted floor.

Step 3: Promoting Self-awareness through a Self-evaluation Process

After describing the incident, each family member (except the baby) was asked to write a letter to a family member (in Chinese or English) to express his or her opinions in four areas: feeling toward the incident; language development or use in the family; attitude toward American culture and Chinese culture; and perception of family functioning. Then, pretending to be another person in the family (such as a parent), each wrote a letter to express that person's perspectives on these four areas. In addition, on behalf of that person, each person also expressed what changes the other person would like to see and what that person would like to maintain within the family. In this case, Mr. Chan wrote about what Tony would think, Tony and Sue wrote about what Mr. Chan would think.

After these self- and projective evaluation exercises, Sue and Tony read their second letters which represented their perception of how Mr. Chan felt and thought. Then Mr. Chan read his first letter which represented his own opinions. The same procedure applied to compare perceptions for Tony and Sue. Through discussions they discovered different expectations among family members. Unconsciously, Sue was jealous of her father-in-law and wanted Tony to know she could handle her new role (as a mother) without assistance. Although it was a difficult process, all of them came to appreciate each other's efforts to be part of this extended family and to appreciate the differences among themselves.

Case 2: A Family Scapegoat

Background

The Ho family included Bah, 65, his wife Bihn, 50, and Bah's four children — Ngor, 33; Ellen, 30; Jack, 24; and Cathy, 20. They were Chinese Vietnamese from Saigon, who migrated to the United States in 1980. The parents and the two older children were born in China. Even though Jack and Cathy were Vietnam-born, Bah claimed that they were all Chinese.[3] Bah and Bihn currently lived in a capitol city with Ngor, who was unmarried. Jack and Cathy were both away in college. Ellen was married

---

[3] According to the definition of immigrants in the United States, irrespective of their ethnic Chinese ancestry, Jack and Cathy should be classified as Vietnamese immigrants.

and living with her husband and two children geographically near her parents.

The Hos appeared to be a relatively low-income family. They lived in a refugee resettlement community thirty miles from the Capitol. Their apartment, which was quite small at five hundred square feet, had two bedrooms. Bah had been a herbal doctor and Bihn a grade school teacher in Saigon. In the States, Bah continued his herbal practice but Bihn did not work because of severe arthritis. All children spoke Vietnamese, Chinese and English.

Ngor reported that she was "rescued" by her father from the communist rule. Her parents were relatively affluent before the escape. They used up their savings and gold to get six seats on a boat. Her mother became very ill during the journey and eventually died before arrival. The boat arrived safely in Hong Kong where they spent a year before resettling in the United States. No grief counseling was given during that time. Bah and Bihn married in the transit camp in Hong Kong. Bihn was alone at that time; her family members had all died in Saigon.

Step 1: Assessing Cultural Identity and Differential Acculturation of Each Family Member

Parents: Bah and Bihn were born and raised in a traditional Chinese family. They were strongly influenced by Confucian teaching on the one hand and affected by the war on the other. They did not like to be identified as "boat people" but were proud of being Chinese. They liked Chinese foods and taught their children about Chinese culture. They did not want to migrate to the United States and preferred the idea of staying in Hong Kong so that they could live in a Chinese community. Their choice was not granted. They had a difficult time adjusting to the United States primarily because of the language barrier. They did not want to learn English because they felt they would look ridiculous when speaking it. They expected their children to be their interpreters.

Children: Ngor was a traditional Chinese who had been socialized to accept family responsibility because she was the oldest child. Her taking on this responsibility began after her mother passed away. She protected her siblings and helped her father do household chores. She identified herself as a traditional person but wanted to learn more about the new country.

Ellen was a bi-cultural person who started to learn about American culture when she entered a pre-college program at the age of 19, the year when they came to the United States. She married a second-generation Chinese who knew a little Chinese. They spoke only English at home because they were afraid that their pre-school children would not catch up with other kids in school. Ellen also did not speak Chinese to other people except to her parents and Ngor. She said this would help get rid of her accent.

Jack and Cathy came to the United States at a critical period of their psychosocial development (as adolescents). In high school, they were socialized (or pressured) by their peers to be independent from their parents although they knew that independence would be impossible if they were not studying out of state. In college, they seldom associated themselves with other Vietnamese or Chinese and explained to their parents that they wanted to concentrate on their studies. Jack did not have close girlfriend and Cathy had been dating a Caucasian man whom she met in a bar near campus. She kept this a secret from her family.

Step 2: Describing a Critical Incident of Family Conflict

Ngor was the identified person in this case. She appeared to be depressed and complained of chronic headaches. Her presenting problem was that she did not know how to take care of her father and stepmother. Her younger brother and sister, Jack and Cathy, persuaded her to enter college and move away from their parents. Last year, she passed the GED test, applied to college and was admitted. However, she found she could not leave her parents and decided to continue her work at a factory. Recently she had been involved with a Vietnamese worker for about three months. She left him because she felt that he did not care about her family.

Ngor had experienced many losses. She lost her country, her mother, her chance of higher education, and her boyfriend. With a deep commitment to filial piety, she viewed herself as the responsible person who would take care of everything in the family, including planning for her father's retirement. Her post-traumatic stress had not been resolved while she took on new, demanding stress.

When asked about her personal needs, Ngor replied that she wanted to provide sufficient income for the family. She also wanted to be a nurse: "maybe going to college after her father passed away." Ngor's denial of feeling about the overwhelming responsibilities created inner conflict within herself. She was facing many dilemmas regarding her roles. On the one hand, she perceived that her family responsibilities made her life meaningful. On the other, she saw herself as a scapegoat because she was the oldest. She expressed the sentiment that her siblings were lucky that they could "try out the new world." Her lack of communication with her family, especially with her stepmother, had made her feel alienated and at times intimidated. She always wanted her parents to reassure her of her importance in the family but had never attempted to express this need. Since her siblings had left home, she felt that she was no longer welcome in the family. She perceived that her parents' wanting her to get married was a hint.

Step 3: *Promoting Self-awareness through a Self-evaluation Process*

Ngor came to family services by herself and did not think about involving her family in counseling. However, after revealing her family information, Ngor agreed that getting the entire family together was important. Ngor's father was invited to the third session and the entire family was invited to the fifth and seventh session. In the joint sessions, an open-ended questioning method was used to clarify family expectations. For example, Ngor and her father were asked to write down self perceptions of each other individually. Then, they shared these perceptions in order to achieve mutual understanding. Some of these questions included:

1. What does your family expect from you?
    Ngor: No clear indications from parents; the oldest child should take care of elderly parents.
    Father: Be productive; care about my children and my wife; don't burden my family with my personal problems.
2. What do you expect from your family?
    Ngor: A warm and caring family; more supportive of my educational goal.
    Father: Cared for by children in old age.
3. What are/were the consequences of these expectations?
    Ngor: Conflicting expectations between self and father's; blaming the culture.
    Father: Kids all moved out; oldest daughter not getting married.
4. Describe each individual's communication style in your family?
    Ngor:

    Self: Shy, not open, non-verbal
    Father: Demanding, emphasizing traditional values and filial piety

> Mother: Interrupting, trying to show understanding
> Ellen: Giving double messages: trying to help but avoiding responsibilities
> Jack: Strong personality, liked father
> Cathy: Encouraging, appreciating American culture
>
> Father:
> Self: Not much to share
> Ngor: Shy, quiet
> Mother: Shared with me any difficulties she had with stepchildren
> Ellen: Always spoke English — didn't understand her at all; used to be quiet
> Jack: Usually said nothing when home
> Cathy: Seldom talked with me

After writing their answers individually, Ngor and Mr. Ho compared them and expressed their agreement or disagreement. Ngor orally shared her agreement. Also, she was encouraged to write down her disagreement because of her discomfort over verbally disputing an elder. The assessment from this mutual questioning and sharing procedure identified minimal conflict between Ngor and her father. However, the inability to communicate and share different expectations was evident. It was also found that cultural expectations were different between them. The different rates of acculturation into a new environment explained their difference in expectations. For example, Ngor was eager to learn about the new country and be released from her family responsibilities, while Bah thought, unconsciously, that his daughter should be taking care of him. Although their expectations might not be in conflict, each of them assumed that accepting a new culture would make them lose their own culture.

Implications of the Cases

Status Quo or Conflict: An Adjustment Difficulty

Although conflict occurred between children and their elderly parents in both cases, the sources of conflict were different. In the first case, "Three generations," the direct source of conflict was the cultural differences between the in-laws, including cultural expectations and language. Other indirect sources included the unfamiliarity of the living environment for the elderly parent and the independent living of the teenage daughter (Yuen-yuen), which made Mr. Chan feel that he had lost control over his family. To Mr. Chan, ability to control one's family was still an important value. However, his children had adopted the value of autonomy American children have. Yuen-yuen's search for a new identity could be seen as a persistent attempt to define and redefine herself. The American ways of encouraging youth to be more expressive, autonomous, and self-determining had become attractive to her (Ho, 1992). Both Tony and Yuen-yuen directed themselves in what they wanted to do rather than receiving their father's guidance, which was perceived as taking the father's power away.

In the second case, "A family scapegoat," conflict seemed to be covert. The heavy responsibilities of an adult child were the major source of conflict. Socialized since childhood, Ngor was presented with different expectations from her family than from her younger siblings. She wanted to maintain her traditional values to make her feel worthy. However, her inner self blamed her siblings for not sharing the responsibilities even though she had not shared this concern with them. She wanted to be independent from her family but found that her parents had been important in her life. Her dilemma created an individual's internal conflict rather than a family conflict. Her silence became the inner voice of resistance to changes.

Maintaining the *status quo* of one's cultural values is difficult to achieve, especially when new values are pushing into one's life. Many internal and external factors interfere with the decision to stay with one's traditional values. External factors include the social and cultural components of the new environment, such as language, socially-defined roles, economic situations, living environment, employment and education. Internal factors include the individual's reactions to acculturation, communication barriers with people of the same culture and of different cultures, and the cultural definition of self-worth.

Compartmental Adjustment

Through the eyes of second-generation Chinese Americans, their ancestors are "strangers from a different shore" (Takaki, 1989). However, they have been raised to identify with two cultures. For example, Sue tried to be a bi-cultural person but felt that Mr. Chan would be a barrier to her adjustment to Chinese culture. She also felt that she was a stranger in this triangular family because of her lack of knowledge of Chinese culture. The outcome of this struggle would be Sue's alignment with her son and resistance to adopting Chinese culture. This outcome would also create difficulties in fulfilling Mr. Chan's expectation of his grandson learning Chinese culture.

In the Ho family, Ngor's cultural adjustment was quite different from her siblings. Her adjustment level was similar to her parents' because of the rooted cultural values and expectations. She felt that a wide "generation gap" would separate her from her brother and sisters if she did not go to college. Education was perceived to be an essential avenue to successful cultural adjustment. On the other hand, she felt that her sense of accomplishment (mainly from assisting her father) could not be maintained if she pursued other "dreams."

When family conflict occurs, the involved individuals often engage in "self-talk" that creates assumptions about other people's feelings and thoughts. They may not realize that their self-talk could shut down the family communication channel and could also slow down their own adjustment process. Awareness of differential acculturation is a first step to gaining mutual understanding among family members. In both case studies, in order to encourage self-evaluation, the helping professional facilitated the family to:

1. understand each individual's attitudes toward his/her own culture and other cultures;
2. assess each individual's need for cultural adjustment; and
3. evaluate the contribution of personal characteristics to the different rate of acculturation, such as age and other sociohistorical factors.

Critical Factors in the Adjustment Process Affecting Children and Their Families

Family conflict occurs when each generation has its unique cultural identity development. This developmental process is different from one generation to another, depending on the socializational process and environmental impact. In the case examples, the cultural identity of each individual was also different. Each individual had his or her own cultural compartment. Mr. Chan and Bah Ho shared the same cultural identity in that they were traditional Chinese who respected the elderly; but their cultural compartments were always locked — refusing differences. Both Tony and Ngor were marginal persons who were caught in between two sets of cultural expectations. Not only were they highly motivated to keep their traditional values, they were also influenced by other people of their generation who had already adopted new cultural values. Their cultural compartments were half open — accepting new values while simultaneously rejecting them in order to maintain ethnic values, which created cultural conflict.

On the other hand, younger immigrants (Yuen-yuen and Ngor's siblings) or American-born Chinese (Sue) usually feel an immediate need to adjust to the new culture. Their cultural compartment is wide open — readily accepting cultural values different from those of their ethnic origin. Based on the known facets of the acculturation process in the U.S., social and peer pressures are contributing factors to this openness. Individuals may try to hide their Chinese cultural identity in order to avoid racial discrimination and minimize cultural conflict with peers. Some of them change their first names and physical appearance to show their attachment to and sense of identity with their peer culture. Sometimes, parents give their children an American name in lieu of a Chinese name with the idea that it may help the child adjust to the mainstream culture. However, their intention may be misinterpreted as giving up their children's Chinese heritage.

In a study of bicultural socialization, DeAnda (1984) studied how minority parents teach their children to function in two distinct socio-cultural environments — at home and in society. Six factors may influence the outcome of bicultural socialization: (1) the degree to which the two cultures share norms, values, perceptions, and beliefs; (2) the availability of cultural models, mediators, and interpreters; (3) the consistency of feedback provided by each culture about one's behaviors; (4) the congruence of problem-solving style between the two cultures; (5) the degree of bilingualism; and (6) physical appearance. When parenting their children at home, many Chinese immigrants (especially if one or both of the parents were American born) focus on the mainstream culture in which some values may not be consistent with the Chinese culture. In addition, bilingualism may not be an emphasis at home but sometimes parents push for it to be part of the youth's extra-curricular activities. Parents who give conflicting messages to children about their perception of Chinese culture have found a wider generation gap between themselves and their children.

In a study of Chinese immigrant children in New York City, Sung (1987) found that the "bicultural conflict" experienced by these youngsters could cause deviant behaviors and gang involvement. The major source of this conflict began in the family where children experienced "feelings about their transplantation from one continent to another and from one culture to another" (p. 6). Although the impact of conflict between parents and grandparents on children is not addressed in Sung's study, the lack of appropriate modeling from one's own culture could be a major concern for the children's psychological adjustment to a new culture. Nevertheless, Sung gave a sample of bicultural conflicts facing Chinese immigrant children. These conflicts had also been experienced by the children in the Chan and Ho families:

> Chinese children are brought up to refrain from aggressive behavior, whereas the masculine image in the United States often stresses the macho stereotype.

> Sexual attractiveness is expressed subtly according to Chinese custom, whereas it is stressed blatantly according to American custom.

> Sport is a consuming pastime for the American people, whereas it takes a backseat to scholastic achievement for the Chinese.

In short, many factors affect the adjustment process of Chinese families into the American culture. The most critical factors demonstrated through these and many other cases fall into three major categories:

1. Bicultural Conflicts
   For example:
   a. Conflict between the family's demand for bilingualism and the perceived need of bilingualism from the child
   b. Conflict between ethnic values and peer cultures
   c. Conflict between family and peer pressures
   d. Conflicting values between the two cultures
   e. Conflicting ideas about living close to or far from Chinatowns
2. Differential Acculturation
   For example:
   a. Different rates of acculturation among family members: the *status quo* vs. moving along with a new set of values
   b. The pace and perception of cultural identity development of each family member
   c. Pushes and pulls from two or more cultures to accept "assimilation"
3. Family Dynamics
   For example:
   a. Lack of mutually agreed-upon goals in the family
   b. Lack of open communication among family members

    c. Lack of social support from the ethnic community
    d. Lack of motivation to seek ethnic support
    e. Differences in perception of family relationships

It is suggested that the qualitative aspects of the parent-child relationship be a focus when family conflict becomes an issue within an immigrant family. Critical factors affecting their relationship should be identified and assessed. Through culturally appropriate assessment of each individual's attitude toward accepting or rejecting others' values or expectations, mutual understanding among family members can be achieved.

Conclusions: Working with Chinese Immigrants

Very few studies have focused on how socialization and changing environments create conflict and how the perception of cultural adjustment effects changes among Chinese families. Half a century after Chen's (1941) study on family conflict among Chinese in the U.S., the author of this chapter suggests that research priority in these areas be placed on Chinese new immigrants based on the following reasons: (1) the numbers of Chinese immigrants have been steadily increasing since the last decade; (2) these immigrants represent diverse socio-economic characteristics and cultural expectations, even among parents and children; and (3) new immigrants usually do not share their problems with others until these problems have become so serious that they require immediate attention. In such studies, second- or third-generation Chinese should be included because the increased quota in immigration preferences has brought relatives of these American-born Chinese to the U.S. These people may experience different rates of acculturation which may contribute to family conflict.

The acculturation experiences of Chinese immigrants provide practice implications for helping professionals. First, we need to evaluate our own cultural biases before assisting our clients in evaluating theirs. Accepting diversity is an important theme of self-evaluation. Green (1982) suggests an approach to working with American minorities. When applying it to the Chinese community, a culturally sensitive worker would utilize the following steps: (1) being aware of the worker's own cultural limitations; (2) being open to cultural differences; (3) practising a client-oriented learning style; (4) utilizing cultural resources; and (5) acknowledging cultural integrity. The most important aspect of these steps is respect for the uniqueness of clients' ethnographic characteristics.

Second, when dealing with family conflict, we can assist a family with a practical approach in mind. This approach has three components. The first component is a cultural identity assessment model that aims at measuring each individual's cultural compartment and adjustment process. The second component is a critical incident analysis which engages family members in sharing their experience in a conflict situation in order to gain insight on differential acculturation among family members. The third component is a self-evaluation process that incorporates a Confucian philosophy — "One should evaluate oneself three times daily" — to promote awareness of cultural differences within a family and with people from the same ethnic group.

The cultural identity assessment model suggests that when we work with children and their families, we need to pay attention to each individual's own pace of adjustment. It also stresses that cultural adjustment is an ongoing process. In many cases, cultural values of children from a three generation family have not been fully assessed because it is a common assumption that children progress quite well with a new culture. However, when it comes to interpersonal relationships within a family, the psychosocial adjustment process of each individual may have caused the conflict and each individual may be affected. Adequate assessment of cultural identity from the developmental perspective will help each person better understand other family members.

The critical incident assessment is a means to achieve mutual understanding rather than to blame each other. Different expectations or value perspectives may create misunderstanding between parents and children. Conflict usually comes from a lack of open communication to clarify such misunderstanding. Many Chinese people have the strong belief that personal problems should not be shared. Skillful and culturally sensitive professionals will move discussions from a broader perspective to a specific incident. If these "personal problems" are re-defined as "cultural adjustment difficulties" that new immigrants usually face, they tend to accept the problem-sharing opportunity. A critical incident can be shared when the involved family members are present in order to identify the source of adjustment difficulties.

The self-evaluation process suggests that the cultural adjustment of an individual can be evaluated on a personal basis, by the individual himself or herself and through the help of his or her significant others, including parents, siblings and children. Through an awareness exercise, such as problem-sharing from a different cultural perspective, each family member would provide information regarding cultural preferences (including language, place of residence), rates of cultural adjustment, and perception of family functioning and conflict. This information allows the helping professionals to assess (1) the level of adjustment of Chinese immigrants to the American culture; (2) whether or not their cultural and social adjustment would clash with other family members' values; (3) interaction patterns with people of the same ethnic backgrounds; and (4) interaction patterns with people of other ethnic backgrounds. They will use this information to facilitate discussions of from where, and how, different adjustment patterns emerge and encourage self and mutual evaluation among family members to widen their perspectives toward others.

The strength of this approach is the application of a multi-cultural perspective within each immigrant family. The uniqueness of each family and the different rates of cultural adjustment among family members are considered. One caution, however, is that many Chinese families do not share problems with an outsider. The helping professional must first establish a rapport with the family and empower the family to develop effective communication skills to resolve conflict. Through the learning process of developing communication skills, family members will feel comfortable sharing their perspectives in front of others. Reframing family conflict with a perspective of cultural differences within the family, that each family member may have different experiences in the process of developing a cultural identity, has been proven helpful.

Similar to the cases presented in this chapter, many immigrant children would like to be part of a new culture to ease their adjustment difficulties, whereas older immigrants usually do not want to be assimilated. Every Chinese person has to deal with some level of cultural adjustment in the U.S. — children often face an immediate need to make cultural adjust-ment; elderly people find adjustment difficult because of cultural conflict; adults who live with both younger children and older parents are caught between the cultures significant to different generations. A missing-link crisis may be present when immigrants cannot or will not identify themselves with the new culture but have to move along with it; or when they do not want to give up their traditional values but have found that their children will not "inherit" them. From a family-oriented perspective, working with Chinese immigrants means working with immigrants of all ages who have experienced different levels of cultural adjustment difficulties.

References

Aronowitz, M. (1984). The social and emotional adjustment of immigrant children: A review of the literature. *International Migration Review*, 18 (2): 237–257.

————. (1992). Adjustment of immigrant children as a function of parental attitudes to change. *International Migration Review*, 26 (1): 89–110.

Atkinson, D. R., Morten, G., and Sue, D. W. (1989). *Counseling American minorities: A cross cultural perspective*. Dubuque, IA: Wm. C. Brown.

Atkinson, M. P., Kivett, V. R., and Campbell, R. T. (1986). Intergenerational solidarity: An examination of a theoretical model. *Journal of Gerontology*, 41 (May): 408–416.

Bengtson, V. L., Mangen, D. J., and Landry, P. H. (1984). The multi-generation family: Concepts and findings. In V. Garms-Homolova, E. M. Hoerning, and D. Schaeffer (Eds.), *Intergenerational relationships* (pp. 63–80). Lewiston, NJ: C. J. Hogrefe.

Berry, J. W. (1980). Acculturation as varieties of adaptation. In A. M. Padilla (Ed.), *Acculturation: Theory, models and some new findings* (pp. 9–25). Boulder, CO: Westview Press.

Chen, J.I.H. (1941). *The Chinese community in New York: A study in their cultural adjustment*. Unpublished doctoral dissertation, American University, Washington, DC.

Chen, P. N. (1979). A study of Chinese–American elderly residing in hotel rooms. *Social Casework*, 60 (2): 89–95.

Cheung, L.Y.S., Cho, E. R., Lum, D., Tang, T. Y., and Yau, H. B., (1980). The Chinese elderly and family structure: Implications for health care. *Public Health Reports*, 95 (5): 491–495.

Cheung, M. (1989). Elderly Chinese living in the United States: Assimilation or adjustment? *Social Work*, 34 (5): 457–461.

Chow, C. (1984). *Immigration and immigrant settlements: The Chinese in New York City*. Unpublished doctoral dissertation, University of Hawaii, Honolulu.

Davis, K. (1940). The sociology of parent–youth conflict. *American Sociological Review*, 5: 523–534.

DeAnda, D. (1984). Bicultural socialization: Factors affecting the minority experience. *Social Work*, 29: 101–107.

Garms-Homolova, V., Hoerning, E. M., and Schaeffer, D. (Eds.). (1984). *Intergenerational relationships*. Lewiston, NY: C. J. Hogrefe.

Gibbs, J. T., and Huang, L. N. (1989). *Children of color: Psychological interventions with minority youth*. San Francisco: Jossey-Bass Publishers.

Green, J. W. (1982). *Cultural awareness in the human services*. Englewood Cliffs, NJ: Prentice-Hall.

Herskovits, M. J. (1958). *Acculturation: The study of culture contact*. Gloucester, MA: Peter Smith.

Hirshorn, B. A. (1991). Sharing or competition: Multiple views of the intergenerational flow of society's resources. *Marriage and Family Review*, 16 (1–2): 175–193.

Ho, M. K. (1992). *Minority children and adolescents in therapy*. Newbury Park, CA: Sage.

Hsu, F. (1971). *The challenge of the American dream*. Belmont, CA: Wadsworth.

Ikels, C. (1983). *Aging and adaptation: Chinese in Hong Kong and the United States*. Hamden, CT: Anchor Books.

————. (1990). The resolution of intergenerational conflict: Perspectives of elders and their family members. *Modern China*, 16 (October): 379–406.

Ip, D. F. (1972). *Motivations and adjustment: An assimilation study of the Chinese immigrants in Honolulu*. A thesis in sociology, University of Hawaii, Honolulu.

Kearl, M. C., and Hermes, M. P. (1984). Grandparents, grandchildren, and the Kondratieff: Thoughts on "period effects" in intergenerational analyses. *International Journal of Aging and Human Development*, 19 (4): 257–265.

Lee, R. H. (1960). *The Chinese in the United States of America*. Hong Kong: Hong Kong University Press.

Lyman, S. (1977). Chinese secret societies in the Occident: Notes and suggestions for research in the sociology of secrecy. In S. Lyman (Ed.), *The Asian in North America* (pp. 13–19). Santa Barbara, CA: ABC-Clio.

Mangiafico, L. (1988). *Contemporary American immigrants: Patterns of Filipino, Korean, and Chinese settlement in the United States*. New York: Praeger.

Mantell, E. H. (1991). Factional conflict through the generations: Theory and measurement. *The American Journal of Economics and Sociology*, 50 (October): 407–419.

Martin, B. (1990). The transmission of relationship difficulties from one generation to the next. *Journal of Youth and Adolescence*, 19 (June): 181–199.

Matsuoka, J. K. (1990). Differential acculturation among Vietnamese refugees. *Social Work*, 35 (4): 341–345.

Pett, M. A., Caserta, M. S., and Hutton, A. P. (1988). Intergenerational conflict: Middle-aged women caring for demented older relatives. *American Journal of Orthopsychiatry*, 58 (July): 405–417.

Price, C. (1969). The study of assimilation. In Jackson, J.A. (Ed.), *Migration* (pp. 181–237). London: Cambridge University Press.

Richardson, A. (1967). A theory and a method for the psychological study of assimilation. *The International Migration Review*, 2 (1): 3–28.

Rosenthal, D. A., and Feldman, S. S. (1991). The acculturation of Chinese immigrants: Perceived effects on family functioning of length of residence in two cultural contexts. *The Journal of genetic psychology*, 151 (4): 495–514.

Simic, A. (1990). Aging, world view, and intergenerational relations in America and Yugoslavia. In J. Sokolovsky (Ed.), *The cultural context of aging: Worldwide perspectives* (pp. 89–107). New York: Bergin & Garvey Publishers.

Statistical abstract of the United States 1991. Washington, DC: U.S. Department of Commerce.

Sue, S., and Sue, D. W. (1973). Chinese–American personality and mental health. In S. Sue and N. N. Wagner (Eds.), *Asian–Americans: Psychological perspectives* (pp. 111–124). Palo Alto, CA: Science and Behavior Books.

Suitor, J. J., and Pillemer, K. (1988). Explaining intergenerational conflict when adult children and elderly parents live together. *Journal of Marriage and the Family,* 50 (November), 1037–1047.

Sung, B. L. (1967). *Mountain of gold.* New York: MacMillan.

——— . (1987). *The adjustment experience of Chinese immigrant children in New York City.* New York: Center for Migration Studies.

Takaki, R. (1989). *Strangers from a different shore: A history of Asian Americans.* Boston: Little, Brown & Co.

Thompson, L., Clark, K., and Gunn, W. (1985). Developmental stage and perceptions of intergencrational continuity. *Journal of Marriage and the Family,* 47 (November): 913–920.

Traub, S. H., and Dodder, R. A. (1988). Intergenerational conflict of values and norms: A theoretical model. *Adolescence,* 23 (Winter): 975–989.

U.S. Census. (1950; 1960; 1970; 1980; 1990). *Population reports.* Washington, DC: Government Printing Office.

Walker, A. (1990). The economic burden of ageing and the prospect of intergenerational conflict. *Ageing and Society,* 10 (December): 377–396.

Wong, B. (1982). *Chinatown: Economic adaptation and ethnic identity of the Chinese.* New York: Holt, Rinehart & Winston.

Wong, B. (1987). The Chinese: New immigrants in New York's Chinatown. In Foner, N. (Ed.), *New immigrants in New York* (pp. 243–271). New York: Columbia University Press.

Self-Concept Development: Is There a Concept of Self in Chinese Culture?

Sing Lau

Introduction

The world is changing, and changing fast; its people are changing, and changing fast. To speak of the world and its people in terms of East and West may soon be a thing of the past, according to some cosmopolitan scholars, novelists, and travelers. It may be too much of an exaggeration to say this. But even if it is, we have to admit that we are entering a new era of the re-marking of cultural boundaries.

The present chapter discusses Chinese people in general, but the issues or questions raised should have much bearing on the self-concept development of Chinese children and adolescents in particular. In fact, most studies done on Chinese people involve the younger rather than the older generation.

Before we embark on a discussion of the self-concept of Chinese people, we need to take note of two perspectives: an East–West cross-cultural perspective, and a past–present historical perspective. These perspectives will not be introduced in great detail as they are beyond the scope of the present chapter. But they will help to set the stage and orient us in examining the self-concept of Chinese people later on.

But why are the two themes, East–West, past–present, given such emphasis? It is because of the pitfalls in contemporary psychological studies of Chinese people that we want to avoid or minimize (Lau, 1994). There are at least two reasons why we should consider such emphasis. First, current research still tends to treat East and West as two separate and distinct worlds. This is partly due to the convenience it affords us in finding a framework and making cognitive categorization (Fiske and Taylor, 1991) and partly due to the historical dominance of such thinking. By its very name, cross-cultural psychology assumes the comparison of two or more distinctly different cultures, where in fact the world is coming closer together rather than growing apart. This does not mean that the whole field of cross-cultural psychology should be disbanded or that its significance should be disregarded. On the contrary, we need to re-examine its role in order to reaffirm its value. A second reason is that in current research, psychologists always resort to ancient thinking in explaining the behaviour of Chinese people, where in fact the Chinese world is not stagnant: Historians and philosophers (especially those not of the Confucian tradition) tell us that the Chinese are no longer governed by what was traditionally practiced (Lau, 1992; Terrill,1992). A brief perusal alone of the last few hundred years of China's history presents us with a telling story: The impact of the experiences the Chinese have endured is hard to fathom (Spence, 1990).

East and West, Past and Present

In recent decades, we have witnessed both East and West undergoing rapid changes. And the distance between them is over diminishing. This is partly due to the more frequent contact, and partly due to the internal reorganization of the political, economic, and societal systems in both parts of the world. The changes, especially in the East, are beyond imagining: How could one have predicted, in such a short period of time, the handshake between the Jewish and Palestinian leaders, the dissolution of the Soviet Union, the human rights movement in 1989 and the Tiananmen incident in China?

These dramatic events aside, just the more frequent contact between East and West, either voluntary or involuntary, intentional or by accident, has tremendous impact on both sides of the world. It is thus a bit simplistic, and may soon be outdated, to separate the world in terms of East and West — though we like to think in this way because of our habitual thinking and our processes of cognitive categorization or schema (Fiske and Taylor, 1991; Wyer and Srull, 1984). For example, it has been reported that people tend to read and comprehend culturally familiar information (Pritchard, 1991). As a mental shortcut, we are inclined to use a representativeness heuristic in the process of personal and cultural perceptions (Tversky and Kahneman, 1973). The effect of cognitive schemas is also gaining greater attention in the fields of anthropology and sociology (e.g., Baron and Byrne, 1994). In all, it is therefore in such a context that we should view Chinese culture and its people. And it is in such a context that we should look at the self-concept of Chinese people. This is one theme that will be espoused in the present chapter.

A second theme that will be emphasized is historical. China has a long history. The distant past and the recent past are so very different (Meisner, 1986; Terrill, 1992). On one hand, the past in totality and the present represent two different realms of life. On the other hand, however, we can find shades or even duplication of the past in the present. As in western history, China's past and present are so intertwined and yet so different. To put it mildly, the turmoil and upheaval within the past few hundred years of China's history are mind-boggling. The struggles China had to endure in those years is certain to have had great impact on the self-development of Chinese people. To ignore the recent past and to focus only on the distant past (which is exactly the attitude adopted in contemporary research) would do little justice to understanding the mentality of Chinese people. Take, for example, what Confucius said thousands of years ago on the hierarchy of authority: to focus on this would help very little in understanding the "sudden" uprising of the demand for human rights and the democracy movement in China and Hong Kong. Moreover, contemporary Chinese philosophers and historians are well aware of the inter-mixing of philosophy and politics in China. Thus, the simple quotation of one saying or concept from Confucius could be very misleading in understanding what Chinese really want and think. It would likewise be equally impossible to picture the present-day life of westerners in term of the Victorian age or under the rubrics of the influence of even Plato or Aristotle. We are not to disregard the impact of past giant figures and major thinkers like Aristotle in philosophy, or Galileo in science, or Queen Victoria in England's social life. In psychology, even today, we do not belittle Freud's influence; but to put him in a proper perspective in psychoanalysis or clinical psychology nowadays is more justified.

Self-Concept and Chinese Culture

There is a fundamental question we should raise that has not been asked often enough: Is there a concept of self in Chinese culture or thinking? If so, how is it construed?

In a nutshell, there can be two very extreme answers to this question: One "yes", the other "no". To simplify matters, two philosophical ways of thinking are aligned with the two answers. Briefly speaking, the affirmative answer can be identified with Confucianism, and the negative answer with Taoism (Chen, 1987; Yu, 1976).

In traditional Confucian thinking, the self is very well defined within the social context or milieu. An Individual's self, identity, and roles derive meaning from his relations with others. Confucianism is noted for the hierarchy of relationships it lays out. There are rules and regulations for almost every behavior in almost every situation; and one is not expected to go beyond the defined boundary of lines. Distinctions are made between the *ta wo* (big me) and *hsaio wo* (small me). There is emphasis on putting *ta wo* before *hsaio wo*. Such emphasis is phrased in terms of sacrificing oneself for the good of a larger entity, such as family and society. Selflessness is encouraged and honored; selfishness is discouraged.

According to Confucianism, there seems to be a concept of self — self as defined in relation to others, self as defined in the hierarchy of relationships. But when one looks closer, it can also be argued that there is no self in actuality. One's own self is so small (*hsaio wo* — small me), so externally defined by rules and relationships, that we can find no real self (in the sense of one's own will and wishes). To go to the extreme, there is only the concept of "we", but not "I". Everything connected with "I" is subsumed under "we".

From the Han dynasty onward, until recent decades, Confucianism was espoused because of its emphasis on the hierarchical structure of authority. Confucianism and politics were so enmeshed that one could not have a good understanding of the reasons for the influence and dominance of Confucianism in Chinese society without simultaneous consideration of the political history of China. This dualistic view is especially emphasized in neo-Confucian thinking.

Then what about Taoism? The picture here is even more intriguing. In Taoist philosophy, there seems to be no concept of self to begin with. To define self is to defy the essence of self. In fact, to define anything, even life, is missing the target. It is characteristic of Taoism to understand life by way of analogies. To attain the level of nothingness is to attain the essence of life and the essence of selfhood. "Things" will come naturally if one looks for "nothing". Virtues like honesty, loyalty, filial piety are the end products of an ideal person. And to be an ideal person is to be true to self and the universe.

It is also worthy of note that Taoism was not mingled with politics, external rules and regulations, hierarchy of relationships, etc. The very nature of Taoist thinking does not fit in with the wishes of the ruling class.

It does not provide sets of rules for the ruler to use (be it in government or in the family).

But is the concept of self so elusive and unfathomable in the Taoist tradition? In a way, it is. But from another perspective, it is not. If one tries to capture the meaning of self in the regular sense, the result is failure. But if one just lets go of oneself, one will find one's self. Moreover, it is emphasized that if one is able to view oneself as part of the universe, the meaning of life and self comes naturally. Taoism also espouses the cultivation of the ideal person. But what is ideal (like loyalty, honesty, filial piety) will come when one becomes natural. This is in contrast to Confucianism where it is asserted that one should nurture all the ideal characteristics before one can become ideal.

So it is interesting to see how self is construed in Confuciaism and Taoism. The process of finding self seems to be in opposite directions in the two philosophies. To put it simply, it seems that in Confucianism, self is well defined to begin with but one can end up with no self at all. In Taoism, self is not to be defined to begin with but one can end up with a real self in the truest sense.

Taoism was and still is a dominant way of thinking in Chinese culture. Nevertheless, it is generally, if not totally, neglected in contemporary Chinese psychological research. The reason why might be due to the fact that Confucianism provides more easily understood and accessible constructs (such as filial piety, obedience to authority) for researchers to apply to Chinese behavior and personality. But to balance this, we should take note of the significance and long history of Taoism's influence on Chinese culture.

In a positive sense, these two philosophies provide complementary views with which to understand the concept of self of Chinese people. If one opts for a structured concept of self, Confucianism can provide a ready framework. The downside, of course, is that it also imposes restrictions on the free development of self. Recent studies indeed have found that the desire for freedom, independence, and individuality is prevalent among young Chinese people (e.g., Feather, 1986; Lau, 1992). On the other hand, if one opts for an unstructured concept of self, Taoism can provide another framework. This framework is exemplified in the works that adopt a spontaneous approach (in which subjects are allowed to give subjective descriptions of themselves freely) in self-concept research (e.g., Bond and Cheung, 1983). To sum up, there is a concept of self on the surface in Confucianism, but underneath there is no individuality. There are rules, regularities, and priorities for every relationship leaving little room to manoeuver in one's mind. Confucianism puts great emphasis on authority and is the thinking that fits in well with the wishes of the ruling class or ruling figures (like parents). In contrast, there seems to be no concept of self on the surface in Taoism. No maps or rules or roads are provided. To find one's inner self is to unite with the universe, and the approach is spontaneous and free-spirited. So underneath, there is certainly a concept of self. The difference is that the Taoist self is more elusive and harder to capture. In fact, the more one lets go and looks inward, the more easily one senses one's true self. So "self-less-ness" has a different meaning in Confucianism and Taoism. In Confucianism, it may be a non-self or no self (a lack of selfhood) in the very extreme. In Taoism, it may mean the opposite.

Confucianism and Taoism (Lin, 1990; Thomas and Niikura, 1990) are two dominant and indigenous Chinese philosophies and, together with other philosophies (e.g., Buddhism, Marek, 1990), have significant bearing on the shaping of Chinese thinking and culture. It is, however, beyond the scope of the present chapter to introduce all these philosophies and their implications. (Buddhism, for example, emphasizes the giving up of any human desires. Through such a process, true happiness and true self can be attained. In some ways, Taoism is very much like Buddhism. In fact, Zen Buddhism is a conglomeration of the two philosophies.) Nonetheless, we should take note of the importance of Taoism and not just focus on Confucianism in contemporary Chinese psychological research. We should also mention that, with the influence of westernization, Christianity has had, and is still gaining, great influence (Thomas, 1990): for example, more self-proclaimed Christians than Confucian and Taoist believers are to be found nowadays in Taiwan and Hong Kong. Most Chinese, including Mainland Chinese, are not practicing believers of any traditional religion. Of course, one may argue that philosophy is a way of life that may infiltrate Chinese people's minds in an unconscious way. The point here is that we should at least take a more balanced look if we are to understand the self-concept of Chinese people through a philosophical magnifying glass.

Contemporary Views of Self-Concept in Western Psychology

Self-concept is a well understood construct that has a long history in Western psychology. It is central to personality. In modern day terms, it is represented as a central self-schema. All in all, self-concept is "a system of affective and cognitive structures (schemas) about the self that lends coherence to each individual's self-relevant experiences" (Baron and Byrne, 1994, p. 214). Through a self-schema, a collection of beliefs and feelings about some aspect of the world, as well as our self-knowledge, is organized (Markus and Nurius, 1986). A person's self-schema serves the function of a cognitive framework, to guide behavior and process information about the self. It represents "... all of our current knowledge and existing memories about ourselves; and our conception of what we were like in the past, what we are like now, and what we may be like in the future" (Baron and Byrne, 1994, p. 175). Self-concept is a collection of self-schemas that are based on self-relevant information (Higgins and Bargh, 1987). Such a collection could help to elaborate and categorize information related to one's self-concept.

With the above broad conceptualization of self-concept, there are many possibly related constructs such as self-esteem (self-evaluation), self-efficacy (self-perceived competency in a given task), self-monitoring (self-regulation), self-focusing (centrality of sense of self), self-characterization (beliefs about the self's character), and sex role. Together, these and other constructs constitute an individual's self-concept or identity.

In contemporary studies related to self-concept, there are several lines of research or theories that are worth mentioning. The following brief introduction to these highlights some points that might be useful in understanding the self-concept of Chinese people.

First, research tends to show that self-concept is based very much on self-relevant information (Higgins and Bargh, 1987). This self-relevance effect has much bearing on how one reacts to others and how one construes oneself. In fact, in-group and out-group discrimination or identification can be viewed as an indirect outcome of such an effect. The contrast is most vividly shown in the study of the identity of Chinese people. It has been found that Chinese overseas (e.g., in the United States) indicate more of a feeling of "Chineseness" than Chinese in local Chinese societies (Abbott, 1970; Fong, 1965; Lee, 1984; Sue, 1973). It seems that the greater the contrast one perceives between oneself and one's environment, the greater the tendency to seek information to reconfirm one's identity or sense of self.

A second line of research is on self-discrepancy (Higgins and Bargh, 1987). Discrepancies can exist between one's actual self, ideal self, and ought self. Research has shown, for example, that despite the higher academic performance of Chinese students than American students, they tend to have a low ability self-concept (Sue and Okazaki, 1990). This might be due to the fact that the Chinese place a higher ideal standard on their offspring so that the actual self might not measure up to the high expectations. This effect of actual-ideal self-discrepancy, however, is yet to be tested.

The third line of research focuses on contrasting self-esteem theory and self-consistency theory (cf. Jones, 1973). In essence, self-esteem theory affirms that individuals seek positive evaluations to bolster their self-image. On the contrary, self-consistency theory predicts that people seek evaluations that are in line with their original self-image: i.e., people high in self-esteem will look for positive evaluations, whereas people low in self-esteem will accept negative evaluations. The controversy between the two theories has not been totally resolved. And no research to test these theories with regard to the Chinese has been done. Thus, the implications of these theories on Chinese people's self-concept formation or development is not yet known.

A fourth line of research is along the lines of the looking-glass-self tradition (Cooley, 1902; Shrauger and Schoeneman, 1979). According to this approach, our concept of self or self-appraisal is very much based on reflected appraisals, which are usually from significant others (such as parents and teachers). In more common terms, how we see ourselves depends to a great extent on how we imagine others see us. This approach has regained much attention in recent research since its original conceptualization (DePaulo, Kenny, Hoover, Webb, and Oliver, 1987; Felson, 1989; Kenny and Albright, 1987). Moreover, the looking-glass self effect may not be confined to any group of people, and this approach may therefore have some bearing on the understanding of Chinese people's self-concept, especially in light of the importance that Chinese people tend to place on how they appear in others' eyes or how they are being judged (Cheung and Lau, 1994).

As a fifth line of research, much attention has been given to the multifaceted and hierarchical nature of self-concept (Harter, 1982; Marsh, Byrne, and Shavelson, 1988; Shavelson, Hubner, and Stanton, 1976). This approach emphasizes that self-concept is composed of different domains or dimensions which can be hierarchically organized (with general self-concept subsuming other facets of the self-concept). Thus, previous reliance on measuring only general self-concept or self-esteem is judged to be inadequate in understanding self-concept. Recent research on Chinese people's self-concept has in fact adopted this multidimensional approach (Lau and Leung, 1992a; Leung and Lau, 1989).

As a final note, it is worth pointing out that, as a new development, there are studies which attempt to combine the looking-glass-self and multidimensional approaches (Cheung and Lau, 1994). In the series of studies by Marsh and his colleagues (Marsh et al., 1988), for example, how one is perceived by others is included in the measure of self-concept. This might develop into a new line of self-concept research on Chinese people in the future.

The Self-Concept of the Chinese

In this section, we are not going to focus on the "findings" of the self-concept of Chinese people but to pinpoint what is lacking in this area of research. As in most studies on the self-concept of Chinese people, there are several characteristics that can be identified. First, a western approach is generally adopted. Current research surpasses previous studies by using a more multidimensional rather than a general or global measure of self-concept. Second, Confucianism is the theoretical base commonly used. Third, cross-cultural comparisons tend to be the major emphasis, and any differences or similarities found are generally explained in terms of Confucian concepts.

In the following discussion section, a review of cross-cultural studies and the use of Confucianism as an explanatory framework are skipped. There are several reasons for such a decision. One reason is that cross-cultural differences are often not consistent — although most studies show that Chinese are lower in self-concept (for example, self-evaluation in academic ability, cf. Stevenson and Stigler, 1992), some recent findings have found the reverse (e.g., Lau, Nicholls, Thorkildsen, and Patashnick, 1994). A second reason is that the Chinese cultural concepts (e.g., the losing and saving of face) used to explain cross-cultural differences are seldom directly measured but are often assumed to be in operation. A third reason is that many of the differences, if they exist, could be explained by using concepts already present in Western social psychology. Take, for example, the concern about face and others' opinions which can be related to self-monitoring (as high self-monitors are more concerned about public approval, Cutler and Wolfe, 1989) or in terms of private and public self differentiation (Scheier and Carver, 1983). When the term "face" was first introduced and used in research on Chinese behavior, it was a novel and exotic term to Western psychologists. But now that the language barrier has been put aside, it has become a common part of the English language. In fact, the concern about saving or losing face may be very important among westerners (especially macho types or gangsters, who might get in fights simply for the sake of face). Similarly, it may appear novel to use the terms *ta wo* (big me) and *hsaio wo* (little me) to describe how Chinese sacrifice self for the sake of their family or country. But the basic mentality of sacrifice (as in being patriotic) is also pertinent to westerners. In all, the cross-cultural differences found may be unjustified when explained on a strong empirical base. Moreover, the differences may be just a matter of timing and the period of societal development / modernization. Specifically, in older times and in rural areas, traditional family and social values (such as caring for the elderly and obedience toward authority) were equally emphasized in past Western society as they are in Chinese society nowadays.

Let us now briefly review the research on the self-concept of Chinese people. Similar interest is found in how self-concept relates to various variables as in the Western literature. In general, the patterns of findings are very much the same for Chinese as for westerners. For example, self-concept has been found to relate positively to academic performance and personal control, and negatively to delinquency (Lau and Leung, 1992a, 1992b; Leung and Lau, 1989).

When self-concept is examined in terms of sex role and sex difference, similar common findings are observed. For example, the masculine sex role is found to relate positively to achievement-related values (Lau and Wong, 1992). Males tend to endorse success as a personal goal more so than females (Wang and Creedon, 1989) and they tend to describe themselves as more competent and agential than do females (Li and Wong, 1982).

Recent research has also shown interest in the socialization of self-concept of Chinese children and adolescents. It has been found, as in the Western literature, that self-concept development benefits from supportive relations with parents and family harmony (Berndt, Cheung, Lau, Hau, and Lew, 1993; Cheung and Lau, 1985; Lau and Cheung, 1987; Lau, Lew, Hau, Cheung, and Berndt, 1990).

It is apparent that many areas of research need attending to other than the correlates of self-concept mentioned above. One area is the relation between self-concept and feelings. In fact, the domain of feelings and emotions is worth exploring in its own right, as it appears to be an untouched and taboo-like area in Chinese custom. Another area that needs greater effort of investigation is the widening of the scope of self-concept related research. Topics like self-consciousness and saliency (Ho, 1992), self-discrepancy (Poon and Lau, 1994), and others, are worthy of attention.

A third area is related to theory building. This is most challenging and urgently needed if we are to have a better indigenous base from which to understand the self-concept of Chinese people. The works by Bond and Cheung (1983), Luk and Bond (1992), and Cheung and Lau (1994) represent some efforts in this direction. For example, in Luk and Bond's (1992) study, a Sino-American Person Perception Scale (Yik and Bond, 1993) was used to assess personality, and the results obtained were used to question the Western masculine model of self-esteem. Another study by Yik and Bond (1993) also examined self-perception in terms of personality factors by contrasting scales developed in the West and by Chinese psychologists. These and other efforts should be continued.

Conclusion: Modern China, Modern World

We are living in a post-modern period, and contemporary theorists take a very critical view of the present and the future. China is a few steps slower, but will be catching up soon with the rest of the world. Again, it is a matter of time. Historians and political scientists tend to have a better sense than psychologists of what is to come. Maybe we can and should learn more from them.

China has been undergoing a series of shock waves. In fact, the whole world is undergoing a series of shock waves, according to futuristic scholars (Toffler, 1970, 1980, 1990). What has yet to come is not certain to anyone. But there is no doubt about the necessity of taking note of the changes occurring both inside and outside of China.

The changes that have taken place in the last two hundred years since the Qing dynasty have significant implications for China in the present and future. Suffice to say, with the influence and invasion of the Western powers and of Japan, China switched from being a self-centred, proud nation to a self-doubting, and humiliated nation (Meisner, 1986; Terrill, 1992). The "Middle Kingdom" became the middle firing target. The desire to turn around this situation in modern China is strong. And this tends to serve as an impetus for the self development and modernization of China as a whole.

From very early on, psychologists like Lewin (1951) indicated that the meaning of one's sense of well-being and confidence depends to a great extent on one's cultural identity. The greater one's pride in identifying with one's cultural or ethnic heritage, the higher one's self-esteem. Thus, the membership of a group (from smaller units like peers and family to larger units like nations) has great psychological meaning. This is especially so in inter-group comparisons. In Western research, the collective self (Luhtanen and Crocker, 1992) and in-group out-group effects (Judd, Ryan, and Parke, 1991; Linville, Fischer, and Salovey, 1989) have received much attention. Thus, consideration of the importance of social identity of individuals is not pertinent only to Chinese people.

However, when we look at the history of China, we can see the periods of pride and shame that Chinese people have experienced (Kwok, 1980; Meisner, 1986; Spence, 1990; Terrill, 1992). Such experiences are clearly associated with the national identity or national self-concept of Chinese people.

The following extracts (cited in Lee, 1987) tell a lot about the feelings the Chinese have had over the last few decades.

> Please tell me who the Chinese are,
> Reveal to me how to firmly cherish the memory,
> Please tell me of the greatness of this people, ...
> — Wen Yiduo (1928)

> We must acknowledge our own mistakes,
> we must acknowledge that in a hundred
> ways we are inferior to others, and that
> it is not only in the material way that
> we are not equal to others politically,
> socially, or morally either ...
> — Hu Shi (1930)

> We really don't know which, if any,
> of our traditional institutions can
> be adapted for survival in the
> modern world. I would rather see
> the destruction of our 'national essence'
> than the final extinction of our race
> because it is unable to adapt.
> The Babylonians are no more; what
> good does their civilization do them
> today?
> — Chen Duxin (1920)

As can be seen from the period of the above quotations, China was at a low ebb of national pride. With Mao Zedong in power, China had revived, and Chinese people welcomed the re-gaining of a sense of national pride (Meisner, 1986; Spence, 1990; Terrill, 1992). They were willing to make any sacrifice and change under Mao's leadership. As pointed out by Lee (1987), many historians and sinologists argued that "the waves of modernization movements carried out in China in the past century have been propelled by national shame as the result of Western imperialistic aggression, and the feeling of cultural inferiority (Ch'en, 1979; Fairbank, 1975; Leslie, 1974; Wu, 1977)" (p. 7). We can take issue with this argument, but shame could be seen as a motivating force for achievement (Pettigrew, 1967).

The picture of China's history has changed. But how proud are the Chinese of being Chinese and of their country? The answer is not forthcoming as no persuasive research has been done on Chinese people's national self-concept. What we know for sure is that Chinese are hard working people. They are trying their best to achieve and to prove to themselves and the world that they are capable and intelligent. In fact, research evidence has shown consistently that Chinese students are high academic achievers (cf. Sue and Okazaki, 1990). Such high achievement certainly draws the attention of the Western world (Stevenson and Stigler, 1992).

But what are the motivating forces underlying such achievements? There are some observations we can make. First, Chinese nowadays are still in search of a self-worth, an identity (Sternberg, Cornbusch, and Brown, 1992). Second, they are in search of a good or better life through migration because of political uncertainty in their homeland (Cheung and Lau, 1995). Such search is made through a narrow channel (in fields they are good at, such as achieving high standards academically). Also, it seems that such search is made through a collective action but in the narrowest sense (such as through the caring for offspring and the passing on of family glory down the family line). For instance, although no less achieving and no fewer in number, Asian Americans are far less cohesive and a less influential politically and socially than other minority groups such as Jewish Americans. As a minority group, they don't seem to do much for their fellow group members. If Chinese are so collective in their life orientation as presumed by some researchers, they should be more collective in their action. Yet studies have found that they uphold self-centred or personal values (Feather, 1986; Lau, 1992). Such discrepancy may indicate the need for further in-depth investigations.

Most Chinese seem very self-assured on the surface. The economic growth and modernization of Hong Kong, Taiwan, and Mainland China plays a significant role in the self-assurance process. But deep down, the need to prove oneself is still there. This may not be unique to the Chinese, but true of most people. Nonetheless, further observation and investigation are awaited. The road that Chinese people, especially the younger generations, have to travel along in this stage of their development is uncertain. And the process and stopping-off points of such travel should have much bearing on the self-concept development of Chinese people.

References

Abbott, K. A. (1970). *Harmony and individualism.* Taipei: Oriental Cultural Press.

Baron, R. A., and Byrne, D. (1994). *Social psychology: Understanding human interaction* (7th ed.). Boston: Allyn & Bacon.

Berndt, T. J., Cheung, P. C., Lau, S., Hau, K. T., and Lew, W.J.F. (1993). Perceptions of parenting in Mainland China, Taiwan, and Hong Kong: Sex differences and societal differences. *Developmental Psychology,* 29: 156–164.

Bond, M. H., and Cheung, T. S. (1983). College students' spontaneous self-concept. *Journal of Cross-Cultural Psychology,* 14: 153–171.

Ch'en, J. (1979). *China and the West: Society and culture 1815–1937.* London: Hutchinson.

Chen, L. F. (1987). *The Confucian Way.* New York: Kegan Paul, Associate Book.

Cheung, P. C., & Lau, S. (1985). Self-esteem: Its relationship to the family and school social environments among Chinese adolescents. *Youth & Society,* 16: 438–456.

————. (1995). *A multi-perspective multi-domain mode of self-concept: Relating two lines of self-concept research.* Manuscript submitted for publication.

Cooley, D. H. (1902). *Human nature and the social order.* New York: Scribners.

Culter, B. L., and Wolfe, R. N. (1989). Self-monitoring and the association between confidence and accurancy. *Journal of Research in Personality,* 23: 410–420.

DePaulo, B. M., Kenny, D. A., Hoover, C. W., Webb, W., and Oliver, P. V. (1987). Accuracy of person perception: Do people know what kinds of impressions they convey? *Journal of Personality and Social Psychology,* 52: 303–315.

Fairbank, J. K. (1975). *Chinese American interactions: A historical summary.* New Brunswick, NJ: Rutgers University Press.

Feather, N. T. (1986). Value systems across cultures: Australia and China. *International Journal of Psychology,* 21: 697–715.

Felson, R. B. (1989). Parents and the reflected appraisal process: A longitudinal analysis. *Journal of Personality and Social Psychology,* 56: 965–971.

Fiske, S. T., and Taylor, S. E. (1991). *Social cognition* (2nd ed.). New York: Random House.

Fong, S.L.M. (1965). Assimilation of Chinese in America: Changes in orientation and social perception. *American Journal of Sociology*, 71: 265–273.

Harter, S. (1982). The perceived competence scale for children. *Child Development*, 53: 87–97.

Higgins, E. T., and Bargh, J. A. (1987). Social cognition and social perception. In M. R. Rosenszweig and L. W. Porter (Eds.), *Annual Review of Psychology*, 38: 369–425. Palo Alto, CA: Annual Reviews Inc.

Ho, S. M. (1992). *Effects of salience and consciousness on the relationship between self concept and school performance.* Unpublished master's thesis, School of Education, The Chinese University of Hong Kong.

Jones S. C. (1973). Self and interpersonal evaluations: Esteem theories versus consistency theories. *Psychological Bulletin.* 79: 185–199.

Judd, C. M., Ryan, C. N., and Parke, B. (1991). Accuracy in the judgment of in-group and out-group variability. *Journal of Personality and Social Psychology*, 61: 366–379.

Kenny, D. A., and Albright, L. (1987). Accuracy in interpersonal perception: A social relations analysis. *Psychological Bulletin*, 102: 390–402.

Kwok, T. Y. (1980). *Modern Chinese history.* Hong Kong: The Chinese University Press.

Lau, S. (1992). Collectivism's individualism: Value preference, personal control, and the desire for freedom among Chinese in Mainland China, Hong Kong, and Singapore. *Personality and Individual Difference*, 13: 361–366.

———. (1994). *The pitfalls in doing cross-cultural research.* Manuscript in Preparation.

Lau, S., and Cheung, P. C. (1987). Relations between Chinese Adolescents' perception of parental control and organization and their perception of parental warmth. *Developmental Psychology*, 23: 726–729.

Lau, S., and Leung, K. (1992a). Relations with parents and school and Chinese adolescents' self-concept, delinquency, and academic performance. *British Journal of Educational Psychology*, 62: 21–30.

———. (1992b). Self-concept, delinquency, relations with parents and school, and Chinese adolescents' perception of personal control. *Personality and Individual Differences*, 13: 615–622.

Lau, S., Lew, W.J.F., Hau, K. T., Cheung, P. C., and Berndt, T. J. (1990). Relations among perceived parental control, warmth, indulgence, and family harmony of Chinese in Mainland China. *Developmental Psychology*, 26 (4): 674–677.

Lau, S., and Li, W. L. (1994). *Peer status and creativity: How popular are creative children as viewed by peers and teachers.* Manuscript submitted for publication.

Lau, S., Nicholls, J. G., Thorkildsen, T. A., and Patashnick, M. (1994). *Chinese and American adolescents' perceptions of the purposes of education and beliefs about the world of work*. Unpublished manuscript.

Lau, S., and Wong, A. K. (1992). Value and sex-role orientation of Chinese adolescents. *International Journal of Psychology*, 27: 3–17.

Lee, W. M. (1984). *Portraits of a challenge: An illustrated history of the Chinese Canadians*. Toronto, Ontario: The Council of the Chinese Canadians in Ontario.

Lee. W. M. (1987). *Academic self-concept, national self-concept, and need for achievement of Chinese students in China and Hong Kong: A Comparative study*. Unpublished master's thesis, School of Education, The Chinese University of Hong Kong.

Leslie, C. (1974). *The Modernization of Asian medical systems*. In J. J. Poggie Jr. and R. N. Lynch (Eds.), *Rethinking modernization: Anthropological perspectives* (pp. 69–108). Westport: Greenwood Press.

Leung, K., and Lau, S. (1989). Effects of self-concept and perceived disapproval on delinquent behavior in school children. *Journal of Youth and Adolescence*, 18: 345–359.

Lewin, K. (1951). *Field theory in social science: Selected theoretical papers*. New York: Harper. (Original work published in 1935).

Li, S. Y., and Wong, S. Y. (1982). A cross-cultural study on sex-role stereotypes and social desirability. *Sex Roles*, 8(5).

Lin, H. Y. (1990). Confucian theory of human development. In R. M. Thomas (Ed.), *The encyclopedia of human development and education theory, research, and studies* (pp. 149–52). New York: Pergamon Press.

Linville, P. W., Fischer, O. W., and Salovey, P. (1989). Perceived distributions of the characteristics of in-group and out-group members: Empirical evidence and a computer simulation. *Journal of Personality and Social Psychology*, 57: 165–188.

Luhtanen, R., and Crocker, J. (1992). A collective self-esteem scale: Self-evaluation of one's social identity. *Personality and Social Psychology Bulletin*, 18: 302–318.

Luk, C. L., and Bond, M. H. (1992). Explaining Chinese self-esteem in terms of the self-concept. *Psychologia*.

Marek, J. C. (1990). Buddhist theory of human development. In R. M. Thomas (Ed.), *The encyclopedia of human development and education theory, research, and studies* (pp. 144–49). New York: Pergamon Press.

Markus, H., and Nurius, P. (1986). Possible selves. *American Psychologist*, 41: 954–969.

Marsh, H. W., Byrne, B. M., and Shavelson, R. J. (1988). A multifaceted self-concept: Its hierarchical structure and its relation to academic achievement. *Journal of Educational Psychology*, 80: 366–380.

Meisner. M. (1986). *Mao's China and after: A history of the People's Republic.* New York: The Free Press.

Pettigrew, T. F. (1967). Social evaluation theory: Convergences and application. *The Nebraska Symposium on Motivation,* 15: 241–311.

Pritchard, R. (1991). The effects of cultural schemata on reading processing strategies. *Reading Research Quarterly,* 25: 273–295.

Poon, W. T., and Lau, S. (1994). *Coping with failure: Effects of attributional style and self-discrepancy.* Unpublished manuscript.

Scheier, M. F., and Carver, C. S. (1983). Two sides of the self: One for you and one for me.

Shavelson, R. J., Hubner, J. J., and Stanton, G. (1976). Self-concept: Validation of construct interpretations. *Review of Educational Research,* 46: 407–441.

Shrauger, J. S., and Schoeneman, T. J. (1979). Symbolic interactionist view of self-concept: Through the looking glass darkly. *Psychological Bulletin,* 86: 549–573.

Spence, J. D. (1990). *The search for modern China.* New York: Norton

Sternberg, L., Dornbusch, S., and Brown, B. B. (1992). Ethnic differences in adolescent achievement: An ecological perspective. *American Psychologist,* 47: 723–729.

Stevenson, H. W., and Stigler, J. W. (1992). *The learning gap.* New York: Summit Books.

Sue, D. W. (1973). Ethnic identity: The impact of two cultures on the psychological development of Asians in American. In S. Sue and N. N. Wagner (Eds.), *Asian–Americans: Psychological Perspectives* (pp. 140–149). Palo Alta, CA: Science and Behavior.

Sue, S., and Okazaki, S. (1990). Asian–American educational achievements: A phenomenon in search of an explanation. *American Psychologist,* 45: 913–920.

Terrill, R. (1992). *China in our time.* New York: Simon & Schuster.

Thomas, R. M. (1990). Christian theory of human development. In R. M. Thomas (Ed.), *The encyclopedia of human development and education theory, research, and studies* (pp. 131–137). New York: Pergamon Press.

Thomas, R. M. (Ed.) (1990). *The encyclopedia of human development and education theory, research, and studies.* New York: Pergamon Press.

Thomas, R. M., and Niikura, R. (1990). Shinto theory of human development. In R. M. Thomas (Ed.), *The encyclopedia of human development and education theory, research, and studies* (pp. 152–55). New York: Pergamon Press.

Toffler A. (1970). *Future shock.* New York: Bantam Books.

———. (1980). *The third wave.* New York: Bantam Books.

———. (1990). *War and antiwar: Survival at the dawn of the 21st Century.* New York: Bantam Books.

Tversky, A., and Kahneman, D. (1973). Availability: A heuristic for judging frequency and probability. *Cognitive Psychology,* 5: 207–232.

Wang, T. H., and Creedon, C. F. (1989). Sex role orientations, attributions for achievement, and personal goals of Chinese youth. *Sex Roles*, 20 (9–10): 473–486.

Wu, T. Y. (1977). Chinese traditional values and modernization. In Seah Chee-Meow (Ed.), *Asian values and modernization* (pp. 47–60). Singapore: Singapore University Press.

Wyer, R. W., and Srull, T. K. (1984). Human cognition in its social context. *Psychological Review*, 93: 322–359.

Yik, M., and Bond, M. H. (1993). Exploring the dimensions of Chinese person perception with indigenous and imported constructs: Creating a culturally balanced scale. *International Journal of Psychology*, 28: 75–95.

Yu, Y. S. (1976). *History and thought*. Taipei: Luen King Press.

In Search of the Course of Chinese Children's Development: An Overall Conclusion

Sing Lau

Introduction

The task of trying to map out the course of Chinese children's development is not an easy one, especially with only very limited reliable and valid data available. Yet it is an exciting one. Modestly and realistically, the authors of the present volume have provided at least some stepping stones for further exploration.

In going through the volume, several themes are evident, some of which are interrelated. This final chapter will attempt to highlight and integrate the ideas put forth by the authors on socialization, academic achievement, social maladjustment, only-child policy, and Chinese overseas.

Culture and Socialization

The significance of culture in socialization is most succinctly highlighted in Wu's study (Chapter 1) of China's only children. Based on an anthropological approach, Wu has not only found that only and non-only children do not differ in most aspects of their development, but has also uncovered some interesting patterns of Chinese parenting practices. Noticeably, *guan*, a means of discipline, is characteristic of how Chinese parents rear their offspring. Parental control or discipline is therefore most prevalent. In Wu's study, no over-indulgence of only children was found, rather a greater demand for performing well. This was especially so with the urban and better educated parents. In child rearing, early moral education or indoctrination is very common. In addition, the pressure for achievement is also notorious. Wu has stated that such pressure for achievement "is a continuation of the emphasis in traditional Chinese culture." If the only child exhibits any difference in behavior, it is because he has to face greater parental demand for proper behavior and higher achievement. Wu has therefore summarized that if single children are seen as a problem, the problem is not with them but with "the parents, grandparents, and political élite."

The connection between culture and socialization is further emphasized by Lau and Yeung in Chapter 2, which focuses on the political and historical changes in recent decades. Such changes are sources of adjustment that younger generations of Chinese have to face. Taking up a very important issue, Cheung (Chapter 3) has brought to our attention the role of women in Chinese history and culture. Sex discrimination against females was, and still is, true of Chinese societies. In the bringing up of young children, Cheung has indicated that girls tend to receive less opportunity or encouragement for higher and better education. With the one-child policy in effect from 1980, the future that girls have to face is not much better. The preference for sons over daughters is still true in present day Chinese families. Even if we only see girls from the point of view of occupying half of China's future generation, Cheung's alarm over the female issue is not to be taken lightly.

Academic Achievement

Western educators and psychologists are astonished by the high academic achievement of Chinese students, and are greatly interested in finding the reasons for it.

The systematic research on this topic by Stevenson and his colleagues is reported by Chen, Lee, and Stevenson in Chapter 4. In their cross-cultural studies, they observe that Chinese students perform consistently higher on numerical tests. They have found that intelligence is not a factor in explaining the Chinese student's superior performance. As an alternative, several cultural factors are proposed. One factor is the high value placed on education. A second factor is the value of hard work, with effort being emphasized over ability. (This explanation may appear controversial: it fails to explain why Japanese students, who attach even greater importance to effort than Chinese student do, perform less well than Chinese students.) A third factor is family involvement — Chinese parents have high aspirations and standards for their children and spend a great deal of time supervising their children's school work, and Chinese children are also aware of their parents' high standards. A fourth factor is homework — Chinese students tend to spend much more time doing homework. A fifth factor is self-evaluation — Chinese students tend to evaluate themselves as being average in ability and this is taken as a more accurate level of self-evaluation. Finally, a sixth factor is adjustment to school — Chinese students tend to be more attentive, calm, and responsive, as well as less psychologically disturbed and tense. In all, the explanations fit in well with the image of the model student.

Chao and Sue (in Chapter 5) discuss the paradox of academic achievement and parenting style. According to Western theories, parental control or restrictiveness in the form of authoritarian parenting is related negatively to academic achievement. However, it has been found that while Chinese students are under high parental control, they nonetheless exhibit high rather than low achievement. This paradoxical phenomenon is the focus of Chao's series of studies. It has been found that Chinese parents have higher expectations, greater dissatisfaction with their children's performance, and greater involvement in their children's homework, and that they provide a more stable home environment (in terms of fewer broken families). These factors are similar to those proposed by Chen et al. in Chapter 4. In addition, Chao and Sue point out that the motivation to achieve and the fear of the consequences of school failure tend to be better predictors of school performance for Chinese students. Interestingly, their studies of Asian Chinese students have shown that the influence of parental style upon achievement is not as important as previous researchers have thought. For Asian Chinese, and other minorities in the U.S., education is seen as a way to advance socially. In addition, Chao and Sue emphasize that child training rather than child rearing is characteristic of the Chinese parenting style. They argue that the concept of the authoritarian parenting style is an incomplete or even a misleading characteristization of Chinese parents. For this, they offer four explanations to support their argument. Furthermore, they argue against the importance of peer influence as suggested in previous research. With evidence both from their study and from the studies of other researchers, parental control (as in authoritarian parenting style) should be further delineated by distinguishing between functional and dysfunctional control. The need for functional control appears to run parallel with the need for *guan* as described by Wu in Chapter 1. Proper discipline is therefore not necessarily bad. In fact, it is viewed as necessary by Chinese parents when children are at a very young age.

Hau and Salili (Chapter 6), from the point of view of motivation, have found that Chinese students tend to attribute their achievement to effort more than to ability. They also emphasize the importance of parental control of Chinese parents in directing their children to perform well academically (i.e. restriction in the positive sense). The importance of education and diligence is stressed by Chinese parents and their children. Hau and Salili state that Chinese children are learning/goal oriented. They hypothesize that the stress on effort and hard work, a self-effacing attributional style, is a result of the collectivistic culture of the Chinese to maintain group harmony. This conjecture, however, needs to be further examined in future research.

In Chapter 7, Biggs raises another interesting paradox. Chinese and other Asian students tend to adopt a rote-learning approach, which is said generally to result in low academic achievement. Yet on the contrary, evidence consistently shows that they perform extremely well in international tests. As Biggs points out, their high performance requires a high cognitive level of learning strategies. In a series of cross-cultural studies, Biggs has devised measures of three learning approaches: surface, deep, and achieving. Results of his studies show that Chinese are lower in the surface, but higher in the deep and achieving approaches.

Therefore, the impression of Chinese being just rote learners, is deceptive. According to Biggs, understanding of material can come through memorization, and the use of repetition is to seek meaning. In other words, "deep-memorizing" is an exam-taking strategy: it uses repetition of material already meaningfully learned. Through such an approach, which is backed by a series of studies, Biggs has offered a convincing explanation for the paradox of rote learning and achievement. The old adage "practice makes perfect" seems to be true, as demonstrated by the performance of Chinese and other Asian students.

Social Adjustment

Apart from the positive side of their development, such as high academic achievement, Chinese children do manifest social-emotional adjustment problems. Shek (Chapter 8) has reviewed data showing that adjustment problems are prevalent in the 16–25 age range. Shek's chapter provides references to many epidemiological studies done in Mainland China. As is commonly the case, the reliability and validity of these studies have yet to be determined.

On a related but more specific topic, J. P. Leung (Chapter 9) has indicated that the problem of hyperactivity has begun to receive greater attention in the last decade. The reason for such concern has tended to start with parents' care about their children's academic performance, which is usually affected negatively by hyperactivity. Leung has indicated that despite claims of comparability, the prevalence rates of hyperactivity are in general smaller in Chinese societies than those found in Western societies. In further exploration, Leung has offered some probable reasons for such a difference. In particular, the lower rates in Chinese societies may reflect the effects of cultural influences on the manifestation or the perception of hyperactivity. Studies have also shown that more boys than girls are diagnosed as having such psychological adjustment problems. As a result of the one-child policy in Mainland China (see Chapter 1, Chapter 3, and Chapter 9), the distribution of boys and girls might not be as normal as in Western societies. Leung has also found age difference to be another differentiating factor. Specifically, in Western societies (with some countries such as Germany and New Zealand as exceptions), hyperactivity tends to increase from age five, peak at eight, and then decline afterward; whereas among Chinese children, an inverted U shape is generally found. The method of assessment and treatment poses another problem. In general, the interviews and tests with Chinese children lack reliability and valid information, and objective laboratory tests are under-used. With respect to treatment, limited data are found in the literature. In all fairness, even in the West, few methods of treatment are proved to be effective. The most popular and frequent method used is drug therapy. In spite of the paucity of treatment methods, Leung has identified two interesting and potentially effective methods. Both originate from Eastern culture: one is the use of acupuncture; another is a group method that uses story telling and the involvement of group members in puppet playing. In essence these point to new ways of treating adjustment problems. Leung then concludes by questioning the use of Western diagnostic methods, which may not be applicable to the specific cultural backgrounds of Chinese children. More indigenous methods may serve as supplements to existing Western methods at the very least.

If we see delinquency as a behavioral manifestation of psychological maladjustment, Leung and Fan's chapter (Chapter 10) provides an interesting source of information and hypotheses. In Western literature, delinquency has generally been viewed as a single dimension. Recent cross-cultural research has tended to expand such thinking. In their study of Hong Kong, Australian, and American adolescents, Feldman, Rosenthal, Mont-Reynaud, Leung, & Lau (1991) have identified three types of delinquency: school-based misconduct, anti-social behavior, and status offense. Yang's (1981) study of Taiwan youth has found two sub-sets of delinquency:

pleasure-seeking and rule-violating behaviors. In both crime statistic comparison and cross-cultural literature on aggression, Leung and Fan indicate that Chinese show lower rates than Western adolescents. They go on to ask an interesting and important question: Why are Chinese adolescents less delinquent? There are no empirical data to answer this question. Leung and Fan, however, propose three post *hoc* explanations. The first possible cause is the suppression of delinquent behavior in socialization. Chinese parents tend to discourage aggression and encourage impulse control in children. However, in the extreme case of too much suppression and control of feelings, mental health problems may surface (see Chapter 8 and Chapter 9; and also Chapter 3). The second possible cause is the pressure to conform. This is especially so in the light of conformity toward authority or high-status figures, and is rule-driven. Such conformity may be a double-edged sword. It may make adolescents law- or rule-abiding students or citizens. Or it may make them become gang members with a blind loyalty. Finally, the third possible cause identified by Leung and Fan is genetic influence. Research evidence tends to show that Chinese newborns are less reactive emotionally, habituate more quickly to adverse stimulation, and are more easily consoled when upset than Western babies. This explanation is comparatively quite convincing because of its empirical base. It should however be noted that because research has shown that boys are more aggressive than girls, and because of the one-child policy in China (which results in an unnatural distribution of boys and girls), the genetic explanation needs to be further explored: China may have disproportionally more girls who tend to be "easy" rather than "difficult" babies. In terms of personality correlates, sensation-seeking, impulsiveness, aggressiveness, and neuroticism are among the major factors. This relationship is partly elaborated in Chapter 8 and Chapter 9. Leung and Fan in their chapter pay great attention to the reviews of theories in delinquency research. In the studies done in Hong Kong and Taiwan, control theory (the break-down of social bonds) has in general received the widest support. Several studies in Taiwan have also found support for the differential association theory (the association or membership of anti-social groups). Other theories, such as the strain theory, the labeling theory, and the conflict theory, are weaker and less consistent in predicting delinquency behaviors. Recently, the self-enhancement theory (the gaining of self-worth through negative or anti-social achievement) has received great attention and empirical support. In recent studies done in Hong Kong, the theory is extended by the incorporation of different domains of self-esteem. Finally, Leung and Fan call for greater attention to indigenous phenomena and hypotheses for theory building. They point out that this is especially necessary in view of the fact that the nature of delinquent behaviors of Chinese adolescents tends to be different from that of Western adolescents.

Only Children

In previous sections, under the heading of culture and tradition, Wu (Chapter 1) and Cheung (Chapter 3) have touched upon the topic of only children. Wu's chapter in particular shows that only children and non-only children do not differ as has previously been thought. Falbo, Poston, and Feng (Chapter 11) have further documented support for such a result. Based on their own research, using a different and more sophisticated research approach, they are able to dispel the label of only children as "little emperors". Their samples are made more representative by including a wider region of China. They also in their research use a control for possible confounding variables, such as parents' education, number of siblings, and site of residence (urban vs. rural). In brief, only children are found to score higher on verbal and maths tests than non-only children. As far as personality attributes are concerned, few differences are found. On physical measures, only children are larger in body build. The truth of the matter is that only children are no worse, and sometimes even better, than non-only children by most measures. This has great significance in our understanding and study of the present generation of Chinese children.

Interestingly enough, Falbo et al. note that even in the West, it was thirty years before Stanley Hall's hasty conclusion about the poor psychological adjustment of only children was challenged by the results of empirical studies and that only children were seen as part of the normal population. Falbo et al. point that today seventy-five percent of all Americans live in urban areas. These perception and social changes have significant implications for the understanding of the development of Chinese children. It may only be a matter of time before Chinese children come to behave like their Western counterparts. The time factor should therefore be taken into consideration in the cross-cultural studies of Chinese and Western children (see Chapter 2 and Chapter 14). As an added outcome, the research on only children has also brought about greater understanding of the parenting style of Chinese parents.

Chinese Overseas

More and more Chinese are found residing in Western countries over recent decades. Their settlement on foreign soil has a long history. As a whole, they are welcomed by the host cultures because of their achievement and hard working style (see Chapter 4). Yet, despite all the success stories, there are problems due to poor adjustment to cultures different from their own. Rosenthal and Feldman (Chapter 12) have pointed out that especially for Chinese adolescents, the bridging of two cultures (their own and that of the host country) is not an easy task. In the process of acculturation, different aspects of adjustment have to be accommodated. For example, there are great differences in parenting style between Chinese and Western cultures. Chinese adolescents are caught in between the discrepancies. Adolescents in general are at the stage of searching for autonomy and independence. Yet they are also in need of family support. Chinese families are in general high on support and cohesiveness but low in granting autonomy and independence to their children. Chinese adolescents living in Western cultures tend to seek the kind of autonomy their Western counterparts have. Another problem posed for these Chinese adolescents is the high parental expectations they have to live up to in terms of academic achievement. This often results in a high level of anxiety and disappointment in both Chinese adolescents and parents if the level of achievement cannot be reached. The model Chinese student image therefore has its dark side. In their studies of Chinese adolescents in the US and Australia, Rosenthal and Feldman have found that the pace of behavioral autonomy is slow, whereas that of values is more rapid. In understanding this phenomenon, Rosenthal and Feldman offer several possible explanations. One is self-selection — the migrant Chinese may be more entrepreneurial and value more highly the Western notions of outward success and achievement. Another is the effect of the persuasive cultural messages of Western mass media that emphasize the values of comfort in the Western style of living. The third possible explanation is the significance of the family unit in Chinese culture that may effectively transmit traditional standards of conduct and behaviors. These explanations all deserve further exploration in the understanding of the acculturation process of values and behaviors of Chinese adolescents in Western cultures.

In Chapter 13, Cheung uses the family approach to understand how overseas Chinese adjust in the host countries. In essence, Cheung postulates different rates of adjustment for different family members (the grandparents, the parents, and the offspring). According to Cheung, conflicts often arise because of differential acculturation. A three-step analysis is introduced in her chapter. The analysis includes assessment of the cultural identity of each family member, a critical incident analysis to discover the source of conflict, and a self-evaluation process for both children and parents to identify their adjustment issues. Cheung likens the uneven assimilation among family members as a compartmental adjustment process: locked, half-open, or wide-open. Age is found to be a major factor which has not been addressed in previous studies. Among overseas Chinese, conflict and its source are often hidden. In her chapter, Cheung introduces two cases to highlight the three-stage analysis and the compartmental adjustment process. In all, Cheung has presented the adjustment problems that overseas Chinese have to face.

Conclusion

China is a vast nation. Both the older and younger generations are in search of a better life, a sense of destiny and self-worth. Amidst all the economic development, there is turmoil underneath (Meisner, 1986; Spence, 1990; Terrill, 1992). The future for China and its young people is not certain. This is epitomized by the high rate of migration overseas to Western countries. There are, however, signs of self-empowerment in different domains of life. With these, a strong China and stronger generations of young children may be in sight. It is hoped that the present volume has clarified and highlighted some of the issues that young Chinese children have to face and overcome.

References

Feldman, S. S., Rosenthal, D. A., Mont-Reynaud, R., Leung, K., & Lau, S. (1991). Ain't misbehavin': Adolescent values and family environments as correlates of misconduct in Australia, Hong Kong, and the United States. *Journal of Research on Adolescence*, 1: 109–134.

Meisner, M. (1986). *Mao's China and after: A history of the People's Republic.* New York: The Free Press.

Spence, J. D. (1990). *The search for modern China.* New York: Norton (W. W.) & Company.

Terrill, R. (1992). *China in our time.* New York: Simon & Schuster.

Yang, K. S. (1981). Problem behavior in Chinese adolescents in Taiwan: A classificatory-factorial-study. *Journal of Cross-cultural Psychology*, 12: 179–193.

Contributors

JOHN B. BIGGS has been Professor of Education, University of Hong Kong, since 1987. Prior to that he was Professor of Education, Newcastle University, Australia, and has held academic posts in Canada, Australia, and England. His main research area is the application of educational psychology to teaching and learning, with particular interests in: students' approaches to learning, learning in Chinese cultures, tertiary teaching, and the effects of assessment on the quality of student learning. Publications include *Evaluating the Quality of Learning* (with K. Collis, 1982), *Why and How Do Hong Kong Students Learn?* (1992), and *Process of Learning* (with P. Moore, 1993), and over one hundred journal articles.

RUTH K. CHAO is Assistant Professor in the Department of Child and Family Studies at Syracuse University. She is currently conducting a research project, funded by the National Academy of Education's Spencer Post-doctoral Fellowship, involving parental influences on academic achievement for Chinese, Japanese, and Koreans in the U.S. She had received her Ph.D. from the University of California, Los Angeles in the Department of Educational Psychology.

CHUAN-SHENG CHEN (Ph.D., 1992, University of Michigan) is Assistant Professor of Psychology and Social Behavior at the School of Social Ecology, University of California, Irvine, California, USA. His major area of interest relates to the role of culture in child and adolescent development.

FANNY M. CHEUNG is Reader in Psychology, and Director of the Gender Research Programme of the Hong Kong Institute of Asia-Pacific Studies at The Chinese University of Hong Kong. She obtained her B.A. from the University of California (Berkeley) and her Ph.D. from the University of Minnesota. Her major research areas include personality assessment, psychopathology, and gender roles and stereotypes. She has pioneered gender research in Hong Kong and set up the first women's centre in the local community. Under her directorship, the Gender Research Programme has organized several conferences on gender issues in Chinese societies, and published proceedings, monographs, and occasional papers on topics including gender and society, rape, sexual harassment, social participation by women, and bibliography on gender studies.

KAM-FONG MONIT CHEUNG is Associate Professor at the Graduate School of Social Work, University of Houston, in Texas, U.S.A. she graduated from the Ohio State University and obtained her Ph.D. and MSW in social work and MA in public administration. Currently, Dr. Cheung is a licensed Advanced Clinical Practitioner (LMSW-ACP), a faculty trainer in the Texas Children's Protective Service Training Institute, and a consultant of the American Association for Protecting Children. Her research and teaching interest includes child abuse and neglect, ethnic-sensitive practice in child protective services, social services for Asian American immigrants, family therapy, and play therapy for sexual abuse survivors.

TONI FALBO is Professor of Educational Psychology and Sociology at the University of Texas at Austin. She has published many studies of only children in scientific journals and is a recognized expert about the impact of family size on children's outcomes. Dr. Falbo is also an expert on social power and has written extensively on the power dynamics within intimate relationships and within parent-child relationships.

RUTH MEI-TAI FAN is a doctoral student at the Department of Psychology, The Chinese University of Hong Kong. Her research interests include adolescent psychology, justice in school, judgemental processes, and conflict resolution.

S. SHIRLEY FELDMAN is the Director of the Stanford Center for the Study of Families, Children, and Youth. She has published extensively in the areas of adolescence, family influences on development, and socialization. Her work has often had a cross-cultural perspective, with comparative studies comparing developmental processes in the United States to those in Hong Kong, Israel, Greece, and Australia. She has published more than one hundred articles, monographs and books.

XIAO-TIAN FENG is Professor of Sociology at Central China Institute of Technology in Wuhan. He holds a Ph.D. in sociology from Peking University. His research focuses on only children in China, survey methods, and sociological methodology. He is an expert in China on the educational characteristics and the families of Chinese only children.

KIT-TAI HAU is Lecturer in the Department of Educational Psychology at The Chinese University of Hong Kong. He obtained his Ph.D. in psychology at the University of Hong Kong. He has great research interest and has published in students' achievement motivation, causal attribution, goal orientation, suicidal behavior, and self concept. In recent years, he has also been actively involved in simulation studies of structural equation modeling.

SING LAU obtained his Ph.D. in social psyschology from Purdue University in 1977. He is currently Director of the Center for Child Development and Professor of psychology and education at Hong Kong Baptist University. He was formerly

Head of the Department of Education Studies of Hong Kong Baptist University. He had also taught at The Chinese University of Hong Kong and was Visiting Scholar at Purdue University, University of Pittsburgh, and State University of New York. He has published many articles in international journals and two books related to the social development of adolescents and children. His research interests cover the areas of self-concept, gender role, and value.

SHIN-YING LEE (Ph.D., 1987, University of Michigan) is Assistant Research Scientist at the Center for Human Growth and Development, University of Michigan, Ann Arbor, Michigan, USA. Her major research interests are cross-cultural differences in instruction and students' school performance.

JIN-PANG LEUNG is Senior Lecturer in Department of Psychology, The Chinese University of Hong Kong. He is currently the Associate Editor for Bulletin of the Hong Kong Psychological Society and he also sits on the Editorial Board of Journal of Behavioral Education. Dr. Leung has a wide scope of research interests including behavior analysis and modification, rehabilitation psychology, choice behavior, life satisfaction in adolescents, children hyperactivity, mental retardation, and autism.

KWOK LEUNG is the Chairman of the Department of Psychology of The Chinese University of Hong Kong. He obtained his Ph.D. from the University of Illinois at Urbana-Champaign, and his research interests include justice, conflict resolution, cross-cultural psychology, and the psychology of the adolescents.

DUDLEY L. POSTON, JR. is Professor and Head of the Department of Sociology, and the Samuel Rhea Gammon Professor of Liberal Arts, at Texas A&M University. He has published widely on various demographic and sociological aspects of China including fertility, migration, infant mortality, only children, and ethnic minorities. In 1992 he published (with David Yaukey) *The Population of Modern China*.

DOREEN A. ROSENTHAL is Professor and Foundation Director of the Centre for the Study of Sexually Transmissible Diseases at La Trobe University. She holds a Ph.D. from the University of Melbourne and is a developmental psychologist, specializing in the psychology of adolescence. Her research interests include gender and cross-cultural issues, and she has published widely in the area of the acculturation and adaptation of adolescents of non-English-speaking background. She is currently researching adolescents' sexual risk-taking.

FARIDEH SALILI is a Senior Lecturer in psychology at the University of Hong Kong. She received her Ph.D. in educational psychology from the University of Illinois. Her research interest and publications are primarily concerned with age, sex, and cultural variations in achievement orientation. She has also conducted research on language development and on exceptional children.

DANIEL T. L. SHEK is Senior Lecturer in the Department of Social Work, The Chinese University of Hong Kong. His basic research interests lie in the areas of adolescent development, family processes, mental health, mental retardation, rehabilitation, psychological assessment, personal construct psychology, and psychophysiology. He has published numerous books, book chapters and papers on these topics and he has been the Associate Editor of the *Hong Kong Journal of Social Work*. He is actively involved in community service and he has recently served as chairman of the Research Sub-Committee of the Action Committee Against Narcotics.

HAROLD W. STEVENSON (Ph.D., 1951, Stanford University) is Professor of Psychology and Fellow at the Center for Human Growth and Development, University of Michigan, Ann Arbor, Michigan. His cross-cultural studies in Japan, Taiwan, China, Hungary, Canada, and Peru have dealt with the influence of culture and environment on children's cognitive development and academic achievement.

STANLEY SUE is Professor of Psychology and Director of the National Research Center on Asian American Mental Health at the University of California, Los Angeles. His research includes the areas of mental health, academic achievements, and personality development among various Asian groups in the United States.

DAVID YEN-HO WU is Reader and Chairperson of the Department of Anthropology, The Chinese University of Hong Kong. Formerly a Senior Fellow of the East-West Center in Honolulu, he has coordinated multi-national team research on Chinese culture and mental health, childhood socialization among Chinese communities, and pan-Asian youth culture.

PATRICIA P. W. YEUNG is a Research Officer at the Center for Child Development of the Hong Kong Baptist University. She obtained her M.A. in Developmental and Educational Psychology from Teachers College, Columbia University. Her research interests are multi-cultural education, Asian-American psychology, creativity and giftedness, and early childhood psychology.

Index